The Literature of American Jews

Orchard Street, looking south from Hester Street, 1898. The
Byron Collection, Museum of the City of New York.

The Literature
of
American
Jews

Edited by
THEODORE L. GROSS

THE FREE PRESS
A Division of Macmillan Publishing Co., Inc.
New York

The Free Press
A Division of Macmillan Publishing Co., Inc.
866 Third Avenue, New York, N.Y. 10022

Collier–Macmillan Canada Ltd.

Library of Congress Catalog Card Number: 72–93311

Printed in the United States of America

printing number
2   3   4   5   6   7   8   9   10

Library of Congress Cataloging in Publication Data

Gross, Theodore L   comp.
    The literature of American Jews.

    1. American literature--Jewish authors. 2. Jews.
in literature. I. Title.
PS508.J4G7   810'.8'08924   72-93311
ISBN 0-02-913190-1

Acknowledgments

Abraham Cahan: Excerpt is from pp. 85, 92, 93–103 in *The Rise of David Levinsky* by Abraham Cahan. Copyright 1917, 1945 by Abraham Cahan. By permission of Harper & Row, Publishers, Inc.

Mary Antin: Excerpt is from *The Promised Land*, copyright renewed 1940 by Mary Antin. Reprinted by permission of the publisher, Houghton Mifflin Company.

Ludwig Lewisohn: Excerpt is from *Upstream* by Ludwig Lewisohn. Permission of Liveright, Publishers, New York. Copyright © 1922 by Boni & Liveright, Inc. Copyright ©R1949 by Ludwig Lewisohn.

Ludwig Lewisohn: Excerpt is reprinted from *The Island Within* by Ludwig Lewisohn with permission of The Jewish Publication Society of America.

Waldo Frank: "The Chosen People" is from *Our America* by Waldo Frank. Permission of Liveright Publishers, New York. Copyright (R) 1947 by Waldo Frank.

Michael Gold: "Did God Make Bedbugs?" is from *Jews Without Money*. Reprinted by permission of Sidney Schrieberg.

Ben Hecht: "My Tribe Is Called Israel" and "The Jews Strike Out" are from *A Child of the Century*, © 1954 by Ben Hecht. Reprinted by permission of Simon & Schuster, Inc.

Henry Roth: Excerpt from *Call It Sleep*. Reprinted by permission of Cooper Square Publishers, Inc., 59 Fourth Avenue, New York, N.Y.

Henry Roth: "Henry Roth: No Longer Home," © 1971 by The New York Times Company. Reprinted by permission.

Daniel Fuchs: Excerpt from *Summer in Williamsburg* is from *Three Novels,* © by Daniel Fuchs. Reprinted by permission of the author.

Clifford Odets: *Awake and Sing.* Copyright © 1933, 1935 by Clifford Odets. Copyright renewed 1961, 1963 by Clifford Odets. Reprinted by permission of Brandt and Brandt, 101 Park Avenue, New York, N.Y. 10017.

Isaac Bashevis Singer: "Gimpel the Fool," translated by Saul Bellow, is from *A Treasury of Yiddish Stories,* edited by Irving Howe and Eliezer Greenberg. Copyright 1953, 1954 by The Viking Press, Inc. All rights reserved. Reprinted by permission of The Viking Press, Inc.

Paul Goodman: "The Facts of Life," copyright 1941 and renewed 1969 by Paul Goodman. Reprinted from *Adam and His Works: Collected Stories of Paul Goodman,* by permission of Random House, Inc. Appeared originally in Partisan Review, vol. 8, no. 5, 1941.

Bernard Malamud: "The Magic Barrel" is reprinted with the permission of Farrar, Straus & Giroux, Inc. from *The Magic Barrel* by Bernard Malamud, copyright © 1958 by Bernard Malamud.

Saul Bellow: Excerpt from *Herzog* by Saul Bellow. Copyright 1961, 1963, 1964 by Saul Bellow. All rights reserved. Reprinted by permission of The Viking Press, Inc.

Arthur Miller: "Mont Sant' Angelo" is from *I Don't Need You Any More* by Arthur Miller. Copyright 1951 by Arthur Miller. All rights reserved. Reprinted by permission of The Viking Press, Inc.

Delmore Schwartz: "America! America!" is from Partisan Review, vol. 7, no. 2, 1940. Copyright © 1940 by Partisan Review.

Grace Paley: "The Loudest Voice" is from *The Little Disturbances of Man* by Grace Paley. Copyright © 1959 by Grace Paley. All rights reserved. Reprinted by permission of The Viking Press, Inc.

Norman Mailer: "The Marshal and the Nazi" is from *Armies of the Night,* copyright © by Norman Mailer. Reprinted by permission of the author and the author's agents, Scott Meredith Literary Agency, Inc.

Herbert Gold: "Aristotle and the Hired Thugs" is reprinted by permission of the author and his agent, James Brown Associates, Inc. Copyright © 1957 by Herbert Gold.

Philip Roth: Excerpt from *Portnoy's Complaint* by Philip Roth. Copyright © 1967, 1968, 1969 by Philip Roth. Reprinted by permission of Random House, Inc.

Irvin Faust: "Jake Bluffstein and Adolph Hitler," copyright © 1962 by Irvin Faust. Reprinted from *Roar Lion Roar and Other Stories* by Irvin Faust, by permission of Random House, Inc.

Elie Wiesel: "Yom Kippur: The Day Without Forgiveness" is from *Legends of Our Time* by Elie Wiesel. Copyright © 1968 by Elie Wiesel. Reprinted by permission of Holt, Rhinehart and Winston, Inc.

Delmore Schwartz: "Once and For All," copyright © 1958 by Delmore Schwartz, and "The Would-Be Hungarian," © 1955 by Delmore Schwartz, are from the book *Summer Knowledge, New and Selected Poems,* by Delmore Schwartz. Reprinted by permission of Doubleday and Company, Inc.

Muriel Rukeyser: "The Blood Is Justified" and "To Be A Jew in the Twentieth Century" are from *Letter to the Front: Selected Poems.* Reprinted by permission of Monica McCall, International Famous Agency, copyright © 1951, Muriel Rukeyser.

Karl Shapiro: "Shylock" is from *Selected Poems* by Karl Shapiro. Copyright © 1968 by Karl Shapiro. Reprinted by permission of Random House, Inc.

Karl Shapiro: "Jew," copyright 1943 by Karl Shapiro. Reprinted from *Selected Poems* by Karl Shapiro, by permission of Random House, Inc.

Karl Shapiro: "The Murder of Moses," copyright 1944 by Karl Shapiro. Reprinted from *Selected Poems* by Karl Shapiro, by permission of Random House, Inc.

Howard Nemerov: "One Forever Alien" and "Debate with the Rabbi" are from *New and Selected Poems* by Howard Nemerov, copyright by the University of Chicago Press, 1960.

Allen Ginsberg: "Kaddish for Naomi Ginsberg 1894–1956," copyright © 1961 by Allen Ginsberg. Reprinted by permission of City Lights Books.

Lionel Trilling: "Under Forty," symposium. Reprinted from the *Contemporary Jewish Record*, February, 1944. Reprinted by permission of Professor Lionel Trilling and The Viking Press, Inc.

Muriel Rukeyser: "Under Forty," symposium. Reprinted from the *Contemporary Jewish Record*, February, 1944, by permission of Monica McCall, International Famous Agency.

Philip Rahv: "Introduction" to *A Malamud Reader*. Reprinted with the permission of Farrar, Straus & Giroux, Inc., from *A Malamud Reader*, copyright © 1967 by Farrar, Straus & Giroux, Inc.

Isaac Rosenfeld: "David Levinsky: The Jew As American Millionaire," is reprinted by permission of the World Publishing Company from *An Age of Enormity* by Isaac Rosenfeld. This edition copyright © 1962 by the World Publishing Company.

Alfred Kazin: "Under Forty," symposium. Reprinted from the *Contemporary Jewish Record*, February, 1944, by permission of the author.

Leslie A. Fiedler: "Zion as Main Street," copyright © 1964 by Leslie A. Fiedler. From the book *Waiting for the End*. Reprinted with permission of Stein and Day Publishers.

Daniel Bell: "Reflections on Jewish Identity," reprinted from *Commentary*, by permission, copyright © 1961 by the American Jewish Committee. Reprinted by permission of the author.

Irving Howe: "Sholom Aleichem: Voice of Our Past" is from *A World More Attractive*. Reprinted by permission of the publisher, Horizon Press, New York, from *A World More Attractive* by Irving Howe, copyright © 1963.

Nathan Glazer: "The Religion of American Jews" is from *American Judaism*. Copyright © 1957, 1972 by The University of Chicago Press. Reprinted by permission of the publisher.

Theodore Solotaroff: "Harry Golden and the American Audience" is from *The Red Hot Vacuum and Other Pieces on the Writing of the Sixties* by Theodore Solotaroff. Copyright © 1961 by Theodore Solotaroff. Appeared originally in *Commentary*. Reprinted by permission of Atheneum Publishers, 122 East 42nd St., New York, N.Y.

Norman Podhoretz: "Jewishness and the Younger Intellectuals," symposium. Reprinted from *Commentary*, by permission; copyright © 1961 by the American Jewish Committee.

Herbert Gold: "Jewishness and the Younger Intellectuals," symposium. Reprinted from *Commentary*, by permission; copyright © 1961 by the American Jewish Committee. Reprinted by permission of the author and his agent, James Brown Associates, Inc.

Wallace Markfield: "Jewishness and the Younger Intellectuals," symposium. Reprinted from *Commentary*, by permission; copyright © 1961 by the American Jewish Committee.

Philip Roth: "Jewishness and the Younger Intellectuals," symposium. Reprinted from *Commentary*, by permission; copyright © 1961 by the American Jewish Committee. Reprinted by permission of the author.

Contents

vii

Contents

Foreword

These survivors and children of survivors, bearers of a haunting memory and an ancient promise, these dreamers and rebels who persist in trying to change the world and man through words—nostalgic, poetic, or frenzied, depending on the circumstances—what do they have in common? Theodore Gross, editor of this important anthology, offers an explanation: they are all Jews.

Yet he does not tell us what this means. No doubt distrusts easy definitions and he is quite right. Through the great variety of his themes and the wide range of his commitments, the Jewish writer transcends all obvious categories.

Whether he celebrates the triumphs or the torments of his people or whether he denigrates them, whether he clings to his past or detaches himself from it, he will reflect his background in more than one way. Jew by conviction or Jew in spite of himself, the Jewish writer *cannot be* anything else. What is most ironic is that even his rejection of his Jewishness identifies him.

A Jewish writer is, in the final analysis, a Jew who has chosen the art of writing to extol or to condemn a certain way of living, believing, fighting, or in one word: being. He remains a Jew even if he writes against Jews. Except that in this case, he will be an apologetic Jew and an inauthentic writer.

For it is in speaking about himself that the Jewish writer broadens the consciousness of others. It is in measuring himself against his own destiny that he expresses himself in the name of everyone. Self rejection leads to universal rejection. He who betrays his own will end up by betraying all others. Writing is an act of fidelity as well as of faith. Certain novelists have understood that, others refuse to understand. Yet all are Jews.

Their literature, presented here in a novel way, is rich and abundant, reflecting their anguish and their joy, real or imaginary. Some communicate a thirst for understanding, others yearn for justice. Some see themselves as creators on the level of consciousness, others draw from their experiences. Poets with an elusive vision, writers of fiction with a burning message: without them, American literature would not be what it aspires to be: the humanizing element in the course of history.

Elie Wiesel

Preface

The Jew has always been a figure of interest to other Americans because of the successful way that he has accommodated himself to his adopted country. Although he has known the poverty of the immigrant, the Jew has burst the boundaries of the ghetto and succeeded wherever permitted: in law, medicine, and teaching; in journalism, public relations, accounting, publishing, and advertising; in business and science; in music, dance, painting, acting, film, and television. The catalogue of the Jew's achievement is extraordinary and largely explains his fascination for those who are fascinated by success; but he would not be so engaging to Americans if he had not imagined himself in a literature of complexity and richness. This book is a testimony to the literary expression of Jewish Americans: its birth in the East-European migration, its later record of that immigrant experience, and its remarkable flowering after World War II.

The authors represented in this volume are of Jewish ancestry. One hesitates to call them Jewish writers—as one might speak, for example, of Black or Asian or Puerto Rican authors in America—for their response to Jewishness varies so greatly that to consider them in terms of religion or nationality alone is to do violence to their idiosyncratic nature. "The truth is," Philip Rahv warned years ago, "that many writers are Jewish in descent without being in any appreciable way 'Jewish' in feeling and sensibility. . . . It is one thing to speak factually of a writer's Jewish extraction and it is something else again to speak of his 'Jewishness' which is a very elusive quality and rather difficult to define." There is no easy definition of Jewishness when a writer identifies marginally with the Jewish religion and culture. Clearly Saul Bellow and Bernard

Malamud are more aware of themselves as Jews than Norman Mailer
and J. D. Salinger; Irving Howe and Leslie Fiedler consider the Jewish
experience in America with a self-consciousness untypical of Lionel
Trilling and Stanley Edgar Hyman. Nevertheless, a stubborn residue of
Jewishness lives in all these writers and gives their work a point of
view and an attitude that is distinct from that of Christian authors. At
one time or another each writer has had to confront his Jewishness: the
expression and meaning of that confrontation is the subject of this book.

There may be no satisfactory definition of Jewishness, but there is
a particular perspective that suggests how these authors are different
from other Americans. The literary and cultural critics share an urban
background, an early radicalism, and a liberal disposition that charges
their writing with social and moral concerns; they are not, for the most
part, "new critics," and their strong intellectual training in universities
and in urban publishing circles causes them to write in a highly
analytical, concrete, nervous style. The novelists create stories often
from an alienated point of view and in an ambiguous, ironic style that
is directed toward the condition of man's suffering, his tragic-comic,
quixotic position in the modern world. The literary expression of Jewish
authors is clearly far more complex and intricate than these remarks
suggest—far more, certainly, than "Jewish"—and in the introductions
to the three sections of this book I have explored the historical roots of
the Jewish-American experience and have attempted to explain more
fully the reasons for the recent flowering of literature by Jewish Americans. I have no desire to reduce these writers to a parochial nationality;
the brilliance of their achievement lies in an ability to draw upon
their Jewishness in varying intensities, as one aspect of complex American lives. But now that the literary achievement of Jews can be
measured with a degree of detachment, one can see that for the past
thirty years these writers did bring a special angle of vision to bear on
American society, as distinct as that of New Englanders in mid-
nineteenth century, Midwesterners in the early twentieth century,
Southerners in the thirties, and black Americans in the 1970's.

"To be a Jew in the twentieth century," writes Muriel Rukeyser, "Is
to be offered a gift. If you refuse / Wishing to be invisible you choose /
Death of the spirit, the stone insanity." Many did choose invisibility
and self-hatred, as the following pages suggest; but many more accepted the gift and used it as one touchstone to an understanding of

America and the Western world. In the shadow of Hitler and the creation of Israel, how could the Jew avoid his place at the center of man's consciousness? And how could the Jewish American, still a man of the book, help but create a literature that drew upon his self-consciousness as a Jew. "The gift is torment," the poem continues, and surely the gift has produced a tormented literature, but also, one hastens to add, a literature of humor and seriousness, of tolerance and misunderstanding, of moral sensitivity, of the repeated assertion that man —in spite of his absurd condition—possesses dignity. Like all great human experiences transfigured into literature, the gift of being Jewish in the twentieth century has been returned as a gift for all people, a token passed on in the form of a permanent literary heritage.

PART I

Early Literature and the East-European Migration

Emigrants coming to America in steerage aboard the S.S. West-
ernland, c. 1890. Museum of the City of New York.

Introduction

Before 1880, Jewish immigrants had a minimal effect on American culture. They had come to colonial New England and established themselves primarily as tradesmen in the cities. Migrating from England and France, Poland, Hungary, Russia, and Germany, Jews were readily accepted into Puritan life, so that by the time of the Revolution they formed a sizable community in Newport, Rhode Island.

The Jews who came to America in the seventeenth and eighteenth centuries enjoyed a better life than they had known in their old countries. They left Europe for traditional reasons: economic deprivation, religious prejudice, and political oppression. Traveling to the New World, they brought with them a sense of adventure, the quest for a quick fortune, and the desire to be released from the tyranny of Europe. "The old master Europe, the masterless America," is D. H. Lawrence's characterization of the immigrant experience. "That's why most people have come to America, and still do come. To get away from everything they are and have been."

In the beginning, most Jews did not become different people in America. They were itinerant peddlers who wanted to own country stores and, if they were successful enough, to move their dry goods businesses into the city. Although some were able to practice a profession, most Jews in the seventeenth, eighteenth, and nineteenth centuries were merchants of one sort or another; and in their eagerness to rise economically, they moved south, from town to town, until Jews were scattered across the entire United States.

Of all European nations, Germany contributed the greatest number of immigrants until the end of the nineteenth century. The mass migration of Germans began in 1836 and ended in 1880, when the Jewish-American population amounted to 250,000. The German Jews were represented by the well-known rabbi, Isaac Mayer Wise (1819–1900), who was particularly concerned with the Americanization of immigrants. Mayer challenged the conservatism of the other German-Jewish leader, Isaac Lesser, and was successful in reforming the synagogue service, modernizing the Hebrew prayer book, and establishing the Hebrew Union College in Cincinnati in 1875.

By the turn of the century, German Jews were remarkably successful businessmen, accountants, salesmen, lawyers, and doctors; they regarded with a certain hostility the orthodox and politically radical immigrants from Eastern Europe who had begun to arrive in the early 1880's. These poverty-stricken people—from Russia, Rumania, and Austria—were fleeing various pogroms, and when they came to America, they settled in the cities and formed communities of orthodox Jews. The East Europeans became laborers and did not assimilate themselves into American society so quickly as the German Jews. Their two outstanding characteristics— religious orthodoxy and political radicalism—threatened the middle-class position of German Jewry; however, the Germans quickly realized that any anti-Semitism inflicted upon new immigrants might soon affect them as well, and they offered assistance to the East Europeans. In time, the religious fervor of the immigrants yielded to a social consciousness that became the central characteristic of Jews in twentieth-century America.

East Europeans represented 75 percent of American Jewry at the turn of the century. Their immigration to this country merged with the rapid development of cities, so that their remarkable success has always been associated with urban life. Gimbel, Altman, Bloomingdale, and Filene were soon famous names in American retailing; Louis D. Brandeis, Benjamin Cardozo, and Felix Frankfurter began careers as lawyers and later served as justices in the Supreme Court; Felix Adler and Morris Raphael Cohen turned to philosophy; Joseph Pulitzer, Adolph S. Ochs, and Walter Lippman became journalists; Abraham Jacobi, Marion B. Sulzberger, and Isaac Levin did brilliant work in their respective fields of pediatrics, dermatology, and cancer. A full list of significant figures who emerged from nineteenth- and early twentieth-century Jewry makes an impressive record of one minority's contribution to American civilization. Indeed, that contribution may partially be the reason why Jews enjoy the status of a major religion in a country whose origins and history are fundamentally Christian: the three major religions in America are Protestant, Catholic, and Jewish, even though the six million Jews here occupy only three-and-one-half percent of the population.

Jews have been particularly prominent in all the arts. The development of theater, film, television, painting, and music in America is marked by brilliant Jewish actors, directors, and performers; indeed, the first real success in the arts was achieved by popular entertainers like Charlie Chaplin, Eddie Cantor, and the Marx Brothers. Of all the arts, however, literature has been the most faithful reflection of the Jewish experience in America, even though its beginnings are limited aesthetically. Nineteenth-century writers, for example, expressed themselves imitatively, but their writing is still of interest as a commentary on the early Jewish experience in America.

I have presented selections from the work of Isaac Mayer Wise and Abraham Cahan, which represent respectively the reactions of a German and an East European immigrant to America; a chapter from Mary Antin's *The Promised Land,* which expresses the idealism that so many youngsters carried with them to the New World; and the poetry of Penina Moise, Adah Isaacs Menken, and Emma Lazarus, which suggests the concerns of three gifted nineteenth-century poets in terms of their Jewish identity in America. Like the early literature of most ethnic groups, this writing is a modest achievement; but it reminds us of some of the roots from which the great flowering of literature by American Jews developed.

ISAAC MAYER WISE (1819–1900)

The leading figure of German-Jewish immigration to America was Isaac Mayer Wise. Born in Bohemia in 1819, he came to America in 1846 and established himself as a rabbi of Congregation Beth-El in Albany, New York. He soon became convinced that traditional Judaism would not survive in America, and he sought to modernize religious practices through a national organization of American Jews. With this objective in mind, Wise moved to Cincinnati, where there was a large Jewish community more amenable to his radical ideas. He created The Israelite, a popular Jewish newspaper, and Die Deborah, a German-language magazine; with the influence he exerted through these journals, Wise established the Union American Hebrew Congregations in 1873, the Hebrew Union College in 1875, and the Central Conference of American Rabbis in 1889.

Wise began to write his memoirs in 1874 and went so far as to trace the first eleven years of his life in America. He never completed the work, however, for many of his opponents were still alive and he did not wish to intensify his disagreements with them. His work was translated into English by David Philipson and published as Reminiscences by Isaac M. Wise in 1901. This volume is one of the best accounts of the German-Jewish immigration to America between 1835 and 1960.

An Immigrant in New York

Upon my arrival in New York I had much luggage, but little money. A countryman of mine, who had a horse and cart at hand, offered to take my luggage to Essex Street for $6. The price seemed to me too high. I spoke with an Irishman, who also had a horse and wagon; he asked $2 for the same service, and I gave the Irishman the preference over my obliging countryman.

I had to make similar arrangements for my fellow-travelers; this incensed a dozen German drivers against me. "Now this confounded Jew has to know English, and take the morsel of bread out of our mouths," cried one of them threateningly, and the chorus joined in with all possible objurgations against the Jews. I did not swear, but I was exceedingly angry. Aha! thought I, you have left home and kindred in order to get away from the disgusting Judaeophobia, and here the first German greeting that sounds in your ears is "Hep! hep!" [Down with the Jews!]. True, in my magnanimity I gave no retort to the gruff drivers. I turned my back on them, but I indulged the right of being angry to my heart's content, for I felt that from now on I was no longer an im-perial-royal, Bohemian *Schutzjude* [protected Jew], but that I was breath-ing a free atmosphere, and no one could prevent me from being as angry as I pleased.

My wife and child were taken from the ship to his home in Staten Island by a certain John Lindheim. This Mr. Lindheim had a clothing store on the Bowery, and my brother-in-law, Edward Bloch [later a founder of the Bloch Publishing Company], a youth of sixteen, clerked for him. Hence the friendship between the Lindheim family and my own. I could not remain in Lindheim's house, because I was compelled to be the guest of Mr. Joseph Cohn. I had married him six months previously in Radnitz [Bohemia]. He was about to emigrate, and in lieu of a fee engaged to have me stop with him on my arrival in New York. The promise was given and kept. Soon, however, we were enabled to move into a house on Broom[e] Street, belonging to Mr. Friedman, where we went to housekeeping.

In 1846, New York was a large village. On Broadway, as far up as Canal Street, and in the business section east of Broadway, the beginnings of the metropolis were perceptible, but elsewhere it was like a village. Small, insignificant-looking people went in and out of small houses, small shops, small institutions. The first impression that the city made upon me was exceedingly unfavorable. The whole city appeared to me like a large shop where everyone buys or sells, cheats or is cheated. I had never before seen a city so bare of all arts and of every trace of good taste; likewise I had never witnessed anywhere such rushing, hurrying, chasing, running. In addition to this, there was the crying, blowing, clamoring, and other noises of the fishmongers, milkmen, ragpickers, newsboys, dealers in popcorn, etc., earsplitting noises which were often drowned in the rumblings of the wagons and the cries of the street gamins.

All this shocked my aesthetic sense beyond expression. In the first five days, I heard the sound of music but once in the street; this was produced by a wandering, mediocre Bohemian band which thundered Turkish music. Yet, on the other hand, I heard, on the very first day, the favorite, and in fact the only dance music known here, played by a negro, who fiddled outrageously and at the same time called the figures of the quadrille in a hoarse voice. Everything seemed so pitifully small and paltry; and I had had so exalted an idea of the land of freedom, that New York seemed to me like a lost station by the sea; on that first day I longed to be away from the city.

An American Judaism

But why have Jews so little regard for one another that they revile and traduce each other? How is it that a highly honored public applauds loudly whenever literary rowdies squabble like street gamins, and throw mud at decent people? Whence comes this wretched imitation of Christian customs, good and bad, by Jews; this cringing to every Christian fashion; this eager association with, this humble attitude towards, every Christian, even though he be a knave, for no other reason than that he is not a Jew? Whence this disgusting phenomenon?

I could find but one answer to these questions. The century-long oppression has demoralized the German and Polish Jew and robbed him of his self-respect. He has no self-respect, no pride left. The hep! hep! [attacks on Jews] times still weigh him down; he bows and scrapes, he crawls and cringes. The Jew respects not the fellow man in another Jew, because he lacks the consciousness of manhood in himself. He parodies and imitates, because he has lost himself. After diagnosing the evil, I set myself to seeking a remedy.

The Jew must be Americanized, I said to myself, for every German book, every German word reminds him of the old disgrace. If he continues under German influences, as they are now in this country, he must become either a bigot or an atheist, a satellite or a tyrant. He will never be aroused to self-consciousness or to independent thought. The Jew must become an American, in order to gain the proud self-consciousness of the free-born man.

From that hour I began to Americanize with all my might and was as enthusiastic for this as I was for Reform. Since then, as a matter of course, the German element here, as well as in Germany, has completely changed, although Judaeophobia and uncouthness have survived in many; but at that time it appeared to me that there was but one remedy that would prove effective for my coreligionists, and that was to Americanize them thoroughly. We must be not only American citizens, but become Americans through and through, outside of the synagogue. This was my cry then and many years thereafter.

PENINA MOISE (1797–1880)

Penina Moise was born on April 23, 1797, in Charleston, South Carolina. Her father died when she was only twelve years of age, and she was forced to leave school permanently. She remained with her mother, who became a paralytic in 1838, and devoted herself to teaching and writing. During the yellow fever epidemic of 1854 and throughout the Civil War she became known to the people of Charleston for her acts of charity. All her life Penina Moise suffered from failing sight, neuralgia and other physical ailments as well as from the effects of poverty, but her deep and sincere religious faith gave her a sense of resignation and humility; these qualities characterize her poetry.

The following two poems are taken from the Hymns which Penina Moise composed for the use of the congregation in the Charleston Synagogue. Her secular verse was published together with her religious works in 1911, but her most important writing remains the Hymns Written for the Use of Hebrew Congregations. These 190 poems are simple expressions of faith whose central theme is almost exclusively the adulation of God and the gratitude Penina Moise felt for His kindness.

Man of the World

Man of the world! wilt thou not pause,
And give thy heart to Heaven's cause?
In paths of interest wilt thou plod,
Forgetful of the Lord thy God?

Oh! turn away from life's parade,
Before thy soul hath been betrayed
From virtue's eminence to stoop,
And forfeit its eternal hope.

What purer pleasures wouldst thou taste,
Than are by piety embraced?
What higher prize couldst thou obtain,
Than thy Creator's love to gain?

The wealth and glory of the skies
Are won, by generous sacrifice,
By him who selfish joy foregoes
To mitigate another's woes;

Whose resignation, calm and meek,
Will humbly of God's chastening speak;
Whose soul from perjury is free,
And worships but one Deity.

Man of the world! no gift of thine
Compares with Mercy's pledge divine,
Which pardon to each sinner yields,
Whose spirit true contrition feels.

Can he who justice has abhorred,
Believe that Power will accord
Pardon to him, who has transgressed
Statutes, that human wrongs redressed?
Sternly the upright spirit frowns
On mortals who o'erleap its bounds.

Oh God! though great my sins may be,
From stains like these my soul is free.
Perverseness, arrogance, and pride
Have oft Thy precepts set aside;
For evil, both in word and deed,
Forgiveness doth Thy servant need.

But Thou the penitent will raise,
Who humbly at thy altar prays,
Stretch out Thy right hand to the meek,
Sustain the desolate and weak;
And in the book of mercy write,
The broken-hearted and contrite.

Exalted Theme of Human Praise

Exalted theme of human praise,
In filial confidence I raise
    To Thee the voice of prayer;
Burthened with guilt and shame and grief,
Father in heaven! for relief
    To Thee I still repair.

Thou seest the shadows of my heart,
To man it turns its sunny part,
    Ashamed of passion's storm.
In Thy compassion I confide,
O gentle Judge and gracious Guide!
    My frailties to reform.

Meekly will I thy chastening bear,
And sackcloth on my spirit wear,
    For trespass to atone;
But pity e'er transcends Thine ire,
When to thy footstool, Holy Sire!
    Sin hath for mercy flown.

Now let that attribute divine,
Upon contrition's tear-drops shine,
    And like a rainbow rest
On the horizon of my soul,
Till ev'ry cloud shall from it roll,
    And leave it pure and blest.

ADAH ISAACS MENKEN (1835-1868)

Adah Isaacs Menken was born on June 15, 1835 near New Orleans. Her father died when she was only two and her stepfather when she was eighteen. She spent a quiet childhood in the South and received a sound education, which included a knowledge of Latin, Hebrew, and French. In 1856 she traveled to Galveston and met the son of a wealthy Cincinnati family, a musician named Alexander Isaacs Menken. They married on April 3rd of the same year and settled in New Orleans.

Adah Menken's talents were expressed in drama and in poetry. Although she had performed in amateur theatricals, she did not appear professionally until her husband lost his fortune in the panic of 1857. When she arrived in Cincinnati, a few years later, to pursue her dramatic career, she was already known to intellectuals and artists through poems published in The Israelite. She soon grew interested in the development of a Jewish homeland, expressing great sympathy for the oppressed Jews of the world and denouncing all varieties of anti-Semitism. She also believed in mysticism and in the advent of a Messiah, envisaging herself as a prophet of the Hebrew people.

Adah Isaacs Menken was an unsettled and erratic person. Shortly after her divorce from Alexander Menken, she married John Carmel Heenan, an Irishman who was heavyweight boxing champion of America. She bore his baby, although he claimed that he had never married her; in a few months, the baby died and Heenan deserted her. Her public humiliation was aggravated when she was involved in a suit that a Bowery hotel brought against Heenan for his failure to pay a bill. Out of these embarrassments—some sparked by Adah Menken's fiery personality, some the result of genuine misfortune—stemmed the poetry for which she is best known.

Adah Menken met Walt Whitman in Pfaff's restaurant on Broadway and was influenced by him. Liberated artistically by Whitman's experiments in free verse and in unconventional subject matter, she wrote poetry that reflected her unstable character. After her divorce from Heenan she married Robert Henry Newell, the literary editor of the Sunday Mercury, in which her poems had appeared; that marriage, however, was short-lived. Her fourth husband was the wealthy New Yorker James Barkley, from whom she was soon separated. After collapsing at a rehearsal in Paris she died on August 10, 1868. Her collection of verse, from which these poems are taken, is Infelicia.

One Year Ago

In feeling I was but a child,
    When first we met—one year ago,
As free and guileless as the bird,
    That roams the dreary woodland through.

My heart was all a pleasant world
    Of sunbeams dewed with April tears:
Life's brightest page was turned to me,
    And naught I read of doubts or fears.

We met—we loved—one year ago,
    Beneath the stars of summer skies;
Alas! I knew not then, as now,
    The darkness of life's mysteries.

You took my hand—one year ago,
    Beneath the azure dome above,
And gazing on the stars you told
    The trembling story of your love.

I gave to you—one year ago,
    The only jewel that was mine;
My heart took off her lonely crown,
    And all her riches gave to thine.

HEAR, O ISRAEL!

"And they shall be my people, and I will be their God."—JEREMIAH xxxii. 38.

From the Hebrew

I.

Hear, O Israel! and plead my cause against the ungodly nation!

'Midst the terrible conflict of Love and Peace, I departed from thee, my people, and spread my tent of many colors in the land of Egypt.

In their crimson and fine linen I girded my white form.

Sapphires gleamed their purple light from out the darkness of my hair.

The silver folds of their temple foot-cloth was spread beneath my sandaled feet.

Thus I slumbered through the daylight.

Slumbered 'midst the vapor of sin,
Slumbered 'midst the battle and din,
Wakened 'midst the strangle of breath,
Wakened 'midst the struggle of death!

II.

Hear, O Israel! my people—to thy goodly tents do I return with unstained hands.

Like as the harts for the water-brooks, in thirst, do pant and bray, so pants and cries my longing soul for the house of Jacob.

My tears have unto me been meat, both in night and day:

And the crimson and fine linen moulders in the dark tents of the enemy.

With bare feet and covered head do I return to thee, O Israel!

With sackcloth have I bound the hem of my garments.

With olive leaves have I trimmed the border of my bosom.

The breaking waves did pass o'er me; yea, were mighty in their strength—

Strength of the foe's oppression.

My soul was cast out upon the waters of Sin: but it has come back to me.

My transgressions have vanished like a cloud.

The curse of Balaam hath turned to a blessing;

And the doors of Jacob turn not on their hinges against me.

Rise up, O Israel! for it is I who passed through the fiery furnace seven times, and come forth unscathed, to redeem thee from slavery, O my nation! and lead thee back to God.

III.

Brothers mine, fling out your white banners over this Red Sea of wrath!

Hear ye not the Death-cry of a thousand burning, bleeding wrongs?

Against the enemy lift thy sword of fire, even thou, O Israel! whose prophet I am.

For I, of all thy race, with these tear-blinded eyes, still see the watch-fire leaping up its blood-red flame from the ramparts of our Jerusalem!

And my heart alone beats and palpitates, rises and falls with the glimmering and the gleaming of the golden beacon flame, by whose light I shall lead thee, O my people! back to freedom!

Give me time—oh give me time to strike from your brows the shadow-crowns of Wrong!

On the anvil of my heart will I rend the chains that bind ye.

Look upon me—oh look upon me, as I turn from the world—from love, and passion, to lead thee, thou Chosen of God, back to the pastures of Right and Life!

Fear me not; for the best blood that heaves this heart now runs for thee, thou Lonely Nation!

Why wear ye not the crown of eternal royalty, that God set down upon your heads?

Back, tyrants of the red hands!

Slouch back to your ungodly tents, and hide the Cain-brand on your foreheads!

Life for life, blood for blood, is the lesson ye teach us.

We, the Children of Israel, will not creep to the kennel graves ye are scooping out with iron hands, like scourged hounds!

Israel! rouse ye from the slumber of ages, and, though Hell welters at your feet, carve a road through these tyrants!

The promised dawn-light is here; and God—O the God of our nation is calling!

Press on—press on!

IV.

Ye, who are kings, princes, priests, and prophets. Ye men of Judah and bards of Jerusalem, hearken unto my voice, and I will speak thy name, O Israel!

Fear not; for God hath at last let loose His thinkers, and their voices now tremble in the mighty depths of this old world!

Rise up from thy blood-stained pillows!

Cast down to dust the hideous, galling chains that bind thy strong hearts down to silence!

Wear ye the badge of slaves?

See ye not the watch-fire?

Look aloft, from thy wilderness of thought!

Come forth with the signs and wonders, and thy strong hands, and stretched-out arms, even as thou didst from Egypt!

Courage, courage! trampled hearts!

Look at these pale hands and frail arms, that have rent asunder the welded chains that an army of the Philistines bound about me!

But the God of all Israel set His seal of fire on my breast, and lighted up, with inspiration, the soul that pants for the Freedom of a nation!

With eager wings she fluttered above the blood-stained bayonet-points of the millions, who are trampling upon the strong throats of God's people.

Rise up, brave hearts!

The sentry cries: "All's well!" from Hope's tower!

Fling out your banners of Right!

The watch fire grows brighter!

All's well! All's well!

Courage! Courage!

The Lord of Hosts is in the field,

The God of Jacob is our shield!

EMMA LAZARUS (1849–1887)

Emma Lazarus was born on July 22, 1849, daughter of a wealthy New York sugar merchant. She began to write poetry in her adolescence and drew the approval of William Cullen Bryant, who felt that her poems were "better than any verses I remember to have seen written by any American girl of eighteen." In her early years she was influenced by Emerson, who thought highly of her Poems and Translations (1866) and who carried on a close correspondence with his young disciple. Her second book of poetry, Admetus and Other Poems (1871), was dedicated to Emerson and clearly reveals his influence. Emma Lazarus was not formally religious, but she shared Emerson's love of nature and devoted much of her creative energy to an exploration of the inner life of man.

The early work of Emma Lazarus, which also included a novel, Alide (1874), and a play, The Spagnoletto (1876), was scarcely distinctive, and she grew dissatisfied with it. Edmund C. Stedman, a well-known poet and editor of the period, suggested that she return to the roots of her Jewish heritage; but Emma told him, in Stedman's words, that "although proud of her blood and lineage, the Hebrew ideals did not appeal to her." She did write a poetic drama, The Dance to Death (1882), concerned with the persecution of the Jews in Germany during the Middle Ages, as well as translate Heine's poetry; but she did not become deeply involved in Jewish subjects until she witnessed the homeless, poverty-stricken Jews who had come to Ward's Island because of Russian persecution in the pogroms of 1880–1881. From 1880 until the end of her life she was intensely concerned with Jewish culture. She contributed essays to The American Hebrew in defense of Russian Jewry; she wrote polemical poems—"The Banner of the Jew" and "The Crowing of the Red Cock"—that celebrated the courage of Jewish people and verse—"In Exile" and "The New Ezekiel"—that called for the unity of all Jews; and she wrote a series of sixteen articles, "An Epistle to the Hebrew," that once again stressed Jewish unity and urged Jews to educate themselves in preparation for the industrial twentieth century.

During the early 1880's Emma Lazarus became an outspoken Zionist. She was convinced that only a Jewish homeland would protect the persecuted Jews of the world. When she visited England in May, 1883, she was considered a leading figure among American Jews and an important poet. At this time her health declined, and after the death of her father in 1884, she grew extremely depressed and weak. She returned to Europe in 1885 but was never able to recover from the cancer that had infected her body, and she died on November 19, 1887, at the age of thirty-eight.

Emma Lazarus's finest verse is collected in The Songs of a Semite.

Her most famous poem, "The New Colossus," is a part of the American imagination because of its inscription on the pedestal of the Statue of Liberty; it reminds us of Emma Lazarus's great humanity and attachment to the immigrants who had come to the United States at the end of the nineteenth century. The other poems reflect her awakening to her Jewish heritage and her belief in a land for oppressed Jews of all nations.

In Exile

"Since that day till now our life is one unbroken paradise. We live a true brotherly life. Every evening after supper we take a seat under the mighty oak and sing our songs."—*Extract from a letter of a Russian refugee in Texas.**

Twilight is here, soft breezes bow the grass,
　　Day's sounds of various toil break slowly off,
The yoke-freed oxen low, the patient ass
　　Dips his dry nostril in the cool, deep trough.
Up from the prairie the tanned herdsmen pass
　　With frothy pails, guiding with voices rough
Their udder-lightened kine. Fresh smells of earth,
The rich, black furrows of the glebe send forth.

After the Southern day of heavy toil,
　　How good to lie, with limbs relaxed, brows bare
To evening's fan, and watch the smoke-wreaths coil
　　Up from one's pipe-stem through the rayless air.
So deem these unused tillers of the soil,
　　Who stretched beneath the shadowing oak-tree, stare
Peacefully on the star-unfolding skies,
And name their life unbroken paradise.

* The letter was shown to Emma Lazarus by Michael Heilprin (1823–1888), who had come to this country in 1856. In 1879–1880 he published the first two volumes of *Historical Poetry of the Ancient Hebrews.* He was very active in aiding the refugees from the pogroms.

The hounded stag that has escaped the pack,
    And pants at ease within a thick-leaved dell;
The unimprisoned bird that finds the track
    Through sun-bathed space, to where his fellows dwell;
The martyr, granted respite from the rack,
    The death-doomed victim pardoned from his cell,—
Such only know the joy these exiles gain,—
Life's sharpest rapture is surcease of pain.

Strange faces theirs, wherethrough the Orient sun
    Gleams from the eyes and glows athwart the skin.
Grave lines of studious thought and purpose run
    From curl-crowned forehead to dark-bearded chin.
And over all the seal is stamped thereon
    Of anguish branded by a world of sin,
In fire and blood through ages on their name,
Their seal of glory and the Gentiles' shame.

Freedom to love the law that Moses brought,
    To sing the songs of David, and to think
The thoughts Gabirol to Spinoza taught,
    Freedom to dig the common earth, to drink
The universal air—for this they sought
    Refuge o'er wave and continent, to link
Egypt with Texas in their mystic chain,
And truth's perpetual lamp forbid to wane.

Hark! through the quiet evening air, their song
    Floats forth with wild sweet rhythm and glad refrain.
They sing the conquest of the spirit strong,
    The soul that wrests the victory from pain;
The noble joys of manhood that belong
    To comrades and to brothers. In their strain
Rustle of palms and Eastern streams one hears,
And the broad prairie melts in mist of tears.

The New Ezekiel

WHAT, can these dead bones live, whose sap is dried
   By twenty scorching centuries of wrong?
Is this the House of Israel, whose pride
   Is as a tale that's told, an ancient song?
Are these ignoble relics all that live
   Of psalmist, priest, and prophet? Can the breath
Of very heaven bid these bones revive,
   Open the graves and clothe the ribs of death?

Yea, Prophesy, the Lord hath said. Again
   Say to the wind, Come forth and breathe afresh,
Even that they may live upon these slain,
   And bone to bone shall leap, and flesh to flesh.

The Spirit is not dead, proclaim the word,
   Where lay dead bones, a host of armed men stand!
I ope your graves, my people, saith the Lord,
   And I shall place you living in your land.

The Banner of the Jew

Wake, Israel, wake! Recall to-day
    The glorious Maccabean rage,
The sire heroic, hoary-gray,
    His five-fold lion-lineage:
The Wise, the Elect, the Help-of-God,
The Burst-of-Spring, the Avenging Rod.*

From Mizpeh's mountain-ridge** they saw
    Jerusalem's empty streets, her shrine
Laid waste where Greeks profaned the Law,
    With idol and with pagan sign.
Mourners in tattered black were there,
With ashes sprinkled on their hair.

Then from the stony peak there rang
    A blast to ope the graves: down poured
The Maccabean clan, who sang
    Their battle-anthem to the Lord.
Five heroes lead, and following, see,
Ten thousand rush to victory!

    * The sons of Mattathias—Jonathan, John, Eleazar, Simon (also called the Jewel), and Judas, the Prince.
    ** The Mizpeh was a place of solemn assembly for the Jews of Palestine at the time of the Maccabean revolt against Antiochus IV, 175–164 B.C.

Oh for Jerusalem's trumpet now,
    To blow a blast of shattering power,
To wake the sleepers high and low,
    And rouse them to the urgent hour!
No hand for vengeance—but to save,
A million naked swords should wave.

O deem not dead that martial fire,
    Say not the mystic flame is spent!
With Moses' law and David's lyre,
    Your ancient strength remains unbent.
Let but an Ezra* rise anew,
To lift the *Banner of the Jew!*

A rag, a mock at first—erelong,
    When men have bled and women wept,
To guard its precious folds from wrong,
    Even they who shrunk, even they who slept,
Shall leap to bless it, and to save.
Strike! for the brave revere the brave!**

* See Book of Ezra, Old Testament.
** This poem was first read at the closing exercises of the Temple Emanu-El-Religious School, New York, then appearing in *The Critic,* June 3, 1882, and was reprinted in *The American Hebrew,* June 9, 1882.

The Crowing of the Red Cock

Across the Eastern sky has glowed
    The flicker of a blood-red dawn,
Once more the clarion cock has crowed,
    Once more the sword of Christ is drawn.
A million burning rooftrees light
The world-wide path of Israel's flight.

Where is the Hebrew's fatherland?
    The folk of Christ is sore bestead;
The Son of Man is bruised and banned,
    Nor finds whereon to lay his head.
His cup is gall, his meat is tears,
His passion lasts a thousand years.

Each crime that wakes in man the beast,
    Is visited upon his kind.
The lust of mobs, the greed of priest,
    The tyranny of kings, combined
To root his seed from earth again,
His record is one cry of pain.

When the long roll of Christian guilt
    Against his sires and kin is known,
The flood of tears, the life-blood spilt,
    The agony of ages shown,

29

What oceans can the stain remove,
From Christian law and Christian love?

Nay, close the book; not now, not here,
    The hideous tale of sin narrate,
Reechoing in the martyr's ear,
    Even he might nurse revengeful hate,
Even he might turn in wrath sublime,
With blood for blood and crime for crime.

Coward? Not he, who faces death,
    Who singly against worlds has fought,
For what? A name he may not breathe,
    For liberty of prayer and thought.
The angry sword he will not whet,
His nobler task is—to forget.

Venus of the Louvre

Down the long hall she glistens like a star,
The foam-born mother of Love, transfixed to stone,
Yet none the less immortal, breathing on.
Time's brutal hand hath maimed but could not mar.
When first the enthralled enchantress from afar
Dazzled mine eyes, I saw not her alone,
Serenely poised on her world-worshipped throne,
As when she guided once her dove-drawn car,—
But at her feet a pale, death-stricken Jew,
Her life adorer, sobbed farewell to love.
Here *Heine* wept! Here still he weeps anew,
Nor ever shall his shadow lift or move,
While mourns one ardent heart, one poet-brain,
For vanished Hellas and Hebraic pain.

The New Colossus

Not like the brazen giant of Greek fame,
With conquering limbs astride from land to land;
Here at our sea-washed, sunset gates shall stand
A mighty woman with a torch, whose flame
Is the imprisoned lightning, and her name
Mother of Exiles. From her beacon-hand
Glows world-wide welcome; her mild eyes command
The air-bridged harbor that twin cities frame.
"Keep, ancient lands, your storied pomp!" cries she
With silent lips. "Give me your tired, your poor,
Your huddled masses yearning to breathe free,
The wretched refuse of your teeming shore.
Send these, the homeless, tempest-tost to me,
I lift my lamp beside the golden door!"

ABRAHAM CAHAN (1860–1951)

The central figure in Jewish-American literature of the early twentieth century was Abraham Cahan. As editor (1902–1951) of the most widely read Yiddish newspaper in the world, The Jewish Daily Forward, Cahan encouraged young immigrants to tell their stories and provided a forum for their work. As a short-story writer, novelist, and literary critic, he reflected the social and cultural life of the Lower East Side in New York when it made its greatest impact on America.

Cahan was born near Vilna, Lithuania, in 1860. The son of a Hebrew teacher, he attended the traditional Hebrew schools; but he soon developed a deep attachment to Russian literature and insisted upon acquiring a Russian public education. Cahan grew interested in socialism and joined a revolutionary organization; when his membership was discovered by the police, he fled to America and became a journalist. His attachment to literature grew once again, and under the influence of Tolstoy and Chekhov, he began to write realistic literature. Aiming for a wide reading public, he composed in Yiddish and established firm connections with the Jewish community in New York. His devotion to the development of Yiddish literature in America lasted all his life.

Cahan's first novel, Yekel: A Tale of the New York Ghetto, was published in 1896. William Dean Howells, the most influential editor in America at the time, had encouraged Cahan to write the novel, and when it appeared Howells hailed it as an important contribution to American literature. The book was not a success, despite the rise of interest in the immigrant experience. In 1913, Cahan wrote four stories about life on the Lower East Side which he later incorporated into The Rise of David Levinsky (1917), his most important single work.

The world of David Levinsky has passed from the American scene. Indeed, Cahan's novel went unread in the 1930's and 1940's as the children of immigrants tried to assimilate themselves into the mainstream of American life. But The Rise of David Levinsky is intrinsically a fine work of art; its clearly defined characters and richly textured milieu recall, with great perception, that East European migration to America which produced some of the most remarkable men and women in twentieth-century American life.

The Rise of David Levinsky

Two WEEKS LATER I was one of a multitude of steerage passengers on a Bremen steamship on my way to New York. Who can depict the feeling of desolation, homesickness, uncertainty, and anxiety with which an emigrant makes his first voyage across the ocean? I proved to be a good sailor, but the sea frightened me. The thumping of the engines was drumming a ghastly accompaniment to the awesome whisper of the waves. I felt in the embrace of a vast, uncanny force. And echoing through it all were the heart-lashing words:

"Are you crazy? You forget your place, young man!"

When Columbus was crossing the Atlantic, on his first great voyage, his men doubted whether they would ever reach land. So does many an American-bound emigrant to this day. Such, at least, was the feeling that was lurking in my heart while the Bremen steamer was carrying me to New York. Day after day passes and all you see about you is an unbroken waste of water, an unrelieved, a hopeless monotony of water. You know that a change will come, but this knowledge is confined to your brain. Your senses are skeptical. . . .

With twenty-nine cents in my pocket (four cents was all that was left of the sum which I had received from Matilda and her mother) I set forth in the direction of East Broadway.

Ten minutes' walk brought me to the heart of the Jewish East Side. The streets swarmed with Yiddish-speaking immigrants. The sign-boards

were in English and Yiddish, some of them in Russian. The scurry and
hustle of the people were not merely overwhelmingly greater, both in
volume and intensity, than in my native town. It was of another sort.
The swing and step of the pedestrians, the voices and manner of the
street peddlers, and a hundred and one other things seemed to testify to
far more self-confidence and energy, to larger ambitions and wider scopes,
than did the appearance of the crowds in my birthplace.

The great thing was that these people were better dressed than the
inhabitants of my town. The poorest-looking man wore a hat (instead of
a cap), a stiff collar and a necktie, and the poorest woman wore a hat
or a bonnet.

The appearance of a newly arrived immigrant was still a novel spec-
tacle on the East Side. Many of the passers-by paused to look at me
with wistful smiles of curiosity.

"There goes a green one!" some of them exclaimed.

The sight of me obviously evoked reminiscences in them of the days
when they had been "green ones" like myself. It was a second birth that
they were witnessing, an experience which they had once gone through
themselves and which was one of the greatest events in their lives.

"Green one" or "greenhorn" is one of the many English words and
phrases which my mother-tongue has appropriated in England and
America. Thanks to the many millions of letters that pass annually between the Jews of Russia and their relatives in the United States, a
number of these words have by now come to be generally known among
our people at home as well as here. In the eighties, however, one who
had not visited any English-speaking country was utterly unfamiliar
with them. And so I had never heard of "green one" before. Still,
"green," in the sense of color, is Yiddish as well as English, so I understood the phrase at once, and as a contemptuous quizzical appellation
for a newly arrived, inexperienced immigrant it stung me cruelly. As I
went along I heard it again and again. Some of the passers-by would
call me "greenhorn" in a tone of blighting gaiety, but these were an
exception. For the most part it was "green one" and in a spirit of sympathetic interest. It hurt me, all the same. Even those glances that offered
me a cordial welcome and good wishes had something self-complacent
and condescending in them. "Poor fellow! he is a green one," these people seemed to say. "We are not, of course. We are Americanized."

For my first meal in the New World I bought a three-cent wedge of
coarse rye bread, off a huge round loaf, on a stand on Essex Street. I
was too strict in my religious observances to eat it without first perform-
ing ablutions and offering a brief prayer. So I approached a bewigged old

woman who stood in the doorway of a small grocery-store to let me wash my hands and eat my small meal in her place. She looked old-fashioned enough, yet when she heard my request she said, with a laugh:

"You're a green one, I see."

"Suppose I am," I resented. "Do the yellow ones or black ones all eat without washing? Can't a fellow be a good Jew in America?"

"Yes, of course he can, but—well, wait till you see for yourself."

However, she asked me to come in, gave me some water and an old apron to serve me for a towel, and when I was ready to eat my bread she placed a glass of milk before me, explaining that she was not going to charge me for it.

"In America people are not foolish enough to be content with dry bread," she said, sententiously.

While I ate she questioned me about my antecedents. I remember how she impressed me as a strong, clever woman of few words as long as she catechised me, and how disappointed I was when she began to talk of herself. The astute, knowing mien gradually faded out of her face and I had before me a gushing, boastful old bore.

My intention was to take a long stroll, as much in the hope of coming upon some windfall as for the purpose of taking a look at the great American city. Many of the letters that came from the United States to my birthplace before I sailed had contained a warning not to imagine that America was a "land of gold" and that treasure might be had in the streets of New York for the picking. But these warnings only had the effect of lending vividness to my image of an American street as a thoroughfare strewn with nuggets of the precious metal. Symbolically speaking, this was the idea one had of the "land of Columbus." It was a continuation of the widespread effect produced by stories of Cortes and Pizarro in the sixteenth century, confirmed by the successes of some Russian emigrants of my time.

I asked the grocery-woman to let me leave my bundle with her, and, after considerable hesitation, she allowed me to put it among some empty barrels in her cellar.

I went wandering over the Ghetto. Instead of stumbling upon nuggets of gold, I found signs of poverty. In one place I came across a poor family who—as I learned upon inquiry—had been dispossessed for non-payment of rent. A mother and her two little boys were watching their pile of furniture and other household goods on the sidewalk while the passers-by were dropping coins into a saucer placed on one of the chairs to enable the family to move into new quarters.

What puzzled me was the nature of the furniture. For in my birthplace chairs and a couch like those I now saw on the sidewalk would be a sign of prosperity. But then anything was to be expected of a country where the poorest devil wore a hat and a starched collar.

I walked on.

The exclamation "A green one" or "A greenhorn" continued. If I did not hear it, I saw it in the eyes of the people who passed me.

When it grew dark and I was much in need of rest I had a street peddler direct me to a synagogue. I expected to spend the night there. What could have been more natural?

At the house of God I found a handful of men in prayer. It was a large, spacious room and the smallness of their number gave it an air of desolation. I joined in the devotions with great fervor. My soul was sobbing to Heaven to take care of me in the strange country.

The service over, several of the worshipers took up some Talmud folio or other holy book and proceeded to read them aloud in the familiar singsong. The strange surroundings suddenly began to look like home to me.

One of the readers, an elderly man with a pinched face and forked little beard, paused to look me over.

"A green one?" he asked, genially.

He told me that the synagogue was crowded on Saturdays, while on week-days people in America had no time to say their prayers at home, much less to visit a house of worship.

"It isn't Russia," he said, with a sigh. "Judaism has not much of a chance here."

When he heard that I intended to stay at the synagogue overnight he smiled ruefully.

"One does not sleep in an American synagogue," he said. "It is not Russia." Then, scanning me once more, he added, with an air of compassionate perplexity: "Where will you sleep, poor child? I wish I could take you to my house, but—well, America is not Russia. There is no pity here, no hospitality. My wife would raise a rumpus if I brought you along. I should never hear the last of it."

With a deep sigh and nodding his head plaintively he returned to his book, swaying back and forth. But he was apparently more interested in the subject he had broached. "When we were at home," he resumed, "she, too, was a different woman. She did not make life a burden to me as she does here. Have you no money at all?"

I showed him the quarter I had received from the cloak contractor.

"Poor fellow! Is that all you have? There are places where you can get a night's lodging for fifteen cents, but what are you going to do afterward? I am simply ashamed of myself."

" 'Hospitality,' " he quoted from the Talmud, " 'is one of the things which the giver enjoys in this world and the fruit of which he relishes in the world to come.' To think that I cannot offer a Talmudic scholar a night's rest! Alas! America has turned me into a mound of ashes."

"You were well off in Russia, weren't you?" I inquired, in astonishment. For, indeed, I had never heard of any but poor people emigrating to America.

"I used to spend my time reading Talmud at the synagogue," was his reply.

Many of his answers seemed to fit, not the question asked, but one which was expected to follow it. You might have thought him anxious to forestall your next query in order to save time and words, had it not been so difficult for him to keep his mouth shut.

"She," he said, referring to his wife, "had a nice little business. She sold feed for horses and she rejoiced in the thought that she was married to a man of learning. True, she has a tongue. That she always had, but over there it was not so bad. She has become a different woman here. Alas! America is a topsy-turvy country."

He went on to show how the New World turned things upside down, transforming an immigrant shoemaker into a man of substance, while a former man of leisure was forced to work in a factory here. In like manner, his wife had changed for the worse, for, lo and behold! instead of supporting him while he read Talmud, as she used to do at home, she persisted in sending him out to peddle. "America is not Russia," she said. "A man must make a living here." But, alas! it was too late to begin now! He had spent the better part of his life at his holy books and was fit for nothing else now. His wife, however, would take no excuse. He must peddle or be nagged to death. And if he ventured to slip into some synagogue of an afternoon and read a page or two he would be in danger of being caught red-handed, so to say, for, indeed, she often shadowed him to make sure that he did not play truant. Alas! America was not Russia.

A thought crossed my mind that if Reb Sender were here, he, too, might have to go peddling. Poor Reb Sender! The very image of him with a basket on his arm broke my heart. America did seem to be the most cruel place on earth.

"I am telling you all this that you may see why I can't invite you to my house," explained the peddler.

All I did see was that the poor man could not help unburdening his mind to the first listener that presented himself.

He pursued his tale of woe. He went on complaining of his own fate, quite forgetful of mine. Instead of continuing to listen, I fell to gazing around the synagogue more or less furtively. One of the readers attracted my special attention. He was a venerable-looking man with a face which, as I now recall it, reminds me of Thackeray. Only he had a finer head than the English novelist.

At last the henpecked man discovered my inattention and fell silent. A minute later his tongue was at work again.

"You are looking at that man over there, aren't you?" he asked.

"Who is he?"

"When the Lord of the World gives one good luck he gives one good looks as well."

"Why, is he rich?"

"His son-in-law is, but then his daughter cherishes him as she does the apple of her eye, and—well, when the Lord of the World wishes to give a man happiness he gives him good children, don't you know."

He rattled on, betraying his envy of the venerable-looking man in various ways and telling me all he knew about him—that he was a widower named Even, that he had been some years in America, and that his daughter furnished him all the money he needed and a good deal more, so that "he lived like a monarch." Even would not live in his daughter's house, however, because her kitchen was not conducted according to the laws of Moses, and everything else in it was too modern. So he roomed and boarded with pious strangers, visiting her far less frequently than she visited him and never eating at her table.

"He is a very proud man," my informant said. "One must not approach him otherwise than on tiptoe."

I threw a glance at Even. His dignified singsong seemed to confirm my interlocutor's characterization of him.

"Perhaps you will ask me how his son-in-law takes it all?" the voluble Talmudist went on. "Well, his daughter is a beautiful woman and well favored." The implication was that her husband was extremely fond of her and let her use his money freely. "They are awfully rich and they live like veritable Gentiles, which is a common disease among the Jews of America. But then she observes the commandment, 'Honor thy father.' That she does."

Again he tried to read his book and again the temptation to gossip was too much for him. He returned to Even's pride, dwelling with con-

siderable venom upon his love of approbation and vanity. "May the
Uppermost not punish me for my evil words, but to see him take his roll
of bills out of his pocket and pay his contribution to the synagogue one
would think he was some big merchant and not a poor devil sponging on
his son-in-law."

A few minutes later he told me admiringly how Even often "loaned"
him a half-dollar to enable him to do some reading at the house of God.

"I tell my virago of a wife I have sold fifty cents' worth of goods," he
explained to me, sadly.

After a while the man with the Thackeray face closed his book, kissed
it, and rose to go. On his way out he unceremoniously paused in front
of me, a silver snuff-box in his left hand, and fell to scrutinizing me. He
had the appearance of a well-paid rabbi of a large, prosperous town. "He
is going to say, 'A green one,'" I prophesied to myself, all but shuddering
at the prospect. And, sure enough, he did, but he took his time about it,
which made the next minute seem a year to me. He took snuff with
tantalizing deliberation. Next he sneezed with great zest and then he
resumed sizing me up. The suspense was insupportable. Another second
and I might have burst out, "For mercy's sake say 'A green one,' and let
us be done with it." But at that moment he uttered it of his own accord:

"A green one, I see. Where from?" And grasping my hand he added
in Hebrew, "Peace be to ye."

His first questions about me were obsequiously answered by the man
with the forked beard, whereupon my attention was attracted by the fact
that he addressed him by his Gentile name—that is, as "Mr. Even," and
not by his Hebrew name, as he would have done in our birthplace.
Surely America did not seem to be much of a God-fearing country.

When Mr. Even heard of my Talmud studies he questioned me
about the tractates I had recently read and even challenged me to explain
an apparent discrepancy in a certain passage, for the double purpose of
testing my "Talmud brains" and flaunting his own. I acquitted myself
creditably, it seemed, and I felt that I was making a good impression
personally as well. Anyhow, he invited me to supper in a restaurant.

On our way there I told him of my mother's violent death, vaguely
hoping that it would add to his interest in me. I did—even more than I
had expected. To my pleasant surprise, he proved to be familiar with the
incident. It appeared that because our section lay far outside the region
of pogroms, or anti-Jewish riots, the killing of my mother by a Gentile
mob had attracted considerable attention. I was thrilled to find myself in
the lime-light of world-wide publicity. I almost felt like a hero.

"So you are her son?" he said, pausing to look me over, as though I had suddenly become a new man. "My poor orphan boy!"

He caused me to recount the incident in every detail. In doing so I made it as appallingly vivid as I knew how. He was so absorbed and moved that he repeatedly made me stop in the middle of the sidewalk so as to look me in the face as he listened.

"Oh, but you must be hungry," he suddenly interrupted me. "Come on."

Arrived at the restaurant, he ordered supper for me. Then he withdrew, commending me to the care of the proprietress until he should return.

He had no sooner shut the door behind him than she took to questioning me: Was I a relative of Mr. Even? If not, then why was he taking so much interest in me? She was a vivacious, well-fed young matron with cheeks of a flaming red and with the consciousness of business success all but spurting from her black eyes. From what she, assisted by one of the other customers present, told me about my benefactor I learned that his son-in-law was the owner of the tenement-house in which the restaurant was located, as well as of several other buildings. They also told me of the landlord's wife, of her devotion to her father, and of the latter's piety and dignity. It appeared, however, that in her filial reverence she would draw the line upon his desire not to spare the rod upon her children, which was really the chief reason why he was a stranger at her house.

I had been waiting about two hours and was growing uneasy, when Mr. Even came back, explaining that he had spent the time taking his own supper and finding lodgings for me.

He then took me to store after store, buying me a suit of clothes, a hat, underclothes, handkerchiefs (the first white handkerchiefs I ever possessed), collars, shoes, and a necktie.

He spent a considerable sum on me. As we passed from block to block he kept saying, "Now you won't look green," or, "That will make you look American." At one point he added, "Not that you are a bad-looking fellow as it is, but then one must be presentable in America." At this he quoted from the Talmud an equivalent to the saying that one must do in Rome as the Romans do.

When all our purchases had been made he took me to a barber shop with bathrooms in the rear.

"Give him a hair-cut and a bath," he said to the proprietor. "Cut off his side-locks while you are at it. One may go without them and yet be a good Jew."

He disappeared again, but when I emerged from the bathroom I found him waiting for me. I stood before him, necktie and collar in hand, not knowing what to do with them, till he showed me how to put them on.

"Don't worry, David," he consoled me. "When I came here I, too, had to learn these things." When he was through with the job he took me in front of a looking-glass. "Quite an American, isn't he?" he said to the barber, beamingly. "And a good-looking fellow, too."

When I took a look at the mirror I was bewildered. I scarcely recognized myself.

I was mentally parading my "modern" make-up before Matilda. A pang of yearning clutched my heart. It was a momentary feeling. For the rest, I was all in a flutter with embarrassment and a novel relish of existence. It was as though the hair-cut and the American clothes had changed my identity. The steamer, Gitelson, and the man who had snatched him up now appeared to be something of the remote past. The day had been so crowded with novel impressions that it seemed an age.

He took me to an apartment in a poor tenement-house and introduced me to a tall, bewhiskered, morose-looking, elderly man and a smiling woman of thirty-five, explaining that he had paid them in advance for a month's board and lodging. When he said, "This is Mr. Levinsky," I felt as though I was being promoted in rank as behooved my new appearance. "Mister" struck me as something like a title of nobility. It thrilled me. But somehow it seemed ridiculous, too. Indeed, it was some time before I could think of myself as a "Mister" without being tempted to laugh.

"And here is some cash for you," he said, handing me a five-dollar bill, and some silver, in addition. "And now you must shift for yourself. That's all I can do for you. Nor, indeed, would I do more if I could. A young man like you must learn to stand on his own legs. Understand? If you do well, come to see me. Understand?"

There was an eloquent pause which said that if I did not do well I was not to molest him. Then he added, aloud:

"There is only one thing I want you to promise me. Don't neglect your religion nor your Talmud. Do you promise that, David?"

I did. There was a note of fatherly tenderness in the way this utter stranger called me David. It reminded me of Reb Sender. I wanted to say something to express my gratitude, but I felt a lump in my throat.

He advised me to invest the five dollars in dry-goods and to take up peddling. Then, wishing me good luck, he left.

My landlady, who had listened to Mr. Even's parting words with pious nods and rapturous grins, remarked that one would vainly search the world for another man like him, and proceeded to make my bed on a lounge.

The room was a kitchen. The stove was a puzzle to me. I wondered whether it was really a stove.

"Is this used for heating?" I inquired.

"Yes, for heating and cooking," she explained, with smiling cordiality. And she added, with infinite superiority, "America has no use for those big tile ovens."

When I found myself alone in the room the feeling of desolation and uncertainty which had tormented me all day seized me once again.

I went to bed and began to say my bed-prayer. I did so mechanically. My mind did not attend to the words I was murmuring. Instead, it was saying to God: "Lord of the Universe, you have been good to me so far. I went out of that grocery-store in the hope of coming upon some good piece of luck and my hope was realized. Be good to me in the future as well. I shall be more pious than ever, I promise you, even if America is a godless country."

I was excruciatingly homesick. My heart went out to my poor dead mother. Then I reflected that it was my story of her death that had led Even to spend so much money on me. It seemed as if she were taking care of me from her grave. It seemed, too, as though she had died so that I might arouse sympathy and make a good start in America. I thought of her and of all Antomir, and my pangs of yearning for her were tinged with pangs of my unrequited love for Matilda.

MARY ANTIN (1882–1949)

Mary Antin was born in Poland in 1882 and grew up under the shadow of Czar Alexander III. The record of her early years in the midst of an orthodox Jewish community and her subsequent migration to Chelsea, Massachusetts, reveals the extent to which a sensitive child thought of America as "the promised land."

Mary Antin's father had a series of financial reversals in Europe, and when he finally settled near Boston in 1894, he experienced further difficulty in establishing himself; but Mary, a gifted child who represented her family in the New England elementary school, remained idealistic and regarded America as the land of infinite possibilities. She shed her religious faith and struggled to assimilate herself into the American mainstream. The Promised Land is a moving account of the difficulties she confronted.

Mary Antin succeeded, for a time, in achieving her goals. She married a Christian professor of paleontology and settled near New York, in an affluent suburb; in 1920, however, her husband went to China, leaving Mary and her daughter alone for more than twenty-five years. Mary Antin became a social worker and, as she grew older, turned increasingly religious.

The Promised Land

Father himself conducted us to school. He would not have delegated that mission to the President of the United States. He had awaited the day with impatience equal to mine, and the visions he saw as he hurried us over the sun-flecked pavements transcended all my dreams. Almost his first act on landing on American soil, three years before, had been his application for naturalization. He had taken the remaining steps in the process with eager promptness, and at the earliest moment allowed by the law, he became a citizen of the United States. It is true that he had left home in search of bread for his hungry family, but he went blessing the necessity that drove him to America. The boasted freedom of the New World meant to him far more than the right to reside, travel, and work wherever he pleased; it meant the freedom to speak his thoughts, to throw off the shackles of superstition, to test his own fate, unhindered by political or religious tyranny. He was only a young man when he landed—thirty-two; and most of his life he had been held in leading-strings. He was hungry for his untasted manhood.

Three years passed in sordid struggle and disappointment. He was not prepared to make a living even in America, where the day laborer eats wheat instead of rye. Apparently the American flag could not protect him against the pursuing Nemesis of his limitations; he must expiate the sins of his fathers who slept across the seas. He had been endowed at birth with a poor constitution, a nervous, restless temperament, and an abundance of hindering prejudices. In his boyhood his body was starved, that his mind might be stuffed with useless learning. In his youth this dearly gotten learning was sold, and the price was the bread and salt which he had not been trained to earn for himself. Under the wedding canopy he was bound for life to a girl whose features were still strange to him; and he was bidden to multiply himself, that sacred learning might be perpetuated in his sons, to the glory of the God of his fathers. All this while he had been led about as a creature without a will, a chattel, an instrument. In his maturity he awoke, and found himself poor in health, poor in purse, poor in useful knowledge, and hampered on all sides. At the first nod of opportunity he broke away from his prison, and strove to atone for his wasted youth by a life of useful labor; while at the same time he sought to lighten the gloom of his narrow scholarship by freely partaking of modern ideas. But his utmost endeavor still left him far from his goal. In business, nothing prospered with him. Some fault of hand or mind or temperament led him to failure where other men found success. Wherever the blame for his disabilities be placed, he reaped their bitter fruit. "Give me bread!" he cried to America. "What will you do to earn it?" the challenge came back. And he found that he was master of no art, of no trade; that even his precious learning was of no avail, because he had only the most antiquated methods of communicating it.

So in his primary quest he had failed. There was left him the compensation of intellectual freedom. That he sought to realize in every possible way. He had very little opportunity to prosecute his education, which, in truth, had never been begun. His struggle for a bare living left him no time to take advantage of the public evening school; but he lost nothing of what was to be learned through reading, through attendance at public meetings, through exercising the rights of citizenship. Even here he was hindered by a natural inability to acquire the English language. In time, indeed, he learned to read, to follow a conversation or lecture; but he never learned to write correctly, and his pronunciation remains extremely foreign to this day.

If education, culture, the higher life were shining things to be worshipped from afar, he had still a means left whereby he could draw one step nearer to them. He could send his children to school, to learn all those things that he knew by fame to be desirable. The common school, at least, perhaps high school; for one or two, perhaps even college! His children should be students, should fill his house with books and intellectual company; and thus he would walk by proxy in the Elysian Fields of liberal learning. As for the children themselves, he knew no surer way to their advancement and happiness.

So it was with a heart full of longing and hope that my father led us to school on that first day. He took long strides in his eagerness, the rest of us running and hopping to keep up.

At last the four of us stood around the teacher's desk; and my father, in his impossible English, gave us over in her charge, with some broken word of his hopes for us that his swelling heart could no longer contain. I venture to say that Miss Nixon was struck by something uncommon in the group we made, something outside of Semitic features and the abashed manner of the alien. My little sister was as pretty as a doll, with her clear pink-and-white face, short golden curls, and eyes like blue violets when you caught them looking up. My brother might have been a girl, too, with his cherubic contours of face, rich red color, glossy black hair, and fine eyebrows. Whatever secret fears were in his heart, remembering his former teachers, who had taught with the rod, he stood up straight and uncringing before the American teacher, his cap respectfully doffed. Next to him stood a starved-looking girl with eyes ready to pop out, and short dark curls that would not have made much of a wig for a Jewish bride.

All three children carried themselves rather better than the common run of "green" pupils that were brought to Miss Nixon. But the figure that challenged attention to the group was the tall, straight father, with his earnest face and fine forehead, nervous hands eloquent in gesture, and a voice full of feeling. . . . I think Miss Nixon guessed what my father's best English could not convey. I think she divined that by the simple act of delivering our school certificates to her he took possession of America.

PART II

Between the Wars
(1920-1940)

Stella Adler and J. E. Bromberg in Clifford Odets' "Awake and Sing." Museum of the City of New York.

Introduction

The most striking feature of literature by Jews between the two world wars is the absence of its Jewishness. The children of immigrants sought to Americanize themselves as quickly as possible, and they were careful not to betray their ethnic origins or heritage. In the 1920's and '30's they divorced themselves almost completely from formal religion, and it seemed as though Judaism could no longer sustain itself in America. Their writing—except for scattered authors like Henry Roth, Michael Gold, Daniel Fuchs, and Clifford Odets—recorded few of the tensions between the first and second generation of Jews, and little of the difficulty involved in the migration from the Lower East Side of New York to the more affluent areas of the city.

This period of American Jewry marked the most rapid economic and social development of any ethnic group in American history. Those who were the children of shopkeepers and needle-trade workers became lawyers, doctors, teachers, accountants, and salesmen: they moved, in many cases, from extreme poverty to middle-class and upper-middle-class comfort and they formed an aggressive Jewish bourgeoisie. Their enormous success in American society resulted largely from their swift adjustment to an urban life that was to present them with the greatest opportunities as well as the most vexing problems of the twentieth century.

When we think of the most characteristic Jewish expression during this period, we do not think of literature but of the popular arts, of the Yiddish theater and vaudeville. Entertainers like the Marx Brothers,

Eddie Cantor, George Jessel, Al Jolson, and Fannie Brice, as well as scores of actors, songwriters, and directors, created a distinct Jewish image that has lasted to this day. This image is the self-conscious clown: man as a loser, an outcast and victim, but man always in the ironical position of knowing what he has lost and why he has been cast out and victimized. This exquisite self-consciousness is turned to literary purposes by the writers in the next generation and has a central place in the work of Nathanael West and Saul Bellow, J. D. Salinger and Philip Roth.

Besides the vaudeville of popular entertainers and an imported Yiddish theater, the Jew was scarcely present in American drama. He was caricatured in *Abie's Irish Rose,* sentimentalized in Elmer Rice's *Street Scene,* and at times viewed with some depth, as in S. N. Behrman's *Rain From Heaven* (1934), a study of the threat of anti-Semitism and fascism. The Jewish playgoer who wanted to see Jewish life on the stage had to go to Maurice Schwartz's Yiddish Art Theater, which produced translations of plays like David Pinsky's *The Treasure* and S. Ansky's *The Dybbuk*—impressive works that grew out of a rich dramatic tradition in Russia and Poland at the end of the nineteenth century. In America, the first significant dramatist who drew upon the complex texture of Jewish life was Clifford Odets, and his most penetrating revelation of that life— particularly the interrelationships in a typical Jewish family—is rendered in *Awake and Sing* (1935). Odets wrote other plays which bear upon the Jewish experience—*Till the Day I Die* (1935) and *The Flowering Peach* (1954)—but *Awake and Sing* is his most successful record of the immigrant experience in a large city.

The roster of Jewish dramatists is long and impressive. It includes S. N. Behrman, George Kaufman, Lillian Hellman, Irwin Shaw, Arthur Miller, Paddy Chayevsky, and Israel Horovitz. But the work of these playrights is so Americanized that, with certain exceptions like Miller's *Incident at Vichy* and Chayevsky's *The Tenth Man,* it scarcely draws upon their Jewishness. Odets was a singular exception: *Awake and Sing* recalls the 1930's with a vividness and an emotional fidelity that can still be felt.

During the twenties and thirties, novelists, short-story writers and essayists were less overtly Jewish than entertainers. As they benefited from an American society that encouraged assimilation, they did not want to remind themselves of their un-American background. Some avoided Jewish subjects altogether; others, however, did return to their youth and described in naturalistic detail the experiences of a poverty-stricken childhood. These few memorable writers saw the immigrant experience through the eyes of a child. Michael Gold's *Jews Without Money* (1930), Henry Roth's *Call It Sleep* (1934), and Daniel Fuch's *Summer in Williamsburg* (1935) filter the power of exact recall through the sensitive intelligence of an introspective boy. The autobiographies of Ben Hecht and Ludwig Lewisohn—portions of which I have included—lack the same creative power, but they do suggest the sudden consciousness of secularized Jews to a religion and a people they have not yet felt deeply.

In the 1930's those intellectual Jews who had abandoned the formal religion of their fathers channeled their moral sensitivity into socialistic causes. Their writing tends to be journalistic and politically rooted, not yet artistically distant from the materials that affected them so much. They had not explored the full impact of Western Christianity on their Jewish experiences: that connection, as well as the fate of Jews in World War II and the migration to Israel, affected the consciousness of American Jews of the next generation so profoundly that they produced what must be considered the most significant body of literature in America since 1940. Between the wars talented Jewish writers recalled their indigent youth or recorded the struggles of their families during the Depression of the 1930's.

LUDWIG LEWISOHN (1882–1955)

Ludwig Lewisohn was born on May 30, 1882, in Berlin. His parents migrated to America in 1890 and settled in Charleston, South Carolina. As he grew up in Charleston, Lewisohn found southern christian life so congenial that he renounced Judaism as well as his German background; soon, however, he fell under the influence of Matthew Arnold's skepticism and lost faith in all formal religion.

Lewisohn attended Columbia University and was a brilliant student. When he sought a professional position, however, he was told that there was no place for him in American universities because he was a Jew. Lewisohn's experience, as recorded in Upstream and reprinted in this volume, is a tragic commentary on the state of higher education in America in the 1920's: he was a victim of that Anglo-Saxon tradition in English departments which dominated academic life until recently. After a brief editorial career, in which he was first drama critic and then associate editor of The Nation, Lewisohn began to write stories and articles; he identified more closely than ever before with the German-American community in New York, and he translated the works of Jacob Wasserman, whose anti-Semitic experiences he felt were kindred to his own.

Lewisohn taught German for a year at the University of Wisconsin and for six years at Ohio State; but he felt that he had no real academic future and not until late in his career did he return to teaching full time. He published many novels—Don Juan (1923), The Case of Mr. Crump (1926), Roman Summer (1927), Stephen Escott (1930), and The Last Day of Shylock (1931); literary and dramatic criticism—Poets of Modern France (1918), Spirit of Modern German Literature (1916), The Drama and the Stage (1922), and Expression in America (1932); and the autobiography—Upstream (1922), Mid-Channel (1929), and Haven (1940). Toward the end of his life he taught literature at Brandeis University and developed a strong interest in Zionism.

The following excerpt from Upstream depicts Lewisohn's experience at Columbia University. The Island Within is Lewisohn's most successful attempt at recreating his Jewish-American experiences.

Upstream

The various experiences which I have set down so briefly extended over two years. At the end of the first year I duly took my master's degree and applied for a fellowship. Among the group of students to which I belonged it was taken for granted that, since Ellard had completed his studies for the doctorate, I would undoubtedly be chosen. I record this, heaven knows, not from motives of vanity but as part of the subtler purpose of this story. The faculty elected my friend G. I went, with a heavy heart, to interview Professor Brewer, not to push my claims to anything, but because I was at my wits' end. I dreaded another year of tutoring and of living wretchedly from hand to mouth, without proper clothes, without books. Brewer leaned back in his chair, pipe in hand, with a cool and kindly smile. "It seemed to us," he stuttered, "that the university hadn't had its full influence on you." He suggested their disappointment in me and, by the subtlest of stresses, their sorrow over their disappointment. I said that I had been struggling for a livelihood and that, nevertheless, my examinations had uniformly received high grades and my papers, quite as uniformly, the public approval of Brent and himself. He avoided a direct answer by explaining that the department had recommended me for a scholarship for the following year. The truth is, I think, that Brewer, excessively mediocre as he was, had a very keen tribal instinct of the self-protective sort and felt in me—what I was hardly yet consciously—the implacable foe of the New England dominance over our national life. I wasn't unaware of his hostility, but I had no way of provoking a franker explanation.

I forgot my troubles in three beautiful months at home—three months seemed so long then—or, rather, I crowded these troubles from my field of consciousness. I wouldn't even permit the fact that I wasn't elected to a scholarship to depress me. Brewer wrote a letter of regret and encouragement that was very kindly in tone. The pleasant implication of that letter was, of course, a spiritual falsehood of the crassest. He knew then precisely what he knew and finally told me ten months later. But his kind has a dread of the bleak weather of the world of truth, and approaches it gingerly, gradually, with a mincing gait. He, poor man, was probably unconscious of all that. In him, as in all like him, the corruption of the mental life is such that the boundaries between the true and the false are wholly obliterated.

In the passionate crises of the second year I often walked as in a dream. And I was encouraged by the fact that the department arranged a loan for my tuition. In truth, I was deeply touched by so unusual a kindness and I feel sure that the suggestion came from Brent. If so, Brewer again did me a fatal injury by not preventing that kindness. For he had then, I must emphasize, the knowledge he communicated to me later—the knowledge that held the grim upshot of my university career.

Spring came and with it the scramble for jobs among the second year men. My friends were called in to conferences with Brewer; I was not. They discussed vacancies, chances here and there. It wasn't the chagrin that hurt so; it wasn't any fear for myself. After all I was only twenty-two and I was careless of material things. I thought of my father and my mother in the cruel sunshine of Queenshaven. Their hope and dream and consolation were at stake. I could see them, not only by day, but in the evening, beside their solitary lamps, looking up from their quiet books, thinking of me and of the future. . . . I remembered how my father had believed in certain implications of American democracy. I remembered . . . I was but a lad, after all. I couldn't face Brewer's cool and careless smile. I wrote him a letter—a letter which, in its very earnestness and passionate veracity must have struck like a discord upon the careful arrangements of his safe and proper nature. For in it I spoke of grave things gravely, not jestingly, as one should to be a New England gentleman: I spoke of need and aspiration and justice. His answer lies before me now and I copy that astonishingly smooth and chilly document verbatim: "It is very sensible of you to look so carefully into your plans at this juncture, because I do not at all believe in the wisdom of your scheme. A recent experience has shown me how terribly hard it is for a man of Jewish birth to get a good position. I had always suspected that it was a matter worth considering, but I had not known how wide-spread and strong it was. While we shall be glad to do anything we can for you, therefore, I cannot help feeling that the chances are going to be greatly against you."

I sat in my boarding-house room playing with this letter. I seemed to have no feeling at all for the moment. By the light of a sunbeam that fell in I saw that the picture of my parents on the mantelpiece was very dusty. I got up and wiped the dust off carefully. Gradually an eerie, lost feeling came over me. I took my hat and walked out and up Amsterdam Avenue, farther and farther to High Bridge and stood on the bridge and watched the swift, tiny tandems on the Speedway below and the skiffs gliding up and down the Harlem River. A numbness held my soul and mutely I watched life, like a dream pageant, float by me. . . . I ate nothing till evening when I went into a bakery and, catching sight of myself in a mirror, noted with dull objectivity my dark hair, my melancholy eyes, my unmistakably Semitic nose. . . . An outcast. . . . A sentence arose in my mind which I have remembered and used ever since. So long as there is discrimination, there is exile. And for the first time in my life my heart turned with grief and remorse to the thought of my brethren in exile all over the world.

The Island Within

There was a clerk at Friedenfeld & Cohn's named Nathan Goldmann. He was a small, thin, tense young man with very black eyes and very black eyebrows growing together over his long inquisitive nose. He had come over with his parents from Tilsit when he was a boy of fifteen and considered himself an authority on American tastes and habits. He was terribly in earnest and gesticulated violently and found a good listener in Jacob. He said that people in America were growing richer and richer; there was an increasing market for a better grade of goods even among working-people; he had a theory, in addition, that the atrocious taste of the period could be mitigated. On an open bookstall in lower Fourth Avenue he had bought a few second-hand copies of European periodicals devoted to the decorative arts. There was a man in England, named William Morris, who had designed some new types of furniture. If one could manufacture such things here one could make a fortune. Goldmann carried about with him photographs of furniture torn out of the stray copies of periodicals that he had bought. He threw up his arms in hard despair. "But without a capital what can you do? I've talked to the boss. A good man but a *shemihl*. He said: 'Why should I change my business? It is a good business.'"

Jacob felt a strange quiver in his entrails. "How much capital is needed?"

Goldmann squinted fiercely. He lifted a tense forefinger. "I have a scheme. If I had one thousand dollars—just one thousand dollars!"

Jacob's face fell. "All I have is three hundred."

Goldmann jumped. "I have two hundred, myself. Wait . . . wait . . . wait."

Two days later he came to Mrs. Bartenwerfer's house in the evening and, sitting on the single chair in Jacob's little room, explained. Mr. Friedenfeld had been persuaded to put five hundred dollars into the scheme of the two young men, since they had the other five hundred between them. He liked to help to set up young men in business, though Goldmann's particular scheme still annoyed him a little. If young men had businesses of their own they could marry, and to promote marriages was a good and a Jewish action. Thus the benevolent Friedenfeld argued. With a wave of his hand Goldmann swept him out of existence and explained his scheme to Jacob. They would rent a shop; they would hire a carpenter, a greener, newly from Poland; Goldmann, who could draw fairly well, would design a new type of easy chair from the cuts he had; the rods and cushions for the Morris chairs they could buy ready made. They would advertise a little. But also they would both canvass from house to house in certain districts. He believed . . . he believed . . . Jacob was swept away by his friend's tense faith. He knew that he would feel rather naked and exposed to the cruelty of the world without either his job or his little capital safe in the bank. But there was no backing out now; there was no possibility of risking the reproaches or the despair of Goldmann. The firm of Goldmann & Levy was founded on that evening; it was, of course, not incorporated until several years later. Hazel Levy, as well as the two Goldmann girls, though thoroughly familiar with this whole story, were to be glad enough in their day that no one would have guessed it from the exquisite advertisements of the Phoenix Art Furniture Company, Creators of Beautiful Homes, which graced the pages of their favorite magazines. . . .

Success did not come to the two young men at once. At first the sale of their chair went very slowly. Then when the orders increased they found it difficult to fill them, for they had no money and little credit. If Mrs. Bartenwerfer had not occasionally waited for her board bill and Goldmann's parents supported him and Friedenfeld said a good word for the young men to wholesalers in wood and upholstery, the firm would have collapsed half a dozen times during its first three years. Nathan and Jacob lived frugally and worked hard; Jacob felt guilty when, occasionally, he sneaked off to a concert. Nathan needed nothing for life but his purpose. He was a more typical Jew than Jacob. Had his education and opportunities been higher his purpose would have been higher, too. His children were to illustrate that amply later on. The point is that he knew no drifting, no turning aside, only his purpose. Jacob, the slightly blond with the broad hands, could not so easily curb his hungers and his outgoings. But the example of his partner kept him frugal and definitely at work. By 1888 the worst struggles were over. A tiny factory had been established on the outskirts of Hoboken and a modest showroom opened on Broadway. After that the expansion of the business was rapid, though it was not until 1898 that the great factory at Grand Rapids, Mich., was built and the permanent Phoenix Exhibit of Art Furniture established on East Fiftieth Street. . . .

In the crucial years of the expansion of the business both Nathan and Jacob were helped by their marriages. Nathan married Sarah Herz in 1889. She was plump and brown and kind and competent, and her father, an importer of silk ribands, gave her a dowry of $5,000, which promptly went, of course, to strengthen the business of Goldmann & Levy. Thereafter Jacob felt that it was, in a sense, his duty to imitate his partner. But he was in a dilemma. For he was in love with Gertrude Oberwarter and Gertrude was one of the two daughters of a widow who could not touch her small capital without dangerously reducing her income. He had met the Oberwarters through the Bartenwerfers. Fanny Oberwarter, the daughter of a well-known German-American journalist of Jewish extraction named Julius Conheim, had been born in America. Her husband had come from Hamburg in his earliest years. The two girls, though they could speak German if necessary, were very conscious Americans. The family lived in a pleasant house in Mount Vernon and it was on their lawn and under their trees that Jacob Levy first perceived the soft brilliance of an American landscape and in some dim way claimed the earth and country as his own.

Gertrude was a little shocked when she found herself attracted by the young immigrant named Levy. She had liked some of the blond young German-Americans with whom she had gone to school. But in her generation the instinct against intermarriage was still forbidding in its strength. Well, Jacob was blond; he was gentle; he loved music. He seemed less Jewish to her than the swarthy young men with their intense and eager air whom she knew. He seemed less emphatic and so more refined. Her mother liked him, too; spring nights in the little Mount Vernon garden did the rest.

Since Gertrude was younger than her sister Ella there was no hurry about marriage. Also Mrs. Oberwerter wanted to see Jacob's business expand a little more. But early in 1891 old Mrs. Conheim died and left each of the girls $8,000. Jacob looked into the velvety brown eyes of

Gertrude; he gazed at her oval face with the burning red lips; he touched her long coils of chestnut hair. She wanted to be a June bride in the American fashion. The minister of a reform congregation read the service over them in Mrs. Oberwarter's parlor. They went to Niagara Falls on their wedding journey.

WALDO FRANK (1889-1967)

"*For my sense of literature is that of an* action. *To me a good book is an* act; *or, if you prefer, an* acting *and an* enacting *individual. That is why, in the long run, a book's formal quality is what counts most— makes it most effective. Where mine comes in, in such a hierarchy, it is too early to say.*"

Waldo Frank occupies a small place in the history of American literature; but he was an interesting figure during the 1920's, a literary radical and idealist who, together with H. L. Mencken and Van Wyck Brooks, sought closer ties between literature and life. In the 1930's, he became a champion of freedom in Spain and Latin America, attempting to establish closer relations between the United States and these countries.

Frank was born in Long Branch, New Jersey, and was educated at Yale University, where he received an M.A. in 1911. He was a journalist and a free-lance writer, and throughout the twenties and thirties wrote voluminously. His fiction includes The Unwelcome Man (*1917*); The Dark Mother (*1920*); City Block (*1922*); Rehab (*1922*); Holiday (*1923*); Chalk Face (*1924*); The Death and Birth of David Markand (*1934*); The Bridegroom Cometh (*1938*); *and* Summer Never Ends (*1941*). *Among his collections of essays are* The Art of the Vieux Colombier (*1918*); Our America (*1919*); Salvos (*1924*); Virgin Spain (*1926*); Time Exposures (*1926*); The Rediscovery of America (*1929*); America Hispana (*1931*); Dawn in Russia (*1932*); In the American Jungle (*1937*); *and* Chart for Rough Water (*1940*).

The following excerpt is taken from his best-known work, Our America.

The Chosen People

The early Puritans came to Massachusetts in the faith that they were the Chosen People. In this faith, they founded their miniature theodicies after the stern manner of the Old Testament. In it, they looked with condescension, often with contempt, upon their neighbors. They were sure that Christ, in his second coming, would snub Europe and land in Boston.

Two centuries passed. New England was breaking up and scattering Westward. Jesus had not arrived. But now another Chosen People, of the race of Jesus, came instead. To-day, more than three million of Jews live in the United States. One million and a half—one quarter of its entire population—live in the city of New York.

The kinship of the Puritan and Jew, as they appear on the American scene, is close. There was no fortuity in the New Englander's obsession with the Hebrew texts, in his quite conscious taking on of the rôle of Israel in a hostile world. Like the Jew, the Puritan was obsessed with the dream of power: elected a career of separatism from the world in order to attain it: took to himself a personal and exacting God in order to justify it: traversed the seas in order to effect it. And as with the Puritan, so with the Jew, once free in a vast country, the urge of power swiftly shook off its religious and pietistic way, and drove untrammeled to material aggression. In their intense and isolated will, the Puritan and Jew were kin. Also, in their function as American pioneers. But one must not press the relationship too far. As occurs so often upon the theater of the world, channels of energy, though flung from widely different sources and tend-ing to diverse points, for a season flowed together and fertilized one field. No more. . . .

There is a Jewish paradox, and this paradox is perhaps the equation of the Jew's survival, of his immense success. Always, he has been moved by these seemingly antagonistic motives: the will-to-power, the need of mystical abnegation, the desire for comfort on the sensuous and mental planes. When these impulses converged and created a resultant philosophy of life, the Jew has functioned. Otherwise not.

In ancient Hebrew times, these forces brought about Jehovah. Jahveh remained a tribal, a proprietory God. As such, he was the true master over Israel. "He has commanded unto each people its ruler. . . . And he has elected Israel for his own portion: he nourishes it in his discipline like a first born."* A stern and jealous father, functioning fully in the Jewish need of self-humiliation. But behold the other force of the Jewish nature making this God the one God, the Lord over all. No more grandiose satisfaction for the Jew's will-to-power could have been imagined. The little tribe at once set itself over the world. Its Lord was the Lord of hosts, and its rôle in human history became divine. Yet, with this satisfaction of the lust for dominance, the equal thirst for suffering, for immolation is not neglected.

In the Dispersion, the equation did not fundamentally change. The Jews were scattered and were suffering. Even the little kingdom was no more, which their genius had lifted up—to their own contentment— above the kingdoms of earth. It became needful, merely, to stress the spiritual part of their syllogism of power and mystical debasement. The belief in Israel's universal Priesthood was an ample response to the most abject reality. Jewish pride, Jewish mysticism, Jewish masochism met on a sublimated plane. To it, the Jew was able, in every trial, to rise up and find the solace of his Reason, the satisfaction of his senses. So he survived. The stiff-necked Jew was actually the most flexible man that the world had ever known. He needed power, comfort, the sense of being lost in a greater Whole. Inordinate needs, and yet, above his brethren, he was able to attain them. He had the genius for *transferring* them, when they encountered obstacles in life, to some other but still *real* plane. And I say *real*, because the Jew never lost the objective balance, never leaped up in the transcendental escape. The plane to which he lifted his needs was ever one upon which his emotions, instincts, experience and activity of life could remain in play. If he was persecuted and despised,

---

* *Jesus, Son of Sirach* (Apocr.): XVIII, 14–15.

he found his sense of power in his religious mission. If he was forced to live in an evil Ghetto, physically tortured, he found his comfort in the joys of suffering and denial. If he was rich and great in the world, his synagogue brought him back to the sweet misery of mystical humiliation.

With modern times, Talmudic Judaism could no longer serve as a complete expression of the Jewish will. Scientific inquiry, the rational method instituted by Descartes, were conquering the world. The immemorial paradox of the Jew needed a modern means. No more perfect paradigm of his adaptability could be conceived than the rational mysticism of Spinoza. It is one of those rare expressions of personality, in which the genius of an entire people culminates and lives. The Book of Isaiah is not more Jewish than the *Ethica Ordine Geometrico Demonstrata.*

In Spinoza, the Jewish paradox comes to this: God is infinite, and man is lost in Him, yet God must be contained within the consciousness of man. The first clause satisfies the need of abnegation, the second the need of power. Spinoza responds by *rationally* proving the infinity and the inscrutability of God. Since the reason is a function of man, and since by this function God has been ascertained, God in all His attributes comes within human reach. God is non-anthropomorphic. Yet he is in man's power, since man's mind proves him. He is universal, yet finite mind encompasses His being. All substance, including man, is a part of God. There is thus no true distinction between finite and infinite. And if man, who is finite knows an infinite world, he is infinite as well. He loses his identity, disappears from the snug center of the universe he had for so long occupied. But he reappears in a far more powerful modification: as an inclusive attribute of the universal.

The third coördinate in the Jewish nature is the need of physical comfort. Life is real and important to the Jew. His asceticism is always a sensual surrogate forced on him by his surroundings. It is never voluntary, never perverse, never dominant like the self-denial of the Anglo-Saxon. The Preacher has put down the immortal balance of the Jew. "In the day of prosperity be joyful, but in the day of adversity consider." The place of *comfort* in the philosophy of Spinoza is clear even to the title of his great book. It was no trivial matter to call a metaphysics "Ethics." The fact points to the Jewish need of practical application. Even the consciousness of God must serve a sensory end. As Spinoza says in another work*: he strives for knowledge "which shall enable him to enjoy continuous and supreme and unending happiness."

The Jew is the indefeasible realist. All his genius for seeing God

---

* *De Intellectus Emendatione.*

must in the last analysis apply to the means of mortal life. The heights of his inspired speculation have ever been determined by the heights of the mundane barriers he needed to transcend in order to survive. So now, with the age of critical philosophy, of scientific method, of increased social toleration, his conditions changed. Gradually, the Christian earth became more real and urgent, the heavens grew dimmer. Gradually, men strove to apply their idea of heaven to the mundane present. The social Revolution stirred on its long and bloody course. And a Jew, Karl Marx, appeared to give it form, substance, the passion of organic hope.

The three elements of which I have spoken reside generically in the Jewish mind. In the Jewish genius they rise coördinately to fruition. The paradox is solved. The masters of the Old Testament, Moses Maimonides, who was philosopher, priest, physician, Baruch Spinoza—were such Jews of genius. And through their like, the Jewish spirit lives. But in the majority of Jews, two of these elements go down before the sovereignty of one.

After all, a majority of Jews doubtless deemed Moses a scatter-brain and preferred Egypt: declined Cyrus' invitation to shake off the prestige and comforts of the Babylonian captivity. A majority of Jews, like a majority of other men and women, respond rather passively and simply to the external impulse of the world they live in. Certainly, a majority of Jews have done just that in the United States.

They came to America—mostly after 1880—with their sharpened wits and will-to-power, and America welcomed them and put these qualities to work. They came to America also with their love of God, but for such seed America was less fertile.

The Jew simply was caught up in the continental rhythm. He became a pioneer: in many ways, as we have seen, he was a Puritan already. He joined hands in the keen task of developing America. The power of wealth, the sanctity of money, were no secret to him. The sweets in the denial of sensuous indulgence when such indulgence was impossible or meant defeat, were no secret to him. The channeling of his mind upon the problems of practical dominion was an old channel to the Jew. Enormous incentives, these, in the American lands. He also poured outward: he also became spiritually poor: he also stripped for action. When the mystical Jew dies, the Jew is dead. The mystical Jew survived. But he slept. While the acquisitive Jew, the power-lusting Jew, the comfort-seeking Jew, at last unbarred from centuries of oppression and restraint, flooded upon a world that thirsted for his gifts.

The three directions of desire whose complex I have called Jewish are, of course, not uniquely so. The Jewish quality is rather their degree. The Jew is intense, high-keyed, above other men whose history has been a less continuous climax. And in his coming to America, he met an intensive need in an intensive land. His own intensity made him equal to the situation. The Jew, moreover, is tremendously adaptable in a superficial way. He can meet conditions: but at the end, he must stamp on them the marks of his own nature. Here again, the American adventurer was auspicious. A vast, crude, virgin continent to bend to: his own passion for power and cultivation to impress upon it. Even the period of his coming was well-timed. His mystical obsession was out of place in pioneering. And he had come to America in an hour of revulsion against revealed theologies. Darwin had dealt the old God a blow. The geometric pace of mechanical power, of physical knowledge, for a time made men think that science was knowledge indeed, and that the shadows were retreating. The Jew in whom the genius for rational and empirical endeavor was always strong was dazzled along with the rest. He responded the more easily to pioneer demands, in an hour when his old mystical equipment seemed particularly futile. In this mystical equipment resided the culture of the Jew. As he dropped the first, the other fell away. Unlike the Latin and the Slav, he had in consequence no painful cultural assimilation to submit to. Like the Puritan's, his old cultural habits were already weak at his coming: his power to face new worlds to that extent enhanced. Thus, like the New Englander again, he played a rôle in the building of America out of all proportion to his numerical strength, because like him he was strategically placed.

The psychological history of the Jew in the United States is the process of his rather frenzied conformation to the land of his new opportunity: the sharpening of his means to power, the perfecting of his taste for comfort, the suppression of the mystical in his heart. For the mystical is never dead. It required the best activities of the Jewish mind to keep it under.

One of the early means was to find a substitute for the synagogue and for religion. The first generation still kept the Sabbath. The third is altogether "free." The middle generation went half way—with substitutes. As an example of this degenerate Judaism, none could serve us better than the "Societies for Ethical Culture," of which the first was founded in 1876 by Dr. Felix Adler. Adler's father was a Rabbi and the son was called to the same service. He went back to Germany—where he was born—to complete his studies. Modern empiricism brought the doubt. The doubt wiped most of the old slate clean. The young Doctor Adler came home to America empty. To what extent, let his own words tell: "Accordingly, on returning from abroad, my first action consisted in founding among men of my own or nearly my own age a little society which we ambitiously called a Union for the Higher Life, based on three tacit assumptions: sex purity, the principle of devoting the surplus of one's income beyond that required by one's own genuine needs to the elevation of the working class, and thirdly, continued intellectual development." Now, there is nothing remarkable about this sterile statement. What is significant is that a generation of American Jews looked upon this man as their spiritual father! Adler proceeded to evolve an adulterate religion. He avoided the concepts of God and Godhood: he declared Faith to be of no importance: he poised the world on an abstract notion of "personal worth" devoid of personality and worthless. Adler had met Socialism in Berlin. The "Moral Order" he came back with was a first worried effort on the part of the still healthy Jewish bourgeoisie to save the pickings for themselves. To it, he sacrificed Jehovah.

The main adherence of these Societies in New York and other American cities was among the prosperous Jews who had shown themselves most apt to run the American race. Religious memories haunted these people. Most of them had been brought up in the Jewish church. They turned to Adler to give them a semblance of creed: one which would still the stirring of the Past, bring them no preoccupation to conflict with their affairs and, on the contrary, fit them the more aptly and the more politely for the life of respectable material dominion which America afforded. A completely commercialized religion: a religion, in other words, which was no religion at all, since all the mystery of life, all the harmony of sense, all the immanence of God were deleted from it: and in their place a quiet, moral code destined to make good citizens of eager pioneers. In Spinoza, *Ethics* had meant the lifting up of consciousness to the universal, since for so great a soul no lesser contemplation could serve human joy. With these others, *Ethics* meant the complete excision of all that was mystical, all that in any way could debauch the human interest from the immediate affairs of a commercial world. These Jews were afraid of religion, even to the extent of not daring openly to do without it. "The Society for Ethical Culture" met their problem. It was free not only of the suppressed demands of the Jewish soul, but even of the odium of the Jewish name.*

---

* It is perhaps only fair to repeat that a similar adulteration had long since gone on in many Protestant churches. One that engages me most is the gospel of the "Finite God," now preached by certain forward-looking ministers, and glorified by no less a man than H. G. Wells. The idea behind the Finite God is to effect a compromise between our Reason which tells us that this is an imperfect world and our lurking

Meantime, the Jew was spreading out. He filled our schools, he filled our public colleges, he filled the laboratories of science. He knew, like any pioneer, that the mystery and the experience of life were poison. He knew that the best defense from the subtle promptings of his race lay in the passionate devotion to rational pursuits. He poured into the medical colleges and law schools. He joined hands with the Irish in Tammany Hall and became a practical politician. He discovered Pragmatism and reduced it to its most acrid and cynical dogmas of utilitarian supineness. And everything he did, he did a little more intensely, a little more like the fanatic, than his brothers. For not alone was his nature intrinsically pitched at a high key: he needed the added stress in order to combat the mystical yearnings which his reason covered.

Here, then, this strange phenomenon of our present day! the anæsthetic Jew. The literal-minded Gentile is as a rule content with his world of facts: secure in it. The literal-minded Jew is a Jew unbalanced. He declared defensive war against the other side: particularly against religion and art. We have seen a similar psychic process in Mark Twain. Himself an intuitive and "tender-minded" man, he held to his forced rank in the frontiering world by denial of his nature—and by violent attack when it appeared in others. So the Jew, electing to worship power, achieve comfort, suppressed the God in him, and by way of it, denied the God in others. Instinctively, he went out in arms against all approach, spiritual, æsthetic, which might stir in himself the senses he denied. A simple process of transference of which the subject only remains unaware.

Jews of this sort have played a great part in the recent intellectual life of the United States. They are bitter, ironic, passionately logical. And the camps of the Enemy fascinate them so, they cannot keep away. They become critics of the arts. They consort with artists: study the anatomy of æsthetic: and from the strategy of close acquaintance subtly inspire the distrust of art, prove art is dying, teach how trivial an affair art has become.

---

desire for some sort of worship. An Infinite God could not be held responsible for such a mess as Science (so they say) tells us this suffering world is. Let a finite God take his place—the credit and the blame. By positing a deity who is almost as weak and fumbling as ourselves, like ourselves "on-the-make"—(a dash here of pseudo-Bergsonianism), we avoid the issue. Of course, such a God is a sop thrown by King Reason to abject intuition. He is a product of a prevailing intellectual arrogance, by no means to be found among superior men of science, which will admit nothing beyond the range of rational adventure. To say that such a God is an absurdity, a distinctly a-religious invention, seems to me not to say too much.

Some of these men are mere disappointed artists: souls bitter at their own self-treachery. Others are deeply sincere and brilliantly equipped.* They have observed the spiritual disarray of the last thirty years: they have become submerged in it, above their eyes. They cannot see beyond the palpable failure of the present. And they are strengthened in their doctrine of despair by the artists whom they know. For those artists are, in large part, weak and loveless. They, too, have innerly given up the fight against the pioneering rhythm: emotionally accepted the prevailing Puritan contempt. But in them, the critical faculties have not harmonized desire and conviction. Their hearts beat to the Puritan command. Their minds disobey. They produce art lacking in love and vision. And the more critical, the stronger-minded Jew seeing their pathetic failures, is encouraged in his at least rational despair.

Not alone the examples of modern life, as well the modern tools of thought are on hand to help—and to create the anæsthetic Jew, the Jew who has turned all the passion of his blood against the vision which has preserved him. He grasps at the discoveries of science—whose philosophical inconsequence the true scientist is foremost in avowing—in order to sneer at the mysteries beyond. He quotes the new analytical psychology in order to prove the spiritual apperceptions of mankind mere symptoms of neurosis.

In their bitter arrogance, the truth about these men is clear enough. They are defending their conscious position against the encroachment of unconscious doubts. For these pragmatic doctrines—these assumptions of the falsity of faith and the futility of art—pander to their need of comfort: *the comfort of the Limit.* Science has put up a nice, small room, and lighted it quite well. Outside, as ever, rolls the illimitable world—the world which Jews have ever needed to explore. But these men have been made weary by their freedom, have become spiritually weak in the new flowing-forth of their desires. The wider universe haunts them and sings to their blood. So they deny it: prove desperately that it does not exist and that the limits of the fitful glow of their experimental candle are the limits of all life. Equally, these doctrines pander to their need of power. A giant, as there have been giants among the Jews, lets his vision out upon infinity and embraces that. These depleted minds are still ambitious, they still yearn to possess what they perceive. Since they are weak, therefore, they solve the problem by per-

* Among them—perhaps the most imposing and influential, by reason of his high integrity, intellectual power and close association with the art movements, here and abroad, of recent years—is Leo Stein.

ceiving less. They exercise power in the little spaces of the reasonable world. It is sweet for them to hold there are no spaces beyond.

So the passive response of the Jew to the traditional American demand is complicated by the vast spiritual sacrifice which the Jew peculiarly must make. The Jewish paradox—the Jewish nature—is broken up. This sacrifice means conflict. This conflict adds to the intensity of Jewish adaptation. For if the Jew went less wilfully on his elected way, the suppressed need of his life would rise and swing him elsewhere, and he might not go that way at all.

This rich element, flung into the many others to make the American chaos. Sons of an ancient Sacrifice—these aggressive and worldly and compromising men who fill our markets and our professions. But let it not be overlooked: the Jew who dwindles himself down to these is sick and restless. The stifled Will is ready to burst forth. And in the most degraded families of Jews, you find them: solitary sons and daughters, stirring and rebellious—outposts—in whom that Will has become once more incarnate.

During eight decades of the Nineteenth Century, the human spirit struggled against the incoming tide of mechanical and industrial aberration. Nietzsche, Flaubert, Whitman, Tolstoi, Dostoievski—such were the last giants to float. Then the world went under. The Machine, the sweep of material aggrandizement which the Machine made possible— offered a delirious game upon which the Occidental world poured its passions. We are beginning to understand what that vast flood has swept away. The old community of art, the old worship of God, the old economic orders. But more: the flood has swept away the frenzied material obsession which first loosed the flood. Quite as dead as the old idolatries is the heresy of the dominion of empirical thought: quite as futile as the art of the old secluded classes, has become the arrogant belief that art and religion can be dispensed with. . . .

In the American chaos the Jew went under. We shall see how, in the American birth, he rises up.

MICHAEL GOLD (1893–1967)

The distinguished literature of Jewish-American life in the early years of the twentieth century is limited to only a few works: Henry Roth's Call It Sleep, Daniel Fuch's novels of Williamsburg, and Michael Gold's brief and compelling Jews Without Money. Like Roth, Gold recalls his youth on the Lower East Side; unlike Roth he presents his early experiences directly, without the self-consciousness of the artist. Jews Without Money is a naturalistic description of poverty, tableaux of immigrant life in the ghetto that are rendered poetic by the haunting, powerful simplicity of Gold's earthy style. The book is one of the genuine autobiographies of Jewish-American culture and a minor classic of proletarian literature.

Michael Gold, the son of a Rumanian father and an Hungarian mother, was born in 1893 on the Lower East Side of New York. His frustration at being poor found its political focus in the years just before World War I when, as he remarks at the conclusion of Jews Without Money, he heard "a man on an East Side soap-box" proclaim "that out of the despair, melancholy and helpless rage of millions, a world movement had been born to abolish poverty." Gold joined the Industrial Workers of the World and worked for the New York Call, a socialist newspaper.

During the 1920's Gold became friendly with radical writers like Max Eastman and Floyd Dell and began to contribute political essays to The Masses. Soon he became editor of The Liberator and The New Masses; in the 1930's, as a leading spokesman for the Communist Party, he insisted that writing be directed toward social reform. His position was excessively rigid, and his political journalism lacked the complexities one finds in the work of liberal contemporaries like Edmund Wilson, William Phillips, and Philip Rahv. With the passing of the thirties, Gold's influence waned and his work, as one views it from the perspective of half a century, scarcely rises above its topicality and narrow interests. In Jews Without Money, however, he recreated the reality of the Lower East Side: the rivalries of minority groups; the lack of privacy; the father's dreams of wealth and the mother's hard work; the hot nights on rooftops, as the family tried to sleep; the gang wars of the ghetto streets; and the anxious confusions of the young children. All these experiences are reported, rather than "written," in a simple style that reflects faithfully the life of the Lower East Side at the turn of the century.

73

Did God Make Bedbugs?

IT RAINED, we squatted dull as frogs on the steps of the rear tenement. What boredom in the backyard; we kids didn't know what to do. Life seemed to flicker out on a rainy day.

The rain was warm and sticky; it spattered on the tin roofs like a gangster's blood. It filled our backyard with a smell of decay, as if some one had dumped a ton of rotten apples.

Rain, rain! The sky was a strip of gray tin above the terraced clotheslines, on which flowery shirts and underwear flapped in the rain. I looked up at them.

I heard the hum of sewing machines, surf on a desolate island. A baby wept feebly. Its hoarse mother answered. The swollen upper half of a fat woman hung from a window, her elbows like hams. She stared with dull eyes at the rain.

A wooden shack occupied a portion of the yard; it was the toilet. A bearded man in suspenders went in.

Masha sang from the next tenement. The deep Russian songs helped her pain; the blind girl was homesick. Other girls sang with her often; many nights I fell asleep to that lullaby. Now she sang alone.

Because there was nothing to do. Rain, rain, we had tired of our marbles, our dice and our playing store games.

The backyard was a curious spot. It had once been a graveyard. Some of the old American headstones had been used to pave our Jewish yard. The inscriptions were dated a hundred years ago. But we had read them all, we were tired of weaving romances around these ruins of America.

Once we had torn up a white gravestone. What an adventure. We scratched like ghouls with our hands deep into the earth until we found moldy dirty human bones. What a thrill that was. I owned chunks of knee bone, and yellow forearms, and parts of a worm-eaten skull. I had them cached in a secret corner of my home, wrapped in burlap with other treasured playthings.

But it would be boring to dig for bones now. And we were sick of trying to sail paper boats in the standing pool above the drain pipe. It was choked with muck, too sluggish for real boat races.

Then a cat appeared in the rain and macabre gloom of the yard. We were suddenly alert as flies.

It was an East Side gutter cat, its head was gaunt, its bones jutted sharply like parts of a strange machine. It was sick. Its belly dragged the ground, it was sick with a new litter. It paused before a garbage can, sniffing out food.

We yelled. In slow agony, its eyes cast about, as if searching for a friend. The starved mother-cat suspected our whoops of joy. It leaped on a garbage can and waited. It did not hump its back, it was too weary to show anger or fear. It waited.

And we pursued it like fiends, pelting it with offal. It scrambled hysterically up the fence. We heard it drop on heavy feet into the next yard. There other bored children sat in the rain.

There is nothing in this incident that ought to be recorded. There were thousands of cats on the East Side; one of the commonplace joys of childhood was to torture cats, chase them, drop them from steep roofs to see whether cats had nine lives.

It was a world of violence and stone, there were too many cats, there were too many children.

The stink of cats filled the tenement halls. Cats fought around each garbage can in the East Side struggle for life. These cats were not the smug purring pets of the rich, but outcasts, criminals and fiends. They were hideous with scars and wounds, their fur was torn, they were smeared with unimaginable sores and filth, their eyes glared dangerously. They were so desperate they would sometimes fight a man. At night they alarmed the tenement with their weird cries like a congress of crazy witches. The obscene heartbreak of their amours ruined our sleep, made us cry and toss in cat nightmares. We tortured them, they tortured us. It was poverty.

When you opened the door of your home there was always a crazy cat or two trying to claw its way inside. They would lie for days outside the door, brooding on the smell of cooking until they went insane.

Kittens died quietly in every corner, rheumy-eyed, feeble and old before they had even begun to learn to play.

Sometimes momma let you pity a kitten, give it a saucer of milk which it lapped madly with its tiny tongue.

But later you had to drive it out again into the cruel street. There were too many kittens. The sorrow of kittens was too gigantic for one child's pity.

I chased and persecuted cats with the other children; I never had much pity; but on this rainy afternoon I pitied the poor mother-cat.

I found myself thinking: Did God make cats?

I was oppressed with thoughts of God because my parents had put me in a *Chaider*. I went to this Jewish religious school every afternoon when the American public school let out.

There is no hell fire in the orthodox Jewish religion. Children are not taught to harrow themselves searching for sin; nor to fear the hereafter. But they must memorize a long rigmarole of Hebrew prayers.

Reb Moisha was my teacher. This man was a walking, belching symbol of the decay of orthodox Judaism. What could such as he teach any one? He was ignorant as a rat. He was a foul smelling, emaciated beggar who had never read anything, or seen anything, who knew absolutely nothing but this sterile memory course in dead Hebrew which he whipped into the heads and backsides of little boys.

He dressed always in the same long black alpaca coat, green and disgusting with its pattern of grease, snuff, old food stains and something worse; for this religious teacher had nothing but contempt for the modern device of the handkerchief. He blew his nose on the floor, then wiped it on his horrible sleeve. Pickled herring and onions were his standard food. The sirocco blast of a thousand onions poured from his beard when he bent over the *Aleph-Beth* with you, his face close and hot to yours.

He was cruel as a jailer. He had a sadist's delight in pinching boys with his long pincer fingers; he was always whipping special offenders with his cat-o'-nine-tails; yet he maintained no real discipline in his hell-hole of Jewish piety.

I was appalled when my parents brought me there, and after paying Reb Moisha his first weekly fee of fifty cents, left me with him.

In the ratty old loft, lit by a gas jet that cast a charnelhouse flare on the strange scene, I beheld thirty boys leaping and rioting like so many tigers pent in the one cage.

Some were spinning tops; others played tag, or wrestled; a group kneeled in a corner, staring at the ground as though a corpse lay there, and screaming passionately. They were shooting craps.

One of these boys saw me. He came over, and without a word, tore the picture of W. J. Bryan from my lapel. The boys gambled in buttons. He wanted my valuable button, so he took it.

At a long table, hacked by many knives, Reb Moisha sat with ten surly boys, the beginners' class. Soon I was howling with them. Over and over again we howled the ancient Hebrew prayers for thunder and lightning and bread and death; meaningless sounds to us. And Reb Moisha would pinch a boy, and scream above the bedlam, "Louder, little thieves! Louder!" He forced us to howl.

There was a smell like dead-dog from the broken toilet in the hall. A burlap curtain hung at one end of the hall to disguise the master's home, for he was the unlucky father of five children. His wife's harpy voice nagged them; we could smell onions frying; always onions for the master.

His face was white and sharp like a corpse's; it was framed in an ink-black beard; he wore a skullcap. His eyes glittered, and roved restlessly like an ogre's hungry for blood of little boys.

I hated this place. Once he tried to whip me, and instead of the usual submission, I ran home. My mother was angry.

"You must go back," she said. "Do you want to grow up into an ignorant *goy?*"

"But why do I have to learn all those Hebrew words? They don't mean anything, momma!"

"They mean a lot," said she severely. "Those are God's words, the way He wants us to pray to Him!"

"Who is God?" I asked. "Why must we pray to Him?"

"He is the one who made the world," said my mother solemnly. "We must obey Him."

"Did He make *everything?*"

"Yes, everything. God made everything in this world."

This impressed me. I returned to the *Chaider.* In the midst of the riot and screaming I would brood on my mother's God, on the strange man in the sky who must be addressed in Hebrew, that man who had created everything on earth.

My mother was very pious. Her face darkened solemnly and mysteriously when she talked about her God. Every one argued about God. Mendel Bum, and Fyfka the Miser, and my Aunt Lena, and Jake Wolf, the saloonkeeper, and the fat janitor woman, and Mrs. Ashkenazi, of the umbrella store, and Mottke Blinder, and Harry the Pimp—all were interested in God. It was an important subject. When I discovered this, it became important for me, too.

I couldn't get the thought out of my head; God made everything. A child carries such thoughts about him unconsciously, the way he carries his body. They grow inside him. He sits quietly; no one knows why; he himself doesn't know. He is thinking. Then one day he will speak.

In the livery stable on our street there was an old truck horse I loved. Every night he came home weary from work, but they did not unhitch him at once. He was made to wait for hours in the street by Vassa.

The horse was hungry. That's why he'd steal apples or bananas from the pushcarts if the peddler was napping. He was kicked and beaten for this, but it did not break him of his bad habit. They should have fed him sooner after a hard day's work. He was always neglected, and dirty, fly-bitten, gall-ridden. He was nicknamed the Ganuf—the old Thief on our street.

I stole sugar from home and gave it to him. I stroked his damp nose, gray flanks, and gray tangled mane. He shook his head, and stared at me with his large gentle eyes. He never shook his head for the other boys; they marveled at my power over Ganuf.

He was a kind, good horse, and wise in many ways. For instance: Jim Bush abused him. Jim Bush was a fiery little Irish cripple who lived by doing odd jobs for the prostitute girls. Jim Bush was a tough guy only from the waist up. His blue fireman's shirt covered massive shoulders and arms. His face was red and leathery like a middle-aged cop's. But his legs were shriveled like a baby's.

He cracked dirty jokes with the girls, he was genial when sober. When he was drunk he wanted to fight every one. He would leap from his crutches at a man's throat and hang there like a bulldog, squeezing for death with his powerful hands, until beaten into unconsciousness. He always began his pugnacious debauches by abusing Ganuf the Horse.

He seemed to hate Ganuf. Why, I don't know. Maybe to show his power. Jim was the height of a boy of seven. He stood there, eyes blood-shot with liquor, mouth foaming, and shouted curses at the horse. Ganuf moved; Jim struck him over the nose with a crutch. Jim grabbed the bridle. "Back up!" he yelled, then he sawed the bit on poor Ganuf's tongue. Then he clutched the horse's nostrils and tried to tear them off.

The poor horse was patient. He looked down from his great height at the screaming little cripple, and seemed to understand. He would have kicked any one else, but I think he knew Jim Bush was a cripple.

People always marveled at this scene. I used to feel sorry for my poor horse, and imagine there were tears in his eyes.

This horse dropped at work one summer day. They loosened his harness, and slopped buckets of water over him. He managed to stand up, but was weak. He dragged the truck back to the stable. Waiting there as usual to be unhitched for his supper, he fell gasping; he died on our street.

His body bloated like a balloon. He was left for a day until the wagon came to haul him to the boneyard.

When a horse lay dead in the street that way, he was seized upon to become another plaything in the queer and terrible treasury of East Side childhood.

Children gathered around Ganuf. They leaped on his swollen body, poked sticks in the vents. They pried open the eyelids, and speculated on those sad, glazed big eyes. They plucked hair from the tail with which to weave good-luck rings.

The fat blue and golden flies swarmed, too, around the body of my kind old friend. They buzzed and sang with furious joy as they attacked this tremendous meal sent them by the God of Flies.

I stood there helplessly. I wanted to cry for my poor old Ganuf. Had God made Ganuf? Then why had He let Ganuf die? And had God made flies?

The millions of East Side flies, that drove us crazy in summer, and sucked at our eyelids, while we slept, drowned in our glass of milk? Why?

Did God make bedbugs? One steaming hot night I couldn't sleep for the bedbugs. They have a peculiar nauseating smell of their own; it is the smell of poverty. They crawl slowly and pompously, bloated with blood, and the touch and smell of these parasites wakens every nerve to disgust.

(Bedbugs are what people mean when they say: Poverty. There are enough pleasant superficial liars writing in America. I will write a truthful book of Poverty; I will mention bedbugs.)

It wasn't a lack of cleanliness in our home. My mother was as clean as any German housewife; she slaved, she worked herself to the bone keeping us fresh and neat. The bedbugs were a torment to her. She doused the beds with kerosene, changed the sheets, sprayed the mattresses in an endless frantic war with the bedbugs. What was the use; nothing could help; it was Poverty; it was the Tenement.

The bedbugs lived and bred in the rotten walls of the tenement, with the rats, fleas, roaches; the whole rotten structure needed to be torn down; a kerosene bottle would not help.

It had been a frightful week of summer heat. I was sick and feverish with heat, and pitched and tossed, while the cats sobbed in the yard. The bugs finally woke me. They were everywhere. I cannot tell the despair, loathing and rage of the child in the dark tenement room, as they crawled on me, and stank.

I cried softly. My mother woke and lit the gas. She renewed her futile battle with the bedbugs. The kerosene smell choked me. My mother tried to soothe me back to sleep. But my brain raced like a sewing machine.

"Momma," I asked, "why did God make bedbugs?"

She laughed at her little boy's quaint question. I was often jollied about it later, but who has answered this question? Did the God of Love create bedbugs, did He also put pain and poverty into the world? Why, a kind horse like my Ganuf would never have done such a thing.

BEN HECHT (1894–1964)

In the histories of American literature, Ben Hecht occupies a small place as a hard-boiled journalist, a popular and realistic author, and a screenwriter who enjoyed extraordinary success. In the history of Jewish-American literature he represents that writer who attacked the Jews in his early work (especially in A Jew in Love, *1931) and then, responding intensely to the rise of Nazism, experienced a kind of conversion as he asserted his allegiance to Jewry.*

Ben Hecht was born in New York on February 28, 1894, and grew up in Racine, Wisconsin. He began his newspaper career with the Chicago Journal *in 1910 and went on to write human interest articles for the* Chicago Daily News *which were later collected in his* 1001 Afternoons in Chicago *(1922). His first novel,* Erik Dorn *(1921), was based on his experiences as Berlin correspondent for the* Daily News *during the revolutionary period in Germany from 1918–1919.*

After returning to the United States in the early twenties, Hecht associated with the "Chicago School" of writers: Pascal Covici, Sherwood Anderson, Maxwell Bodenheim, and Margaret Anderson, editor of the Little Review. *During this period he published voluminously in all genres. His novels include* Gargoyles *(1922);* Humpty-Dumpty *(1924);* The Kingdom of Evil *(1924);* Count Bruga *(1926); and* Broken Necks *(1926). His early plays—*The Egotist *(1923),* The Stork *(1923), and* The Great Magoo *(1933)—were not successful; but* The Front Page, *which he wrote in 1928 with Charles MacArthur, was so great a hit on Broadway that it was converted into a film and then revived as a play in 1971. Throughout this period Hecht was also writing short stories, collected in* Actor's Blood *(1936). His real commercial success came as the film writer of* Scarface, Nothing Sacred, *and a score of other movies.*

In the late 1930's, Hecht became increasingly self-conscious as a Jew. He wrote for the New York newspaper, PM, *scolding readers who did not hate Hitler enough and Jews who were not sufficiently proud of their heritage. His tough, cynical attitude yielded to an idealism that was a deep expression of his identification with European Jews. The following essay, "The Lost Tribe," is the best-known example of Hecht's religious chauvinism.*

The Lost Tribe

My MEETING with Peter Bergson was the result of my having turned into a Jew in 1939. I had before then been only related to Jews. In that year I became a Jew and looked on the world with Jewish eyes.

The German mass murder of the Jews, recently begun, had brought my Jewishness to the surface. I felt no grief or vicarious pain. I felt only a violence toward the German killers. I saw the Germans as murderers with red hands. Their fat necks and round, boneless faces became the visages of beasts. Their descent from humanity was as vivid in my eyes as if they had grown four legs and a snout.

I was too old to enlist in the battle in Europe. But I was not too old for anger. I went through the days holding my anger like a hot stove in my arms. There seemed nothing to do with it but carry it and suffer its heat.

The anger led me to join an organization for the first time in my life. It was called "Fight for Freedom" and was dedicated to bringing the U.S.A. into the war against the Germans. Herbert Agar, a handsome and eloquent fellow, was at its head. My work in the organization consisted of writing war propaganda speeches and a pageant called "Fun To Be Free," which MacArthur collaborated on and Billy Rose put on in Madison Square Garden. I wrote and staged other similar shows for the Red Cross and the War Bond Drive.

I was aware that I was doing all these things as a Jew. My eloquence in behalf of democracy was inspired chiefly by my Jewish anger. I had been no partisan of democracy in my earlier years. Its sins had seemed to me more prominent than its virtues. But now that it was the potential enemy of the new German Police State I was its uncarping disciple. Thus, oddly, in addition to becoming a Jew in 1939 I became also an American—and remained one.

I dreamed day and night of a German collapse but I desired something more than their military defeat as a nation. I desired their ostracism from the human family. How could the Germans, in 1940 already methodically launched on torturing and murdering millions of harmless Jews, ever be allowed to sit in the conclaves of men again? I knew, bitterly, that they would be allowed, that their crime against the Jews would be overlooked as if it had been an unfortunate bit of war strategy and not a befoulment of the human spirit.

Another bitter thought was in my head—how could the Jews whose butchery was going on before an indifferent world ever be a people of dignity again?

I knew, and wrote, that the Germans would be beaten in battle if the U.S. joined against them, and I was certain their miserable megalomania would be knocked out of them—for another few decades. But I felt there would be no victory for Jews in this. As I walked the street, a million Jewish men, women and children had been butchered and four million more were yet to be fed to the lime kilns and bonfires. Yet there was no voice of importance anywhere, Jewish or non-Jewish, protesting this foulest of history's crimes.

A people to whom I belonged, who had produced my mother, father and all the relatives I had loved, was being turned into an exterminator's quarry, and there was no outcry against the deed. No statesmen or journalists spoke out. Art was also silent. Was the Jew so despised that he could be murdered en masse without protest from onlookers, or was humanity so despicable that it could witness the German crime without moral wince?

Ten years after the massacre a bitterness still comes to me when I write of it. But I am no longer wholly bitter. I know now that the silence during the massacre was caused by many things other than I thought of then. Chief among them was the indifference to death which an era of wars had bred into the world. The American of yesterday watched American soldiers suffer and die in Korea with the same lack of emotional response he had for the massacre of Jews a decade ago. Individual life is not sacred, death is not important. The modern soul thus conditions itself for the great battles to come, the battles of H-Bombs, which Professor Einstein prophecies will number their dead in the hundreds of millions; a war which William Laurence, science reporter for *The New York Times,* prophecies will count as a casualty not nations but a planet.

These half-understandings were not in me in the years of the Jewish massacre. The silence, then, shamed me. It contained for me an anti-Semitism more sinister than the massacre. I felt the most deeply shamed by the silence of the American Jews. Around me the most potent and articulate Jews in the world kept their mouths fearfully closed.

The unassimilated Jews—the Yiddish Jews—were speaking their horror in the Jewish newspapers. In the synagogues the Jews were weeping and praying. In thousands of homes where Yiddish was spoken the German murderers and their deeds were cursed. But these were the locked-away Jews who had only the useless ear of other Jews and, possibly, of God.

The Americanized Jews who ran newspapers and movie studios, who wrote plays and novels, who were high in government and powerful in the financial, industrial and even social life of the nation were silent.

Talking of these things at home in Nyack one evening, I received an unexpected gift from Rose. She had been conferring with Ralph Ingersoll, editor of *P.M.*, and Ingersoll had agreed to take me on as a daily columnist, at seventy-five dollars a week.

I went to work at once, grateful for a forum larger than my dinner table. I wrote of the city as I had done years before on the *Daily News* in Chicago, but only part of me was a newspaperman now. I was as much Jew as reporter, and I wrote often of Jews. My column reported the incredible silence of New York's Jews in this time of massacre.

I continued the column while writing movie scripts in Hollywood. There the movie chieftains, nearly all Jews, protested that I was on the wrong track with my Jewish articles. They told me that Ambassador Joseph Kennedy, lately returned from beleaguered London, had spoken to fifty of Hollywood's leading Jewish movie makers in a secret meeting in one of their homes. He had told them sternly that they must not protest as Jews, and that they must keep their Jewish rage against the Germans out of print.

Any Jewish outcries, Kennedy explained, would impede victory over the Germans. It would make the world feel that a "Jewish War" was going on.

As a result of Kennedy's cry for silence, all of Hollywood's top Jews went around with their grief hidden like a Jewish fox under their Gentile vests. In New York, the influential Jews I met had also espoused the Kennedy hide-your-Jewish-head psychology. I argued that a moral outcry against the massacre, regardless of who raised it, would fill the Germans with doubts and fears. It would make them realize they were acting outside the human family. Such a single avaunt from the King of Denmark was to frighten off the Germans from murdering the Jews of that land.

I argued too that the sound of moral outrage over the extinction of the Jews would restore human stature to the name Jew. In the silence this stature was vanishing. We Jews in America were fast becoming the relatives of a garbage pile of Jewish dead. There would be no respect for the living Jew when there was no regret for a dead one.

I wrote in a column called "My Tribe Is Called Israel":

I write of Jews today [1941], I who never knew himself as one before, because that part of me which is Jewish is under a violent and apelike attack. My way of defending myself is to answer as a Jew. . . . My angry critics all write that they are proud of being Americans and of wearing carnations, and that they are sick to death of such efforts as mine to Judaize them and increase generally the Jew-consciousness of the world.

Good Jews with carnations, it is not I who am bringing this Jew-consciousness back into the world. It is back of all the radios of the world. I don't advise you to take off your carnations. I only suggest that you don't hide behind them too much. They conceal very little.

It was a few days after the foregoing was printed that the letter from Peter Bergson arrived. The letter contained a mysterious ferment that led me to invite for a drink, unknowingly, the political head of the not yet notorious Palestinian underground called the Irgun Zvai Leumi.

But now that it had come, the outcry seemed to make little sense and hold less victory. It had reached German ears and done no good. My theory had been wrong. The Germans, made aware that the murder of the Jews was humanly distasteful to the world, had not stayed their reddened hands. They had continued killing Jews.

But my theory had been, possibly, only half wrong. For there had been only half an outcry against the massacre of the Jews. The political outcry had been missing. With all our mass meetings and stinging propaganda we had managed to rouse no protest against the Jewish massacre from Roosevelt, Churchill, Stalin, or their official governments.

THE WAR for the rescue of humanity from German defilement ended "triumphantly" with all the Jews of Europe exterminated and the great victors still indifferent to that amazing fact. The word Jew lay lusterless in its horrid grave.

I knew now that rhetoric was no better than tears as a solution for my "Jewish Problem"—the rescue of the word Jew from the garbage can into which the Germans had dumped it. I had had faith in eloquence as a historical force. History had disproved my faith. I saw that propaganda was incapable of altering anything around it. It might incubate in time, it might mold the future. But it could only confuse the present or irritate it, or be lost entirely in all the other word noises of its own day.

I began to wonder if the cause I had tried to serve was even sensible. Did such a cause even exist—the salvaging of the word Jew? What did it mean? Obviously one of its meanings was the fact that my ego had identified itself with this historic word. Something in me, as well as in Europe, was being removed and befouled. Since it had been always my habit to answer insults, I had answered back to the Germans. But was an outraged ego a cause?

I kept avoiding something I knew, because it was contrary to my version of myself. In this version I had been always a sort of detached fellow who believed in nothing or, at least, in very little—in a few good human traits, in the charms of love and gallant friendship and in the single dictum—let your neighbors alone as you would like to be let alone. I was, also, a man of much negative kindness. The only prayer I had ever heard that had appealed to me was a line by the Hindu pundit Acharya. He had written, "I pray each day that I may be made strong enough not to hurt anyone."

I found it difficult now to face the all-too-human fact that the "cause" I had tried to serve was not what I had kept telling myself it was. The egoistic concern for the word Jew was there. But the compelling thing that had thrown me into the Jewish fight was that I loved Jews. It may have been mostly the memory of my parents and tantes and uncles that I loved—I find it hard even now to understand where this love came from and for whom it was. But there rose up before the eyes of my soul a world that I loved, that was Jewish; a world of fine-smelling kitchens, fascinating little candy stores, crowded tenement streets with infants crawling over hot pavements; a Jewish world of tearooms, amusement parks, cloak and suit factories, huge holiday dinners, jokes and curses in broken English and even of whiskered rabbis and tiny synagogues smelling of musty books and candle grease.

I had lived in such a world only for the first ten years of my life, but it was as vivid as if I had never stepped out of it.

The fact that the torture and massacre of Jews had failed ever to bring any tears to my eyes, that it was rage against the brute I felt rather than pity for his victim, had helped conceal from me why I was in the Jewish cause. I had looked on myself and seen a man hot with angers. He seemed as lacking in love and sentiment for Jewish memories as if he had been born on the moon, rather than in the New York ghetto.

But when I saw now that the Jews were forever done for, a wail came into my heart. Who could save them now—the dead and dishonored? What words were there that could make the cold world tip its hat to their grave—their disowned and unkept grave?

I looked at the Jews around me still trying to believe themselves intact. But the intactness was gone. However they twisted about to evade the truth, they were members of a race, a tribe, a religion or whatever the Jews are, that had been burned alive in a great public bonfire with no friend in the world to cry "shame" or "stop." They were Americans, too, these Jews around me. But wounded ones. The wound was big.

The American in me came to a painful conclusion: "The Jew isn't much good as a Jew. But he's fine and brave as anything else. The best thing a Jew can do is forget there is any Jewish cause—and stick to causes that he can back up under a flag—and with a gun."

I nodded to my honest American counselor—myself from Racine and Chicago. It was sensible advice. I would go back to being an American, full of American pride and victory. There would remain a small, private area of defeat in me called Jew. On the Jewish holy days that I never had observed before, I would make certain observances now. I would remember that all the people to whom, in a curious way, I belonged had been slaughtered and that they had been too lowly a people for the world to regret. And too spiritless a people to raise a fist or a gun against their enemies.

Except the Jews of the Warsaw ghetto. I would remember them on the Jewish holidays. There had not been many—some thirty thousand. But they had faced the German exterminators with more than prayers on their lips. They had old guns and oaken staves, and iron crowbars, and bombs made out of tin cans. Armed with these almost playful weapons, they had met the German Panzer tanks, the German cannon, gas, machine-gun fire and fought them to a standstill for three very military weeks. During these weeks the Jews of Warsaw had issued their communiqués over a single radio. They were standing firm but the need for guns and bullets was growing. Would somebody in the world drop them some ammunition out of the skies, or perhaps even a cannon or two.

Nobody in the world answered. Not a bullet, a bomb or even a cap pistol fell out of the skies. The day of Jewish manna was a long time ago. Thus the Jews of Warsaw were finally reduced to fighting with stones, hot water and sticks. They continued the battle until they were either all slain or too maimed to move.

The Germans carted the wounded quickly to the always ready lime pits, tossed them in and covered them up; and the slaughter of Jews went on as if nothing had happened. Which was not entirely true. I and many Jews like me would remember these Warsaw Jews on the Pesach and, in the security of our American protected homes, drink to them. They were the little souvenir of Jewish pride that glinted in Europe's garbage can.

HENRY ROTH (1906–   )

Henry Roth was born in 1906 and attended the City College of New York. Directly after his graduation, he began to write Call It Sleep. *The novel was published in December, 1934, and received high critical praise, although it was not as popular as Roth had hoped it would be. Roth never succeeded in finishing another work and settled on a farm in Maine to raise ducks and geese.*

In a symposium which appeared in The American Scholar *in 1956, Alfred Kazin and Leslie Fiedler characterized* Call It Sleep *as one of "The Most Neglected Books of the Past 25 Years." Since that time the novel has enjoyed a wide audience. Published in 1960, it was reprinted as a paperback in 1962 by Avon Books. It now is an established classic of immigrant literature, and Fiedler's judgment may serve as a valid commentary on the importance of the book:* Call It Sleep *"is a specifically Jewish book, the best single book by a Jew about Jewishness written by an American, certainly through the 'thirties and perhaps ever."*

Call It Sleep

(I pray thee ask no questions this is that
Golden Land)

THE SMALL WHITE STEAMER, Peter Stuyvesant, that delivered the
immigrants from the stench and throb of the steerage to the stench and
the throb of New York tenements, rolled slightly on the water beside
the stone quay in the lee of the weathered barracks and new brick buildings of Ellis Island. Her skipper was waiting for the last of the officials,
laborers and guards to embark upon her before he cast off and started
for Manhattan. Since this was Saturday afternoon and this the last trip
she would make for the week-end, those left behind might have to stay
over till Monday. Her whistle bellowed its hoarse warning. A few figures in overalls sauntered from the high doors of the immigration quarters and down the grey pavement that led to the dock.

It was May of the year 1907, the year that was destined to bring the
greatest number of immigrants to the shores of the United States. All
that day, as on all the days since spring began, her decks had been
thronged by hundreds upon hundreds of foreigners, natives from almost
every land in the world, the jowled close-cropped Teuton, the full-
bearded Russian, the scraggly-whiskered Jew, and among them Slovack
peasants with docile faces, smooth-cheeked and swarthy Armenians,
pimply Greeks, Danes with wrinkled eyelids. All day her decks had been
colorful, a matrix of the vivid costumes of other lands, the speckled green-
and-yellow aprons, the flowered kerchief, embroidered homespun, the
silver-braided sheepskin vest, the gaudy scarfs, yellow boots, fur caps,
caftans, dull gabardines. All day the guttural, the high-pitched voices,
the astonished cries, the gasps of wonder, reiterations of gladness had
risen from her decks in a motley billow of sound. But now her decks were

empty, quiet, spreading out under the sunlight almost as if the warm boards were relaxing from the strain and the pressure of the myriads of feet. All those steerage passengers of the ships that had docked that day who were permitted to enter had already entered—except two, a woman and a young child she carried in her arms. They had just come aboard escorted by a man.

About the appearance of these late comers there was very little that was unusual. The man had evidently spent some time in America and was now bringing his wife and child over from the other side. It might have been thought that he had spent most of his time in lower New York, for he paid only the scantest attention to the Statue of Liberty or to the city rising from the water or to the bridges spanning the East River—or perhaps he was merely too agitated to waste much time on these wonders. His clothes were the ordinary clothes the ordinary New Yorker wore in that period—sober and dull. A black derby accentuated the sharpness and sedentary pallor of his face; a jacket, loose on his tall spare frame, buttoned up in a V close to the throat; and above the V a tightly-knotted black tie was mounted in the groove of a high starched collar. As for his wife, one guessed that she was a European more by the timid wondering look in her eyes as she gazed from her husband to the harbor, than by her clothes. For her clothes were American—a black skirt, a white shirt-waist and a black jacket. Obviously her husband had either taken the precaution of sending them to her while she was still in Europe or had brought them with him to Ellis Island where she had slipped them on before she left.

Only the small child in her arms wore a distinctly foreign costume, an impression one got chiefly from the odd, outlandish, blue straw hat on his head with its polka dot ribbons of the same color dangling over each shoulder.

Except for this hat, had the three newcomers been in a crowd, no one probably, could have singled out the woman and child as newly arrived immigrants. They carried no sheets tied up in huge bundles, no bulky wicker baskets, no prized feather beds, no boxes of delicacies, sausages, virgin-olive oils, rare cheeses; the large black satchel beside them was their only luggage. But despite this, despite their even less than commonplace appearance, the two overalled men, sprawled out and smoking cigarettes in the stern, eyed them curiously. And the old peddler woman, sitting with basket of oranges on knee, continually squinted her weak eyes in their direction.

The truth was there was something quite untypical about their behavior. The old peddler woman on the bench and the overalled men in the stern had seen enough husbands meeting their wives and children after a long absence to know how such people ought to behave. The most volatile races, such as the Italians, often danced for joy, whirled each other around, pirouetted in an ecstasy; Swedes sometimes just looked at each other, breathing through open mouths like a panting dog; Jews wept, jabbered, almost put each other's eyes out with the recklessness of their darting gestures; Poles roared and gripped each other at arm's length as though they meant to tear a handful of flesh; and after one pecking kiss, the English might be seen gravitating toward, but never achieving an embrace. But these two stood silent, apart; the man staring with aloof, offended eyes grimly down at the water—or if he turned his face toward his wife at all, it was only to glare in harsh contempt at the blue straw hat worn by the child in her arms, and then his hostile eyes would sweep about the deck to see if anyone else were observing them. And his wife beside him regarding him uneasily, appealingly. And the child against her breast looking from one to the other with watchful, frightened eyes. Altogether it was a very curious meeting.

They had been standing in this strange and silent manner for several minutes, when the woman, as if driven by the strain into action, tried to smile, and touching her husband's arm said timidly, "And this is the Golden Land." She spoke in Yiddish.

The man grunted, but made no answer.

She took a breath as if taking courage, and tremulously, "I'm sorry, Albert, I was so stupid." She paused waiting for some flicker of unbending, some word, which never came. "But you look so lean, Albert, so haggard. And your mustache—you've shaved."

His brusque glance stabbed and withdrew. "Even so."

"You must have suffered in this land." She continued gentle despite his rebuke. "You never wrote me. You're thin. Ach! Then here in the new land is the same old poverty. You've gone without food. I can see it. You've changed."

"Well that don't matter," he snapped, ignoring her sympathy. "It's no excuse for your not recognizing me. Who else would call for you? Do you know anyone else in this land?"

"No," placatingly. "But I was so frightened, Albert. Listen to me. I was so bewildered, and that long waiting there in that vast room since morning. Oh, that horrible waiting! I saw them all go, one after the other. The shoemaker and his wife. The coppersmith and his children from Strij. All those on the Kaiserin Viktoria. But I—I remained. Tomorrow will be Sunday. They told me no one could come to fetch me. What if they sent me back? I was frantic!"

"Are you blaming me?" His voice was dangerous.

"No! No! Of course not Albert! I was just explaining."

"Well then let me explain," he said curtly. "I did what I could. I took the day off from the shop. I called that cursed Hamburg-American Line four times. And each time they told me you weren't on board."

"They didn't have any more third-class passage, so I had to take the steerage—"

"Yes, now I know. That's all very well. That couldn't be helped. I came here anyway. The last boat. And what do you do? You refused to recognize me. You don't know me." He dropped his elbows down on the rail, averted his angry face. "That's the greeting I get."

"I'm sorry, Albert," she stroked his arm humbly. "I'm sorry."

"And as if those blue-coated mongrels in there weren't mocking me enough, you give them that brat's right age. Didn't I write you to say seventeen months because it would save the half fare! Didn't you hear me inside when I told them?"

"How could I, Albert?" she protested. "How could I? You were on the other side of that—that cage."

"Well why didn't you say seventeen months anyway? Look!" he pointed to several blue-coated officials who came hurrying out of a doorway out of the immigration quarters. "There they are." An ominous pride dragged at his voice. "If he's among them, that one who questioned me so much, I could speak to him if he came up here."

"Don't bother with him, Albert," she exclaimed uneasily. "Please, Albert! What have you against him? He couldn't help it. It's his work."

"Is it?" His eyes followed with unswerving deliberation the blue-coats as they neared the boat. "Well he didn't have to do it so well."

"And after all, I did lie to him, Albert," she said hurriedly trying to distract him.

"The truth is you didn't," he snapped, turning his anger against her. "You made your first lie plain by telling the truth afterward. And made a laughing-stock of me!"

"I didn't know what to do." She picked despairingly at the wire grill beneath the rail. "In Hamburg the doctor laughed at me when I said seventeen months. He's so big. He was big when he was born." She smiled, the worried look on her face vanishing momentarily as she stroked her son's cheek. "Won't you speak to your father, David, beloved?"

The child merely ducked his head behind his mother.

His father stared at him, shifted his gaze and glared down at the officials, and then, as though perplexity had crossed his mind he frowned absently. "How old did he say he was?"

"The doctor? Over two years—and as I say he laughed."

"Well what did he enter?"

"Seventeen months—I told you."

"Then why didn't you tell them seventeen—" He broke off, shrugged violently. "Baah! You need more strength in this land." He paused, eyed her intently and then frowned suddenly. "Did you bring his birth certificate?"

"Why—" She seemed confused. "It may be in the trunk—there on the ship. I don't know. Perhaps I left it behind." Her hand wandered uncertainly to her lips. "I don't know. Is it important? I never thought of it. But surely father could send it. We need only write."

"Hmm! Well, put him down." His head jerked brusquely toward the child. "You don't need to carry him all the way. He's big enough to stand on his own feet."

She hesitated, and then reluctantly set the child down on the deck. Scared, unsteady, the little one edged over to the side opposite his father, and hidden by his mother, clung to her skirt.

"Well, it's all over now." She attempted to be cheerful. "It's all behind us now, isn't it, Albert? Whatever mistakes I made don't really matter any more. Do they?"

"A fine taste of what lies before me!" He turned his back on her and leaned morosely against the rail. "A fine taste!"

They were silent. On the dock below, the brown hawsers had been slipped over the mooring posts, and the men on the lower deck now dragged them dripping from the water. Bells clanged. The ship throbbed. Startled by the hoarse bellow of her whistle, the gulls wheeling before her prow rose with slight creaking cry from the green water, and as she churned away from the stone quay skimmed across her path on indolent, scimitar wing. Behind the ship the white wake that stretched to Ellis Island grew longer, raveling wanly into melon-green. On one side curved the low drab Jersey coast-line, the spars and mast on the waterfront fringing the sky; on the other side was Brooklyn, flat, water-towered; the horns of the harbor. And before them, rising on her high pedestal from the scaling swarmy brilliance of sunlit water to the west, Liberty. The spinning disk of the late afternoon sun slanted behind her, and to those on board who gazed, her features were charred with shadow, her depths exhausted, her masses ironed to one single plane. Against the luminous sky the rays of her halo were spikes of darkness roweling the air; shadow flattened the torch she bore to a black cross against flawless light—the blackened hilt of a broken sword. Liberty. The child and his mother stared again at the massive figure in wonder.

The ship curved around in a long arc toward Manhattan, her bow sweeping past Brooklyn and the bridges whose cables and pillars super-imposed by distance, spanned the East River in diaphanous and rigid waves. The western wind that raked the harbor into brilliant clods blew fresh and clear—a salt tang in the lull of its veerings. It whipped the polka-dot ribbons on the child's hat straight out behind him. They caught his father's eye.

"Where did you find that crown?"

Startled by his sudden question his wife looked down. "That? That was Maria's parting gift. The old nurse. She bought it herself and then sewed the ribbons on. You don't think it's pretty?"

"Pretty? Do you still ask?" His lean jaws hardly moved as he spoke. "Can't you see that those idiots lying back there are watching us already? They're mocking us! What will the others do on the train? He looks like a clown in it. He's the cause of all this trouble anyway!"

The harsh voice, the wrathful glare, the hand flung toward the child frightened him. Without knowing the cause, he knew that the stranger's anger was directed at himself. He burst into tears and pressed closer to his mother.

"Quiet!" the voice above him snapped.

Cowering, the child wept all the louder.

"Hush, darling!" His mother's protecting hands settled on his shoulders.

"Just when we're about to land!" her husband said furiously "He begins this! This howling! And now we'll have it all the way home, I suppose! Quiet! You hear?"

"It's you who are frightening him, Albert!" she protested.

"Am I? Well, let him be quiet. And take that straw gear off his head."

"But Albert, it's cool here."

"Will you take that off when I—" A snarl choked whatever else he would have uttered. While his wife looked on aghast, his long fingers scooped the hat from the child's head. The next instant it was sailing over the ship's side to the green water below. The overalled men in the stern grinned at each other. The old orange-peddler shook her head and clucked.

"Albert!" his wife caught her breath. "How could you?"

"I could!" he rapped out. "You should have left it behind!" His teeth clicked, and he glared about the deck.

She lifted the sobbing child to her breast, pressed him against her. With a vacant stunned expression, her gaze wandered from the grim smouldering face of her husband to the stern of the ship. In the silvery-green wake that curved trumpet-wise through the water, the blue hat still bobbed and rolled, ribbon stretched out on the waves. Tears sprang to her eyes. She brushed them away quickly, shook her head as if shaking off the memory, and looked toward the bow. Before her the grimy cupolas and towering square walls of the city loomed up. Above the jagged roof tops, the white smoke, whitened and suffused by the slanting sun, faded into the slots and wedges of the sky. She pressed her brow against her child's, hushed him with whispers. This was that vast incredible land, the land of freedom, of immense opportunity, that Golden Land. Again she tried to smile.

"Albert," she said timidly, "Albert."

"Hm?"

"Gehen vir voinen du? In Nev York?"

"Nein. Bronzeville. Ich hud dir schoin geschriben."

She nodded uncertainly, sighed . . .

Screws threshing, backing water, the Peter Stuyvesant neared her dock—drifting slowly and with canceled momentum as if reluctant.

No Longer Home*

Continuity was destroyed when his family moved from snug, orthodox 9th Street, from the homogeneous East Side to rowdy, hetero-geneous Harlem, normal continuity was destroyed. The tenets, the ways, the faith were discarded too drastically, too rapidly. That may have been what he sensed when he wrote his novel, that may have been a kind of subliminal theme, dominating him without his knowing it. And once continuity was destroyed, there would always be a sense of loss afterward, an insecurity—even though he might ultimately say good riddance to all that was so abruptly terminated. Therein perhaps lay the explanation for the failure, not only his own, but of so many gifted literary people, his contemporaries, who in one way or another, for one "reason" or another ceased to develop creatively. The whole question needed exploration and study. . . .

He unscrewed the brass-plated top of his mini-cuspidor, and spat. A new, unexplored realm this of chewing tobacco—for the modern writer (now cramped and irked by the awareness that everything pertaining to the minutiae of smoking had been exhausted). A new unexplored realm. For example, the liquid in the glass cuspidor gradually accrued in amber. Yes. He had forgotten in the preoccupation of writing the foregoing a thought of greater significance than the one he dwelled on, a thought, an

---

* In early 1971, the *New York Times* asked Henry Roth "why he chose to stop writing and to remain silent all these years." Roth offered a suggestive explanation, one that could clearly have been written only in retrospect.

insight rather into the meaning of an event long past. It had to do with his writing of 35 years ago, with his second novel, the novel he had destroyed unfinished. (He could still visualize himself in his study in E. L.'s Greenwich Village apartment, seated at his desk, writing.) A peculiar dichotomy had asserted itself, only vaguely apprehended at the time, a dichotomy of purpose, or was it direction? between his striving in the novel and his personal inclinations. It was an interesting revelation— he gazed absently at the diminished waters of the pond—about 35 years too late, but would it have helped any if he had realized it then? In the novel, based on the life of a certain B.C., an illiterate and picturesque proletarian, the central character was essentially a wholesome individual, for all his rugged experiences still sound at the core, seeking a better world for himself and his fellows. (His pilferings and shopliftings, the armed robberies he committed in his younger days, and his brawlings either were justified or could be justified by the compulsions of Capital-ism, committed before the illuminations of Communism, of Marx, the man with the busted mattress on his face, as B.C. called him, before class-consciousness, in short.)

While on the one hand the author dedicated his creativity to the portrayal of proletarian virtue, on the other he desired what his character eschewed. He yearned for the tainted, the perverse, for the pornographic, as it would be termed today, and detested himself as degenerate for doing so. This was the dichotomy. More and more drawn to things sensual, more and more imaginatively kindled by vileness, at the same time as he strained to project a party hero. And with apparent success in this latter aim, be it said, for none other than Maxwell Perkins approved the open-ing sections of the author's novel.

He sat examining the gilt imprint on his pencil. Eagle Mirado 3. Gilt, yes guilt. What guilt that dichotomy could engender! A party stalwart in letter, a satyr in proclivity. The proclivity condemned as degenerate. Per-haps it was. Perhaps pornography was degenerate, presaged another Rome in decline. At all events the outcome was stasis, stasis, immobility, desuetude. It was time to eject his quid, rinse his little cuspidor. Shaped like an hour-glass, wasp-waisted, why hadn't that even been used as a simile for the svelte female figure of a corseted by-gone age? His land-lord's gray guinea-fowl paraded before the window snickering raucously.

. . . That which informed him, connective tissue of his people, inculcated by cheder, countenanced by the street, sanctioned by God, all that dissolved when his parents moved from the East Side to Mick Harlem. The struts went and the staves. It would have to follow that the personality became amorphous, ambiguous, at once mystical and soiled, at once unbridled, inquisitive, shrinking. No longer at home. I guess that's the word, after this smother of words. *No longer at home.*

I'll tell you though, I have now adopted one, out of need, a symbolic home, one where symbols can lodge, whatever it is in actuality, whatever waverings and residual reservations I may have: Israel.

DANIEL FUCHS (1909–   )

Daniel Fuchs was born in Manhattan in 1909 and his family moved to Brooklyn when he was only three days old. He studied at the Eastern District High School and the City College of New York. After graduation he taught in Brooklyn schools, wrote three novels—Summer in Williamsburg (1935), Homage to Blenholt (1936), Low Company (1937)—and published stories in The New Yorker, The Saturday Evening Post, Colliers, Harper's Bazaar, and other popular magazines of the time.

Fuchs went to Hollywood and became a successful screenwriter. His three novels were reissued in one volume in 1961, of which the following essay is the introduction. The fictional extract is from the conclusion to Summer in Williamsburg.

Author's Preface to
Summer in Williamsburg

We moved into Williamsburg the summer I was five. I remember the troop of us going past the elementary school; my oldest brother said to me, "That's where you'll be going to school." The kitchen had a pair of washtubs in it, and the first night my mother put me to sleep on top of the tin covers. The rooms were lit by gas jets, gas mantles; Welsbach. The world was new.

The tenement, 366 South Second Street, was just completed but it was called a tenement from the start. We lived in five small rooms, cubicles. That building, the number 366, have a magic for me which can make me tremble. It was amazing how industriously we combed the building. We were everywhere, the halls, the yards, the cellars, the roofs. Everything people do they did in those places. Outside on the streets were great wide bins of white plaster; I watched the laborers slice into the plaster, pack it in slabs on their hods, and then carry the hods in files up into the new tenements still building around us. I became lost and couldn't find my way back to my apartment. I remember once running in panic through the halls, opening doors: a woman looked up at me from the floor, cleaning a gas range. I took long walks as I grew older. In one direction were low-lying wooden structures; the airy expanse of the sky and clouds; a storybook idleness; store windows with odd, faraway-sounding names on them, Faulkner, Brown, and Jones. I had an image in my mind, in connection with this place, of a hangman's noose. I don't know why, never did; I mention it. In another direction, going into Greenpoint, there were small red-brick factories; the smells of dyes; pony-carts with Shetland ponies hitched to them, standing in the sun; Italian cafes, men inside smoking cigarettes and staring out at the bright patch-work of sunshine on the pavements. Pinocchio. Above us, cutting across the numbered streets—South Second, South Third, South Fourth—and putting an end to them, was a street called Union Avenue. Trolley cars ran here; nearby lived a wonderful girl whose name was Dorothy Kirsch-enbaum. Beyond Union Avenue began a new maze of streets, and this limitless stretch of territory became, in my mind, Greenland, Norway, and Sweden—don't ask me why, the hangman's noose again. Nor can I really explain why in time I was impelled to write pieces about these long walks I took, the things I saw on them and the things I liked to make up and imagine. One of these pieces, a forty-page account, was submitted to the *New Republic*. They accepted two thousand words of it and the editor there kindly suggested that I expand the account into a novel.

Summer in Williamsburg was written in a state of sheer terror. I didn't understand what I was doing and had read somewhere that authors often wrote books not understanding what they were writing but hoping that the reader would. This is really as it should be and no offense. But I didn't know it then. I was determined to write fairly. I wanted to be like the man from Mars. I wanted to examine everything with an absolutely clear view, unencumbered and unaffected. Everyone's adolescence is no doubt precious and important to him, but I don't think it was Williams-burg or my adolescence there which caused my terror; although years later, driving through Williamsburg, I found myself shaking all over. No, what caused my troubles was that I was trying to find a design. A seed is put into the ground, the plant and flower emerge—everything directed from the beginning, according to a plan and purpose, with nothing left to vagary. I was trying to find a similar direction and plan to the life I had witnessed in Williamsburg. I was struggling with form. I was strug-gling with mystery. I was young and intent and met my problem head-on. And what I didn't know was that if I was successful, I would not come up with meaning but with fantasy. The material in *Summer in Williamsburg* is in many ways dear to me. I often thought of rewriting the novel, but then I realized that this would be tampering and wrong. The book, such as it is, has value perhaps only because of my ignorance or innocence at the time I wrote it, and I am led to offer it again without apologies for these reasons.

The books were failures. Nobody seemed to care for them when they came out. I saw a man once on the subway, reading *Homage to Blenholt* and chuckling aloud; that was the only clean appreciation I can remember—unsolicited, true. A friend told me regretfully he could read my novels while he was reading them; but that when he put them down, there was nothing to make him go back to them. The books didn't sell— 400 copies, 400, 1200. The reviews were scanty, inmaterial. The books became odious to me. My young wife and I were living at Saratoga Springs then and I remember fussing and complaining, asking who wanted stories, who really read them. It suddenly occurred to me that great numbers of people read the *Saturday Evening Post* each week. Right then and there I undertook to write a short story for the *Post*. Ten days or two weeks later they sent me a check for six hundred dollars. I decided to become rich. I was in the middle of a fourth novel but broke it up and swiftly turned it into three or four short stories. I worked away all spring, one story after the other—perhaps a dozen or fifteen in all. I rested. It was July. Nothing happened. I had a lovely young lady as my agent but didn't know her very well at that time and was too uncertain and abashed to disturb her with my inquiries. I assumed the stories were rejected. It was August now and the racing season had begun. My wife and I went to the track every day. We bicycled out for the early morning workouts, were often given tips, and won—sixty dollars one day, a hundred dollars, one day two hundred. I had visions of spending the rest of our lives at the races, traveling from track to track with the seasons. Suddenly I heard from my agent. The editors had simply been away on their summer vacations, that was all. They took the stories, all of them—one afternoon three acceptances in the same mail. I had my race-track winnings in cash all over me in different pockets; I had checks from the magazines laid away in envelopes. The stories began to appear. Promptly a barrage fell upon me, friends and strangers and well-wishers, wondering what had become of me, why I had sold out, and so on.

How fast the time goes. We are given only a few decades apiece. I didn't become rich. I went to Hollywood. The popular notions about the movies aren't true. It takes a good deal of energy and hard sense to write stories over an extended period of time, and it would be foolish to expect writers not to want to be paid a livelihood for what they do. But we are engaged here on the same problems that perplex writers everywhere. We grapple with the daily mystery. We struggle with form, with chimera, and to seize upon the elusive, fast-gliding image of Dorothy Kirschenbaum. "Poesy," my father used to call it, and I know I will keep at it for as long as I can, because surely there is nothing else to do. Of course I am always flattered when people ask about me and I am sincerely grateful for their kindness and interest.

I want to acknowledge the help I have received, in the writing of these novels and everything, from the one who has been with me all the years, the one who is part of me, my talisman, my love, my wife.

DANIEL FUCHS

Hollywood, California
April, 1961

Summer in Williamsburg

The air was soft and cool. It was one of those rare springlike days that comes in early September to relieve the hot monotony of summer. All the young women had their babies out sunning in carriages. The sun came into Philip's room like a flood, brightening the bed, the table, the book he was reading. Then it disappeared, hidden not behind clouds but behind the summer blankets airing on the clotheslines in the backyard, bellying with the breeze and then falling flat. The recurrence of the brightness and the dimness was a melancholy thing, and somehow, with the departure of the sweating heat, Philip longed for the cold winter times. He was impatient. The gray sky, the clouds like frozen water on the window-pane, the lonely walks in cold weather—Philip remembered the images and he longed for the winter because then life in Williamsburg grew less exposed, less crude, and a little gentle.

In Williamsburg the summer was getting over, but, on the other hand, in Tasmania it was the winter which was leaving for the soft winds of spring. Philip, waiting for his mother to give him his dinner, went to lie on the bed. The halls of the building were still marked with the black scars and everywhere one went the fire smell of smoke and damp wood persisted, but after the first days it was all the same, no one noticed those signs. The fire was beginning to be forgotten.

Mahler had been dug out of the debris in the cellar unrecognizable and all black like a charred pole. Cohen they found stiff, sitting on the bed with his hands drawing the pajama pants over his knees, fixed in that peculiar pose when the heated air had killed him. To read about a fire in a book was always an exciting thing, but actually Philip felt

cheated. He regretted the passing of Cohen and Mahler as sincerely as
a man could miss people he had known, but they had disappointed him.
For Mahler was certainly an extraordinary man, and Cohen as well, if
less honest. And the incident was unusual. Had Philip read about these
characters and their situations in a book he would have been easily drawn
by their romantic flavor. He would probably have been envious because
his own life would have seemed so empty by comparison. Yet knowing
these people in the flesh and going through the story with them, it was
all, at the bottom, strikingly unremarkable, commonplace, and even flat.
When you met people and lived there was no heroism, no romance, no
poetry. Cohen, of course, would have objected, Philip thought, but that
was how he felt. Or perhaps there was something wrong with him.

The scars and smell of smoke persisted, but the children running
through the halls in play paid no attention. The fire was beginning to
be forgotten. It was as his mother always said. Many things took place
all the time but it was nothing. People grew excited, and then it passed.
It was over, you forgot about it. In a book, Philip said, a fire could be
an important event, it could be used to bind together a setting and a story,
it offered a neat end. But actually there was no climax, no end. It went
on. Here he was himself, lying on a bed. . . .

Philip had been sitting at his table reading a novel by Thackeray
and marveling at the clean delineations of the people therein. How
wonderfully crisp were the characters. The author knew all about them
and said it. He knew everything. All authors knew everything because
they were like God. Thackeray told you what the people did, and then
he said what caused the action. Old Miller, God rest his wizened soul,
used to say, in his funny, smiling fashion, "Va-cha-choo-loo, va-cha-choo-
loo," and that meant, when the wind will blow, the cradle will rock.
How marvelously writers were able to perceive, clear-cut and with sure-
ness, the causes and the actions of their characters. In life no man was
known, even to himself, but in these novels the authors were able to
explain their people logically. What wonder-makers! What liars.

Someone had just begun to play chopsticks on the piano. Two women
were talking across the yard, in scrappy, raw voices. Philip's book rested
on a glass top. When the sun hit the glass there came colors of weak
green, light brown, and lemon yellow. About four or five babies were
crying miserably, and about four or five radios dispensed cracked music
simultaneously.

"Va-cha-choo-loo, va-cha-choo-loo," Old Miller used to say. "Men
are the sum of a million infinitesimal phenomena and experiences. A
million atoms of a certain type produce, in the end, wood just as a

million of another make stone and iron and gold. The same is true of these men.

"To find out, you must make a laboratory out of Williamsburg to learn what touches people here, why these details affect, and in what manner. A tremendous task. If you would really discover the reason for people's actions you must pick Williamsburg to pieces until you have them all spread out before you on your table, a dictionary of Williamsburg. Then select. Pick and discard. Collect and analyze."

How were people revealed? How could one discover what made them go? In books like Thackeray's there was always pertinent dialogue, action developing logically, and the subtle, deftly inserted comment of description. Actually, people said, "Good morning" or "It's a hot day"; they went to work and sat on the sidewalk in the evenings. People did small, inconsequential things, they crooked their small fingers becomingly as they drank vanilla seltzer, they wiped their noses in absent-minded slow moments and they said, "All right, all right, don't holler. I'll be up in a minute." Writers selected, but their imaginations insisted, and was their judgment divine? Why did they pick certain things and overlook others? To present a man honestly you would really have to give him entire.

Philip went to the parlor and looked out of the window. The sun shone brightly across the street. His side was dark because the building in which he lived was blotting out the light. Along his side of the street houses were of different heights and on the sidewalk opposite, the shadows of the buildings formed an uneven line. Philip looked at the group of women around the baby carriages. Mrs. Linck, heated and angry, was involved in fierce conversation. The eyes went up and down savagely, the mouth sawed, the floppy individual raged.

"I don't want children in the yard, missus," she stared with great positiveness and in a voice that carried. "It's my yard. If you don't like the way I take care of it you know what you can do."

"Never mind," said the woman. "I don't care what you do with your yard. You can put it somewhere I don't have to tell you. But nobody can curse my child. I don't need you to say such terrible things. After all, he's my boy. No mother likes to hear anybody curse her baby like that."

"Listen, missus, you like him so much, why don't you take good care of him? Why do you think I keep him out of the yard? Because I like to holler? I'm a mother too, I had children in my time. All the women keep bottles and God knows what else on the window-sills. Would you like it if a bottle fell down, God forbid, and hit your boy on the head?"

That ended the argument, Mrs. Linck certainly had the women

there, and she stamped across the street back into her house with a defiantly triumphant air. Her kindness to the neighborhood's children was unappreciated? To hell with the woman.

Philip looked down the street. The carriages on the sidewalk formed an exhibition. A middle-aged woman was dancing in clumsy, hopping movements to please a baby hidden among its blankets. The woman popped up and down and clapped her hands. Her face was creased with joy, for babies were wonderful things, everyone loved them, they were simply adorable. The dancing lady spoke kindly to a pregnant woman to indicate the joys of motherhood. How often Philip had heard them tell their syrupy philosophy to an expectant woman. It was hard, they said, it was very hard, but once you had them a mother's heart et cetera. They grew up, they went away, they forgot the pain they had caused and the worry when they had been sick, they went on, selfish, ungrateful, and forgetting, but after all, a mother's heart et cetera. The pregnant woman sighed with proud resignation and shook her head in sad concurrence. Look, she as good as said, I suffer for humanity, the world owes me something for it. A woman lifted her breast out of her waist and placed it in position. For the sake of delicacy she partly covered the soft flesh with a handkerchief. The pregnant woman and the one with the breast exposed conversed in the sunshine. Before and after. But we must not be disrespectful.

These were people as God made them and as they were. They sat in the sunshine going through the stale operations of living, they were real, but a novelist did not write a book about them. No novel, no matter how seriously intentioned, was real. The progressive development, the delineated episodes, the artificial climax, the final conclusion, setting the characters at rest and out of the lives of the readers, these were logical devices and they were false. People did not live in dramatic situations. You might even isolate some event in their lives, extract its drama and labor over it according to the rules, but in the end you would still have an incomplete portrait of them, it would be unfaithful to the whole. Even by isolating one episode there was exaggeration. The trouble with writers was that they knew too much. They made life too simple. They could say of the women at their carriages in the sunshine that they rose at ten, made their hurried breakfasts, tidied the rooms, went downstairs, bought candy and soda water, gossiped, went to the movies, and made delicatessen suppers for their husbands; a writer could say that and get away with it, but it wouldn't be the whole thing. They could say that Cohen was a nut who tried to commit suicide because he head was growing bald, that Philip's father was an old Chinaman who hadn't been around, that Tessie was one of those girls who live by *The New Yorker,* they could say that Philip himself was an adolescent in the agonies of awakening inquiry, in the stage when one was occupied with gaudy abstractions like life, meaning, and the grave. They could say that and be sufficiently understood, but it wasn't enough, it wasn't the whole thing. What was all the excitement about? Philip asked himself. Literature was not reality. That was all there was to it. Writers who said otherwise were fakers, claiming more than they could do. A book was an artificial synthesis, the product of a man's idea, to illustrate through his stress on characters and situations certain principles in which he was interested. Take Ripple Street, with Halper's Stable, Yozowitz's laundry, the Auburn S. C., the life on the roofs, in the cellars and in lots, Davey and his gang, Miller, Mrs. Linck and her family, Cohen, his own father and mother, Mahler and Yente Maldick, together with the hundreds of other persons who lived in the tenements on the block; take Ripple Street with the merry-go-rounds in the sunshine, the Italians coming down the street with cheap ice-cream bricks in the small carts; take the whole of Ripple Street from morning to night and back again; take it and reproduce it faithfully and you would have a great formless mass of petty incident, the stale product of people who were concerned completely with the tremendous job of making a living so that tomorrow they would be able to make a living another day. Everything here was petty. Love was a hot joke, a soiled business in worn bed sheets, a sedative interlude in the omnipresent struggle of making a living. There was never time enough. Poetry and heroism did not exist, but the movies did. People in tenements lived in a circle without significance, one day the duplicate of the next until the end, which occurred without meaning but accidentally, cutting the procession short as pointlessly as Cohen's life had been cut. People were born, grew tired and calloused, struggled and died. That was all, and no book was large enough to include the entire picture, to give the completely truthful impression, the exact feeling.

And what is to become of me? Philip asked. These problems we ask to wait a while, in good time we shall worry; these problems persist and never cease, in their inarticulate way, to torment. He remembered his brother Harry's advice. He remembered what Miller used to say. A man must be active, he must make money. What was Philip kidding around for, exploring the cavities of his teeth and pondering his eternal soul after the fashion of poor Cohen? This was something definite and concrete. It meant release and time for life. Money, thought Philip, and remembering Papravel he admired his father for his fine serenity. Was there no way out between the dirty preoccupations of fast money and the deadness of his father's example?

Vainly, said Philip (Lo! and also, Behold!), do I seek within me something magnificent, worth enthusiasm, worth labor, to guide me for the next forty or fifty years to come.

Shall I continue in my quiet anesthesia and contemplate myself imperturbably? Self-possessed, controlled, and analytical, above and indifferent to everything, but really dead years before my time?

Shall I continue to tramp the streets covered in a sunny tranquillity while a vague and aching nostalgia permeates me, nostalgia for places I have never seen because they do not exist, for persons completely unaffected, warm and kind and unreal?

Shall I fool around with Tessie Schlausser and dream at the same time of unearthly women fascinating and wonderful because at twenty I cannot have Ruth Kelman?

Shall I wallow in this gentle sadness in the darkness of moving picture houses, over ruminative cigarettes, like one allowing warm water to run through one's fingers on a cold morning?

And shall I, too, continue to inspect my comb in the light before my eyes for fallen hairs?

Dammit, Philip almost cried aloud. He tried to rouse himself from his mood and went back to his table. He opened *Pendennis,* but it was hard to read. It was getting late already and the sun had moved upward on the tenement wall, beyond the reach of his window, and there would be no more light and the crazy colors on his glass top. The women were going upstairs one by one as their husbands came home from work. Someone began to play chopsticks on the piano. Two women were talking or arguing in raw scrappy tones from windows across the yard. Philip tried to read, but with the sun gone he felt alone and depressed. He thought of winter, the quiet, and empty streets. About four or five babies were crying miserably and the radios kept on sending out the chirpingly cheerful music. Philip's head ached. He lay down again over the bed.

Mrs. Hayman came bustling in to give him his dinner.

"What do you think, Philip? They just found Mrs. Sussman's boy," she said at the gas range. "After all this time. I just heard the news. The poor baby, they found him all the way in Queens some place. In all my life I never witnessed anything so terrible."

"That means they're all found now," Phillip said from the bedroom.

"Yes, but what good does that do anybody?"

If you want to discover the reason, the sage in the long beard had said, the sage in whose skinny body all the cold wisdom of the world dwelt, if you want to discover the reason, you must pick Williamsburg to pieces until you have them all spread out on the table before you, a dictionary. And then select, look for cause and effect.

"Come," Mrs. Hayman called. "Come, Philip, it's ready on the table."

And Philip, waiting for the years to come to see what would happen to him, went to his dinner.

"Eat," his mother said. "Eat with bread. Don't touch only the fancy stuff."

It was night at the boarding house in Aligerville where Papravel kept his boys. Outside the full-starred sky resembled a huge ceiling in a Brooklyn burlesque house. The summer was already leaving and in the coolness of the night air could be discerned the gentle sad quality of autumn. But Mrs. Van Curen had the big living room all lit, the boys half sat, half lay in the chairs, and everyone smoked cigars. After war came peace, quiet, and content.

"Listen, boys," said Papravel from a full heart and with exuberant satisfaction, "it's a party. Tonight we celebrate because all that comes, knock wood, is good news. Morantz, he's quit not only in Williamsburg but in the mountains altogether. We bought him out. As for Gilhooley, let no one say Papravel don't take good care of his boys for Anschele Nussbaum here has everything fixed right, only give us a little time and God's help. And just this morning the railroad company sent out an announcement they take no more passengers, only freight. And it is only a beginning, because, remember, there is still a God over America."

Papravel interrupted the monologue long enough to relight his cigar. The boys listened with their eyes almost closed, but Mrs. Van Curen, that pious old lady, watched him intensely, listening with awe. As he held the match, Papravel turned serious. His eyebrows became constricted, and he waved the match vigorously to kill the flame.

"America," he repeated with conviction through the smoke, "I don't care what anybody says, America is a wonderful country. Seriously, seriously, I mean it. Look at me, look how I worked myself up in four short years. In America everyone has an equal chance. I don't know how things are in Russia now, even God Himself don't know what's going on there these days, but even so, where, I want to know, where in the world could a Jew make such a man of himself as right here in America?"

He had to say that last part quickly for most of his breath was gone and now Papravel waited with his eyes opened wide for an answer from him who dared. But in the pause Mrs. Van Curen suddenly took it into her head to cry. She was very sleepy and wept noiselessly but with many tears.

"What's the matter?" Papravel asked concerned. "What's the matter, what's the old lady crying about?"

Mrs. Van Curen looked up sadly. "I'm crying because you're such a fine, upstanding, kind young man, and yet when you die you won't go to Heaven."

"Why?" Papravel wanted to know. "Why should you say a thing like that?"

"You've never been baptized, Mr. Papravel."

"Oh," he said with great relief. "Don't you worry your little gray head over that." He didn't know whether this was a joke or what. "Just you leave this to me, Mrs. Van Curen, and everything will be all right," Papravel said, and he smiled happily.

CLIFFORD ODETS (1906–1963)

More than any other American playwright, Clifford Odets is identified with the social problems of the 1930's. In Waiting for Lefty, Awake and Sing, *and* Golden Boy, *Odets captured the language and customs of middle-class people during the Depression, their anxiety about poverty, their humor, their ambivalent attitudes toward idealism and materialism. * Awake and Sing *is a particularly accurate record of that period, a significant work that rises above "proletarian drama" through its close examination of a Jewish family in the Bronx.*

Odets was born in Philadelphia on July 18, 1906. During his early years, his family was poor—his father sold salt and peddled newspapers while his mother worked in a factory—but in time his father went into the printing business and became financially successful. When Odets was six years old, his family settled in the Bronx. Impatient with formal education, the boy left Morris High School in New York at the end of his sophomore year and went into his father's printing business; but his real interest was in drama, and he was soon involved with various theatrical groups. For a short period, he acted, then turned to writing radio scripts, and finally became both an actor and a playwright in the Group Theatre in 1930. At the outset, Odets was not successful, but as he grew to understand and sympathize with the working and middle classes, he found subject matter that was compatible to his sensibility: the crushing effects of a materialistic society on average people who seek to express their idealism. He wrote Waiting for Lefty, Awake and Sing, *and* Till the Day I Die *in the early 1930's, and their production in 1935 received critical and commercial acclaim.*

Because of his success, Odets was offered a lucrative position as a scriptwriter in Hollywood; but he remained with the Group Theatre so that he could guide his next play, Paradise Lost, *into production. The play failed commercially and Odets went to Hollywood, where he remained until his death. His last plays for the Group Theatre were* Golden Boy *(1937),* Rocket to the Moon *(1938–1939), and* Night Music *(1939–1940). Throughout the forties, Odets was almost completely absorbed in writing film scripts—*Humoresque *(1942),* None but the Lonely Heart *(1943),* Deadline at Dawn *(1949), and others. His later plays of importance include* The Big Knife *(1948–1949),* The Country Girl *(1949), and* The Flowering Peach *(1954).*

Clifford Odets died in 1963. His career never developed significantly beyond his work of the thirties, although The Country Girl *and* The Flowering Peach *are less programmatic and more exploratory in their examination of character. He remains the most important playwright of* the 1930's, a creator of memorable plays concerned with the Jewish immigrant experience. Awake and Sing is a striking portrayal of one family's economic and moral struggle against an oppressively materialistic culture. It vindicates the judgment that Robert Warshow made of Odets when he characterized him as "the poet of the Jewish middle class."

Awake and Sing

Awake and Sing was presented by the Group Theatre at the Belasco Theatre on the evening of February 19th, 1935, with the following members of the Group Theatre Acting Company:

	Played by
MYRON BERGER	ART SMITH
BESSIE BERGER	STELLA ADLER
JACOB	MORRIS CARNOVSKY
HENNIE BERGER	PHOEBE BRAND
RALPH BERGER	JULES GARFIELD
SCHLOSSER	ROMAN BOHNEN
MOE AXELROD	LUTHER ADLER
UNCLE MORTY	J. E. BROMBERG
SAM FEINSCHREIBER	SANFORD MEISNER

The entire action takes place in an apartment in the Bronx, New York City

The production was directed by HAROLD CLURMAN

The setting was designed by BORIS ARONSON

THE CHARACTERS OF THE PLAY

All of the characters in Awake and Sing *share a fundamental activity: a struggle for life amidst petty conditions.*

BESSIE BERGER, *as she herself states, is not only the mother in this home but also the father. She is constantly arranging and taking care of her family. She loves life, likes to laugh, has great resourcefulness and enjoys living from day to day. A high degree of energy accounts for her quick exasperation at ineptitude. She is a shrewd judge of realistic qualities in people in the sense of being able to gauge quickly their effectiveness. In her eyes all of the people in the house are equal. She is naïve and quick in emotional response. She is afraid of utter poverty. She is proper according to her own standards, which are fairly close to those of most middle-class families. She knows that when one lives in the jungle one must look out for the wild life.*

MYRON, *her husband, is a born follower. He would like to be a leader. He would like to make a million dollars. He is not sad or ever depressed. Life is an even sweet event to him, but the "old days" were sweeter yet. He has a dignified sense of himself. He likes people. He likes everything. But he is heartbroken without being aware of it.*

HENNIE *is a girl who has few friends, male or female. She is proud of her body. She won't ask favors. She travels alone. She is fatalistic about being trapped, but will escape if possible. She is self-reliant in the best sense. Till the day she dies she will be faithful to a loved man. She inherits her mother's sense of humor and energy.*

RALPH *is a boy with a clean spirit. He wants to know, wants to learn. He is ardent, he is romantic, he is sensitive. He is naïve too. He is trying to find why so much dirt must be cleared away before it is possible to "get to first base."*

JACOB, *too, is trying to find a right path for himself and the others. He is aware of justice, of dignity. He is an observer of the others, compares their activities with his real and ideal sense of life. This produces a reflective nature. In this home he is a constant boarder. He is a sentimental idealist with no power to turn ideal to action.*
With physical facts—such as housework—he putters. But as a barber he demonstrates the flair of an artist. He is an old Jew with living eyes in his tired face.

UNCLE MORTY *is a successful American business man with five good senses. Something sinister comes out of the fact that the lives of others seldom touch him deeply. He holds to his own line of life. When he is generous he wants others to be aware of it. He is pleased by attention—a rich relative to the* BERGER *family. He is a shrewd judge of material values. He will die unmarried. Two and two make four, never five with him. He can blink in the sun for hours, a fat tomcat. Tickle him, he laughs. He lives in a penthouse with a real*

Japanese butler to serve him. He sleeps with dress models, but not from his own showrooms. He plays cards for hours on end. He smokes expensive cigars. He sees every Mickey Mouse cartoon that appears. He is a 32-degree Mason. He is really deeply intolerant finally.

MOE AXELROD *lost a leg in the war. He seldom forgets that fact. He has killed two men in extra-martial activity. He is mordant, bitter. Life has taught him a disbelief in everything, but he will fight his way through. He seldom shows his feelings: fights against his own sensitivity. He has been everywhere and seen everything. All he wants is* HENNIE. *He is very proud. He scorns the inability of others to make their way in life, but he likes people for whatever good qualities they possess. His passionate outbursts come from a strong but contained emotional mechanism.*

SAM FEINSCHREIBER *wants to find a home. He is a lonely man, a foreigner in a strange land, hypersensitive about this fact, conditioned by the humiliation of not making his way alone. He has a sense of others laughing at him. At night he gets up and sits alone in the dark. He hears acutely all the small sounds of life. He might have been a poet in another time and place. He approaches his wife as if he were always offering her a delicate flower. Life is a high chill wind weaving itself around his head.*

SCHLOSSER, *the janitor, is an overworked German whose wife ran away with another man and left him with a young daughter who in turn ran away and joined a burlesque show as chorus girl. The man suffers rheumatic pains. He has lost his identity twenty years before.*

THE SCENE

Exposed on the stage are the dining room and adjoining front room of the BERGER *apartment. These two rooms are typically furnished. There is a curtain between them. A small door off the front room leads to* JACOB'S *room. When his door is open one sees a picture of* SACCO *and* VANZETTI *on the wall and several shelves of books. Stage left of this door presents the entrance to the foyer hall of the apartment. The two other bedrooms of the apartment are off this hall, but not necessarily shown.*

Stage left of the dining room presents a swinging door which opens on the kitchen.

Awake and Sing, ye that dwell in dust:

ISAIAH—26:19

ACT ONE

Time: The present; the family finishing supper.
Place: An apartment in the Bronx, New York City.

RALPH: Where's advancement down the place? Work like crazy! Think they see it? You'd drop dead first.

MYRON: Never mind, son, merit never goes unrewarded. Teddy Roosevelt used to say——

HENNIE: It rewarded you—thirty years a haberdashery clerk! (JACOB *laughs.*)

RALPH: All I want's a chance to get to first base!

HENNIE: That's all?

RALPH: Stuck down in that joint on Fourth Avenue—a stock clerk in a silk house! Just look at Eddie. I'm as good as he is—pulling in two-fifty a week for forty-eight minutes a day. A headliner, his name in all the papers.

JACOB: That's what you want, Ralphie? Your name in the paper?

RALPH: I wanna make up my own mind about things . . . be something! Didn't I want to take up tap dancing, too?

BESSIE: So take lessons. Who stopped you?

RALPH: On what?

BESSIE: On what? Save money.

RALPH: Sure, five dollars a week for expenses and the rest in the house. I can't save even for shoe laces.

BESSIE: You mean we shouldn't have food in the house, but you'll make a jig on the street corner?

RALPH: I mean something.

BESSIE: You also mean something when you studied on the drum, Mr. Smartie!

RALPH: I don't know. . . . Every other day to sit around with the blues and mud in your mouth.

MYRON: That's how it is—life is like that—a cake-walk.

RALPH: What's it get you?

HENNIE: A four-car funeral.

RALPH: What's it for?

JACOB: What's it for? If this life leads to a revolution it's a good life. Otherwise it's for nothing.

BESSIE: Never mind, Pop! Pass me the salt.

RALPH: It's crazy—all my life I want a pair of black and white shoes and can't get them. It's crazy!

BESSIE: In a minute I'll get up from the table. I can't take a bite in my mouth no more.

MYRON (*restraining her*): Now, Momma, just don't excite yourself——

BESSIE: I'm so nervous I can't hold a knife in my hand.

MYRON: Is that a way to talk, Ralphie? Don't Momma work hard enough all day? (BESSIE *allows herself to be reseated.*)

BESSIE: On my feet twenty-four hours?

MYRON: On her feet——

RALPH (*jumps up*): What do I do—go to night-clubs with Greta Garbo? Then when I come home can't even have my own room? Sleep on a day-bed in the front room! (*Choked, he exits to front room.*)

BESSIE: He's starting up that stuff again. (*Shouts to him*): When Hennie here marries you'll have her room—I should only live to see the day.

HENNIE: Me, too. (*They settle down to serious eating.*)

MYRON: This morning the sink was full of ants. Where they come from I just don't know. I thought it was coffee grounds . . . and then they began moving.

BESSIE: You gave the dog eat?

JACOB: I gave the dog eat. (HENNIE *drops a knife and picks it up again.*)

BESSIE: You got dropsy tonight.

HENNIE: Company's coming.

MYRON: You can buy a ticket for fifty cents and win fortunes. A man came in the store—it's the Irish Sweepstakes.

BESSIE: What?

MYRON: Like a raffle, only different. A man came in——

BESSIE: Who spends fifty-cent pieces for Irish raffles? They threw out a family on Dawson Street today. All the furniture on the sidewalk. A fine old woman with gray hair.

JACOB: Come eat, Ralph.

MYRON: A butcher on Beck Street won eighty thousand dollars.

BESSIE: Eighty thousand dollars! You'll excuse my expression, you're bughouse!

MYRON: I seen it in the paper—on one ticket—765 Beck Street.

BESSIE: Impossible!

MYRON: He did . . . yes he did. He says he'll take his old mother to Europe . . . an Austrian——

HENNIE: Europe . . .

MYRON: Six per cent on eighty thousand—forty-eight hundred a year.

BESSIE: I'll give you money. Buy a ticket in Hennie's name. Say, you can't tell—lightning never struck us yet. If they win on Beck Street we could win on Longwood Avenue.

JACOB (*ironically*): If it rained pearls—who would work?

BESSIE: Another country heard from. (RALPH *enters and silently seats himself.*)

MYRON: I forgot, Beauty—Sam Feinschreiber sent you a present. Since I brought him for supper he just can't stop talking about you.

HENNIE: What's that "mockie" bothering about? Who needs him?

MYRON: He's a very lonely boy.

HENNIE: So I'll sit down and bust out crying " 'cause he's lonely."

BESSIE (*opening candy*): He'd marry you one two three.

HENNIE: Too bad about him.

BESSIE (*naïvely delighted*): Chocolate peanuts.

HENNIE: Loft's week-end special, two for thirty-nine.

BESSIE: You could think about it. It wouldn't hurt.

HENNIE (*laughing*): To quote Moe Axelrod, "Don't make me laugh."

BESSIE: Never mind laughing. It's time you already had in your head a serious thought. A girl twenty-six don't grow younger. When I was your age it was already a big family with responsibilities.

HENNIE (*laughing*): Maybe that's what ails you, Mom.

BESSIE: Don't you feel well?

HENNIE: 'Cause I'm laughing? I feel fine. It's just funny—that poor guy sending me presents 'cause he loves me.

BESSIE: I think it's very, very nice.

HENNIE: Sure . . . swell!

BESSIE: Mrs. Marcus' Rose is engaged to a Brooklyn boy, a dentist. He came in his car today. A little dope should get such a boy. (*Finished with the meal,* BESSIE, MYRON *and* JACOB *rise. Both* HENNIE *and* RALPH *sit silently at the table, he eating. Suddenly she rises.*)

HENNIE: Tell you what, Mom. I saved for a new dress, but I'll take you and Pop to the Franklin. Don't need a dress. From now on I'm planning to stay in nights. Hold everything!

BESSIE: What's the matter—a bedbug bit you suddenly?

HENNIE: It's a good bill—Belle Baker. Maybe she'll sing "Eli, Eli."

BESSIE: We was going to a movie.

HENNIE: Forget it. Let's go.

MYRON: I see in the papers (*as he picks his teeth*) Sophie Tucker took off twenty-six pounds. Fearful business with Japan.

HENNIE: Write a book, Pop! Come on, we'll go early for good seats.

MYRON: Moe said you had a date with him for tonight.

BESSIE: Axelrod?

HENNIE: I told him no, but he don't believe it. I'll tell him no for the next hundred years, too.

MYRON: Don't break appointments, Beauty, and hurt people's feelings. (BESSIE *exits.*)

HENNIE: His hands got free wheeling. (*She exits.*)

MYRON: I don't know . . . people ain't the same. N-O- The whole world's changing right under our eyes. Presto! No manners. Like the great Italian lover in the movies. What was his name? The Sheik. . . . No one remembers? (*Exits, shaking his head.*)

RALPH (*unmoving at the table*): Jake . . .

JACOB: Noo?

RALPH: I can't stand it.

JACOB: There's an expression—"strong as iron you must be."

RALPH: It's a cock-eyed world.

JACOB: Boys like you could fix it some day. Look on the world, not on yourself so much. Every country with starving millions, no? In Germany and Poland a Jew couldn't walk in the street. Everybody hates, nobody loves.

RALPH: I don't get all that.

JACOB: For years, I watched you grow up. Wait! You'll graduate from my university. (*The others enter, dressed.*)

MYRON (*lighting*): Good cigars now for a nickel.

BESSIE (*to* JACOB): After take Tootsie on the roof. (*To* RALPH): What'll you do?

RALPH: Don't know.

BESSIE: You'll see the boys around the block?

RALPH: I'll stay home every night!

MYRON: Momma don't mean for you——

RALPH: I'm flying to Hollywood by plane, that's what I'm doing. (*Doorbell rings.* MYRON *answers it.*)

BESSIE: I don't like my boy to be seen with those tramps on the corner.

MYRON (*without*): Schlosser's here, Momma, with the garbage can.

BESSIE: Come in here, Schlosser. (*Sotto voce*) Wait, I'll give him a piece of my mind. (MYRON *ushers in* SCHLOSSER *who carries a garbage can in each hand.*) What's the matter the dumbwaiter's broken again?

SCHLOSSER: Mr. Wimmer sends new ropes next week. I got a sore arm.

BESSIE: He should live so long your Mr. Wimmer. For seven years already he's sending new ropes. No dumbwaiter, no hot water, no steam—— In a respectable house, they don't allow such conditions.

SCHLOSSER: In a decent house dogs are not running to make dirty the hallway.

BESSIE: Tootsie's making dirty? Our Tootsie's making dirty in the hall?

SCHLOSSER (to JACOB): I tell you yesterday again. You must not leave her——

BESSIE (indignantly): Excuse me! Please don't yell on an old man. He's got more brains in his finger than you got—I don't know where. Did you ever see—he should talk to you an old man?

MYRON: Awful.

BESSIE: From now on we don't walk up the stairs no more. You keep it so clean we'll fly in the windows.

SCHLOSSER: I speak to Mr. Wimmer.

BESSIE: Speak! Speak. Tootsie walks behind me like a lady any time, any place. So good-bye . . . good-bye, Mr. Schlosser.

SCHLOSSER: I tell you dot—I verk verry hard here. My arms is. . . . (Exits in confusion.)

BESSIE: Tootsie should lay all day in the kitchen maybe. Give him back if he yells on you. What's funny?

JACOB (laughing): Nothing.

BESSIE: Come. (Exits.)

JACOB: Hennie, take care. . . .

HENNIE: Sure.

JACOB: Bye-bye. (HENNIE exits. MYRON pops head back in door.)

MYRON: Valentino! That's the one! (He exits.)

RALPH: I never in my life even had a birthday party. Every time I went and cried in the toilet when my birthday came.

JACOB (seeing RALPH remove his tie): You're going to bed?

RALPH: No, I'm putting on a clean shirt.

JACOB: Why?

RALPH: I got a girl. . . . Don't laugh!

JACOB: Who laughs? Since when?

RALPH: Three weeks. She lives in Yorkville with an aunt and uncle. A bunch of relatives, but no parents.

JACOB: An orphan girl—tch, tch.

RALPH: But she's got me! Boy, I'm telling you I could sing! Jake, she's like stars. She's so beautiful you look at her and cry! She's like French words! We went to the park the other night. Heard the last band concert.

JACOB: Music. . . .

RALPH (stuffing shirt in trousers): It got cold and I gave her my coat to wear. We just walked along like that, see, without a word, see. I never was so happy in all my life. It got late . . . we just sat there.

She looked at me—you know what I mean, how a girl looks at you—right in the eyes? "I love you," she says, "Ralph." I took her home. . . . I wanted to cry. That's how I felt!

JACOB: It's a beautiful feeling.

RALPH: You said a mouthful!

JACOB: Her name is——

RALPH: Blanche.

JACOB: A fine name. Bring her sometimes here.

RALPH: She's scared to meet Mom.

JACOB: Why?

RALPH: You know Mom's not letting my sixteen bucks out of the house if she can help it. She'd take one look at Blanche and insult her in a minute—a kid who's got nothing.

JACOB: Boychick!

RALPH: What's the diff?

JACOB: It's no difference—a plain bourgeois prejudice—but when they find out a poor girl—it ain't so kosher.

RALPH: They don't have to know I've got a girl.

JACOB: What's in the end?

RALPH: Out I go! I don't mean maybe!

JACOB: And then what?

RALPH: Life begins.

JACOB: What life?

RALPH: Life with my girl. Boy, I could sing when I think about it! Her and me together—that's a new life!

JACOB: Don't make a mistake! A new death!

RALPH: What's the idea?

JACOB: Me, I'm the idea! Once I had in *my* heart a dream, a vision, but came marriage and then you forget. Children come and you forget because——

RALPH: Don't worry, Jake.

JACOB: Remember, a woman insults a man's soul like no other thing in the whole world!

RALPH: Why get so excited? No one——

JACOB: Boychick, wake up! Be something! Make your life something good. For the love of an old man who sees in your young days his new life, for such love take the world in your two hands and make it like new. Go out and fight so life shouldn't be printed on dollar bills. A woman waits.

RALPH: Say, I'm no fool!

JACOB: From my heart I hope not. In the meantime—— (*Bell rings.*)

RALPH: See who it is, will you? (*Stands off.*) Don't want Mom to catch me with a clean shirt.

JACOB (*calls*): Come in. (*Sotto voce*) Moe Axelrod. (MOE *enters.*)

MOE: Hello girls, how's your whiskers? (*To* RALPH): All dolled up. What's it, the weekly visit to the cat house?

RALPH: Please mind your business.

MOE: Okay, sweetheart.

RALPH (*taking a hidden dollar from a book*): If Mom asks where I went——

JACOB: I know. Enjoy yourself.

RALPH: Bye-bye. (*He exits.*)

JACOB: Bye-bye.

MOE: Who's home?

JACOB: Me.

MOE: Good. I'll stick around a few minutes. Where's Hennie?

JACOB: She went with Bessie and Myron to a show.

MOE: She what?!

JACOB: You had a date?

MOE (*hiding his feelings*): Here—I brought you some halavah.

JACOB: Halavah? Thanks. I'll eat a piece after.

MOE: So Ralph's got a dame? Hot stuff—a kid can't even play a card game.

JACOB: Moe, you're a no-good, a bum of the first water. To your dying day you won't change.

MOE: Where'd you get that stuff, a no-good?

JACOB: But I like you.

MOE: Didn't I go fight in France for democracy? Didn't I get my goddamn leg shot off in that war the day before the armistice? Uncle Sam give me the Order of the Purple Heart, didn't he? What'd you mean, a no-good?

JACOB: Excuse me.

MOE: If you got an orange I'll eat an orange.

JACOB: No orange. An apple.

MOE: No oranges, huh?—what a dump!

JACOB: Bessie hears you once talking like this she'll knock your head off.

MOE: Hennie went with, huh? She wantsa see me squirm, only I don't squirm for dames.

JACOB: You came to see her?

MOE: What for? I got a present for our boy friend, Myron. He'll drop dead when I tell him his gentle horse galloped in fifteen to one. He'll die.

JACOB: It really won? The first time I remember.

MOE: Where'd they go?

JACOB: A vaudeville by the Franklin.

MOE: What's special tonight?

JACOB: Someone tells a few jokes . . . and they forget the street is filled with starving beggars.

MOE: What'll they do—start a war?

JACOB: I don't know.

MOE: You oughta know. What the hell you got all the books for?

JACOB: It needs a new world.

MOE: That's why they had the big war—to make a new world, they said—safe for democracy. Sure every big general laying up in a Paris hotel with a half dozen broads pinned on his mustache. Democracy! I learned a lesson.

JACOB: An imperial war. You know what this means?

MOE: Sure, I know everything!

JACOB: By money men the interests must be protected. Who gave you such a rotten haircut? Please (*fishing in his vest pocket*), give me for a cent a cigarette. I didn't have since yesterday——

MOE (*giving one*): Don't make me laugh. (*A cent passes back and forth between them,* MOE *finally throwing it over his shoulder.*) Don't look so tired all the time. You're a wow—always sore about something.

JACOB: And you?

MOE: You got one thing—you can play pinochle. I'll take you over in a game. Then you'll have something to be sore on.

JACOB: Who'll wash dishes? (MOE *takes deck from buffet drawer.*)

MOE: Do 'em after. Ten cents a deal.

JACOB: Who's got ten cents?

MOE: I got ten cents. I'll lend it to you.

JACOB: Commence.

MOE (*shaking cards*): The first time I had my hands on a pack in two days. Lemme shake up these cards. I'll make 'em talk. (JACOB *goes to his room where he puts on a Caruso record.*)

JACOB: You should live so long.

MOE: Ever see oranges grow? I know a certain place—— One summer I laid under a tree and let them fall right in my mouth.

JACOB (*off, the music is playing; the card game begins*): From "L'Africana" . . . a big explorer comes on a new land—"O Paradiso." From act four this piece. Caruso stands on the ship and looks on a Utopia. You hear? "Oh paradise! Oh paradise on earth! Oh blue sky, oh fragrant air——"

MOE: Ask him does he see any oranges? (BESSIE, MYRON *and* HENNIE *enter.*)

JACOB: You came back so soon?

BESSIE: Hennie got sick on the way.

MYRON: Hello, Moe. . . . (MOE *puts cards back in pocket.*)

BESSIE: Take off the phonograph, Pop. (*To* HENNIE): Lay down . . . I'll call the doctor. You should see how she got sick on Prospect Avenue. Two weeks already she don't feel right.

MYRON: Moe . . .?

BESSIE: Go to bed, Hennie.

HENNIE: I'll sit here.

BESSIE: Such a girl I never saw! Now you'll be stubborn?

MYRON: It's for your own good, Beauty. Influenza——

HENNIE: I'll sit here.

BESSIE: You ever seen a girl should say no to everything. She can't stand on her feet, so——

HENNIE: Don't yell in my ears. I hear. Nothing's wrong. I ate tuna fish for lunch.

MYRON: Canned goods. . . .

BESSIE: Last week you also ate tuna fish?

HENNIE: Yeah, I'm funny for tuna fish. Go to the show—have a good time.

BESSIE: I don't understand what I did to God He blessed me with such children. From the whole world——

MOE (*coming to aid of* HENNIE): For Chris' sake, don't kibitz so much!

BESSIE: You don't like it?

MOE (*aping*): No, I don't like it.

BESSIE: That's too bad, Axelrod. Maybe it's better by your cigarstore friends. Here we're different people.

MOE: Don't gimme that cigar store line, Bessie. I walked up five flights——

BESSIE: To take out Hennie. But my daughter ain't in your class, Axelrod.

MOE: To see Myron.

MYRON: Did he, did he, Moe?

MOE: Did he what?

MYRON: "Sky Rocket"?

BESSIE: You bet on a horse!

MOE: Paid twelve and a half to one.

MYRON: There! You hear that, Momma? Our horse came in. You see, it happens, and twelve and a half to one. Just look at that!

MOE: What the hell, a sure thing. I told you.

BESSIE: If Moe said a sure thing, you couldn't bet a few dollars instead of fifty cents?

JACOB (*laughs*): "Aie, aie, aie."

MOE (*at his wallet*): I'm carrying six hundred "plunks" in big denominations.

BESSIE: A banker!

MOE: Uncle Sam sends me ninety a month.

BESSIE: So you save it?

MOE: Run it up, Run-it-up-Axelrod, that's me.

BESSIE: The police should know how.

MOE (*shutting her up*): All right, all right—— Change twenty, sweetheart.

MYRON: Can you make change?

BESSIE: Don't be crazy.

MOE: I'll meet a guy in Goldman's restaurant. I'll meet 'im and come back with change.

MYRON (*figuring on paper*): You can give it to me tomorrow in the store.

BESSIE (*acquisitive*): He'll come back, he'll come back!

MOE: Lucky I bet some bucks myself. (*In derision to* HENNIE): Let's step out tomorrow night, Par-a-dise. (*Thumbs his nose at her, laughs mordantly and exits.*)

MYRON: Oh, that's big percentage. If I picked a winner every day. . . .

BESSIE: Poppa, did you take Tootsie on the roof?

JACOB: All right.

MYRON: Just look at that—a cake walk. We can make——

BESSIE: It's enough talk. I got a splitting headache. Hennie, go in bed. I'll call Dr. Cantor.

HENNIE: I'll sit here . . . and don't call that old Ignatz 'cause I won't see him.

MYRON: If you get sick Momma can't nurse you. You don't want to go to a hospital.

JACOB: She don't look sick, Bessie, it's a fact.

BESSIE: She's got fever. I see in her eyes, so he tells me no. Myron, call Dr. Cantor. (MYRON *picks up phone, but* HENNIE *grabs it from him.*)

HENNIE: I don't want any doctor. I ain't sick. Leave me alone.

MYRON: Beauty, it's for your own sake.

HENNIE: Day in and day out pestering. Why are you always right and no one else can say a word?

BESSIE: When you have your own children——

HENNIE: I'm not sick! Hear what I say? I'm not sick! Nothing's the matter with me! I don't want a doctor. (BESSIE *is watching her with slow progressive understanding.*)

BESSIE: What's the matter?

HENNIE: Nothing, I told you!

BESSIE: You told me, but—— (*A long pause of examination follows.*)

HENNIE: See much?

BESSIE: Myron, put down the . . . the. . . . (*He slowly puts the phone down.*) Tell me what happened. . . .

HENNIE: Brooklyn Bridge fell down.

BESSIE (*approaching*): I'm asking a question. . . .

MYRON: What's happened, Momma?

BESSIE: Listen to me!

HENNIE: What the hell are you talking?

BESSIE: Poppa—take Tootsie on the roof.

HENNIE (*holding* JACOB *back*): If he wants he can stay here.

MYRON: What's wrong, Momma?

BESSIE (*her voice quivering slightly*): Myron, your fine Beauty's in trouble. Our society lady. . . .

MYRON: Trouble? I don't under—is it——?

BESSIE: Look in her face. (*He looks, understands and slowly sits in a chair, utterly crushed.*) Who's the man?

HENNIE: The Prince of Wales.

BESSIE: My gall is busting in me. In two seconds——

HENNIE (*in a violent outburst*): Shut up! Shut up! I'll jump out the window in a minute! Shut up! (*Finally she gains control of herself, says in a low, hard voice*): You don't know him.

JACOB: Bessie. . . .

BESSIE: He's a Bronx boy?

HENNIE: From out of town.

BESSIE: What do you mean?

HENNIE: From out of town!!

BESSIE: A long time you know him? You were sleeping by a girl from the office Saturday nights? You slept good, my lovely lady. You'll go to him . . . he'll marry you.

HENNIE: That's what you say.

BESSIE: That's what I say! He'll do it, take MY word he'll do it!

HENNIE: Where? (*To* JACOB): Give her the letter. (JACOB *does so.*)

BESSIE: What? (*Reads.*) "Dear sir: In reply to your request of the 14th inst., we can state that no Mr. Ben Grossman has ever been connected with our organization . . ." You don't know where he is?

HENNIE: No.

BESSIE (*walks back and forth*): Stop crying like a baby, Myron.

MYRON: It's like a play on the stage. . . .

BESSIE: To a mother you couldn't say something before. I'm old-fashioned—like your friends I'm not smart—I don't eat chop suey and run around Coney Island with tramps. (*She walks reflectively to buffet, picks up a box of candy, puts it down, says to* MYRON): Tomorrow night bring Sam Feinschreiber for supper.

HENNIE: I won't do it.

BESSIE: You'll do it, my fine beauty, you'll do it!

HENNIE: I'm not marrying a poor foreigner like him. Can't even speak an English word. Not me! I'll go to my grave without a husband.

BESSIE: You don't say! We'll find for you somewhere a millionaire with a pleasure boat. He's going to night school, Sam. For a boy only three years in the country he speaks very nice. In three years he put enough in the bank, a good living.

JACOB: This is serious?

BESSIE: What then? I'm talking for my health? He'll come tomorrow night for supper. By Saturday they're engaged.

JACOB: Such a thing you can't do.

BESSIE: Who asked your advice?

JACOB: Such a thing——

BESSIE: Never mind!

JACOB: The lowest from the low!

BESSIE: Don't talk! I'm warning you! A man who don't believe in God— with crazy ideas——

JACOB: So bad I never imagined you could be.

BESSIE: Maybe if you didn't talk so much it wouldn't happen like this. You with your ideas—I'm a mother. I raise a family they should have respect.

JACOB: Respect? (*Spits.*) Respect! For the neighbors' opinion! You insult me, Bessie!

BESSIE: Go to your room, Papa. Every job he ever had he lost because he's got a big mouth. He opens his mouth and the whole Bronx could fall in. Everybody said it——

MYRON: Momma, they'll hear you down the dumbwaiter.

BESSIE: A good barber not to hold a job a week. Maybe you never heard charity starts at home. You never heard it, Pop?

JACOB: All you know, I heard, and more yet. But Ralph you don't make like you. Before you do it, I'll die first. He'll find a girl. He'll go in a fresh world with her. This is a house? Marx said it—abolish such families.

BESSIE: Go in your room, Papa.

JACOB: Ralph you don't make like you!

BESSIE: Go lay in your room with Caruso and the books together.

JACOB: All right!

BESSIE: Go in the room!

JACOB: Some day I'll come out I'll—— (*Unable to continue, he turns, looks at* HENNIE, *goes to his door and there says with an attempt at humor*): Bessie, some day you'll talk to me so fresh . . . I'll leave the house for good! (*He exits.*)

BESSIE (*crying*): You ever in your life seen it? He should dare! He should just dare say in the house another word. Your gall could bust from such a man. (*Bell rings,* MYRON *goes.*) Go to sleep now. It won't hurt.

HENNIE: Yeah? (MOE *enters, a box in his hand.* MYRON *follows and sits down.*)

MOE (*looks around first—putting box on table*): Cake. (*About to give* MYRON *the money, he turns instead to* BESSIE): Six fifty, four bits change . . . come on, hand over half a buck. (*She does so. Of* MYRON): Who bit him?

BESSIE: We're soon losing our Hennie, Moe.

MOE: Why? What's the matter?

BESSIE: She made her engagement.

MOE: Zat so?

BESSIE: Today it happened . . . he asked her.

MOE: Did he? Who? Who's the corpse?

BESSIE: It's a secret.

MOE: In the bag, huh?

HENNIE: Yeah. . . .

BESSIE: When a mother gives away an only daughter it's no joke. Wait, when you'll get married you'll know. . . .

MOE (*bitterly*): Don't make me laugh—when I get married! What I think of women? Take 'em all, cut 'em in little pieces like a herring in Greek salad. A guy in France had the right idea—dropped his wife in a bathtub fulla acid. (*Whistles.*) Sss, down the pipe! Pfft—not even a corset button left!

MYRON: Corsets don't have buttons.

MOE (*to* HENNIE): What's the great idea? Gone big time, Paradise? Christ, it's suicide! Sure, kids you'll have, gold teeth, get fat, big in the tangerines——

HENNIE: Shut your face!

MOE: Who's it—some dope pullin' down twenty bucks a week? Cut your throat, sweetheart. Save time.

BESSIE: Never mind your two cents, Axelrod.

MOE: I say what I think—that's me!

HENNIE: That's you—a lousy fourflusher who'd steal the glasses off a blind man.

MOE: Get hot!

HENNIE: My God, do I need it—to listen to this mutt shoot his mouth off?

MYRON: Please. . . .

MOE: Now wait a minute, sweetheart, wait a minute. I don't have to take that from you.

BESSIE: Don't yell at her!

HENNIE: For two cents I'd spit in your eye.

MOE (*throwing coin to table*): Here's two bits. (HENNIE *looks at him and then starts across the room.*)

BESSIE: Where are you going?

HENNIE (*crying*): For my beauty nap, Mussolini. Wake me up when it's apple blossom time in Normandy. (*Exits.*)

MOE: Pretty, pretty—a sweet gal, your Hennie. See the look in her eyes?

BESSIE: She don't feel well. . . .

MYRON: Canned goods. . . .

BESSIE: So don't start with her.

MOE: Like a battleship she's got it. Not like other dames—shove 'em and they lay. Not her. I got a yen for her and I don't mean a Chinese coin.

BESSIE: Listen, Axelrod, in my house you don't talk this way. Either have respect or get out.

MOE: When I think about it . . . maybe I'd marry her myself.

BESSIE (*suddenly aware of* MOE): You could—— What do you mean, Moe?

MOE: You ain't sunburnt—you heard me.

BESSIE: Why don't you, Moe? An old friend of the family like you. It would be a blessing on all of us.

MOE: You said she's engaged.

BESSIE: But maybe she don't know her own mind. Say, it's——

MOE: I need a wife like a hole in the head. . . . What's to know about women, I know. Even if I asked her. She won't do it! A guy with one leg—it gives her the heebie-jeebies. I know what she's looking for. An arrow-collar guy, a hero, but with a wad of jack. Only the two don't go together. But I got what it takes . . . plenty, and more where it comes from. . . . (*Breaks off, snorts and rubs his knee. A pause. In his room* JACOB *puts on Caruso singing the lament from "The Pearl Fishers."*)

BESSIE: It's right—she wants a millionaire with a mansion on Riverside Drive. So go fight City Hall. Cake?

MOE: Cake.

BESSIE: I'll make tea. But one thing—she's got a fine boy with a business brain. Caruso! (*Exits into the front room and stands in the dark, at the window.*)

MOE: No wet smack . . . a fine girl. . . . She'll burn that guy out in a month. (MOE *retrieves the quarter and spins it on the table.*)

MYRON: I remember that song . . . beautiful. Nora Bayes sang it at the old Proctor's Twenty-third Street—"When It's Apple Blossom Time in Normandy." . . .

MOE: She wantsa see me crawl—my head on a plate she wants! A snow-ball in hell's got a better chance. (*Out of sheer fury he spins the quarter in his fingers.*)

MYRON (*as his eyes slowly fill with tears*): Beautiful . . .

MOE: Match you for a quarter. Match you for any goddam thing you got. (*Spins the coin viciously.*) What the hell kind of house is this it ain't got an orange!!

Slow Curtain

ACT TWO

SCENE I

One year later, a Sunday afternoon. The front room. JACOB *is giving his son* MORDECAI (UNCLE MORTY) *a haircut, newspapers spread around the base of the chair.* MOE *is reading a newspaper, leg propped on a chair.* RALPH, *in another chair, is spasmodically reading a paper.* UNCLE MORTY *reads colored jokes. Silence, then* BESSIE *enters.*

BESSIE: Dinner's in half an hour, Morty.

MORTY (*still reading jokes*): I got time.

BESSIE: A duck. Don't get hair on the rug, Pop. (*Goes to window and pulls down shade.*) What's the matter the shade's up to the ceiling?

JACOB (*pulling it up again*): Since when do I give a haircut in the dark? (*He mimics her tone.*)

BESSIE: When you're finished, pull it down. I like my house to look respectable. Ralphie, bring up two bottles seltzer from Weiss.

RALPH: I'm reading the paper.

BESSIE: Uncle Morty likes a little seltzer.

RALPH: I'm expecting a phone call.

BESSIE: Noo, if it comes you'll be back. What's the matter? (*Gives him money from apron pocket.*) Take down the old bottles.

RALPH (*to* JACOB): Get that call if it comes. Say I'll be right back. (JACOB *nods assent.*)

MORTY (*giving change from vest*): Get grandpa some cigarettes.

RALPH: Okay. (*Exits.*)

JACOB: What's new in the paper, Moe?

MOE: Still jumping off the high buildings like flies—the big shots who lost all their cocoanuts. Pfft!

JACOB: Suicides?

MOE: Plenty can't take it—good in the break, but can't take the whip in the stretch.

MORTY (*without looking up*): I saw it happen Monday in my building. My hair stood up how they shoveled him together—like a pancake— a bankrupt manufacturer.

MOE: No brains.

MORTY: Enough . . . all over the sidewalk.

JACOB: If someone said five-ten years ago I couldn't make for myself a living, I wouldn't believe——

MORTY: Duck for dinner?

BESSIE: The best Long Island duck.

MORTY: I like goose.

BESSIE: A duck is just like a goose, only better.

MORTY: I like a goose.

BESSIE: The next time you'll be for Sunday dinner I'll make a goose.

MORTY (*sniffs deeply*): Smells good. I'm a great boy for smells.

BESSIE: Ain't you ashamed? Once in a blue moon he should come to an only sister's house.

MORTY: Bessie, leave me live.

BESSIE: You should be ashamed!

MORTY: Quack quack!

BESSIE: No, better to lay around Mecca Temple playing cards with the Masons.

MORTY (*with good nature*): Bessie, don't you see Pop's giving me a haircut?

BESSIE: You don't need no haircut. Look, two hairs he took off.

MORTY: Pop likes to give me a haircut. If I said no he don't forget for a year, do you, Pop? An old man's like that.

JACOB: I still do an A-1 job.

MORTY (*winking*): Pop cuts hair to fit the face, don't you, Pop?

JACOB: For sure, Morty. To each face a different haircut. Custom built, no ready made. A round face needs special——

BESSIE (*cutting him short*): A graduate from the B.M.T. (*going*): Don't forget the shade. (*The phone rings. She beats* JACOB *to it.*) Hello? Who is it, please? . . . Who is it please? . . . Miss Hirsch? No, he ain't here. . . . No, I couldn't say when. (*Hangs up sharply.*)

JACOB: For Ralph?

BESSIE: A wrong number. (JACOB *looks at her and goes back to his job.*)

JACOB: Excuse me!

BESSIE (*to* MORTY): Ralphie took another cut down the place yesterday.

MORTY: Business is bad. I saw his boss Harry Glicksman Thursday. I bought some velvets . . . they're coming in again.

BESSIE: Do something for Ralphie down there.

MORTY: What can I do? I mentioned it to Glicksman. He told me they squeezed out half the people. . . . (MYRON *enters dressed in apron.*)

BESSIE: What's gonna be the end? Myron's working only three days a week now.

MYRON: It's conditions.

BESSIE: Hennie's married with a baby . . . money just don't come in. I never saw conditions should be so bad.

MORTY: Times'll change.

MOE: The only thing'll change is my underwear.

MORTY: These last few years I got my share of gray hairs. (*Still reading jokes without having looked up once.*) Ha, ha, ha—Popeye the sailor ate spinach and knocked out four bums.

MYRON: I'll tell you the way I see it. The country needs a great man now—a regular Teddy Roosevelt.

MOE: What this country needs is a good five-cent earthquake.

JACOB: So long labor lives it should increase private gain——

BESSIE (*to* JACOB): Listen, Poppa, go talk on the street corner. The government'll give you free board the rest of your life.

MORTY: I'm surprised. Don't I send a five-dollar check for Pop every week?

BESSIE: You could afford a couple more and not miss it.

MORTY: Tell me jokes. Business is so rotten I could just as soon lay all day in the Turkish bath.

MYRON: Why'd I come in here? (*Puzzled, he exits.*)

MORTY (*to* MOE): I hear the bootleggers still do business, Moe.

MOE: Wake up! I kissed bootlegging bye-bye two years back.

MORTY: For a fact? What kind of racket is it now?

MOE: If I told you, you'd know something. (HENNIE *comes from bedroom.*)

HENNIE: Where's Sam?

BESSIE: Sam? In the kitchen.

HENNIE (*calls*): Sam. Come take the diaper.

MORTY: How's the Mickey Louse? Ha, ha, ha. . . .

HENNIE: Sleeping.

MORTY: Ah, that's life to a baby. He sleeps—gets it in the mouth—sleeps some more. To raise a family nowadays you must be a damn fool.

BESSIE: Never mind, never mind, a woman who don't raise a family—a girl—should jump overboard. What's she good for? (*To* MOE—*to change the subject*): Your leg bothers you bad?

MOE: It's okay, sweetheart.

BESSIE (*to* MORTY): It hurts him every time it's cold out. He's got four legs in the closet.

MORTY: Four wooden legs?

MOE: Three.

MORTY: What's the big idea?

MOE: Why not? Uncle Sam gives them out free.

MORTY: Say, maybe if Uncle Sam gave out less legs we could balance the budget.

JACOB: Or not have a war so they wouldn't have to give out legs.

MORTY: Shame on you, Pop. Everybody knows war is necessary.

MOE: Don't make me laugh. Ask me—the first time you pick up a dead one in the trench—then you learn war ain't so damn necessary.

MORTY: Say, you should kick. The rest of your life Uncle Sam pays you ninety a month. Look, not a worry in the world.

MOE: Don't make me laugh. Uncle Sam can take his *seventy* bucks and—— (*Finishes with a gesture.*) Nothing good hurts. (*He rubs his stump.*)

HENNIE: Use a crutch, Axelrod. Give the stump a rest.

MOE: Mind your business, Feinschreiber.

BESSIE: It's a sensible idea.

MOE: Who asked you?

BESSIE: Look, he's ashamed.

MOE: So's your Aunt Fanny.

BESSIE (*naïvely*): Who's got an Aunt Fanny? (*She cleans a rubber plant's leaves with her apron.*)

MORTY: It's a joke!

MOE: I don't want my paper creased before I read it. I want it fresh. Fifty times I said that.

BESSIE: Don't get so excited for a five-cent paper—our star boarder.

MOE: And I don't want no one using my razor either. Get it straight. I'm not buying ten blades a week for the Berger family. (*Furiously, he limps out.*)

BESSIE: Maybe I'm using his razor too.

HENNIE: Proud!

BESSIE: You need luck with plants. I didn't clean off the leaves in a month.

MORTY: You keep the house like a pin and I like your cooking. Any time Myron fires you, come to me, Bessie. I'll let the butler go and you'll be my housekeeper. I don't like Japs so much—sneaky.

BESSIE: Say, you can't tell. Maybe any day I'm coming to stay. (HENNIE *exits.*)

JACOB: Finished.

MORTY: How much, Ed. Pinaud? (*Disengages self from chair.*)

JACOB: Five cents.

MORTY: Still five cents for a haircut to fit the face?

JACOB: Prices don't change by me. (*Takes a dollar.*) I can't change——

MORTY: Keep it. Buy yourself a Packard. Ha, ha, ha.

JACOB (*taking large envelope from pocket*): Please, you'll keep this for me. Put it away.

MORTY: What is it?

JACOB: My insurance policy. I don't like it should lay around where something could happen.

MORTY: What could happen?

JACOB: Who knows, robbers, fire . . . they took next door. Fifty dollars from O'Reilly.

MORTY: Say, lucky a Berger didn't lose it.

JACOB: Put it downtown in the safe. Bessie don't have to know.

MORTY: It's made out to Bessie?

JACOB: No, to Ralph.

MORTY: To Ralph?

JACOB: He don't know. Some day he'll get three thousand.

MORTY: You got good years ahead.

JACOB: Behind. (RALPH *enters.*)

RALPH: Cigarettes. Did a call come?

JACOB: A few minutes. She don't let me answer it.

RALPH: Did Mom say I was coming back?

JACOB: No. (MORTY *is back at new jokes.*)

RALPH: She started that stuff again? (BESSIE *enters.*) A call come for me?

BESSIE (*waters pot from milk bottle*): A wrong number.

JACOB: Don't say a lie, Bessie.

RALPH: Blanche said she'd call me at two—was it her?

BESSIE: I said a wrong number.

RALPH: Please, Mom, if it was her tell me.

BESSIE: You call me a liar next. You got no shame—to start a scene in front of Uncle Morty. Once in a blue moon he comes——

RALPH: What's the shame? If my girl calls I wanna know it.

BESSIE: You made enough mish mosh with her until now.

MORTY: I'm surprised, Bessie. For the love of Mike tell him yes or no.

BESSIE: I didn't tell him? No!

MORTY (*to* RALPH): No! (RALPH *goes to a window and looks out.*)

BESSIE: Morty, I didn't say before—he runs around steady with a girl.

MORTY: Terrible. Should he run around with a foxie-woxie?

BESSIE: A girl with no parents.

MORTY: An orphan?

BESSIE: I could die from shame. A year already he runs around with her. He brought her once for supper. Believe me, she didn't come again, no!

RALPH: Don't think I didn't ask her.

BESSIE: You hear? You raise them and what's in the end for all your trouble?

JACOB: When you'll lay in a grave, no more trouble. (*Exits.*)

MORTY: Quack quack!

BESSIE: A girl like that he wants to marry. A skinny consumptive-looking . . . six months already she's not working—taking charity from an aunt. You should see her. In a year she's dead on his hands.

RALPH: You'd cut her throat if you could.

BESSIE: That's right! Before she'd ruin a nice boy's life I would first go to prison. Miss Nobody should step in the picture and I'll stand by with my mouth shut.

RALPH: Miss Nobody! Who am I? Al Jolson?

BESSIE: Fix your tie!

RALPH: I'll take care of my own life.

BESSIE: You'll take care? Excuse my expression, you can't even wipe your nose yet! He'll take care!

MORTY (*to* BESSIE): I'm surprised. Don't worry so much, Bessie. When it's time to settle down he won't marry a poor girl, will you? In the long run common sense is thicker than love. I'm a great boy for live and let live.

BESSIE: Sure, it's easy to say. In the meantime he eats out my heart. You know I'm not strong.

MORTY: I know . . . a pussy cat . . . ha, ha, ha.

BESSIE: You got money and money talks. But without the dollar who sleeps at night?

RALPH: I been working for years, bringing in money here—putting it in your hand like a kid. All right, I can't get my teeth fixed. All right, that a new suit's like trying to buy the Chrysler Building. You never in your life bought me a pair of skates even—things I died for when I was a kid. I don't care about that stuff, see. Only just remember I pay some of the bills around here, just a few . . . and if my girl calls me on the phone I'll talk to her any time I please. (*He exits.* HENNIE *applauds.*)

BESSIE: Don't be so smart, Miss America! (*To* MORTY): He didn't have skates! But when he got sick, a twelve-year-old boy, who called a big specialist for the last $25 in the house? Skates!

JACOB (*just in. Adjusts window shades*): It looks like snow today.

MORTY: It's about time—winter.

BESSIE: Poppa here could talk like Samuel Webster, too, but it's just talk. He should try to buy a two-cent pickle in the Burland Market without money.

MORTY: I'm getting an appetite.

BESSIE: Right away we'll eat. I made chopped liver for you.

MORTY: My specialty!

BESSIE: Ralph should only be a success like you, Morty. I should only live to see the day when he rides up to the door in a big car with a chauffeur and a radio. I could die happy, believe me.

MORTY: Success she says. She should see how we spend thousands of dollars making up a winter line and winter don't come—summer in January. Can you beat it?

JACOB: Don't live, just make success.

MORTY: Chopped liver—ha!

JACOB: Ha! (*Exits.*)

MORTY: When they start arguing, I don't hear. Suddenly I'm deaf. I'm a great boy for the practical side. (*He looks over to* HENNIE *who sits rubbing her hands with lotion.*)

HENNIE: Hands like a raw potato.

MORTY: What's the matter? You don't look so well . . . no pep.

HENNIE: I'm swell.

MORTY: You used to be such a pretty girl.

HENNIE: Maybe I got the blues. You can't tell.

MORTY: You could stand a new dress.

HENNIE: That's not all I could stand.

MORTY: Come down to the place tomorrow and pick out a couple from the "eleven-eighty" line. Only don't sing me the blues.

HENNIE: Thanks. I need some new clothes.

MORTY: I got two thousand pieces of merchandise waiting in the stock room for winter.

HENNIE: I never had anything from life. Sam don't help.

MORTY: He's crazy about the kid.

HENNIE: Crazy is right. Twenty-one a week he brings in—a nigger don't have it so hard. I wore my fingers off on an Underwood for six years. For what? Now I wash baby diapers. Sure, I'm crazy about the kid too. But half the night the kid's up. Try to sleep. You don't know how it is, Uncle Morty.

MORTY: No, I don't know. I was born yesterday. Ha, ha, ha. Some day I'll leave you a little nest egg. You like eggs? Ha?

HENNIE: When? When I'm dead and buried?

MORTY: No, when *I'm* dead and buried. Ha, ha, ha.

HENNIE: You should know what I'm thinking.

MORTY: Ha, ha, ha, I know. (MYRON *enters.*)

MYRON: I never take a drink. I'm surprised at myself, I——

MORTY: I got a pain. Maybe I'm hungry.

MYRON: Come inside, Morty. Bessie's got some schnapps.

MORTY: I'll take a drink. Yesterday I missed the Turkish bath.

MYRON: I get so bitter when I take a drink, it just surprises me.

MORTY: Look how fat. Say, you live once. . . . Quack, quack. (*Both exit.* MOE *stands silently in the doorway.*)

SAM (*entering*): I'll make Leon's bottle now!

HENNIE: No, let him sleep, Sam. Take away the diaper. (*He does. Exits.*)

MOE (*advancing into the room*): That your husband?

HENNIE: Don't you know?

MOE: Maybe he's a nurse you hired for the kid—it looks it—how he tends it. A guy comes howling to your old lady every time you look cock-eyed. Does he sleep with you?

HENNIE: Don't be so wise!

MOE (*indicating newspaper*): Here's a dame strangled her hubby with wire. Claimed she didn't like him. Why don't you brain Sam with an axe some night?

HENNIE: Why don't you lay an egg, Axelrod?

MOE: I laid a few in my day, Feinschreiber. Hard-boiled ones too.

HENNIE: Yeah?

MOE: Yeah. You wanna know what I see when I look in your eyes?

HENNIE: No.

MOE: Ted Lewis playing the clarinet—some of those high crazy notes! Christ, you coulda had a guy with some guts instead of a cluck stands around boilin' baby nipples.

HENNIE: Meaning you?

MOE: Meaning me, sweetheart.

HENNIE: Think you're pretty good.

MOE: You'd know if I slept with you again.

HENNIE: I'll smack your face in a minute.

MOE: You do and I'll break your arm. (*Holds up paper.*) Take a look. (*Reads*): "Ten-day luxury cruise to Havana." That's the stuff you coulda had. Put up at ritzy hotels, frenchie soap, champagne. Now you're tied down to "Snake-Eye" here. What for? What's it get you? . . . a 2 x 4 flat on 108th Street . . . a pain in the bustle it gets you.

HENNIE: What's it to you?

MOE: I know you from the old days. How you like to spend it! What I mean! Lizard-skin shoes, perfume behind the ears. . . . You're in a mess, Paradise! Paradise—that's a hot one—yah, crazy to eat a knish at your own wedding.

HENNIE: I get it—you're jealous. You can't get me.

MOE: Don't make me laugh.

HENNIE: Kid Jailbird's been trying to make me for years. You'd give your other leg. I'm hooked? Maybe, but you're in the same boat. Only it's worse for you. I don't give a damn no more, but you gotta yen makes you——

MOE: Don't make me laugh.

HENNIE: Compared to you I'm sittin' on top of the world.

MOE: You're losing your looks. A dame don't stay young forever.

HENNIE: You're a liar. I'm only twenty-four.

MOE: When you comin' home to stay?

HENNIE: Wouldn't you like to know?

MOE: I'll get you again.

HENNIE: Think so?

MOE: Sure, whatever goes up comes down. You're easy—you remember—two for a nickel—a pushover! (*Suddenly she slaps him. They both seem stunned.*) What's the idea?

HENNIE: Go on ... break my arm.

MOE (*as if saying "I love you"*): Listen, lousy.

HENNIE: Go on, do something!

MOE: Listen——

HENNIE: You're so damn tough!

MOE: You like me. (*He takes her.*)

HENNIE: Take your hand off! (*Pushes him away.*) Come around when it's a flood again and they put you in the ark with the animals. Not even then—if you was the last man!

MOE: Baby, if you had a dog I'd love the dog.

HENNIE: Gorilla! (*Exits.* RALPH *enters.*)

RALPH: Were you here before?

MOE (*sits*): What?

RALPH: When the call came for me?

MOE: What?

RALPH: The call came. (JACOB *enters.*)

MOE (*rubbing his leg*): No.

JACOB: Don't worry, Ralphie, she'll call back.

RALPH: Maybe not. I think somethin's the matter.

JACOB: What?

RALPH: I don't know. I took her home from the movies last night. She asked me what I'd think if she went away.

JACOB: Don't worry, she'll call again.

RALPH: Maybe not, if Mom insulted her. She gets it on both ends, the poor kid. Lived in an orphan asylum most of her life. They shove her around like an empty freight train.

JACOB: After dinner go see her.

RALPH: Twice they kicked me down the stairs.

JACOB: Life should have some dignity.

RALPH: Every time I go near the place I get heart failure. The uncle drives a bus. You oughta see him—like Babe Ruth.

MOE: Use your brains. Stop acting like a kid who still wets the bed. Hire a room somewhere—a club room for two members.

RALPH: Not that kind of proposition, Moe.

MOE: Don't be a bush leaguer all your life.

RALPH: Cut it out!

MOE (*on a sudden upsurge of emotion*): Ever sleep with one? Look at 'im blush.

RALPH: You don't know her.

MOE: I seen her—the kind no one sees undressed till the undertaker works on her.

RALPH: Why give me the needles all the time? What'd I ever do to you?

MOE: Not a thing. You're a nice kid. But grow up! In life there's two kinds—the men that's sure of themselves and the ones who ain't! It's time you quit being a selling-plater and got in the first class.

JACOB: And you, Axelrod?

MOE (*to* JACOB): Scratch your whiskers! (*To* RALPH): Get independent. Get what-it-takes and be yourself. Do what you like.

RALPH: Got a suggestion? (MORTY *enters, eating.*)

MOE: Sure, pick out a racket. Shake down the cocoanuts. See what that does.

MORTY: We know what it does—puts a pudding on your nose! Sing Sing! Easy money's against the law. Against the law don't win. A racket is illegitimate, no?

MOE: It's all a racket—from horse racing down. Marriage, politics, big business—everybody plays cops and robbers. You, you're a racketeer yourself.

MORTY: Who? Me? Personally I manufacture dresses.

MOE: Horse feathers!

MORTY (*seriously*): Don't make such remarks to me without proof. I'm a great one for proof. That's why I made a success in business. Proof —put up or shut up, like a game of cards. I heard this remark before—a rich man's a crook who steals from the poor. Personally, I don't like it. It's a big lie!

MOE: If you don't like it, buy yourself a fife and drum—and go fight your own war.

MORTY: Sweatshop talk. Every Jew and Wop in the shop eats my bread and behind my back says, "a sonofabitch." I started from a poor boy who worked on an ice wagon for two dollars a week. Pop's right here —he'll tell you. I made it honest. In the whole industry nobody's got a better name.

JACOB: It's an exception, such success.

MORTY: Ralph can't do the same thing?

JACOB: No, Morty, I don't think. In a house like this he don't realize even the possibilities of life. Economics comes down like a ton of coal on the head.

MOE: Red rover, red rover, let Jacob come over!

JACOB: In my day the propaganda was for God. Now it's for success. A boy don't turn around without having shoved in him he should make success.

MORTY: Pop, you're a comedian, a regular Charlie Chaplin.

JACOB: He dreams all night of fortunes. Why not? Don't it say in the movies he should have a personal steamship, pyjamas for fifty dollars a pair and a toilet like a monument? But in the morning he wakes up and for ten dollars he can't fix the teeth. And millions more worse off in the mills of the South—starvation wages. The blood from the worker's heart. (MORTY *laughs loud and long.*) Laugh, laugh . . . tomorrow not.

MORTY: A real, a real Boob McNutt you're getting to be.

JACOB: Laugh, my son. . . .

MORTY: Here is the North, Pop.

JACOB: North, south, it's one country.

MORTY: The country's all right. A duck quacks in every pot!

JACOB: You never heard how they shoot down men and women which ask a better wage? Kentucky 1932?

MORTY: That's a pile of chopped liver, Pop. (BESSIE *and others, enter.*)

JACOB: Pittsburgh, Passaic, Illinois—slavery—it begins where success begins in a competitive system. (MORTY *howls with delight.*)

MORTY: Oh Pop, what are you bothering? Why? Tell me why? Ha ha ha. I bought you a phonograph . . . stick to Caruso.

BESSIE: He's starting up again.

MORTY: Don't bother with Kentucky. It's full of moonshiners.

JACOB: Sure, sure——

MORTY: You don't know practical affairs. Stay home and cut hair to fit the face.

JACOB: It says in the Bible how the Red Sea opened and the Egyptians went in and the sea rolled over them. (*Quotes two lines of Hebrew.*) In this boy's life a Red Sea will happen again. I see it!

MORTY: I'm getting sore, Pop, with all this sweatshop talk.

BESSIE: He don't stop a minute. The whole day, like a phonograph.

MORTY: I'm surprised. Without a rich man you don't have a roof over your head. You don't know it?

MYRON: Now you can't bite the hand that feeds you.

RALPH: Let him alone—he's right!

BESSIE: Another country heard from.

RALPH: It's the truth. It's——

MORTY: Keep quiet, snotnose!

JACOB: For sure, charity, a bone for an old dog. But in Russia an old man don't take charity so his eyes turn black in his head. In Russia they got Marx.

MORTY (*scoffingly*): Who's Marx?

MOE: An outfielder for the Yanks. (MORTY *howls with delight.*)

MORTY: Ha ha ha, it's better than the jokes. I'm telling you. This is Uncle Sam's country. Put it in your pipe and smoke it.

BESSIE: Russia, he says! Read the papers.

SAM: Here is opportunity.

MYRON: People can't believe in God in Russia. The papers tell the truth, they do.

JACOB: So you believe in God . . . you got something for it? You! You worked for all the capitalists. You harvested the fruit from your labor? You got God! But the past comforts you? The present smiles on you, yes? It promises you the future something? Did you found a piece of earth where you could live like a human being and die with the sun on your face? Tell me, yes, tell me. I would like to know myself. But on these questions, on this theme—the struggle for existence—you can't make an answer. The answer I see in your face . . . the answer is your mouth can't talk. In this dark corner you sit and you die. But abolish private property!

BESSIE (*settling the issue*): Noo, go fight City Hall!

MORTY: He's drunk!

JACOB: I'm studying from books a whole lifetime.

MORTY: That's what it is—he's drunk. What the hell does all that mean?

JACOB: If you don't know, why should I tell you.

MORTY (*triumphant at last*): You see? Hear him? Like all those nuts, don't know what they're saying.

JACOB: I know, I know.

MORTY: Like Boob McNutt you know! Don't go in the park, Pop—the squirrels'll get you. Ha, ha, ha. . . .

BESSIE: Save your appetite, Morty. (*To* MYRON): Don't drop the duck.

MYRON: We're ready to eat, Momma.

MORTY (*to* JACOB): Shame on you. It's your second childhood. (*Now they file out.* MYRON *first with the duck, the others behind him.*)

BESSIE: Come eat. We had enough for one day. (*Exits.*)

MORTY: Ha, ha, ha. Quack, quack. (*Exits.*)

(JACOB *sits there trembling and deeply humiliated.* MOE *approaches him and thumbs the old man's nose in the direction of the dining room.*)

MOE: Give 'em five. (*Takes his hand away.*) They got you pasted on the wall like a picture, Jake. (*He limps out to seat himself at the table in the next room.*)

JACOB: Go eat, boychick. (RALPH *comes to him.*) He gives me eat, so I'll climb in a needle. One time I saw an old horse in summer . . . he wore a straw hat . . . the ears stuck out on top. An old horse for hire. Give me back my young days . . . give me fresh blood . . . arms . . . give me—— (*The telephone rings. Quickly* RALPH *goes to it.* JACOB *pulls the curtains and stands there, a sentry on guard.*)

RALPH: Hello? . . . Yeah, I went to the store and came right back, right after you called. (*Looks at* JACOB.)

JACOB: Speak, speak. Don't be afraid they'll hear.

RALPH: I'm sorry if Mom said something. You know how excitable Mom is . . . Sure! What? . . . Sure, I'm listening . . . Put on the radio, Jake. (JACOB *does so. Music comes in and up, a tango, grating with an insistent nostalgic pulse. Under the cover of the music* RALPH *speaks more freely.*) Yes . . . yes . . . What's the matter? Why're you crying? What happened? (*To* JACOB:) She's putting her uncle on. Yes? . . . Listen, Mr. Hirsch, what're you trying to do? What's the big idea? Honest to God. I'm in no mood for joking! Lemme talk to her! Gimme Blanche! (*Waits.*) Blanche? What's this? Is this a joke? Is that true? I'm coming right down! I know, but—— You wanna do that? . . . I know, but—— I'm coming down . . . tonight! Nine o'clock . . . sure . . . sure . . . sure. . . . (*Hangs up.*)

JACOB: What happened?

MORTY (*enters*): Listen, Pop. I'm surprised you didn't—— (*He howls, shakes his head in mock despair, exits.*)

JACOB: Boychick, what?

RALPH: I don't get it straight. (*To* JACOB): She's leaving. . . .

JACOB: Where?

RALPH: Out West—— To Cleveland.

JACOB: Cleveland?

RALPH: . . . In a week or two. Can you picture it? It's a put-up job. But they can't get away with that.

JACOB: We'll find something.

RALPH: Sure, the angels of heaven'll come down on her uncle's cab and whisper in his ear.

JACOB: Come eat. . . . We'll find something.

RALPH: I'm meeting her tonight, but I know—— (BESSIE *throws open the curtain between the two rooms and enters.*)

BESSIE: Maybe we'll serve for you a special blue plate supper in the garden?

JACOB: All right, all right. (BESSIE *goes over to the window, levels the shade and on her way out, clicks off the radio.*)

MORTY (*within*): Leave the music, Bessie. (*She clicks it on again, looks at them, exits.*)

RALPH: I know . . .

JACOB: Don't cry, boychick. (*Goes over to* RALPH.) Why should you make like this? Tell me why you should cry, just tell me. . . . (JACOB *takes* RALPH *in his arms and both, trying to keep back the tears, trying fearfully not to be heard by the others in the dining room, begin crying.*) You mustn't cry. . . .

(*The tango twists on. Inside the clatter of dishes and the clash of cutlery sound.* MORTY *begins to howl with laughter.*)

Curtain

SCENE II

That night. The dark dining room.

AT RISE JACOB *is heard in his lighted room, reading from a sheet, declaiming aloud as if to an audience.*

JACOB: They are there to remind us of the horrors—under those crosses lie hundreds of thousands of workers and farmers who murdered each other in uniform for the greater glory of capitalism. (*Comes out of his room.*) The new imperialist war will send millions to their death, will bring prosperity to the pockets of the capitalist—aie, Morty—and will bring only greater hunger and misery to the masses of workers and farmers. The memories of the last world slaughter are still vivid in our minds. (*Hearing a noise he quickly retreats to his room.* RALPH *comes in from the street. He sits with hat and coat on.* JACOB *tentatively opens door and asks*): Ralphie?

RALPH: It's getting pretty cold out.

JACOB (*enters room fully, cleaning hair clippers*): We should have steam till twelve instead of ten. Go complain to the Board of Health.

RALPH: It might snow.

JACOB: It don't hurt . . . extra work for men.

RALPH: When I was a kid I laid awake at nights and heard the sounds of trains . . . far-away lonesome sounds . . . boats going up and down the river. I used to think of all kinds of things I wanted to do. What was it, Jake? Just a bunch of noise in my head?

JACOB (*waiting for news of the girl*): You wanted to make for yourself a certain kind of world.

RALPH: I guess I didn't. I'm feeling pretty, pretty low.

JACOB: You're a young boy and for you life is all in front like a big mountain. You got feet to climb.

RALPH: I don't know how.

JACOB: So you'll find out. Never a young man had such opportunity like today. He could make history.

RALPH: Ten P.M. and all is well. Where's everybody?

JACOB: They went.

RALPH: Uncle Morty too?

JACOB: Hennie and Sam he drove down.

RALPH: I saw her.

JACOB (*alert and eager*): Yes, yes, tell me.

RALPH: I waited in Mount Morris Park till she came out. So cold I did a buck'n wing to keep warm. She's scared to death.

JACOB: They made her?

RALPH: Sure. She wants to go. They keep yelling at her—they want her to marry a millionaire, too.

JACOB: You told her you love her?

RALPH: Sure. "Marry me," I said. "Marry me tomorrow." On sixteen bucks a week. On top of that I had to admit Mom'd have Uncle Morty get me fired in a second. . . . Two can starve as cheap as one!

JACOB: So what happened?

RALPH: I made her promise to meet me tomorrow.

JACOB: Now she'll go in the West?

RALPH: I'd fight the whole goddamn world with her, but not her. No guts. The hell with her. If she wantsa go—all right—I'll get along.

JACOB: For sure, there's more important things than girls. . . .

RALPH: You said a mouthful . . . and maybe I don't see it. She'll see what I can do. No one stops me when I get going. . . . (*Near to tears, he has to stop.* JACOB *examines his clippers very closely.*)

JACOB: Electric clippers never do a job like by hand.

RALPH: Why won't Mom let us live here?

JACOB: Why? Why? Because in a society like this today people don't love. Hate!

RALPH: Gee, I'm no bum who hangs around pool parlors. I got the stuff to go ahead. I don't know what to do.

JACOB: Look on me and learn what to do, boychick. Here sits an old man polishing tools. You think maybe I'll use them again! Look on this failure and see for seventy years he talked, with good ideas, but only in the head. It's enough for me now I should see your happiness. This is why I tell you—DO! Do what is in your heart and you carry in yourself a revolution. But you should act. Not like me. A man who had golden opportunities but drank instead a glass tea. No. . . . (*A pause of silence.*)

RALPH (*listening*): Hear it? The Boston air mail plane. Ten minutes late. I get a kick the way it cuts across the Bronx every night. (*The bell rings:* SAM, *excited, disheveled, enters.*)

JACOB: You came back so soon?

SAM: Where's Mom?

JACOB: Mom? Look on the chandelier.

SAM: Nobody's home?

JACOB: Sit down. Right away they're coming. You went in the street without a tie?

SAM: Maybe it's a crime.

JACOB: Excuse me.

RALPH: You had a fight with Hennie again?

SAM: She'll fight once . . . some day. . . . (*Lapses into silence.*)

JACOB: In my day the daughter came home. Now comes the son-in-law.

SAM: Once too often she'll fight with me, Hennie. I mean it. I mean it like anything. I'm a person with a bad heart. I sit quiet, but inside I got a——

RALPH: What happened?

SAM: I'll talk to Mom. I'll see Mom.

JACOB: Take an apple.

SAM: Please . . . he tells me apples.

RALPH: Why hop around like a billiard ball?

SAM: Even in a joke she should dare say it.

JACOB: My grandchild said something?

SAM: To my father in the old country they did a joke . . . I'll tell you: One day in Odessa he talked to another Jew on the street. They didn't like it, they jumped on him like a wild wolf.

RALPH: Who?

SAM: Cossacks. They cut off his beard. A Jew without a beard! He came home—I remember like yesterday how he came home and went in bed for two days. He put like this the cover on his face. No one should see. The third morning he died.

RALPH: From what?

SAM: From a broken heart. . . . Some people are like this. Me too. I could die like this from shame.

JACOB: Hennie told you something?

SAM: Straight out she said it—like a lightning from the sky. The baby ain't mine. She said it.

RALPH: Don't be a dope.

JACOB: For sure, a joke.

RALPH: She's kidding you.

SAM: She should kid a policeman, not Sam Feinschreiber. Please . . . you don't know her like me. I wake up in the nighttime and she sits watching me like I don't know what. I make a nice living from the store. But it's no use—she looks for a star in the sky. I'm afraid like anything. You could go crazy from less even. What I shall do I'll ask Mom.

JACOB: "Go home and sleep," she'll say. "It's a bad dream."

SAM: It don't satisfy me more, such remarks, when Hennie could kill in the bed. (JACOB *laughs.*) Don't laugh. I'm so nervous—look, two times I weighed myself on the subway station. (*Throws small cards to table.*)

JACOB: (*examining one*): One hundred and thirty-eight—also a fortune. (*Turns it and reads*): "You are inclined to deep thinking, and have a high admiration for intellectual excellence and inclined to be very exclusive in the selection of friends." Correct! I think maybe you got mixed up in the wrong family, Sam. (MYRON *and* BESSIE *now enter.*)

BESSIE: Look, a guest! What's the matter? Something wrong with the baby? (*Waits.*)

SAM: No.

BESSIE: Noo?

SAM (*in a burst*): I wash my hands from everything.

BESSIE: Take off your coat and hat. Have a seat. Excitement don't help. Myron, make tea. You'll have a glass tea. We'll talk like civilized people. (MYRON *goes.*) What is it, Ralph, you're all dressed up for a party? (*He looks at her silently and exits. To* SAM): We saw a very good movie, with Wallace Beery. He acts like life, very good.

MYRON (*within*): Polly Moran too.

BESSIE: Polly Moran too—a woman with a nose from here to Hunts Point, but a fine player. Poppa, take away the tools and the books.

JACOB: All right. (*Exits to his room.*)

BESSIE: Noo, Sam, why do you look like a funeral?

SAM: I can't stand it. . . .

BESSIE: Wait. (*Yells*): You took up Tootsie on the roof.

JACOB (*within*): In a minute.

BESSIE: What can't you stand?

SAM: She said I'm a second fiddle in my own house.

BESSIE: Who?

SAM: Hennie. In the second place, it ain't my baby, she said.

BESSIE: What? What are you talking? (MYRON *enters with dishes*.)

SAM: From her own mouth. It went like a knife in my heart.

BESSIE: Sam, what're you saying?

SAM: Please, I'm making a story? I fell in the chair like a dead.

BESSIE: Such a story you believe?

SAM: I don't know.

BESSIE: How you don't know?

SAM: She told me even the man.

BESSIE: Impossible!

SAM: I can't believe myself. But she said it. I'm a second fiddle, she said.
  She made such a yell everybody heard for ten miles.

BESSIE: Such a thing Hennie should say—impossible!

SAM: What should I do? With my bad heart such a remark kills.

MYRON: Hennie don't feel well, Sam. You see, she——

BESSIE: What then?—a sick girl. Believe me, a mother knows. Nerves.
  Our Hennie's got a bad temper. You'll let her she says anything. She
  takes after me—nervous. (*To* MYRON): You ever heard such a remark in all your life? She should make such a statement! Bughouse.

MYRON: The little one's been sick all these months. Hennie needs a rest.
  No doubt.

BESSIE: Sam don't think she means it——

MYRON: Oh, I know he don't, of course——

BESSIE: I'll say the truth, Sam. We didn't half the time understand her
  ourselves. A girl with her own mind. When she makes it up, wild
  horses wouldn't change her.

SAM: She don't love me.

BESSIE: This is sensible, Sam?

SAM: Not for a nickel.

BESSIE: What do you think? She married you for your money? For your
  looks? You ain't no John Barrymore, Sam. No, she liked you.

SAM: Please, not for a nickel. (JACOB *stands in the doorway*.)

BESSIE: We stood right here the first time she said it. "Sam Feinschreiber's a nice boy," she said it, "a boy he's got good common sense,
  with a business head." Right here she said it, in this room. You sent
  her two boxes of candy together, you remember?

MYRON: Loft's candy.

BESSIE: This is when she said it. What do you think?

MYRON: You were just the only boy she cared for.

BESSIE: So she married you. Such a world . . . plenty of boy friends she had, believe me!

JACOB: A popular girl. . . .

MYRON: Y-e-s.

BESSIE: I'll say it plain out—Moe Axelrod offered her plenty—a servant, a house . . . she don't have to pick up a hand.

MYRON: Oh, Moe? Just wild about her. . . .

SAM: Moe Axelrod? He wanted to——

BESSIE: But she didn't care. A girl like Hennie you don't buy. I should never live to see another day if I'm telling a lie.

SAM: She was kidding me.

BESSIE: What then? You shouldn't be foolish.

SAM: The baby looks like my family. He's got Feinschreiber eyes.

BESSIE: A blind man could see it.

JACOB: Sure . . . sure. . . .

SAM: The baby looks like me. Yes. . . .

BESSIE: You could believe me.

JACOB: Any day. . . .

SAM: But she tells me the man. She made up his name too?

BESSIE: Sam, Sam, look in the phone book—a million names.

MYRON: Tom, Dick and Harry. (JACOB *laughs quietly, soberly.*)

BESSIE: Don't stand around, Poppa. Take Tootsie on the roof. And you don't let her go under the water tank.

JACOB: Schmah Yisroeal. Behold! (*Quietly laughing he goes back into his room, closing the door behind him.*)

SAM: I won't stand he should make insults. A man eats out his——

BESSIE: No, no, he's an old man—a second childhood. Myron, bring in the tea. Open a jar of raspberry jelly. (MYRON *exits.*)

SAM: Mom, you think——?

BESSIE: I'll talk to Hennie. It's all right.

SAM: Tomorrow, I'll take her by the doctor. (RALPH *enters.*)

BESSIE: Stay for a little tea.

SAM: No, I'll go home. I'm tired. Already I caught a cold in such weather. (*Blows his nose.*)

MYRON (*entering with stuffs*): Going home?

SAM: I'll go in bed. I caught a cold.

MYRON: Teddy Roosevelt used to say, "When you have a problem, sleep on it."

BESSIE: My Sam is no problem.

MYRON: I don't mean . . . I mean he said——

BESSIE: Call me tomorrow, Sam.

SAM: I'll phone supper time. Sometime I think there's something funny about me. (MYRON *sees him out. In the following pause Caruso is heard singing within.*)

BESSIE: A bargain! Second fiddle. By me he don't even play in the orchestra—a man like a mouse. Maybe she'll lay down and die 'cause he makes a living?

RALPH: Can I talk to you about something?

BESSIE: What's the matter—I'm biting you?

RALPH: It's something about Blanche.

BESSIE: Don't tell me.

RALPH: Listen now——

BESSIE: I don't wanna know.

RALPH: She's got no place to go.

BESSIE: I don't want to know.

RALPH: Mom, I love this girl. . . .

BESSIE: So go knock your head against the wall.

RALPH: I want her to come here. Listen, Mom, I want you to let her live here for a while.

BESSIE: You got funny ideas, my son.

RALPH: I'm as good as anyone-else. Don't I have some rights in the world? Listen, Mom, if I don't do something, she's going away. Why don't you do it? Why don't you let her stay here for a few weeks? Things'll pick up. Then we can——

BESSIE: Sure, sure. I'll keep her fresh on ice for a wedding day. That's what you want?

RALPH: No, I mean you should——

BESSIE: Or maybe you'll sleep here in the same bed without marriage. (JACOB *stands in his doorway, dressed.*)

RALPH: Don't say that, Mom. I only mean. . . .

BESSIE: What you mean, I know . . . and what I mean I also know. Make up your mind. For your own good, Ralphie. If she dropped in the ocean I don't lift a finger.

RALPH: That's all, I suppose.

BESSIE: With me it's one thing—a boy should have respect for his own future. Go to sleep, you look tired. In the morning you'll forget.

JACOB: "Awake and sing, ye that dwell in dust, and the earth shall cast out the dead." It's cold out?

MYRON: Oh, yes.

JACOB: I'll take up Tootsie now.

MYRON (*eating bread and jam*): He come on us like the wild man of Borneo, Sam. I don't think Hennie was fool enough to tell him the truth like that.

BESSIE: Myron! (*A deep pause.*)

RALPH: What did he say?

BESSIE: Never mind.

RALPH: I heard him. I heard him. You don't needa tell me.

BESSIE: Never mind.

RALPH: You trapped that guy.

BESSIE: Don't say another word.

RALPH: Just have respect? That's the idea?

BESSIE: Don't say another word. I'm boiling over ten times inside.

RALPH: You won't let Blanche here, huh. I'm not sure I want her. You put one over on that little shrimp. The cat's whiskers, Mom?

BESSIE: I'm telling you something!

RALPH: I got the whole idea. I get it so quick my head's swimming. Boy, what a laugh! I suppose you know about this, Jake?

JACOB: Yes.

RALPH: Why didn't you do something?

JACOB: I'm an old man.

RALPH: What's that got to do with the price of bonds? Sits around and lets a thing like that happen! You make me sick too.

MYRON (*after a pause*): Let me say something, son.

RALPH: Take your hand away! Sit in a corner and wag your tail. Keep on boasting you went to law school for two years.

MYRON: I want to tell you——

RALPH: You never in your life had a thing to tell me.

BESSIE (*bitterly*): Don't say a word. Let him, let him run and tell Sam. Publish in the papers, give a broadcast on the radio. To him it don't matter nothing his family sits with tears pouring from the eyes. (*To* JACOB): What are you waiting for? I didn't tell you twice already about the dog? You'll stand around with Caruso and make a bughouse. It ain't enough all day long. Fifty times I told you I'll break every record in the house. (*She brushes past him, breaks the records, comes out.*) The next time I say something you'll maybe believe it. Now maybe you learned a lesson. (*Pause.*)

JACOB (*quietly*): Bessie, new lessons . . . not for an old dog. (MOE *enters.*)

MYRON: You didn't have to do it, Momma.

BESSIE: Talk better to your son, Mr. Berger! Me, I don't lay down and die for him and Poppa no more. I'll work like a nigger? For what?

Wait, the day comes when you'll be punished. When it's too late you'll remember how you sucked away a mother's life. Talk to him, tell him how I don't sleep at night. (*Bursts into tears and exits.*)

MOE (*sings*): "Good-by to all your sorrows. You never hear them talk about the war, in the land of Yama Yama. . . ."

MYRON: Yes, Momma's a sick woman, Ralphie.

RALPH: Yeah?

MOE: We'll be out of the trenches by Christmas. Putt, putt, putt . . . here, stinker. . . . (*Picks up Tootsie, a small, white poodle that just then enters from the hall.*) If there's reincarnation in the next life I wanna be a dog and lay in a fat lady's lap. Barrage over? How 'bout a little pinochle, Pop?

JACOB: Nnno.

RALPH (*taking dog*): I'll take her up. (*Conciliatory.*)

JACOB: No, I'll do it. (*Takes dog.*)

RALPH (*ashamed*): It's cold out.

JACOB: I was cold before in my life. A man sixty-seven. . . . (*Strokes the dog.*) Tootsie is my favorite lady in the house. (*He slowly passes across the room and exits. A settling pause.*)

MYRON: She cried all last night—Tootsie—I heard her in the kitchen like a young girl.

MOE: Tonight I could do something. I got a yen . . . I don't know.

MYRON (*rubbing his head*): My scalp is impoverished.

RALPH: Mom bust all his records.

MYRON: She didn't have to do it.

MOE: Tough tit! Now I can sleep in the morning. Who the hell wantsa hear a wop air his tonsils all day long!

RALPH (*handling the fragment of a record*): "O Paradiso!"

MOE (*gets cards*): It's snowing out, girls.

MYRON: There's no more big snows like in the old days. I think the whole world's changing. I see it, right under our very eyes. No one hardly remembers any more when we used to have gaslight and all the dishes had little fishes on them.

MOE: It's the system, girls.

MYRON: I was a little boy when it happened—the Great Blizzard. It snowed three days without a stop that time. Yes, and the horse cars stopped. A silence of death was on the city and little babies got no milk . . . they say a lot of people died that year.

MOE (*singing as he deals himself cards*):
"Lights are blinking while you're drinking,
   That's the place where the good fellows go.

Good-by to all your sorrows,
You never hear them talk about the war,
In the land of Yama, Yama
Funicalee, funicala, funicalo. . . ."

MYRON: What can I say to you, Big Boy?

RALPH: Not a damn word.

MOE (goes "ta ra ta ra" throughout.)

MYRON: I know how you feel about all those things, I know.

RALPH: Forget it.

MYRON: And your girl. . . .

RALPH: Don't soft soap me all of a sudden.

MYRON: I'm not foreign born. I'm an American, and yet I never got close to you. It's an American father's duty to be his son's friend.

RALPH: Who said that—Teddy R.?

MOE (dealing cards): You're breaking his heart, "Litvak."

MYRON: It just happened the other day. The moment I began losing my hair I just knew I was destined to be a failure in life . . . and when I grew bald I was. Now isn't that funny, Big Boy?

MOE: It's a pisscutter!

MYRON: I believe in Destiny.

MOE: You get what-it-takes. Then they don't catch you with your pants down. (Sings out): Eight of clubs. . . .

MYRON: I really don't know. I sold jewelry on the road before I married.. It's one thing to—— Now here's a thing the druggist gave me. (Reads): "The Marvel Cosmetic Girl of Hollywood is going on the air. Give this charming little radio singer a name and win five thousand dollars. If you will send——"

MOE: Your old man still believes in Santy Claus.

MYRON: Someone's got to win. The government isn't gonna allow everything to be fake.

MOE: It's a fake. There ain't no prizes. It's a fake.

MYRON: It says——

RALPH (snatching it): For Christ's sake, Pop, forget it. Grow up. Jake's right—everybody's crazy. It's like a zoo in this house. I'm going to bed.

MOE: In the land of Yama Yama. . . . (Goes on with ta ra.)

MYRON: Don't think life's easy with Momma. No, but she means for your good all the time. I tell you she does, she——

RALPH: Maybe, but I'm going to bed. (Downstairs doorbell rings violently.)

MOE (ring): Enemy barrage begins on sector eight seventy-five.

RALPH: That's downstairs.

MYRON: We ain't expecting anyone this hour of the night.

MOE: "Lights are blinking while you're drinking, that's the place where the good fellows go. Good-by to ta ra tara ra," etc.

RALPH: I better see who it is.

MYRON: I'll tick the button. (*As he starts, the apartment doorbell begins ringing, followed by large knocking.* MYRON *goes out.*)

RALPH: Who's ever ringing means it. (*A loud excited voice outside.*)

MOE: "In the land of Yama Yama, Funicalee, funicalo, funic——" MYRON *enters followed by* SCHLOSSER *the janitor.* BESSIE *cuts in from the other side.*)

BESSIE: Who's ringing like a lunatic?

RALPH: What's the matter?

MYRON: Momma. . . .

BESSIE: Noo, what's the matter? (*Downstairs bell continues.*)

RALPH: What's the matter?

BESSIE: Well, well . . .?

MYRON: Poppa. . . .

BESSIE: What happened?

SCHLOSSER: He shlipped maybe in de snow.

RALPH: Who?

SCHLOSSER (*to* BESSIE): Your fadder fall off de roof. . . . Ja. (*A dead pause.* RALPH *then runs out.*)

BESSIE (*dazed*): Myron. . . . Call Morty on the phone . . . call him. MYRON *starts for phone.*) No. I'll do it myself. I'll . . . do it. (MYRON *exits.*)

SCHLOSSER (*standing stupidly*): Since I was in dis country . . . I was pudding out de ash can . . . The snow is vet. . . .

MOE (*to* SCHLOSSER): Scram. (SCHLOSSER *exits.*)

(BESSIE *goes blindly to the phone, fumbles and gets it.* MOE *sits quietly, slowly turning cards over, but watching her.*)

BESSIE: He slipped. . . .

MOE (*deeply moved*): Slipped?

BESSIE: I can't see the numbers. Make it, Moe, make it. . . .

MOE: Make it yourself. (*He looks at her and slowly goes back to his game of cards with shaking hands.*)

BESSIE: Riverside 7— . . . (*Unable to talk she dials slowly. The dial whizzes on.*)

MOE: Don't . . . make me laugh. . . . (*He turns over cards.*)

Curtain

ACT THREE

A week later in the dining room. MORTY, BESSIE *and* MYRON *eating. Sitting in the front room is* MOE *marking a "dope sheet," but really listening to the others.*

BESSIE: You're sure he'll come tonight—the insurance man?

MORTY: Why not? I shtupped him a ten-dollar bill. Everything's hot delicatessen.

BESSIE: Why must he come so soon?

MORTY: Because you had a big expense. You'll settle once and for all. I'm a great boy for making hay while the sun shines.

BESSIE: Stay till he'll come, Morty. . . .

MORTY: No, I got a strike downtown. Business don't stop for personal life. Two times already in the past week those bastards threw stink bombs in the showroom. Wait! We'll give them strikes—in the kishkas we'll give them. . . .

BESSIE: I'm a woman. I don't know about policies. Stay till he comes.

MORTY: Bessie—sweetheart, leave me live.

BESSIE: I'm afraid, Morty.

MORTY: Be practical. They made an investigation. Everybody knows Pop had an accident. Now we'll collect.

MYRON: Ralphie don't know Papa left the insurance in his name.

MORTY: It's not his business. And I'll tell him.

BESSIE: The way he feels. (*Enter* RALPH *into front room.*) He'll do something crazy. He thinks Poppa jumped off the roof.

MORTY: Be practical, Bessie. Ralphie will sign when I tell him. Everything is peaches and cream.

BESSIE: Wait for a few minutes. . . .

MORTY: Look, I'll show you in black on white what the policy says. *For God's sake, leave me live!* (*Angrily exits to kitchen. In parlor,* MOE *speaks to* RALPH *who is reading a letter.*)

MOE: What's the letter say?

RALPH: Blanche won't see me no more, she says. I couldn't care very much, she says. If I didn't come like I said. . . . She'll phone before she leaves.

MOE: She don't know about Pop?

RALPH: She won't ever forget me she says. Look what she sends me . . . a little locket on a chain . . . if she calls I'm out.

MOE: You mean it?

RALPH: For a week I'm trying to go in his room. I guess he'd like me to have it, but I can't. . . .

MOE: Wait a minute! (*Crosses over.*) They're trying to rook you—a freeze-out.

RALPH: Who?

MOE: That bunch stuffin' their gut with hot pastrami. Morty in particular. Jake left the insurance—three thousand dollars—for you.

RALPH: For me?

MOE: Now you got wings, kid. Pop figured you could use it. That's why. . . .

RALPH: That's why what?

MOE: It ain't the only reason he done it.

RALPH: He done it?

MOE: You think a breeze blew him off? (HENNIE *enters and sits.*)

RALPH: I'm not sure what I think.

MOE: The insurance guy's coming tonight. Morty's "shtupped" him.

RALPH: Yeah?

MOE: I'll back you up. You're dead on your feet. Grab a sleep for yourself.

RALPH: No!

MOE: Go on! (*Pushes boy into room.*)

SAM (*whom* MORTY *has sent in for the paper*): Morty wants the paper.

HENNIE: So?

SAM: You're sitting on it. (*Gets paper.*) We could go home now, Hennie! Leon is alone by Mrs. Strasberg a whole day.

HENNIE: Go on home if you're so anxious. A full tub of diapers is waiting.

SAM: Why should you act this way?

HENNIE: 'Cause there's no bones in ice cream. Don't touch me.

SAM: Please, what's the matter. . . .

MOE: She don't like you. Plain as the face on your nose. . . .

SAM: To me, my friend, you talk a foreign language.

MOE: A quarter you're lousy. (SAM *exits*). Gimme a buck, I'll run it up to ten.

HENNIE: Don't do me favors.

MOE: Take a chance. (*Stopping her as she crosses to doorway.*)

HENNIE: I'm a pushover.

MOE: I say lotsa things. You don't know me.

HENNIE: I know you—when you knock 'em down you're through.

MOE (*sadly*): You still don't know me.

HENNIE: I know what goes in your wise-guy head.

MOE: Don't run away. . . . I ain't got hydrophobia. Wait. I want to tell you. . . . I'm leaving.

HENNIE: Leaving?

MOE: Tonight. Already packed.

HENNIE: Where?

MORTY (*as he enters followed by the others*): My car goes through snow like a dose of salts.

BESSIE: Hennie, go eat. . . .

MORTY: Where's Ralphie?

MOE: In his new room. (*Moves into dining room.*)

MORTY: I didn't have a piece of hot pastrami in my mouth for years.

BESSIE: Take a sandwich, Hennie. You didn't eat all day. . . . (*At window*): A whole week it rained cats and dogs.

MYRON: Rain, rain, go away. Come again some other day. (*Puts shawl on her.*)

MORTY: Where's my gloves?

SAM (*sits on stool*): I'm sorry the old man lays in the rain.

MORTY: Personally, Pop was a fine man. But I'm a great boy for an honest opinion. He had enough crazy ideas for a regiment.

MYRON: Poppa never had a doctor in his whole life. . . . (*Enter* RALPH.)

MORTY: He had Caruso. Who's got more from life?

BESSIE: Who's got more? . . .

MYRON: And Marx he had.

(MYRON *and* BESSIE *sit on sofa.*)

MORTY: Marx! Some say Marx is the new God today. Maybe I'm wrong. Ha ha ha. . . . Personally I counted my ten million last night. . . . I'm sixteen cents short. So tomorrow I'll go to Union Square and yell no equality in the country! Ah, it's a new generation.

RALPH: You said it!

MORTY: What's the matter, Ralphie? What are you looking funny?

RALPH: I hear I'm left insurance and the man's coming tonight.

MORTY: Poppa didn't leave no insurance for you.

RALPH: What?

MORTY: In your name he left it—but not for you.

RALPH: It's my name on the paper.

MORTY: Who said so?

RALPH (*to his mother*): The insurance man's coming tonight?

MORTY: What's the matter?

RALPH: I'm not talking to you. (*To his mother*): Why?

BESSIE: I don't know why.

RALPH: He don't come in this house tonight.

MORTY: That's what *you* say.

RALPH: I'm not talking to you, Uncle Morty, but I'll tell you, too, he
   don't come here tonight when there's still mud on a grave. (*To his
   mother*): Couldn't you give the house a chance to cool off?

MORTY: Is this a way to talk to your mother?

RALPH: Was that a way to talk to your father?

MORTY: Don't be so smart with me, Mr. Ralph Berger!

RALPH: Don't be so smart with *me*.

MORTY: What'll you do? I say he's coming tonight. Who says no?

MOE (*suddenly, from the background*): Me.

MORTY: Take a back seat, Axelrod. When you're in the family——

MOE: I got a little document here. (*Produces paper.*) I found it under his
   pillow that night. A guy who slips off a roof don't leave a note before
   he does it.

MORTY (*starting for* MOE *after a horrified silence*): Let me see this note.

BESSIE: Morty, don't touch it!

MOE: Not if you crawled.

MORTY: It's a fake. Poppa wouldn't——

MOE: Get the insurance guy here and we'll see how—— (*The bell
   rings.*) Speak of the devil. . . . Answer it, see what happens. (MORTY
   starts for the ticker.)

BESSIE: Morty, don't!

MORTY (*stopping*): Be practical, Bessie.

MOE: Sometimes you don't collect on suicides if they know about it.

MORTY: You should let. . . . You should let him. . . . (*A pause in which*
   ALL *seem dazed. Bell rings insistently.*)

MOE: Well, we're waiting.

MORTY: Give me the note.

MOE: I'll give you the head off your shoulders.

MORTY: Bessie, you'll stand for this? (*Points to* RALPH.) Pull down his
   pants and give him with a strap.

RALPH (*as bell rings again.*) How about it?

BESSIE: Don't be crazy. It's not my fault. Morty said he should come
   tonight. It's not nice so soon. I didn't——

MORTY: I said it? Me?

BESSIE: Who then?

MORTY: You didn't sing a song in my ear a whole week to settle quick?

BESSIE: I'm surprised. Morty, you're a big liar.

MYRON: Momma's telling the truth, she is!

MORTY: Lissen. In two shakes of a lamb's tail, we'll start a real fight and then nobody won't like nobody. Where's my fur gloves? I'm going downtown. (*To* SAM): You coming? I'll drive you down.

HENNIE (*to* SAM, *who looks questioningly at her*): Don't look at me. Go home if you want.

SAM: If you're coming soon, I'll wait.

HENNIE: Don't do me any favors. Night and day he pesters me.

MORTY: You made a cushion——sleep!

SAM: I'll go home. I know . . . to my worst enemy I don't wish such a life——

HENNIE: Sam, keep quiet.

SAM (*quietly; sadly*): No more free speech in America? (*Gets his hat and coat.*) I'm a lonely person. Nobody likes me.

MYRON: I like you, Sam.

HENNIE (*going to him gently; sensing the end*): Please go home, Sam. I'll sleep here. . . . I'm tired and nervous. Tomorrow I'll come home. I love you . . . I mean it. (*She kisses him with real feeling.*)

SAM: I would die for you. . . . (SAM *looks at her. Tries to say something, but his voice chokes up with a mingled feeling. He turns and leaves the room.*)

MORTY: A bird in the hand is worth two in the bush. Remember I said it. Good night. (*Exits after* SAM.) (HENNIE *sits depressed.* BESSIE *goes up and looks at the picture calendar again.* MYRON *finally breaks the silence.*)

MYRON: Yesterday a man wanted to sell me a saxophone with pearl buttons. But I——

BESSIE: It's a beautiful picture. In this land, nobody works. . . . Nobody worries. . . . Come to bed, Myron. (*Stops at the door, and says to* RALPH): Please don't have foolish ideas about the money.

RALPH: Let's call it a day.

BESSIE: It belongs for the whole family. You'll get your teeth fixed——

RALPH: And a pair of black and white shoes?

BESSIE: Hennie needs a vacation. She'll take two weeks in the mountains and I'll mind the baby.

RALPH: I'll take care of my own affairs.

BESSIE: A family needs for a rainy day. Times is getting worse. Prospect Avenue, Dawson, Beck Street—every day furniture's on the sidewalk.

RALPH: Forget it, Mom.

BESSIE: Ralphie, I worked too hard all my years to be treated like dirt. It's no law we should be stuck together like Siamese twins. Summer shoes you didn't have, skates you never had, but I bought a new dress every week. A lover I kept—Mr. Gigolo! Did I ever play a game of cards like Mrs. Marcus? Or was Bessie Berger's children always the cleanest on the block?! Here I'm not only the mother, but also the father. The first two years I worked in a stocking factory for six dollars while Myron Berger went to law school. If I didn't worry about the family who would? On the calendar it's a different place, but here without a dollar you don't look the world in the eye. Talk from now to next year—this is life in America.

RALPH: Then it's wrong. It don't make sense. If life made you this way, then it's wrong!

BESSIE: Maybe you wanted me to give up twenty years ago. Where would you be now? You'll excuse my expression—a bum in the park!

RALPH: I'm not blaming you, Mom. Sink or swim—I see it. But it can't stay like this.

BESSIE: My foolish boy. . . .

RALPH: No, I see every house lousy with lies and hate. He said it, Grandpa— Brooklyn hates the Bronx. Smacked on the nose twice a day. But boys and girls can get ahead like that, Mom. We don't want life printed on dollar bills, Mom!

BESSIE: So go out and change the world if you don't like it.

RALPH: I will! And why? 'Cause life's different in my head. Gimme the earth in two hands. I'm strong. There . . . hear him? The air mail off to Boston. Day or night, he flies away, a job to do. That's us and it's no time to die. (*The airplane sound fades off as* MYRON *gives alarm clock to* BESSIE *which she begins to wind.*)

BESSIE: "Mom, what does she know? She's old-fashioned!" But I'll tell you a big secret: My whole life I wanted to go away too, but with children a woman stays home. A fire burned in *my* heart too, but now it's too late. I'm no spring chicken. The clock goes and Bessie goes. Only my machinery can't be fixed. (*She lifts a button: the alarm rings on the clock; she stops it, says "Good night" and exits.*)

MYRON: I guess I'm no prize bag. . . .

BESSIE (*from within*): Come to bed, Myron.

MYRON (*tears page off calendar*): Hmmm. . . . (*Exits to her.*)

RALPH: Look at him, draggin' after her like an old shoe.

MOE: Punch drunk. (*Phone rings.*) That's for me. (*At phone.*) Yeah? . . . Just a minute. (*To* RALPH): Your girl . . .

RALPH: Jeez, I don't know what to say to her.

MOE: Hang up? (RALPH *slowly takes phone.*)

RALPH: Hello. . . . Blanche, I wish. . . . I don't know what to say. . . .
Yes . . . Hello? . . . (*Puts phone down.*) She hung up on me . . .

MOE: Sorry?

RALPH: No girl means anything to me until. . . .

MOE: Till when?

RALPH: Till I can take care of her. Till we don't look out on an airshaft.
Till we can take the world in two hands and polish off the dirt.

MOE: That's a big order.

RALPH: Once upon a time I thought I'd drown to death in bolts of silk
and velour. But I grew up these last few weeks. Jake said a lot.

MOE: Your memory's okay?

RALPH: But take a look at this. (*Brings armful of books from* JACOB'S
room—dumps them on table.) His books, I got them too—the pages
ain't cut in half of them.

MOE: Perfect.

RALPH: Does it prove something? Damn tootin'! A ten-cent nailfile cuts
them. Uptown, downtown, I'll read them on the way. Get a big
lamp over the bed. (*Picks up one.*) My eyes are good. (*Puts book in
pocket.*) Sure, inventory tomorrow. Coletti to Driscoll to Berger—
that's how we work. It's a team down the warehouse. Driscoll's a
show-off, a wiseguy, and Joe talks pigeons day and night. But they're
like me, looking for a chance to get to first base too. Joe razzed me
about my girl. But he don't know why. I'll tell him. Hell, he might
tell me something I don't know. Get teams together all over. Spit on
your hands and get to work. And with enough teams together maybe
we'll get steam in the warehouse so our fingers don't freeze off.
Maybe we'll fix it so life won't be printed on dollar bills.

MOE: Graduation Day.

RALPH (*starts for door of his room, stops*): Can I have . . . Grandpa's
note?

MOE: Sure you want it?

RALPH: Please— (MOE *gives it.*) It's blank!

MOE (*taking note back and tearing it up*): That's right.

RALPH: Thanks! (*Exits.*)

MOE: The kid's a fighter! (*To* HENNIE): Why are you crying?

HENNIE: I never cried in my life. (*She is now.*)

MOE (*starts for door. Stops*): You told Sam you love him. . . .

HENNIE: If I'm sore on life, why take it out on him?

MOE: You won't forget me to your dyin' day—I was the first guy. Part of your insides. You won't forget. I wrote my name on you—indelible ink!

HENNIE: One thing I won't forget—how you left me crying on the bed like I was two for a cent!

MOE: Listen, do you think——

HENNIE: Sure. Waits till the family goes to the open air movie. He brings me perfume. . . . He grabs my arms——

MOE: You won't forget me!

HENNIE: How you left the next week?

MOE: So I made a mistake. For Chris' sake, don't act like the Queen of Roumania!

HENNIE: Don't make me laugh!

MOE: What the hell do you want, my head on a plate?! Was my life so happy? Chris', my old man was a bum. I supported the whole damn family—five kids and Mom. When they grew up they beat it the hell away like rabbits. Mom died. I went to the war; got .clapped down like a bedbug; woke up in a room without a leg. What the hell do you think, anyone's got it better than you? I never had a home either. I'm lookin' too!

HENNIE: So what?!

MOE: So you're it—you're home for me, a place to live! That's the whole parade, sickness, eating out your heart! Sometimes you meet a girl—she stops it—that's love. . . . So take a chance! Be with me, Paradise. What's to lose?

HENNIE: My pride!

MOE (grabbing her): What do you want? Say the word—I'll tango on a dime. Don't gimme ice when your heart's on fire!

HENNIE: Let me go! (He stops her.)

MOE: WHERE?!!

HENNIE: What do you want, Moe, what do you want?

MOE: You!

HENNIE: You'll be sorry you ever started——

MOE: You!

HENNIE: Moe, lemme go—— (Trying to leave): I'm getting up early—lemme go.

MOE: No! . . . I got enough fever to blow the whole damn town to hell. (He suddenly releases her and half stumbles backwards. Forces himself to quiet down.) You wanna go back to him? Say the word. I'll know what to do. . . .

HENNIE (helplessly): Moe, I don't know what to say.

MOE: Listen to me.

HENNIE: What?

MOE: Come away. A certain place where it's moonlight and roses. We'll lay down, count stars. Hear the big ocean making noise. You lay under the trees. Champagne flows like—— (*Phone rings.* MOE *finally answers the telephone*): Hello? . . . Just a minute. (*Looks at* HENNIE.)

HENNIE: Who is it?

MOE: Sam.

HENNIE (*starts for phone, but changes her mind*): I'm sleeping. . . .

MOE (*in phone*): She's sleeping. . . . (*Hangs up. Watches* HENNIE *who slowly sits.*) He wants you to know he got home O.K. . . . What's on your mind?

HENNIE: Nothing.

MOE: Sam?

HENNIE: They say it's a palace on those Havana boats.

MOE: What's on your mind?

HENNIE (*trying to escape*): Moe, I don't care for Sam—I never loved him——

MOE: But your kid—?

HENNIE: All my life I waited for this minute.

MOE (*holding her*): Me too. Made believe I was talkin' just bedroom golf, but you and me forever was what I meant! Christ, baby, there's one life to live! Live it!

HENNIE: Leave the baby?

MOE: Yeah!

HENNIE: I can't. . . .

MOE: You can!

HENNIE: No. . . .

MOE: But you're not sure!

HENNIE: I don't know.

MOE: Make a break or spend the rest of your life in a coffin.

HENNIE: Oh God, I don't know where I stand.

MOE: Don't look up there. Paradise, you're on a big boat headed south. No more pins and needles in your heart, no snake juice squirted in your arm. The whole world's green grass and when you cry it's because you're happy.

HENNIE: Moe, I don't know. . . .

MOE: Nobody knows, but you do it and find out. When you're scared the answer's zero.

HENNIE: You're hurting my arm.

MOE: The doctor said it—cut off your leg to save your life! And they done it—one thing to get another. (*Enter* RALPH.)

RALPH: I didn't hear a word, but do it, Hennie, do it!

MOE: Mom can mind the kid. She'll go on forever, Mom. We'll send money back, and Easter eggs.

RALPH: I'll be here.

MOE: Get your coat . . . get it.

HENNIE: Moe!

MOE: I know . . . but get your coat and hat and kiss the house good-bye.

HENNIE: The man I love. . . . (MYRON *entering.*) I left my coat in Mom's room. (*Exits.*)

MYRON: Don't wake her up, Beauty. Momma fell asleep as soon as her head hit the pillow. I can't sleep. It was a long day. Hmmm. (*Examines his tongue in buffet mirror*): I was reading the other day a person with a thick tongue is feeble-minded. I can do anything with my tongue. Make it thick, flat. No fruit in the house lately. Just a lone apple. (*He gets apple and paring knife and starts paring.*) Must be something wrong with me—I say I won't eat but I eat. (HENNIE *enters dressed to go out.*) Where you going, little Red Riding Hood?

HENNIE: Nobody knows, Peter Rabbit.

MYRON: You're looking very pretty tonight. You were a beautiful baby too. 1910, that was the year you was born. The same year Teddy Roosevelt came back from Africa.

HENNIE: Gee, Pop; you're such a funny guy.

MYRON: He was a boisterous man, Teddy. Good night. (*He exits, paring apple.*)

RALPH: When I look at him, I'm sad. Let me die like a dog, if I can't get more from life.

HENNIE: Where?

RALPH: Right here in the house! My days won't be for nothing. Let Mom have the dough. I'm twenty-two and kickin'! I'll get along. Did Jake die for us to fight about nickels? No! "Awake and sing," he said. Right here he stood and said it. The night he died, I saw it like a thunderbolt! I saw he was dead and I was born! I swear to God, I'm one week old! I want the whole city to hear it—fresh blood, arms. We got 'em. We're glad we're living.

MOE: I wouldn't trade you for two pitchers and an outfielder. Hold the fort!

RALPH: So long.

MOE: So long.

(*They go and* RALPH *stands full and strong in the doorway seeing them off as the curtain slowly falls.*)

Curtain

PART III

After the War:
A Creative
Awakening

KADDISH
AND OTHER POEMS
1958-1960
ALLEN GINSBERG

Elie Wiesel

Yom Kippur: The Day
Without Forgiveness

HERZOG

Isaac Singer SAUL
BELLOW

GIMPEL
THE
FOOL

The Situation of the

Jewish Writer

ALFRED KAZIN

THE
ARMIES
OF THE
NIGHT
NORMAN MAILER

Portnoy's
Complaint
Philip
Roth

Jake Bluffstein
and Adolph Hitler
IRVING FAUST

MAGIC BARREL - MALAMUD

Introduction

Although Jews represent only three-and-one-half percent of the American population, the range and depth of their cultural achievement since World War II has been profound. In our age, many of the artists have been Jews: Bellow, Malamud, Salinger, and Mailer, the novelists; Ginsberg, Rukeyser, Shapiro, Nemerov, the poets; Odets and Miller, the dramatists. Beyond authorship—in journalism, music, art, dance, film, television, the universities, the sciences, advertising, and all the communications arts—the catalogue seems endless, perplexing and, for some, even threatening, as one realizes that six million people in a population of two hundred million have become preeminent in so many fields of human expression so quickly.

The position of the Jewish intellectual who grew up after World War I and matured in the 1930's was paradoxical. In personal terms, he had been raised by parents or grandparents who spoke of the old country in accents foreign and often embarrassing to his ears. He brought little of this immigrant sensibility into his professional life and, in most cases, sought to Americanize himself as quickly as possible. The history of anti-Semitism in those professions which Jews first entered—law, medicine, and education—is well-known, one of the less attractive scars on the face of twentieth-century America; but a deeper, far more troubling expression of anti-Semitism was its presence in the writing of those authors who were celebrated for their exploration of humanistic values and who influenced—at least aesthetically—the writing of Jewish Americans. And, in speaking of the rather complex relationship between the older and younger generations, between Christians and Jews, between the heirs of American civilization and the sons of immigrants, one moves more closely to the heart of the paradox.

The anti-Semitism of American authors has not been fully examined: it is a characteristic that appears with Jewish immigration into the United States and it persists well into the 1930's—until, in fact, Jewish-American literature begins to rise from its ashes. One could reach back into the late nineteenth century and trace the pathological attitudes of James Russell Lowell, who, in his later years, "detected a Jew in every hiding-place and under every disguise"; or the persistent, overwhelming hatred of Brooks and Henry Adams who spoke of "the international Jew" as the enemy to the Anglo-Saxon tradition; or the anxious prejudice of Lafcadio Hearn who, toward the end of his life, wanted "to escape from the shadow of the Jew." The Jew became the "universal scapegoat" in the eyes of these and other writers, a figure who symbolized the decline in America of the Protestant, rural tradition that represented homogeneity, innocence, Anglo-Saxon manners and morality—qualities reflected in the literature of New England and the South. Certain writers, like Howells, Twain, and to a lesser extent Henry James, were striking exceptions; but by the First World War, the Jew in American literature was an unappealing caricature. Theodore Dreiser's correspondence is burdened by derogatory remarks: "New York to me is a scream—a kyke's dream of a Ghetto. The lost tribe has taken the island"; and during the 1930's he was consistently anti-Semitic as Hitler rose to power. Dreiser's anti-Semitism was mirrored, in a more or less sophisticated fashion, directly or obliquely, by Sherwood Anderson, Pound, Eliot, Hemingway, Fitzgerald, Cummings, Wyndham Lewis, Henry Miller, and Wolfe— by those authors who shaped the aesthetic sensibility of young Jewish writers emerging in the 1940's.

The influence did remain primarily aesthetic. The major authors of the twenties and thirties—Christian almost entirely, for Jews like Ben Hecht, Michael Gold, and Nathanael West either denied their Jewishness altogether or substituted socialism for their parents' religious fervor —were Midwesterners or Southerners from small towns who had made their way to the cities: their social tension was between rural and urban life, between the West and the East, between the residue of their own Anglo-Saxon morality and a twentieth-century industrial society. The

Jewish writers of the forties read Pound and Eliot, Hemingway, Fitzgerald, and the new critics, and fell under their influence; but they
refused to acknowledge the full significance of an anti-Semitism that
was—in the work of Pound, Eliot, and Wolfe—pernicious. These
Jewish-American authors had developed in the thirties, when Jewish
identity was, in many cases, self-consciously denied, and they arrived
in the forties so fully liberated from the accents of their ancestors that
Lionel Trilling could say, "as the Jewish community now exists, it can
give no sustenance to the American artist or intellectual who is born a
Jew."

Although Trilling's remark reflected the position of the Jewish writer
of the thirties and early forties, it was swiftly contradicted by a burst of
Jewish-American literature directly and profoundly nourished by the
Jewish community in America and Western Europe. The sense that a
community existed—whether the young Jewish writer was orthodox or
atheistic, rebellious or accommodating—sharpened his awareness of himself in American society, gave him a point of view, a critical and creative
point d'appui; Werner Cohen spoke for many Jews when he remarked
that "I like to regard my Jewishness as a source of strength in my relationship to the world," and Herbert Gold expressed the sentiments of
Jewish writers when he admitted that "The American Jewish community
is most important to me because it is a mirror in which the rest of America can be seen. Like all mirrors, it invites distortion." At the very least,
the American artist or intellectual who was born a Jew thought of himself as a Jew, and the reasons for his self-consciousness may help us to
understand the intensity, variousness, and extraordinary quality of Jewish-
American writing in this past generation.

Trilling's remarks were made in 1944, when the persecution of
European Jews provoked a recognition of Judaism that many American
Jews had avoided during the thirties. Their strong desire to shed ethnic
characteristics—a common tendency among second-generation minority
groups—seemed like a form of betrayal, given the events of the war; even
Christian authors like Dreiser and Wolfe, whose anti-Semitism was
fashionable in the twenties and early thirties, recanted—only Ezra
Pound persisted, but by the late forties he was indeed a singular case,
defensible only in terms of a kind of insanity or (to repeat the cliché)
the higher demands of art, the most striking instance of a man whose
aesthetics and politics raised a controversy unimaginable fifteen or twenty

years earlier. The young Jewish writers who began their careers in the late forties—Bellow, Mailer, Malamud, and others—accepted their Jewishness without apology; it was, they knew, an undeniable aspect of their personalities. Suffering, one of the central themes of Jewish writing, had found its objective correlative in the concentration camp; the postwar Jewish-American writers created their work against that shadow as well as against the shadow of a failed radicalism that had been aborted by Stalin and was entirely altered by the war.

As Jewish authors began to recreate their war experiences into fiction —*The Naked and the Dead, The Young Lions,* and *The Caine Mutiny* were all best sellers—the state of Israel was established; the connection for some was tenuous, but there was a connection, a homeland now, a place that would not cease to be at the center of the world's problems, through the Suez crisis to the seven days' war and the Eichmann trial. For the most part, American Jews responded deeply to Israel and the new country sharpened the image of the Jew so that assimilation in America seemed less attractive, less facile than formerly: one had to come to terms with one's Jewishness by the historical fact of Israel and all that it symbolized for an imaginative people. Visitors to Israel were struck by a lifestyle unlike that of Americans, neither cynical nor phlegmatic: Israelis fought with a purpose—Americans struggled to escape the Vietnam war; Israeli youth seemed strengthened by specific goals—Americans drifted and revolted against institutions like the universities which once had sustained them. The image of the Jew was inevitably modified. In their new and unfamiliar posture of embattled nationalists, the Israelis exhibited a toughness that denied the myth of passivity which Hannah Arendt and others had attributed to the Jews of the concentration camp. It is true that Leon Uris, Robert Nathan and other novelists sentimentalized Jewish heroism in the manner of popular fiction—Theodore Solotaroff and Philip Roth quickly condemned them for their distortions, for "swapping one stereotype for another" in an attempt at "the improvement of public relations"; but still there was a power to the Israelis, a concentration of desire, even, one might say, a "vision," that had never been a characteristic of American Jews and that elicited their pride. Whatever the arguments, Israel led Jewish writers in America to another, still deeper level of reevaluation and self-consciousness.

The black revolution in America also renewed the self-awareness of Jews. As Stanley Kaufmann remarked several years ago, "The question

of the acceptance of Jews is no longer on the frontier of Gentile consciousness, it is well behind the lines, has been swept—by the urgency of
Negro problems—into the state of being quite *passé*. Readers feel that
they ought to be well past it. If, for example, they can't identify with
Moses Herzog, who is white, how are they ever going to achieve brotherhood with black men?" This perception is given greater credence as one
considers the concentration on ethnicity among Indians, Italians, the
Irish, Puerto Ricans, and Mexican Americans. The threat of technocracy
and computerization that has diminished the humanity of the individual
American—the conflict between the machine and the garden which
calls into question the very premises of American civilization and which
most perturbs the youth today—has driven people back to their roots: the
central question that Herzog asks himself is what it means "to be a man.
In a city. In a century. In transition. In a mass. Transformed by science.
Under organized power. Subject to tremendous controls. In a condition
caused by mechanization. After the late failure of radical hopes. In a
society that devalued the person." The assimilation that appeared to be so
attractive forty years ago is now associated with the death of uniqueness,
with the destruction of the individual; and one way of returning to a
period before assimilation and of maintaining a distinctiveness that
dissociates the individual from mass man is by evoking ethnicity. It is no
accident that Bellow's *Herzog,* Baldwin's *The Fire Next Time,* N. Scott
Momaday's *House of Dawn,* and Piri Thomas's *Down These Mean
Streets*—to cite only four examples—should have so great a popularity at
the same time; and in the universities, departments of ethnic affairs—
Jewish studies prominent among them—have become increasingly popular.

It is, in fact, the universities that have provided the most compatible
setting for the Jewish-American renaissance. Universities offer a home
for authors, who enjoy privileged positions among admiring students and
solicitous colleagues—they are, as Charles Fenton pointed out years ago,
the Brahmins and celebrities of the academic world. Some have permanent appointments, like Saul Bellow at the University of Chicago or
Bernard Malamud at Bennington; others have been visiting professors
at one point or another in their careers, staying when they wish to teach
selected groups of students, withdrawing as they need to write. The
American university has indeed served as a most generous patron of the
arts.

The tension that once existed between the university and the artist has now become a conflict between the university "establishment"—poets, sociologists, historians, novelists, dramatists, literary and cultural critics who, at their finest, have written what must be considered "creative" literature—and the military or governmental establishment. Some of the most articulate voices in the universities are Jews. Consider, for example, the remarkable achievement of Lionel Trilling, Irving Howe, Alfred Kazin, Leslie Fiedler, Daniel Bell, Nathan Glazer, David Reisman, and Oscar Handlin. These scholars and critics have produced some of the most cogent commentaries on American civilization, and their work is at least as impressive as that of writers who are more narrowly termed creative artists; it has, furthermore, deeply influenced a generation of readers and forced us, as Norman Podhoretz once suggested, to "return to the old idea of literature as a category that includes the best writing on any subject in any form." This cultural criticism is qualitatively different from that of the mid-nineteenth century, when Emerson and Thoreau considered man in a natural setting; and it is different from that of the new critics, who attended so exclusively to the literary text. It is a criticism directly social and cultural, highly concerned with ethical questions, and intensely analytical. Of greatest importance, it derives its special point of view and feeling from authors who have spent their lives in the cities—it is first and last an urban criticism; and this social coincidence—the emergence of the Jewish intellectual at the same time as America transforms itself into an urban society—is surely the most dynamic reason for the richness of Jewish-American literature.

Until the twentieth century, the great American writers—with certain exceptions like Edgar Allan Poe and Henry James—were concerned primarily with man's relationship to nature. Cooper's novels, the essays of Emerson and Thoreau, Whitman's poetry, and Twain's fiction view man against the American landscape and explore the correspondences between physical and human nature. Even the writers of the 1920's and '30's remember that moment when the American was associated with a virgin land—Faulkner, Fitzgerald, Hemingway, and Eliot contrast the modern wasteland with a time before industrialization; but the Jew, spawned in a ghetto, has known only a city life and his creative imagination has been shaped exclusively by urban problems. Now that the city is the center of consciousness in American culture and determines its quality of life, Jewish writing is important in the same sense that the literature of nineteenth-century Romantics was crucial when the West was still unexplored, the South still rural, even New England an area in which Thoreau's *Walden* was not altogether unnatural. Events move swiftly in the cities and the leisurely conditions of country life that once permitted authors to create long novels and poems, that developed patient readers, no longer exist. Some of the most brilliant writing of our time is a social commentary on the moment: the review, the article, the essay, the monograph. And this is a form which the Jew, diverted like others by his many activities as teacher and committee member and publicist, has found particularly congenial.

But even as we attempt to describe and codify the sources of the literature by modern American Jews—by citing the influence of World War II, the creation of Israel, the loss of radical hopes in the forties followed by a revival of ethnicity, the ever-increasing power of the universities, and the centrality of the city in American life—even as we assent to certain common roots from which this rich and varied literature has flowered, we must remember that it is highly sophisticated and secular; it is a literature born of the freedom from parochialism. "Like many Jewish intellectuals of my time and place brought up to revere the universalism of the Socialist ideal and of modern culture," Alfred Kazin writes, "I had equated 'Jewish' magazines with a certain insularity of tone, subject matter, writers' names—with mediocrity. To be a 'Jewish writer'. . . was somehow to regress, to strike attitudes, to thwart the natural complexities of truth. There were just too many imprecisions and suppressions in the parochially satisfied 'Jewish' writer. It was enough to be a Jew *and* a writer."

It would be a great mistake then to speak of Jewish-American authors as if they formed a school or a distinct type of artist different from all others—"many writers," as Philip Rahv reminds us, "are Jewish in descent without being in any appreciable way 'Jewish' in feeling and sensibility." If these authors do share one common characteristic it is their idiosyncratic nature, their rebellion against homogenization and facile stereotypes. Yet it is also worth remembering that we speak of clusters of other writers who share a common point of view toward American society: of New Englanders during the American renaissance of the mid-nineteenth century, for example, or of realists and writers of the twenties and the Southern renaissance since the 1930's, of Black and

Italian and Spanish Americans—our finest criticism does analyze the work of American authors thematically and archetypically, creating patterns that do, at times, violate the individuality of a given author but that nevertheless illuminate aspects of American literature as does no other kind of criticism. If the author is intrinsically important, he will survive the pattern he has partially revealed. And so it is with Jewish Americans. They share a confluence of cultural forces, as I have suggested, that distinguish them from large groups of other Americans: their creativity is born of a twentieth-century, urban society, of a war in which Jews were central figures, and of an American society in which those qualities always ascribed to Jews seem to reveal the central quality of the society so profoundly that the Jew finds himself, for the first time in his history—and certainly for the first time in the history of America—a representative man, even a cultural hero.

What are the essential qualities of Jews, at least in the writing of Jewish-American authors? Suffering, certainly, attended by pathos, humor, and compassion; a feeling for ambiguity and irony, controlled by reason and expressed usually from an alienated point of view; a self-conscious, highly intellectualized morality that carries a burden of individual righteousness, responsibility, guilt, and social concern.

Clearly these qualities are present in all literature of consequence, but, when grouped together, they serve to distinguish Jewish-American writing from that of other ethnic groups and particularly from the mainstream of American literature. Jewish-American writing is rooted in the specific human being who is suffering or pathetic, humorous or compassionate, ambiguous or righteous or guilt-ridden—there is a strong element of naturalistic detail in this work, the smell and taste and feel of human life. The classics of American literature are marked by a highly metaphoric and fabulistic imaginativeness—a forest, a whale, a scarlet letter or a river which bears a heavy moral freight of good and evil, sin and guilt, life and death; Jewish-American writing, with its constant return to the reason, analyzes the disparate emotional experiences on the human level before applying to them universal referents. Emotion is everywhere—emotion in excess—but it is framed by a recurrent reference to the intellect and by a quixotic sense of humor that humanizes an emotion before it can become an abstraction. Bellow's first novel, *Dangling Man* (1944), opens with a complaint that can almost be considered a prolegomena to the writing of American Jews since World War II; it is a criticism of the tendency, on the part of the previous generation, to romanticize heroism: "to keep a journal nowadays is considered a kind of self-indulgence, a weakness, and in poor taste. For this is an era of hard-boileddom. Today, the code of the athlete, of the tough boy—an American inheritance, I believe, from the English gentleman—that curious mixture of striving, aestheticism, and rigor, the origins of which some trace back to Alexander the Great—is stronger than ever. Do you have feelings? There are correct and incorrect ways of indicating them. Do you have an inner life? It is nobody's business but your own. Do you have emotions? Strangle them. To a degree, everyone obeys this code."

Bellow creates an anti-heroic type in *Dangling Man,* the first of a line of figures that culminate in Herzog, a man whose reason and humor are finally able to temper his excesses of emotion. Malamud's writing is marked by its compassion and humor, ambiguity and irony, and he is fond of finding fabulistic referents, but he always returns to human considerations. Roth fuses all these characteristics, even as he satirizes them; Portnoy's complaint is waged against the entire Jewish-American tradition in the degree to which it inhibits and constricts the boy who wants to be free from self-torture, suffering, righteousness, guilt, and the reason—from all that he considers to be Jewish. Passion boils up only to be thwarted by inherited guilt, moral rectitude, and the sanctions of an outworn religion. And when the tension between the heart and the head, between the past and the present, between those lovely Christian girls and the surreptitious, ogling Jewish boy—when that lifelong, unbearable, exquisite tension breaks, what will follow in its place? It is difficult to predict—for Roth as well as for his readers—but one senses that the pressures that produce creativity will pass with the struggle to still them.

Indeed one feels that the intense creativity has already passed. If *Dangling Man* marks the beginning of the extraordinary literary expression of modern American Jews then *Portnoy's Complaint* can be considered its definitive end. With this novel, the circle of creativity that one might designate as Jewish-American has been fully drawn—the rest, one suspects, will be repetitious, an afterthought. Already one speaks of this quarter-century, as I have, in historical terms. The energy of creativity has faded, its outer limits reached, its essence awaiting definition, codification, and description. Jewish-American writing deserves this study, for it has been the most important literary expression in our time, American in its broadest contours, but Jewish in its silent, intimate furrows, in its buried places and hidden, half-forgotten echoes of immigration, childhood, family and religion. American, certainly, but somewhere in its tangled roots, Jewish. Stubbornly Jewish.

ISAAC BASHEVIS SINGER (1904–   )

More than any other writer in America, Isaac Bashevis Singer re-captures the essence of Jewish life in Poland at the turn of the twentieth century. He is the last and perhaps the greatest living Yiddish author, a weaver of folk tales, myths, and fables of extraordinary force.

Born on July 14, 1904, in Radzymin, Poland, Isaac Singer grew up in Warsaw, the son of a rabbi. At the age of seventeen, he enrolled in a seminar; but he was strongly influenced by his older brother, Israel Joshua, who had rebelled against the family's orthodoxy to become a secular writer. By 1923 Singer was proofreader for a Yiddish literary journal and began to write short stories for the Warsaw magazines. His first novel, Satan in Goray, *appeared in 1934.*

Singer moved to New York in 1935 and wrote for the Yiddish news-paper, the Jewish Daily Forward, *in which his novel,* The Family Moskat, *was published from 1945 to 1948. It was translated into English in 1950 and won the Louis Lamed Prize. From that time until today Singer has been a prolific writer. His works include* Gimpel the Fool, and other Stories *(1957),* The Magician of Lublin *(1959),* The Spinoza of Market Street, *(1961),* The Slave *(1962),* Short Friday and Other Stories *(1964),* In My Father's Court *(1966),* The Manor *(1967),* The Seance and Other Stories *(1968),* The Estate *(1969), and* A Friend of Kafka *(1970).*

Saul Bellow's translation of "Gimpel the Fool," which appeared in Partisan Review *in 1953, was largely responsible for attracting attention to Singer's work. By now the story has become almost a classic of its kind, the recreation of the "wise fool," in the words of one critic, the "representative of poor, bewildered, suffering humanity."*

Gimpel the Fool

I AM GIMPEL the fool. I don't think myself a fool. On the contrary. But that's what folks call me. They gave me the name while I was still in school. I had seven names in all: imbecile, donkey, flax-head, dope, glump, ninny, and fool. The last name stuck. What did my foolishness consist of? I was easy to take in. They said, "Gimpel, you know the rabbi's wife has been brought to childbed?" So I skipped school. Well, it turned out to be a lie. How was I supposed to know? She hadn't had a big belly. But I never looked at her belly. Was that really so foolish? The gang laughed and hee-hawed, stomped and danced and chanted a good-night prayer. And instead of the raisins they give when a woman's lying in, they stuffed my hands full of goat turds. I was no weakling. If I slapped someone he'd see all the way to Cracow. But I'm really not a slugger by nature. I think to myself: Let it pass. So they take advantage of me.

I was coming home from school and heard a dog barking. I'm not afraid of dogs, but of course I never want to start up with them. One of them may be mad, and if he bites there's not a Tartar in the world who can help you. So I made tracks. Then I looked around and saw the whole market place wild with laughter. It was no dog at all but Wolf-Leib the Thief. How was I supposed to know it was he? It sounded like a howling bitch.

When the pranksters and leg-pullers found that I was easy to fool, every one of them tried his luck with me. "Gimpel, the Czar is coming to Frampol; Gimpel, the moon fell down in Turbeen; Gimpel, little Hodel Furpiece found a treasure behind the bathhouse." And I like a golem believed everyone. In the first place, everything is possible, as it is written in the Wisdom of the Fathers, I've forgotten just how. Second, I had to believe when the whole town came down on me! If I ever dared to say, "Ah, you're kidding!" there was trouble. People got angry. "What do you mean! You want to call everyone a liar?" What was I to do? I believed them, and I hope at least that did them some good.

I was an orphan. My grandfather who brought me up was already bent toward the grave. So they turned me over to a baker, and what a time they gave me there! Every woman or girl who came to bake a batch of noodles had to fool me at least once. "Gimpel, there's a fair in heaven; Gimpel, the rabbi gave birth to a calf in the seventh month; Gimpel, a cow flew over the roof and laid brass eggs." A student from the yeshiva came once to buy a roll, and he said, "You, Gimpel, while you stand here scraping with your baker's shovel the Messiah has come. The dead have arisen." "What do you mean?" I said. "I heard no one blowing the ram's horn!" He said, "Are you deaf?" And all began to cry, "We heard it, we heard!" Then in came Rietze the Candle-dipper and called out in her hoarse voice, "Gimpel, your father and mother have stood up from the grave. They're looking for you."

To tell the truth, I knew very well that nothing of the sort had happened, but all the same, as folks were talking, I threw on my wool vest and went out. Maybe something had happened. What did I stand to lose by looking? Well, what a cat music went up! And then I took a vow to believe nothing more. But that was no go either. They confused me so that I didn't know the big end from the small.

I went to the rabbi to get some advice. He said, "It is written, better to be a fool all your days than for one hour to be evil. You are not a fool. They are the fools. For he who causes his neighbor to feel shame loses Paradise himself." Nevertheless the rabbi's daughter took me in. As I left the rabbinical court she said, "Have you kissed the wall yet?" I said, "No; what for?" She answered, "It's the law; you've got to do it after every visit." Well, there didn't seem to be any harm in it. And she burst out laughing. It was a fine trick. She put one over on me, all right.

I wanted to go off to another town, but then everyone got busy matchmaking, and they were after me so they nearly tore my coat tails off. They talked at me and talked until I got water on the ear. She was no chaste maiden, but they told me she was virgin pure. She had a limp, and they said it was deliberate, from coyness. She had a bastard, and they told me the child was her little brother. I cried, "You're wasting your time. I'll never marry that whore." But they said indignantly, "What a way to talk! Aren't you ashamed of yourself? We can take you to the rabbi and have you fined for giving her a bad name." I saw then that I wouldn't escape them so easily and I thought: They're set on making me their butt. But when you're married the husband's the master, and if that's all right with her it's agreeable to me too. Besides, you can't pass through life unscathed, nor expect to.

I went to her clay house, which was built on the sand, and the whole gang, hollering and chorusing, came after me. They acted like bear-baiters. When we came to the well they stopped all the same. They were afraid to start anything with Elka. Her mouth would open as if it were on a hinge, and she had a fierce tongue. I entered the house. Lines were strung from wall to wall and clothes were drying. Barefoot she stood by the tub, doing the wash. She was dressed in a worn hand-me-down gown of plush. She had her hair put up in braids and pinned across her head. It took my breath away, almost, the reek of it all.

Evidently she knew who I was. She took a look at me and said, "Look who's here! He's come, the drip. Grab a seat."

I told her all; I denied nothing. "Tell me the truth," I said, "are you really a virgin, and is that mischievous Yechiel actually your little brother? Don't be deceitful with me, for I'm an orphan."

"I'm an orphan myself," she answered, "and whoever tries to twist you up, may the end of his nose take a twist. But don't let them think they can take advantage of me. I want a dowry of fifty guilders, and let them take up a collection besides. Otherwise they can kiss my you-know-what." She was very plainspoken. I said, "It's the bride and not the groom who gives a dowry." Then she said, "Don't bargain with me. Either a flat 'yes' or a flat 'no'—Go back where you came from."

I thought: No bread will ever be baked from *this* dough. But ours is not a poor town. They consented to everything and proceeded with the wedding. It so happened that there was a dysentery epidemic at the time. The ceremony was held at the cemetery gates, near the little corpse-washing hut. The fellows got drunk. While the marriage contract was being drawn up I heard the most pious high rabbi ask, "Is the bride a widow or a divorced woman?" And the sexton's wife answered for her, "Both a widow and divorced." It was a black moment for me. But what was I to do, run away from under the marriage canopy?

There was singing and dancing. An old granny danced opposite me, hugging a braided white *chalah*. The master of revels made a "God 'a mercy" in memory of the bride's parents. The schoolboys threw burrs, as on Tishe b'Av fast day. There were a lot of gifts after the sermon; a noodle board, a kneading trough, a bucket, brooms, ladles, household articles galore. Then I took a look and saw two strapping young men carrying a crib. "What do we need this for?" I asked. So they said, "Don't rack your brains about it. It's all right, it'll come in handy." I realized I was going to be rooked. Take it another way though, what did I stand to lose? I reflected: I'll see what comes of it. A whole town can't go altogether crazy.

At night I came where my wife lay, but she wouldn't let me in. "Say, look here, is this what they married us for?" I said. And she said, "My monthly has come." "But yesterday they took you to the ritual bath, and that's afterward, isn't it supposed to be?" "Today isn't yesterday," said she, "and yesterday's not today. You can beat it if you don't like it." In short, I waited.

Not four months later she was in childbed. The townsfolk hid their laughter with their knuckles. But what could I do? She suffered intolerable pains and clawed at the walls. "Gimpel," she cried, "I'm going. Forgive me!" The house filled with women. They were boiling pans of water. The screams rose to the welkin.

The thing to do was to go to the House of Prayer to repeat Psalms, and that was what I did.

The townsfolk liked that, all right. I stood in a corner saying Psalms and prayers, and they shook their heads at me. "Pray, pray!" they told me. "Prayer never made any woman pregnant." One of the congregation put a straw to my mouth and said, "Hay for the cows." There was something to that too, by God!

She gave birth to a boy. Friday at the synagogue the sexton stood up before the Ark, pounded on the reading table, and announced, "The wealthy Reb Gimpel invites the congregation to a feast in honor of the birth of a son." The whole House of Prayer rang with laughter. My face was flaming. But there was nothing I could do. After all, I *was* the one responsible for the circumcision honors and rituals.

Half the town came running. You couldn't wedge another soul in. Women brought peppered chick-peas, and there was a keg of beer from the tavern. I ate and drank as much as anyone, and they all congratulated me. Then there was a circumcision, and I named the boy after my father, may he rest in peace. When all were gone and I was left with my wife alone, she thrust her head through the bed-curtain and called me to her.

"Gimpel," said she, "why are you silent? Has your ship gone and sunk?"

"What shall I say?" I answered. "A fine thing you've done to me! If my mother had known of it she'd have died a second time."

She said, "Are you crazy, or what?"

"How can you make such a fool," I said, "of one who should be the lord and master?"

"What's the matter with you?" she said. "What have you taken it into your head to imagine?"

I saw that I must speak bluntly and openly. "Do you think this is the way to use an orphan?" I said. "You have borne a bastard."

She answered, "Drive this foolishness out of your head. The child is yours."

"How can he be mine?" I argued. "He was born seventeen weeks after the wedding."

She told me then that he was premature. I said, "Isn't he a little too premature?" She said, she had had a grandmother who carried just as short a time and she resembled this grandmother of hers as one drop of water does another. She swore to it with such oaths that you would have believed a peasant at the fair if he had used them. To tell the plain truth, I didn't believe her; but when I talked it over next day with the schoolmaster he told me that the very same thing had happened to Adam and Eve. Two they went up to bed, and four they descended.

"There isn't a woman in the world who is not the granddaughter of Eve," he said.

That was how it was; they argued me dumb. But then, who really knows how such things are?

I began to forget my sorrow. I loved the child madly, and he loved me too. As soon as he saw me he'd wave his little hands and want me to pick him up, and when he was colicky I was the only one who could pacify him. I bought him a little bone teething ring and a little gilded cap. He was forever catching the evil eye from someone, and then I had to run to get one of those abracadabras for him that would get him out of it. I worked like an ox. You know how expenses go up when there's an infant in the house. I don't want to lie about it; I didn't dislike Elka either, for that matter. She swore at me and cursed, and I couldn't get enough of her. What strength she had! One of her looks could rob you of the power of speech. And her orations! Pitch and sulphur, that's what they were full of, and yet somehow also full of charm. I adored her every word. She gave me bloody wounds though.

In the evening I brought her a white loaf as well as a dark one, and also poppyseed rolls I baked myself. I thieved because of her and swiped everything I could lay hands on: macaroons, raisins, almonds, cakes. I hope I may be forgiven for stealing from the Saturday pots the women left to warm in the baker's oven. I would take out scraps of meat, a chunk of pudding, a chicken leg or head, a piece of tripe, whatever I could nip quickly. She ate and became fat and handsome.

I had to sleep away from home all during the week, at the bakery. On Friday nights when I got home she always made an excuse of some sort. Either she had heartburn, or a stitch in the side, or hiccups, or headaches. You know what women's excuses are. I had a bitter time of it. It was rough. To add to it, this little brother of hers, the bastard, was growing bigger. He'd put lumps on me, and when I wanted to hit back she'd open her mouth and curse so powerfully I saw a green haze floating before my eyes. Ten times a day she threatened to divorce me. Another man in my place would have taken French leave and disappeared. But I'm the type that bears it and says nothing. What's one to do? Shoulders are from God, and burdens too.

One night there was a calamity in the bakery; the oven burst, and we almost had a fire. There was nothing to do but go home, so I went home. Let me, I thought, also taste the joy of sleeping in bed in mid-week. I didn't want to wake the sleeping mite and tiptoed into the house. Coming in, it seemed to me that I heard not the snoring of one but, as it were, a double snore, one a thin enough snore and the other like the snoring of a slaughtered ox. Oh, I didn't like that! I didn't like it at all. I went up to the bed, and things suddenly turned black. Next to Elka lay a man's form. Another in my place would have made an uproar, and enough noise to rouse the whole town, but the thought occurred to me that I might wake the child. A little thing like that—why frighten a little swallow, I thought. All right then, I went back to the bakery and stretched out on a sack of flour and till morning I never shut an eye. I shivered as if I had had malaria. "Enough of being a donkey," I said to myself. "Gimpel isn't going to be a sucker all his life. There's a limit even to the foolishness of a fool like Gimpel."

In the morning I went to the rabbi to get advice, and it made a great commotion in the town. They sent the beadle for Elka right away. She came, carrying the child. And what do you think she did? She denied it, denied everything, bone and stone! "He's out of his head," she said. "I know nothing of dreams or divinations." They yelled at her, warned her, hammered on the table, but she stuck to her guns: it was a false accusation, she said.

The butchers and the horse-traders took her part. One of the lads from the slaughterhouse came by and said to me, "We've got our eye on you, you're a marked man." Meanwhile the child started to bear down and soiled itself. In the rabbinical court there was an Ark of the Covenant, and they couldn't allow that, so they sent Elka away.

I said to the rabbi, "What shall I do?"

"You must divorce her at once," said he.

"And what if she refuses?" I asked.

He said, "You must serve the divorce. That's all you'll have to do."

I said, "Well, all right, Rabbi. Let me think about it."

"There's nothing to think about," said he. "You mustn't remain under the same roof with her."

"And if I want to see the child?" I asked.

"Let her go, the harlot," said he, "and her brood of bastards with her."

The verdict he gave was that I mustn't even cross her threshold—never again, as long as I should live.

During the day it didn't bother me so much. I thought: It was bound to happen, the abscess had to burst. But at night when I stretched out upon the sacks I felt it all very bitterly. A longing took me, for her and for the child. I wanted to be angry, but that's my misfortune exactly, I don't have it in me to be really angry. In the first place—this was how my thoughts went—there's bound to be a slip sometimes. You can't live without errors. Probably that lad who was with her led her on and gave her presents and what not, and women are often long on hair and short on sense, and so he got around her. And then since she denies it so, maybe I was only seeing things? Hallucinations do happen. You see a figure or a mannikin or something, but when you come up closer it's nothing, there's not a thing there. And if that's so, I'm doing her an injustice. And when I got so far in my thoughts I started to weep. I sobbed so that I wet the flour where I lay. In the morning I went to the rabbi and told him that I had made a mistake. The rabbi wrote on with his quill, and he said that if that were so he would have to reconsider the whole case. Until he had finished I wasn't to go near my wife, but I might send her bread and money by messenger.

Nine months passed before all the rabbis could come to an agreement. Letters went back and forth. I hadn't realized that there could be so much erudition about a matter like this.

Meanwhile Elka gave birth to still another child, a girl this time. On the Sabbath I went to the synagogue and invoked a blessing on her. They called me up to the Torah, and I named the child for my mother-in-law—may she rest in peace. The louts and loudmouths of the town

who came into the bakery gave me a going over. All Frampol refreshed
in spirits because of my trouble and grief. However, I resolved that I
would always believe what I was told. What's the good of *not* believing?
Today it's your wife you don't believe; tomorrow it's God Himself you
won't take stock in.

By an apprentice who was her neighbor I sent her daily a corn or a
wheat loaf, or a piece of pastry, rolls or bagels, or, when I got the
chance, a slab of pudding, a slice of honeycake, or wedding strudel—
whatever came my way. The apprentice was a goodhearted lad, and more
than once he added something on his own. He had formerly annoyed
me a lot, plucking my nose and digging me in the ribs, but when he
started to be a visitor to my house he became kind and friendly. "Hey,
you, Gimpel," he said to me, "you have a very decent little wife and
two fine kids. You don't deserve them."

"But the things people say about her," I said.

"Well, they have long tongues," he said, "and nothing to do with
them but babble. Ignore it as you ignore the cold of last winter."

One day the rabbi sent for me and said, "Are you certain, Gimpel,
that you were wrong about your wife?"

I said, "I'm certain."

"Why, but look here! You yourself saw it."

"It must have been a shadow," I said.

"The shadow of what?"

"Just of one of the beams, I think."

"You can go home then. You owe thanks to the Yanover rabbi. He
found an obscure reference in Maimonides that favored you."

I seized the rabbi's hand and kissed it.

I wanted to run home immediately. It's no small thing to be separated for so long a time from wife and child. Then I reflected: I'd better
go back to work now, and go home in the evening. I said nothing to
anyone, although as far as my heart was concerned it was like one of
the Holy Days. The women teased and twitted me as they did every day,
but my thought was: Go on, with your loose talk. The truth is out, like
the oil upon the water. Maimonides says it's right, and therefore it is
right!

At night, when I had covered the dough to let it rise, I took my
share of bread and a little sack of flour and started homeward. The
moon was full and the stars were glistening, something to terrify the
soul. I hurried onward, and before me darted a long shadow. It was
winter, and a fresh snow had fallen. I had a mind to sing, but it was
growing late and I didn't want to wake the householders. Then I felt

like whistling, but I remembered that you don't whistle at night because it brings the demons out. So I was silent and walked as fast as I could.

Dogs in the Christian yards barked at me when I passed, but I thought: Bark your teeth out! What are you but mere dogs? Whereas I am a man, the husband of a fine wife, the father of promising children.

As I approached the house my heart started to pound as though it were the heart of a criminal. I felt no fear, but my heart went thump! thump! Well, no drawing back. I quietly lifted the latch and went in. Elka was asleep. I looked at the infant's cradle. The shutter was closed, but the moon forced its way through the cracks. I saw the newborn child's face and loved it as soon as I saw it—immediately—each tiny bone.

Then I came nearer to the bed. And what did I see but the apprentice lying there beside Elka. The moon went out all at once. It was utterly black, and I trembled. My teeth chattered. The bread fell from my hands, and my wife waked and said, "Who is that, ah?"

I muttered, "It's me."

"Gimpel?" she asked. "How come you're here? I thought it was forbidden."

"The rabbi said," I answered and shook as with a fever.

"Listen to me, Gimpel," she said, "go out to the shed and see if the goat's all right. It seems she's been sick." I have forgotten to say that we had a goat. When I heard she was unwell I went into the yard. The nannygoat was a good little creature. I had a nearly human feeling for her.

With hesitant steps I went up to the shed and opened the door. The goat stood there on her four feet. I felt her everywhere, drew her by the horns, examined her udders, and found nothing wrong. She had probably eaten too much bark. "Good night, little goat," I said. "Keep well." And the little beast answered with a "Maa" as though to thank me for the good will.

I went back. The apprentice had vanished.

"Where," I said, "is the lad?"

"What lad?" my wife answered.

"What do you mean?" I said. "The apprentice. You were sleeping with him."

"The things I have dreamed this night and the night before," she said, "may they come true and lay you low, body and soul! An evil spirit has taken root in you and dazzles your sight." She screamed out, "You hateful creature! You moon calf! You spook! You uncouth man! Get out, or I'll scream all Frampol out of bed!"

Before I could move, her brother sprang out from behind the oven and struck me a blow on the back of the head. I thought he had broken my neck. I felt that something about me was deeply wrong, and I said, "Don't make a scandal. All that's needed now is that people should accuse me of raising spooks and *dybbuks*." For that was what she had meant. "No one will touch bread of my baking."

In short, I somehow calmed her.

"Well," she said, "that's enough. Lie down, and be shattered by wheels."

Next morning I called the apprentice aside. "Listen here, brother!" I said. And so on and so forth. "What do you say?" He stared at me as though I had dropped from the roof or something.

"I swear," he said, "you'd better go to an herb doctor or some healer. I'm afraid you have a screw loose, but I'll hush it up for you." And that's how the thing stood.

To make a long story short, I lived twenty years with my wife. She bore me six children, four daughters and two sons. All kinds of things happened, but I neither saw nor heard. I believed, and that's all. The rabbi recently said to me, "Belief in itself is beneficial. It is written that a good man lives by his faith."

Suddenly my wife took sick. It began with a trifle, a little growth upon the breast. But she evidently was not destined to live long; she had no years. I spent a fortune on her. I have forgotten to say that by this time I had a bakery of my own and in Frampol was considered to be something of a rich man. Daily the healer came, and every witch doctor in the neighborhood was brought. They decided to use leeches, and after that to try cupping. They even called a doctor from Lublin, but it was too late. Before she died she called me to her bed and said, "Forgive me, Gimpel."

I said, "What is there to forgive? You have been a good and faithful wife."

"Woe, Gimpel!" she said. "It was ugly how I deceived you all these years. I want to go clean to my Maker, and so I have to tell you that the children are not yours."

If I had been clouted on the head with a piece of wood it couldn't have bewildered me more.

"Whose are they?" I asked.

"I don't know," she said. "There were a lot . . . but they're not yours." And as she spoke she tossed her head to the side, her eyes turned glassy, and it was all up with Elka. On her whitened lips there remained a smile.

I imagined that, dead as she was, she was saying, "I deceived Gimpel. That was the meaning of my brief life."

One night, when the period of mourning was done, as I lay dreaming on the flour sacks, there came the Spirit of Evil himself and said to me, "Gimpel, why do you sleep?"

I said, "What should I be doing? Eating *kreplach?*"

"The whole world deceives you," he said, "and you ought to deceive the world in your turn."

"How can I deceive all the world?" I asked him.

He answered, "You might accumulate a bucket of urine every day and at night pour it into the dough. Let the sages of Frampol eat filth."

"What about the judgment in the world to come?" I said.

"There is no world to come," he said. "They've sold you a bill of goods and talked you into believing you carried a cat in your belly. What nonsense!"

"Well then," I said, "and is there a God?"

He answered, "There is no God either."

"What," I said, "*is* there, then?"

"A thick mire."

He stood before my eyes with a goatish beard and horn, long-toothed, and with a tail. Hearing such words, I wanted to snatch him by the tail, but I tumbled from the flour sacks and nearly broke a rib. Then it happened that I had to answer the call of nature, and, passing, I saw the risen dough, which seemed to say to me, "Do it!" In brief, I let myself be persuaded.

At dawn the apprentice came. We kneaded the bread, scattered caraway seeds on it, and set it to bake. Then the apprentice went away, and I was left sitting in the little trench by the oven, on a pile of rags. Well, Gimpel, I thought, you've revenged yourself on them for all the shame they've put on you. Outside the frost glittered, but it was warm beside the oven. The flames heated my face. I bent my head and fell into a doze.

I saw in a dream, at once, Elka in her shroud. She called to me, "What have you done, Gimpel?"

I said to her, "It's all your fault," and started to cry.

"You fool!" she said. "You fool! Because I was false is everything false too? I never deceived anyone but myself. I'm paying for it all, Gimpel. They spare you nothing here."

I looked at her face. It was black; I was startled and waked, and remained sitting dumb. I sensed that everything hung in the balance. A false step now and I'd lose Eternal Life. But God gave me His help. I seized the long shovel and took out the loaves, carried them into the yard, and started to dig a hole in the frozen earth.

My apprentice came back as I was doing it. "What are you doing boss?" he said, and grew pale as a corpse.

"I know what I'm doing," I said, and I buried it all before his very eyes.

Then I went home, took my hoard from its hiding place, and divided it among the children. "I saw your mother tonight," I said. "She's turning black, poor thing."

They were so astounded they couldn't speak a word.

"Be well," I said, "and forget that such a one as Gimpel ever existed." I put on my short coat, a pair of boots, took the bag that held my prayer shawl in one hand, my stock in the other, and kissed the *mezzuzah*. When people saw me in the street they were greatly surprised.

"Where are you going?" they said.

I answered, "Into the world." And so I departed from Frampol.

I wandered over the land, and good people did not neglect me. After many years I became old and white; I heard a great deal, many lies and falsehoods, but the longer I lived the more I understood that there were really no lies. Whatever doesn't really happen is dreamed at night. It happens to one if it doesn't happen to another, tomorrow if not today, or a century hence if not next year. What difference can it make? Often I heard tales of which I said, "Now this is a thing that cannot happen." But before a year had elapsed I heard that it actually had come to pass somewhere.

Going from place to place, eating at strange tables, it often happens that I spin yarns—improbable things that could never have happened—about devils, magicians, windmills, and the like. The children run after me, calling, "Grandfather, tell us a story." Sometimes they ask for particular stories, and I try to please them. A fat young boy once said to me, "Grandfather, it's the same story you told us before." The little rogue, he was right.

So it is with dreams too. It is many years since I left Frampol, but as soon as I shut my eyes I am there again. And whom do you think I see? Elka. She is standing by the washtub, as at our first encounter, but her face is shining and her eyes are as radiant as the eyes of a saint, and she speaks outlandish words to me, strange things. When I wake I have forgotten it all. But while the dream lasts I am comforted. She answers all my queries, and what comes out is that all is right. I weep and implore, "Let me be with you." And she consoles me and tells me to be patient. The time is nearer than it is far. Sometimes she strokes and kisses me and weeps upon my face. When I awaken I feel her lips and taste the salt of her tears.

No doubt the world is entirely an imaginary world, but it is only once removed from the true world. At the door of the hovel where I lie, there stands the plank on which the dead are taken away. The gravedigger Jew has his spade ready. The grave waits and the worms are hungry; the shrouds are prepared—I carry them in my beggar's sack. Another *shnorrer* is waiting to inherit my bed of straw. When the time comes I will go joyfully. Whatever may be there, it will be real, without complication, without ridicule, without deception. God be praised: there even Gimpel cannot be deceived.

Translated by Saul Bellow

PAUL GOODMAN (1911–1972)

"*Everything I do has exactly the same subject—the organism and the environment. Anything I write on society is pragmatic—it aims to accomplish something. . . . I am a man of letters. . . . or an artist-humanist.*" This self-description characterizes Paul Goodman's work as a poet, novelist, short-story writer, playwright, social critic, city planner, pacifist, and anarchist. A prominent leader of the New Left and a tireless critic of American bureaucracy, Goodman was one of the most perceptive moral critics of the past generation and a father figure for many in the younger generation.

He did not always enjoy popularity. Indeed it was not until the publication of Growing Up Absurd in 1960 that he was able to emerge from a life of relative poverty. Goodman's father deserted the family shortly after the writer's birth in 1911 and Goodman grew up in a slum near Mt. Sinai hospital. He graduated from the City College and received his Ph.D. from the University of Chicago in 1954. Goodman's work is in almost every genre. He has written social studies—Growing Up Absurd (1960), The Community of Scholars (1962), Compulsory Mis-Education (1964), and People or Personnel (1965); plays—Jonah (1960), The Young Disciple (1965), and Faustina (1965); novels—The Empire City (1959) and Making Do (1963); books of short stories—The Breakup of Our Camp (1949) and Our Visit to Niagara (1960); literary criticism—Kafka's Prayer (1949) and The Structure of Literature (1954); television criticism for The New Republic; and city planning—Communitas (1947–1961).

Goodman's chief concern, as expressed in Growing Up Absurd, is that American society exists primarily to preserve its own bureaucracies. His social criticism touches upon almost every aspect of American civilization, including the different conflicts that arise between Christians and Jews. The following story suggests Goodman's sensitivity to his own Jewish identity.

The Facts of Life

:

Childish Ronnie Morris has a wife Martha and a daughter Marcia, aged nine.

Ronnie is middle-aged, as we say of any one ten years older than ourselves, and he has invented a wonderful scheme to milk money from those who make $20,000 a year: he sells them Fine Editions with odd associations, as *The Golden Ass* bound in a donkey's hide or *The New Testament* signed by the designer in the blood of a lamb. (He is childish enough to go through with such a profitable idea, instead of dismissing it like the rest of us fools.) He has a two-masted sailboat; he moves in the circle of his clients. In a business way, he knows Picasso and Thomas Benton, and is the expert at the Club in the trade-secrets of the Muses. In the acts of love, he is medium; he went to Dartmouth; but in fact he is only moderately fixated on the period when he was fifth oar, for he had had an even prior period of ease and lust, which has saved him for philosophy and the arts, rather than the brokerage.

Martha Morris is an Andalusian type. When she arranges flowers she keeps them under control with wires. She drives at high speeds. Her relations with Ronnie are as usual; she is her little daughter's friend, and every Xmas she and Marcia design a gift-volume for Ronnie's clientèle. She is more political than her husband and her position is slightly to the left of the right wing of the left-center: a group that finds no representation in Washington, but used to have thirty seats in Paris. I could write forever, as it would seem, about Martha's teeth as they flash under her nose. Aren't the rhythms delightful, of the description of the upper middle class?

Now little Marcia goes to the University Progressive School where many of her schoolmates have fathers in the embassies, but Marcia too has been to the Near East in search of that lamb. At school they are taught to express themselves freely. Little Marcia, when she does so—she takes after her mother—is delightful!

Marcia has a fight in school today with one of the little gentlemen, her contemporaries. He breaks her photographic plate. The fight is about the nature of chickens' eggs. She stamps on his foot. Being a girl, she still has an advantage in mental age and more words to say; she says a sentence in French. He can't punch her in the nose because it is ungentlemanly. He is inhibited from drawing on his best knowledge because it is dirty; but worse, it is gloomily indistinct, and even on these matters she seems to have more definite information, is about to mention it.

"Shut up!" he argues, "shut up! you're just an old-time Jew."

This perplexing observation, of which she understands neither head nor tail, brings her to a momentary pause; for up to now, at least with Harry—though certainly not with Terry or Larry—she has maintained a queenly advantage. But he has brought her to a pause by drawing on absolutely new information.

Now she does a reckless thing: she dismisses his remark from her mind and launches into a tirade which devastatingly combines contempt and the ability to form complete sentences, till Harry goes away in order not to cry. A reckless, a dangerous thing: because what we thus dismiss enters the regions of anxiety, of loss and unfulfilled desire, and there makes strange friends. This is the prologue to fanatic interests and to falling in love. How new and otherwise real is this observation on its next appearance!

Marcia calls her mother sometimes Momsy and sometimes Martha.

"What did Harry mean," she asks her, "when he called me an old-time shoe?"

"Jew?"

"Yes, he stated I was just an old-time Joo."

Across the woman's face passes, for ever so many reasons, the least perceptible tightening. "Oh oh!" feels Marcia along her ears and scalp; and now she is confirmed and doubly confirmed in the suspicions she did not know she had. When she now has to express herself with colored chalks, new and curious objects will swim into the foreground alongside the pool, the clock will become a grandfather's clock, and all be painted Prussian blue, even though Miss Coyle is trying to cajole especially the little girls into using warm bright colors, because that is their natural bent.

"Well he was right, you are a Jewess," says Martha. "It's nothing to be ashamed of."

"Said Joo, not Juice."

"A Jew is a boy; a Jewess is a girl."

"Oh! there are two kinds!"

It's worse and worse. She never dreamed that Harry was up on anything, but perhaps even his veiled hints conceal something. She feels, it seems inescapable to her, that boys have a power, surely not obvious in school—and the grown-ups even take it for granted! She sees it every day, that these same boys when they become men are superior to the women. Yet men's clothes don't *express* anything, and actresses are better than actors. But just this *contradiction* confirms it all the more, for the explanations of contradictions are in the indistinct region—and everything there is mutually involved. Marcia is already working on a system of the mysteries. Especially when Momsy now tries to tell her some reasonable anecdote about Jewesses and Jews, just like a previous astringent account of the chickens and the flowers.

Martha never happens to have told little Marcia that they are all Jews.

"Is Ronnie a Joo?"

"Of course."

"Are Louis and Bernie Joos?"

"Louis is a Jew but Bernie is a Gentile."

It's a lie, thinks Marcia; they are both the same. (She means they are both effeminate.) Why is Martha lying to her?

"What is ser-cum-si-zhun?" asks Marcia, calling the lie.

This inquisition has now become intolerable to Martha. "Good night, Marcia," she explains.

"Is Rosina a Juice?" Marcia cries, asking about Ronnie's mistress.

"Marcia! I said good night!"

"Tell me! tell me! is Rosina Juice?"

"No."

"Ah!"

"Why Ah?"

"Good night, Momsy," says Marcia, kissing her.

Since the habits are formed speediest where necessity constrains and yet conscious and deliberate adjustment is embarrassing or tedious,

Martha has speedily and long ago learned the few adjustments belonging particularly to Jews of a certain class of money. The other hotel; not on this list; the right to more chic and modernity, but please no associations with Betsy Ross in tableaux or on committees. Of course habits learned by this mechanism are subject to amazing breaches, when submerged desire suddenly asserts itself and the son of Jacob becomes Belmont or Ronnie becomes, as he is, an honorary colonel in the militia. But on the whole, where money is so exchangeable, there are very few special adjustments; for instance, they never even came to Marcia's keen perception, especially since none of the Jews whom she is so often with without knowing it, do not mention them. Of course, on the other hand, in the more critical social episodes, such as marriage—but forget that. And there are many other meanings, archaically forgotten.

"Since you have to put up with the handicap whether you like it or not," decides Mrs. Ronnie Morris, "why not make an advantage of it, and be proud of it?" And at once she writes out a check for a subscription to *The Menorah Journal,* the *Harper's Monthly* of reformed Jews.

"Never heard such a stupid argument in my life!" says Ronnie. He is very angry, like any one who has played the game like a perfect gentleman and then finds that the other side goes too far and calls his daughter an old-time Jew. "What's the use of *pretending* you're a Jew, when you're *not* a Jew?" he shouts.

"We are Jews. Don't shout," says Martha.

"I'll go to school and punch that brat's nose."

Martha says nothing.

"Do I pay $300 a year for him to tell Marcia that she's a Jew?"

"But we are Jews," says Martha, with a new loyalty.

"Since when?" says Ronnie scientifically. "To be a Jew means one of three things: It means first to belong to a certain Race; but there isn't any Jewish race in anthropology. Look at me, do I look like a Jewish race?"

He looks like a highly brushed and polished moujik.

"No. Secondly: it means a Nationality. But even if some Jews think they have a nationality, do I? I went to Jerusalem to pick out a Gentile lamb. Anyway, I can't speak the language. Hebrew isn't the same as Yiddish, you know, even though it looks the same; but I can't speak that either.

"Third: it's a Religion. So you see," he concludes triumphantly, "it's not a matter of not *wanting* to be a Jew or trying to *hide* that you're a Jew, but you *can't* be a Jew if you're *not* a Jew!"

"Don't be a fool," says Martha. "A person's a Jew if his grandparents were Jews; even one's enough sometimes, depending."

"What sense does that make?"

"Do you think it's by accident," says Martha flatly, "that your mama and papa came to marry Jews and we married Jews?"

She means, thinks Ronnie, when our desire is toward Gentiles, toward retroussé noses and moon-face Hungarians. Does she mean Rosina? She means Bernie. We mean—but there is no time to think of that.

"I'll ask Louis," says Ronnie; for though he holds sway at the luncheon club, all his ideas come from this poet.

"He's taking Marshy to the Picassos tomorrow."

"Let him tell her, then."

"What! are you going to let your daughter find out the facts from a stranger?"

Having slept over it all night, by morning the little girl has contrived the following working theory:

In the beginning, of course, all babies are alike. Her deep-seated conviction on this point has never been in the least shaken by Momsy's anecdotes about the chickens, for it is plain to observe that all babies are alike. (Nor is this the chief reason for her conviction.) But then comes the moment when the thing is cut off the girls. When this takes place, is not yet clear; but it is planned from the beginning, because you can tell by the names; although sometimes even there is a change of names; with some names you still can't tell; and others are easy to change, like Robert and Roberta or Bernie and Bernice. All of this is an old story to Marcia.

But now, there are some *chosen* ones, who are supposed to be cut but somehow they get off. Why? They are only *partly* cut—and this is ser-cum-si-zhun, because they use a scissors. These are Joos. For a moment, starting from "Louis," Marcia thinks that she can tell by the names, but then when she thinks of "Ronnie" and of "Terry" and "Larry," two boys in school whom she now knows are Joos (in fact, Terry is and Larry is not), she sees that she can't. The *last* names are connected with marrying and have nothing to do with ser-cum-si-zhun.

Now, she sees in a flash, it is *better* to be a Joo, for then you still have the secret power and the thing, but at the same time you can be cleverer like a girl. This is why Larry and Terry are always able to beat her, they have an unfair advantage; but Harry, the dope, is only a boy and not a Joo.

There are also differences among Joos; for instance, Louis is much smarter than Papa. But this *proves* it, for Louis is more like Martha; that is, they cut the *best* amount off him, but not so much from Papa. Anyway, she hates Louis and loves her poor papa. And now an enormous love for poor Harry suffuses her and she begins to tremble and wants to go to school; he has so much secret power.

But more important—and, lying in bed, Marcia begins to tremble as she thinks about herself—what is a Juice? and besides all these, there are Gen-tiles. Martha and Marcia are Juice and Bernie is a Gen-tile. Oh! what a mean thing to say about poor Bernie, that he is not even a Juice, but even worse than a girl; he is not even clever. It is nice of Louis to be so kind to him. So it seems that things go in the following order: Boys, Joos, Juices, Girls, Gen-tiles. Except that it is smartest to be a Joo. But what is it! What is it that they did to Marcia to be a Juice? As she lets her fingers move between her thighs, she breaks into a cold sweat, and an urgency of longing loosens her strength. With a violent dismissal, she leaps from bed.

But while she is eating breakfast, an awful emptiness for her boy Harry spreads within her, and she bursts into tears.

Louis, who is quite intelligent, often cannot resist being cruel and supercilious to Ronnie, so that Ronnie feels like punching him in the nose—but then suddenly, at a poignant touch, even suggested by his own monologue, he relapses into natural melancholia. "To me of course," says he suavely to Ronnie, "your Jewish problem doesn't exist. My paternal parent twelfth removed was Joseph Karo, the author of the *Shulchan Aruch,* or *Table* of the observances; he had established the lineage back to Joseph, son of Eli, so that obviously, if we may lend any credence to the Gentile gospels, we go back to David the son of Jesse and further; but you're a Russian Jew. On my mother's side, I am related to the convert Leo the Hebrew; but that blood throughout is tainted by conversions; my three cousins, Georges de Duchesse, Georges Catala, and Georges Catala-de Duchesse were all converts of Maritain. My cousin Georges Catala-de Duchesse is the Abbot of St. Germain des Prés, an *idol*-worshipper, as I told him last summer. It ought to be clear by now, I said, that only Maimonides conceived the relation of God and Man in a way helpful and necessary to the Modern Age. This is my faith. 'If every Jew would read the *Mishneh Torah,* he would become a perfect snob,' cries Louis Parigi with pride, 'and would set tradition against tradition and not take the insults lying down or by appealing merely to good sense!' Besides, in our poetry both the Parigis and the de Duchesses look for inspiration to the Prophets. My cousin Georges de Duchesse, on the very eve of his baptism wrote his rime royal *Habakuk*; but 'Habakuk,' as Voltaire says, *'était capable de tout!'* But even in writing my *Anacreontics* I have drawn on the dipsomaniac rhythms of your Chassidim. And by the way, my cousin Georges Catala was married to an eighth removed descendant of the Vilna Gaon, and her suicide was the cause of his conversion, which goes to show what comes of marrying with the Ashkenazim. (Are you also related to the Vilna Gaon, like all the other Lithuanians?) On the National issue, I am like Judah ha-Levi an allegorical Zionist; but the vulgar desire of a temporal habitation— this destroys, as I see it, just our sacred distinction from the *Goyim*"— (he pronounces *Go-yeem* as if he had stepped from a Christian fastness in Aragon where never a Moor or Jew had once set foot);—"but God said—but *God* said," says Louis, raising a forefinger, "Make *Succoth*, Booths." At this quotation, suddenly, tears glisten in his eyes and he sinks into the deepest gloom. "Besides," he finishes airily, "except the purity of our Jewish morals, what defense do I have against adultery and sodomy?"

It is especially this breezy ending that makes Ronnie punch him in the nose—almost; yet this happens to be his only heart-felt remark, though in the form of a wish.

In the afternoon, in front of the impassive checkerboard of *The Three Musicians*, the little girl again bursts into tears. Louis, who has with some skill been pointing out to her only such features of the difficult paintings as she is adequate to, an underfed and melancholy face, a marvelous mother bathed in rose, the fact that in 1920 the colors are no longer blended, and enveloping it all in fanciful anecdotes—he looks at her in stupefaction.

"It's not fair! It's not fair!" she sobs.

They are alone in the room.

"What's not fair?" says Louis.

"It's not fair 'cause it's a myst'ry, and I won't *ever* be able to understand it."

"Why you've been understanding it very well, Marcia. What you said about the colors I didn't know myself, because you're a painter and I'm not."

"You're *lying* to me—'cause it's a secret myst'ry, and I won't ever be able to understand it 'cause I'm only a girl, even if I'm a Juice."

? ?

I understand about the colors and the poor boy, but I can't understand it *all*, 'cause they cut my thing off when I was little and Picass' is a man— An' I have nothing left but to be an actress."

He takes her hand, for the tears are rolling down her cheeks.

"—I won't ever be able to make 'em any more with a myst'ry if I live to be a million years old."

She hides her face in her other arm, and she cries with the pent-up anxiety of her third to her ninth years.

A guard comes in and hastily goes out the other door.

On the walls, the impassive objects, which are indeed a secret mystery, stare from side to side.

The tears glisten in Louis's eyes. "This Holy Spirit," he says—he thinks he says—"is given to us and not made by us. It's not my fault if I cannot any more."

"Ah," she says (he thinks), "maybe if it weren't for the Bernies and the Jackies, the prophetic voice of the Lord of Hosts would not prove so disheartened at the third and fourth verse."

"What a despicable argument!" he cries (he thinks), "if I'm finally tired of that boy, why don't I think so right off and not need these thin arguments to bolster up my courage? Stop staring, you," says he to the unblinking middle Musician, "or I'll punch you in the nose."

"Look Marshy," he says reasonably to the little girl whose hand he is holding tight, "you can't expect to make these things right off! You have to develop your power. Just as when you learn to play the piano, you see you have to begin with finger-exercises."

"Oh!" she cries in fright and pulls her hand away. "How could he tell so quick?" she thinks in terror; "Momsy couldn't tell."

"See, this one is easy to understand," he says, pointing to those Three Musicians. "You see, this is an oboe."

"What's a Obo?"

"An oboe is a kind of wooden instrument with stops. This part is what the oboe looks like from underneath, which you can't ordinarily see. This is a guitar; he broke it into two pieces in order to make the pattern here with this red business—"

"Can you, Louis?" she seizes his hand. "I mean can you? Can you develop your power by finger-exercises?"

? ?

"Can you? Can you?"

"Certainly. Every day you'll be able to paint a little better."

"Hurrah!"

Two women come in, tittering at a pyramidal creature that is like one of the works of the Six Days.

But the silence is twangling with the music of the guitars of Picasso, with the guitars of Catalonia, with the cubist harmony by which the acrobats drift away.

In the school-field, the fourth-year boys, in maroon sweat-suits, are playing the in-tra-mur-al ball-game, while Mr. Donlin is umpiring and keeping order. From time to time some of the little boys have the minds completely on the game. When his side is at bat, Harry is sitting on the lowest bench of the stands and Marcia bounces pebbles on him from above. Outside the iron fence around the field, Timmy and Page Mc-Croskey, who go to Holy Name Academy, are staring at the clean and distinguished boys within. Mr. Donlin looks like a perfect fool, full of manly baby-talk such as, "Gooood try!" or "C'mon *Terry*, let's see what you can do!" Sometimes he loses his temper. One of the boys takes off his clothes and to the amazement of the Irish boys discloses his delicate limbs in another maroon uniform of shorts and a shirt with a big U. Amid a loud chorus, Mr. Donlin has to assert his authority to keep the children from exposing themselves to the cold air.

"Mr. Donlin, Mr. Donlin," mimic the two outside the bars, "kin I take off my drawers?"

A local merchant-prince, a great contributor to the University, has the exclusive franchise for the manufacture and sale of these many uniforms. Timmy and Page and their friends call the U-school the Jew-school. They are envious of the boundless wealth behind the bars and of the fact that the girls and boys go to school together. "Why doncha let the girls play with youse?" shouts little Timmy. Page, who is a year younger and much bolder, cries, "Mr. Donlin, kin I take off my drawers and show the girls my p——?"

On the large field, which is used for the high-school games, the base-ball, thrown by weak arms and tapped by little bats, makes ridiculous little hops and arcs. Terry, distracted by the remark from the fence, drops a little pop-fly and the runners stream across the plate. Mr. Donlin advances to the fence shouting without profanity, go away or he'll punch them in the nose. From a little distance, they shout in chorus: "Jew School Jew School!" and some of the little scholars, who at other times announce proudly that they go to the University P'rgressive School (as if they went to college), now turn pink. "Play ball!" shouts Mr. Donlin in a manly voice.

Now all the little feelings are afire.

Marcia and Harry, however, have heard nothing; but they have now progressed from the first stage of touching-yet-not-touching by throwing things at each other, to the next stage of punching and pulling shoe-laces.

To the Irish boys, so systematically kept in order by their father and by the priest and Brothers to whom even their father defers, there is no way of doubting that non-Catholics enjoy a full sexual freedom. They *know*, in fact, that the Reformation *began* with fornication; and even more enviable are the Jews, as is proved by the anti-Semitism, otherwise incomprehensible, that forms so large a part of the instruction by the Brothers. And along with this yearning, they observe this wealth and beauty and privilege through the bars; and so is consolidated that deep sentiment of inferiority which will tomorrow need firearms to soothe.

To the little rich boys, on the other hand, it is obvious that freedom lies outside the bars among those wild boys whose dirty language makes them tremble with terror and stirs unconquerable lust in each one when he is alone; who can stay out late and wear hats decorated with paper-clips, and beg for pennies from strangers. So even before the first clash, the rich boys feel physically and morally powerless and would like to be the slaves of the poor ones, and it will require all the machinery of the state to treat them with an iron hand.

But why should I make the case any simpler than is necessary? For Timmy also hates little Page, just as he hates the Brothers in school; and among the U-boys there are the families going up and the families falling down, and the case, for instance, of weedy Tom, whose parents are slipping and climbing at the same time, and who will tomorrow be satisfied and avenged by burning for the lowest hustler, if his name happens to be Woodrow, until with a sinking heart he one day learns that Woodrow isn't a family name, but a war-name, after President Wilson.

Fascinated, Timmy is watching Marcia wrestling with Harry and pulling his hair, while he is trying to concentrate on his teammate at bat: "Make it be a good one! Make it be a good one!" he cries; and then he suddenly chases Marcia up the stands. Pressed between the bars till he is white, Timmy follows them with his stare, above him, through the stands. But she jumps down and runs across the field toward the building, and then they both disappear. Poor Timmy stares at the gray door which has just closed.—So in each heart are fixed the types of love, after the girls who seem to be easy, who have the reputation of being available, who are easy and available in idea though never in fact. The Jewish girls to the Irish boys like Timmy, and the Irish girls to the Jewish boys like Ronnie, and the sailors to Louis. But for the most part, it is just one's own kind that is really available (and really desirable, and absolutely forbidden!), and that we live with in the end, as Ronnie with Martha, and Louis with Bernie; these are no doubt still deeper types of love, though far too deep to give us any pleasure.

"Knock Knock!" cries Page McCroskey.

"Play Ball!" shouts Mr. Donlin.

"Knock Knock, Mr. Donlin, Knock Knock!" he screams.

"Don't pay any attention, play ball," says Mr. Donlin.

"Who's there?" answers Larry.

"Cohen!"

"Don't pay any attention!" cries Mr. Donlin.

"Cohen who?" answers a voice.

"Who said it?" shouts Mr. Donlin authoritatively.

"Cohen f—— yourself!" cry Page and Timmy together.

One of the boys throws a stone at them.

"You c—— s——!" says Timmy, casting his eyes about for some resource.

"Shut up, McCroskey," says Terry, "or I'll tell somethin' on you, but I don't want to make you ashamed."

"Do you believe that pile o' s—— that O'Hara said?" says Timmy wildly.

"Naw, I *saw* it!" says Terry.

"What did O'Hara say?" says Page.

But at this instant a foul-ball jumps out over the fence.

"*H'yaann! H'yaann!*" sing Page and Timmy and run down the block with the ball, grasping off their hats.

"Where's Harry Riesling? He's supposed to be coaching on first," says the beaten Mr. Donlin.

But Marcia and Harry are in one of the empty rooms where they have never been before (it is part of the High School), and she is telling him all about Picass'. He explains to her that he likes Terry and Larry swell, but he hates his big brother; but he promises just not to notice him any more. "He probably hates your papa as much as you hate *him*," Marcia observes judiciously, "so that's something you know on *him*." This insight, this knowledge, casts such an angel light on Harry's usually puzzled countenance that Marcia turns and stares at him. He explains to her that he likes geography and history, but Miss Jensen doesn't make it interesting the way Mr. Bee used to, and that's why he's not smart;

and when Marcia tells him that she was in Egypt and the Near—East (as opposed to the Far—East), he is struck with admiration. But how different now is this admiration and his pleasure and pride in her ability to form complete sentences, as if she were a teacher whom he can kiss and lick and not even have to discuss certain things with, from the animosity he felt yesterday when she was so God-damned smart. She draws on the blackboard the dolphins playing at the *Ile de France's* prow.

"There are geniuses in every race," says Ronnie passionately, with all the energy of his desire for Rosina; "but both per capita and absolutely there are more of them among the Jews."

"I thought you said there was no Jewish race?"

"That's what I thought, but facts are facts and you can't get around it. Einstein Ehrlich Freud."

"Yes, the Jews are always going in for syphilis or psychoanalysis or the fourth dimension," says Martha.

"Picasso—"

"Ha, the same thing!"

"Proust—"

"There you have it!" says Martha triumphantly. "I'm not saying the Jews are not geniuses, but they're *queer,* they're just queer, that's all."

"What about Dali? He's not a Jew."

"Will you please tell me what you're trying to prove by that? I thought you were trying to prove that all the Jews, including yourself, were geniuses."

"No, but you said that Proust and Picasso were Jews."

"*I* said it? *I* said it?"

"I didn't say you said it especially; they *are* Jews, *half*-Jews."

"Oh, don't be a fool."

Ronnie says nothing.

"And let me tell you another thing," says Martha, "you Jews are not doing yourselves any favor by putting yourselves forward so much. If Felix Frankfurter is so smart as he's supposed to be, he knows that especially just now there's no place for another Jew on the Supreme Court bench. Every Jew that gets on the Supreme Court makes it just so much harder for us and Marcia. Where do you think I'm going to be able to send her to college?"

"That's a fine way of looking at it!" cries Ronnie. "It's true enough," he thinks; but Martha has always been ahead of him on national and international affairs.

"You're a Jew, so all right!" says Mrs. Ronnie Morris née de Havilland. "It's nothing to be ashamed of. But why bring it up in public? Who asks you?"

"Who?" says Ronnie bewildered.

"But trust a Jew to put himself forward as if he were something peculiar! If it weren't for the Jews, there wouldn't be any anti-Semitism."

"Who?" asks Ronnie.

1941

BERNARD MALAMUD (1914-   )

"I write about Jews," Bernard Malamud has remarked, "because I know them. But more important I write about them because the Jews are absolutely the very stuff of drama." The dramatic "stuff" of Malamud's fiction contains the elements traditionally identified with Jewish literature: suffering and laughter, sentiment, morality, and righteousness. These elements, expressed by an author who is ordinarily sympathetic toward people and couched in a highly idiomatic language, characterize Malamud's work and suggest the extent to which he is self-conscious about Jewish-American life. More than any prose artist of the post-war period, Malamud has concerned himself with the Jew in America.

Bernard Malamud was born in Brooklyn, New York, in 1914. He received his B.A. from the City College of New York in 1936 and his M.A. from Columbia University in 1942. Malamud's first novel was The Natural *(1952), which used a background of baseball to satirize American life. His distinctive fusion of old-world Judaism in a modern Christian setting was expressed in* The Assistant *(1957), which won the Rosenthal Award;* The Magic Barrel *(1958), a collection of stories which had appeared in the fifties and which won the National Book Award; A New Life (1961); Idiot's First (1963);* The Fixer *(1967); Pictures of Fidelman (1969); and* The Tenants *(1971).*

Malamud's fiction, as Philip Rahv has noted, differs from that of other authors of Jewish extraction in that he fills his "Jewishness with a positive content. . . . 'Jewishness,' as he understands and above all feels it, is one of the principal sources of value in his work as it affects both his conception of experience in general and his conception of imaginative writing in particular." The elements of Malamud's novels and stories are traditional, even homespun; but his technique transfigures his subject matter and creates a tension that is uniquely his own. This tension rests upon the human suffering of his characters—always sympathetically portrayed—as it manifests itself in their comic qualities. Whereas so many Jewish-American authors are satiric, Malamud is always comic; he never laughs at his characters, though he may see them ironically and whimsically. His compassion for their vulnerability is the attitude which the reader carries away from a typical Malamud story like "The Magic Barrel."

The Magic Barrel

Not long ago there lived in uptown New York, in a small, almost meager room, though crowded with books, Leo Finkle, a rabbinical student in the Yeshivah University. Finkle, after six years of study, was to be ordained in June and had been advised by an acquaintance that he might find it easier to win himself a congregation if he were married. Since he had no present prospects of marriage, after two tormented days of turning it over in his mind, he called in Pinye Salzman, a marriage broker whose two-line advertisement he had read in the *Forward*.

The matchmaker appeared one night out of the dark fourth-floor hallway of the graystone rooming house where Finkle lived, grasping a black, strapped portfolio that had been worn thin with use. Salzman, who had been long in the business, was of slight but dignified build, wearing an old hat, and an overcoat too short and tight for him. He smelled frankly of fish, which he loved to eat, and although he was missing a few teeth, his presence was not displeasing, because of an amiable manner curiously contrasted with mournful eyes. His voice, his lips, his wisp of beard, his bony fingers were animated, but give him a moment of repose and his mild blue eyes revealed a depth of sadness, a characteristic that put Leo a little at ease although the situation, for him, was inherently tense.

He at once informed Salzman why he had asked him to come, explaining that his home was in Cleveland, and that but for his parents, who had married comparatively late in life, he was alone in the world. He had for six years devoted himself almost entirely to his studies, as a result of which, understandably, he had found himself without time for a social life and the company of young women. Therefore·he thought it the better part of trial and error—of embarrassing fumbling—to call in an experienced person to advise him on these matters. He remarked in passing that the function of the marriage broker was ancient and honorable, highly approved in the Jewish community, because it made practical the necessary without hindering joy. Moreover, his own parents had been brought together by a matchmaker. They had made, if not a financially profitable marriage—since neither had possessed any worldly goods to speak of—at least a successful one in the sense of their everlasting devotion to each other. Salzman listened in embarrassed surprise, sensing a sort of apology. Later, however, he experienced a glow of pride in his work, an emotion that had left him years ago, and he heartily approved of Finkle.

The two went to their business. Leo had led Salzman to the only clear place in the room, a table near a window that overlooked the lamp-lit city. He seated himself at the matchmaker's side but facing him, attempting by an act of will to suppress the unpleasant tickle in his throat. Salzman eagerly unstrapped his portfolio and removed a loose rubber band from a thin packet of much-handled cards. As he flipped through them, a gesture and sound that physically hurt Leo, the student pretended not to see and gazed steadfastly out the window. Although it was still February, winter was on its last legs, signs of which he had for the first time in years begun to notice. He now observed the round white moon, moving high in the sky through a cloud menagerie, and watched with half-open mouth as it penetrated a huge hen, and dropped out of her like an egg laying itself. Salzman, though pretending through eye-glasses he had just slipped on, to be engaged in scanning the writing on the cards, stole occasional glances at the young man's distinguished face, noting with pleasure the long, severe scholar's nose, brown eyes heavy with learning, sensitive yet ascetic lips, and a certain, almost hollow quality of the dark cheeks. He gazed around at shelves upon shelves of books and let out a soft, contented sigh.

When Leo's eyes fell upon the cards, he counted six spread out in Salzman's hand.

"So few?" he asked in disappointment.

"You wouldn't believe me how much cards I got in my office," Salzman replied. "The drawers are already filled to the top, so I keep them now in a barrel, but is every girl good for a new rabbi?"

Leo blushed at this, regretting all he had revealed of himself in a curriculum vitae he had sent to Salzman. He had thought it best to acquaint him with his strict standards and specifications, but in having done so, felt he had told the marriage broker more than was absolutely necessary.

He hesitantly inquired, "Do you keep photographs of your clients on file?"

"First comes family, amount of dowry, also what kind promises," Salzman replied, unbuttoning his tight coat and settling himself in the chair. "After come pictures, rabbi."

"Call me Mr. Finkle. I'm not yet a rabbi."

Salzman said he would, but instead called him doctor, which he changed to rabbi when Leo was not listening too attentively.

Salzman adjusted his horn-rimmed spectacles, gently cleared his throat and read in an eager voice the contents of the top card:

"Sophie P. Twenty four years. Widow one year. No children. Educated high school and two years college. Father promises eight thousand dollars. Has wonderful wholesale business. Also real estate. On the mother's side comes teachers, also one actor. Well known on Second Avenue."

Leo gazed up in surprise. "Did you say a widow?"

"A widow don't mean spoiled, rabbi. She lived with her husband maybe four months. He was a sick boy she made a mistake to marry him."

"Marrying a widow has never entered my mind."

"This is because you have no experience. A widow, especially if she is young and healthy like this girl, is a wonderful person to marry. She will be thankful to you the rest of her life. Believe me, if I was looking now for a bride, I would marry a widow."

Leo reflected, then shook his head.

Salzman hunched his shoulders in an almost imperceptible gesture of disappointment. He placed the card down on the wooden table and began to read another:

"Lily H. High school teacher. Regular. Not a substitute. Has savings and new Dodge car. Lived in Paris one year. Father is successful dentist thirty-five years. Interested in professional man. Well Americanized family. Wonderful opportunity."

"I knew her personally," said Salzman. "I wish you could see this girl. She is a doll. Also very intelligent. All day you could talk to her about books and theyater and what not. She also knows current events."

"I don't believe you mentioned her age?"

"Her age?" Salzman said, raising his brows. "Her age is thirty-two years."

Leo said after a while, "I'm afraid that seems a little too old."

Salzman let out a laugh. "So how old are you, rabbi?"

"Twenty-seven."

"So what is the difference, tell me, between twenty-seven and thirty-two? My own wife is seven years older than me. So what did I suffer?—Nothing. If Rothschild's a daughter wants to marry you, would you say on account her age, no?"

"Yes," Leo said dryly.

Salzman shook off the no in the yes. "Five years don't mean a thing. I give you my word that when you will live with her for one week you will forget her age. What does it mean five years—that she lived more and knows more than somebody who is younger? On this girl, God bless her, years are not wasted. Each one that it comes makes better the bargain."

"What subject does she teach in high school?"

"Languages. If you heard the way she speaks French, you will think it is music. I am in the business twenty-five years, and I recommend her with my whole heart. Believe me, I know what I'm talking, rabbi."

"What's on the next card?" Leo said abruptly.

Salzman reluctantly turned up the third card:

"Ruth K. Nineteen years. Honor student. Father offers thirteen thousand cash to the right bridegroom. He is a medical doctor. Stomach specialist with marvelous practice. Brother in law owns own garment business. Particular people."

Salzman looked as if he had read his trump card.

"Did you say nineteen?" Leo asked with interest.

"On the dot."

"Is she attractive?" He blushed. "Pretty?"

Salzman kissed his finger tips. "A little doll. On this I give you my word. Let me call the father tonight and you will see what means pretty."

But Leo was troubled. "You're sure she's that young?"

"This I am positive. The father will show you the birth certificate."

"Are you positive there isn't something wrong with her?" Leo insisted.

"Who says there is wrong?"

"I don't understand why an American girl her age should go to a marriage broker."

A smile spread over Salzman's face.

"So for the same reason you went, she comes."

Leo flushed. "I am pressed for time."

Salzman, realizing he had been tactless, quickly explained. "The father came, not her. He wants she should have the best, so he looks around himself. When we will locate the right boy he will introduce him and encourage. This makes a better marriage than if a young girl without experience takes for herself. I don't have to tell you this."

"But don't you think this young girl believes in love?" Leo spoke uneasily.

Salzman was about to guffaw but caught himself and said soberly, "Love comes with the right person, not before."

Leo parted dry lips but did not speak. Noticing that Salzman had snatched a glance at the next card, he cleverly asked, "How is her health?"

"Perfect," Salzman said, breathing with difficulty. "Of course, she is a little lame on her right foot from an auto accident that it happened to her when she was twelve years, but nobody notices on account she is so brilliant and also beautiful."

Leo got up heavily and went to the window. He felt curiously bitter and upbraided himself for having called in the marriage broker. Finally, he shook his head.

"Why not?" Salzman persisted, the pitch of his voice rising.

"Because I detest stomach specialists."

"So what do you care what is his business? After you marry her do you need him? Who says he must come every Friday night in your house?"

Ashamed of the way the talk was going, Leo dismissed Salzman, who went home with heavy, melancholy eyes.

Though he had felt only relief at the marriage broker's departure, Leo was in low spirits the next day. He explained it as arising from Salzman's failure to produce a suitable bride for him. He did not care for his type of clientele. But when Leo found himself hesitating whether to seek out another matchmaker, one more polished than Pinye, he wondered if it could be—his protestations to the contrary, and although he honored his father and mother—that he did not, in essence, care for the matchmaking institution? This thought he quickly put out of mind yet found himself still upset. All day he ran around in the woods—missed an important appointment, forgot to give out his laundry, walked out of a Broadway cafeteria without paying and had to run back with the ticket in his hand; had even not recognized his landlady in the street when she passed with a friend and courteously called out, "A good evening to you, Doctor Finkle." By nightfall, however, he had regained sufficient calm to sink his nose into a book and there found peace from his thoughts.

Almost at once there came a knock on the door. Before Leo could say enter, Salzman, commercial cupid, was standing in the room. His face was gray and meager, his expression hungry, and he looked as if he would expire on his feet. Yet the marriage broker managed, by some trick of the muscles, to display a broad smile.

"So good evening. I am invited?"

Leo nodded, disturbed to see him again, yet unwilling to ask the man to leave.

Beaming still, Salzman laid his portfolio on the table. "Rabbi, I got for you tonight good news."

"I've asked you not to call me rabbi. I'm still a student."

"Your worries are finished. I have for you a first-class bride."

"Leave me in peace concerning this subject." Leo pretended lack of interest.

"The world will dance at your wedding."

"Please, Mr. Salzman, no more."

"But first must come back my strength," Salzman said weakly. He fumbled with the portfolio straps and took out of the leather case an oily paper bag, from which he extracted a hard, seeded roll and a small, smoked white fish. With a quick motion of his hand he stripped the fish out of its skin and began ravenously to chew. "All day in a rush," he muttered.

Leo watched him eat.

"A sliced tomato you have maybe?" Salzman hesitantly inquired.

"No."

The marriage broker shut his eyes and ate. When he had finished he carefully cleaned up the crumbs and rolled up the remains of the fish, in the paper bag. His spectacled eyes roamed the room until he discovered, amid some piles of books, a one-burner gas stove. Lifting his hat he humbly asked, "A glass tea you got, rabbi?"

Conscience-stricken, Leo rose and brewed the tea. He served it with a chunk of lemon and two cubes of lump sugar, delighting Salzman.

After he had drunk his tea, Salzman's strength and good spirits were restored.

"So tell me, rabbi," he said amiably, "you considered some more the three clients I mentioned yesterday?"

"There was no need to consider."

"Why not?"

"None of them suits me."

"What then suits you?"

Leo let it pass because he could give only a confused answer.

Without waiting for a reply, Salzman asked, "You remember this girl I talked to you—the high school teacher?"

"Age thirty-two?"

But, surprisingly, Salzman's face lit in a smile. "Age twenty-nine."

Leo shot him a look. "Reduced from thirty-two?"

"A mistake," Salzman avowed. "I talked today with the dentist. He took me to his safety deposit box and showed me the birth certificate. She was twenty-nine years last August. They made her a party in the mountains where she went for her vacation. When her father spoke to me the first time I forgot to write the age and I told you thirty-two, but now I remember this was a different client, a widow."

"The same one you told me about? I thought she was twenty-four?"

"A different. Am I responsible that the world is filled with widows?"

"No, but I'm not interested in them, nor for that matter, in school teachers."

Salzman pulled his clasped hands to his breast. Looking at the ceiling he devoutly exclaimed, "Yiddishe kinder, what can I say to somebody that he is not interested in high school teachers? So what then you are interested?"

Leo flushed but controlled himself.

"In what else will you be interested," Salzman went on, "if you not interested in this fine girl that she speaks four languages and has personally in the bank ten thousand dollars? Also her father guarantees further twelve thousand. Also she has a new car, wonderful clothes, talks on all subjects, and she will give you a first-class home and children. How near do we come in our life to paradise?"

"If she's so wonderful, why wasn't she married ten years ago?"

"Why?" said Salzman with a heavy laugh. "—Why? Because she is *partikiler*. This is why. She wants the *best*."

Leo was silent, amused at how he had entangled himself. But Salzman had aroused his interest in Lily H., and he began seriously to consider calling on her. When the marriage broker observed how intently Leo's mind was at work on the facts he had supplied, he felt certain they would soon come to an agreement.

Late Saturday afternoon, conscious of Salzman, Leo Finkle walked with Lily Hirschorn along Riverside Drive. He walked briskly and erectly, wearing with distinction the black fedora he had that morning taken with trepidation out of the dusty hat box on his closet shelf, and the heavy black Saturday coat he had thoroughly whisked clean. Leo also owned a walking stick, a present from a distant relative, but quickly put temptation aside and did not use it. Lily, petite and not unpretty, had on something signifying the approach of spring. She was au courant, animatedly, with all sorts of subjects, and he weighed her words and found her surprisingly sound—score another for Salzman, whom he uneasily sensed to be somewhere around, hiding perhaps high in a tree along the street, flashing the lady signals with a pocket mirror; or perhaps a cloven-hoofed Pan, piping nuptial ditties as he danced his invisible way before them, strewing wild buds on the walk and purple grapes in their path, symbolizing fruit of a union, though there was of course still none.

Lily startled Leo by remarking, "I was thinking of Mr. Salzman, a curious figure, wouldn't you say?"

Not certain what to answer, he nodded.

She bravely went on, blushing, "I for one am grateful for his introducing us. Aren't you?"

He courteously replied, "I am."

"I mean," she said with a little laugh—and it was all in good taste, or at least gave the effect of being not in bad—"do you mind that we came together so?"

He was not displeased with her honesty, recognizing that she meant to set the relationship aright, and understanding that it took a certain amount of experience in life, and courage, to want to do it quite that way. One had to have some sort of past to make that kind of beginning.

He said that he did not mind. Salzman's function was traditional and honorable—valuable for what it might achieve, which, he pointed out, was frequently nothing.

Lily agreed with a sigh. They walked on for a while and she said after a long silence, again with a nervous laugh, "Would you mind if I asked you something a little bit personal? Frankly, I find the subject fascinating." Although Leo shrugged, she went on half embarrassedly, "How was it that you came to your calling? I mean was it a sudden passionate inspiration?"

Leo, after a time, slowly replied, "I was always interested in the Law."

"You saw revealed in it the presence of the Highest?"

He nodded and changed the subject. "I understand that you spent a little time in Paris, Miss Hirschorn?"

"Oh, did Mr. Salzman tell you, Rabbi Finkle?" Leo winced but she went on, "It was ages ago and almost forgotten. I remember I had to return for my sister's wedding."

And Lily would not be put off. "When," she asked in a trembly voice, "did you become enamored of God?"

He stared at her. Then it came to him that she was talking not about Leo Finkle, but of a total stranger, some mystical figure, perhaps even passionate prophet that Salzman had dreamed up for her—no relation to the living or dead. Leo trembled with rage and weakness. The trickster had obviously sold her a bill of goods, just as he had him, who'd expected to become acquainted with a young lady of twenty-nine, only to behold, the moment he laid eyes upon her strained and anxious face, a woman past thirty-five and aging rapidly. Only his self control had kept him this long in her presence.

"I am not," he said gravely, "a talented religious person," and in seeking words to go on, found himself possessed by shame and fear. "I think," he said in a strained manner, "that I came to God not because I loved Him, but because I did not."

This confession he spoke harshly because its unexpectedness shook him.

Lily wilted. Leo saw a profusion of loaves of bread go flying like ducks high over his head, not unlike the winged loaves by which he had counted himself to sleep last night. Mercifully, then, it snowed, which he would not put past Salzman's machinations.

He was infuriated with the marriage broker and swore he would throw him out of the room the minute he reappeared. But Salzman did not come that night, and when Leo's anger had subsided, an unaccountable despair grew in its place. At first he thought this was caused by his disappointment in Lily, but before long it became evident that he had involved himself with Salzman without a true knowledge of his own intent. He gradually realized—with an emptiness that seized him with six hands—that he had called in the broker to find him a bride because he was incapable of doing it himself. This terrifying insight he had derived as a result of his meeting and conversation with Lily Hirschorn. Her probing questions had somehow irritated him into revealing—to himself more than her—the true nature of his relationship to God, and from that it had come upon him with shocking force, that apart from his parents, he had never loved anyone. Or perhaps it went the other way, that he did not love God so well as he might, because he had not loved man. It seemed to Leo that his whole life stood starkly revealed and he saw himself for the first time as he truly was—unloved and loveless. This bitter but somehow not fully unexpected revelation brought him to a point of panic, controlled only by extraordinary effort. He covered his face with his hands and cried.

The week that followed was the worst of his life. He did not eat and lost weight. His beard darkened and grew ragged. He stopped attending seminars and almost never opened a book. He seriously considered leaving the Yeshivah, although he was deeply troubled at the thought of the loss of all his years of study—saw them like pages torn from a book, strewn over the city—and at the devastating effect of this decision upon his parents. But he had lived without knowledge of himself, and never in the Five Books and all the Commentaries—mea culpa—had the truth been revealed to him. He did not know where to turn, and in all this desolating loneliness there was no *to whom*, although he often thought of Lily but not once could bring himself to go downstairs and make the call. He became touchy and irritable, especially with his landlady, who asked him all manner of personal questions; on the other hand, sensing his own disagreeableness, he waylaid her on the stairs and apologized abjectly, until mortified, she ran from him. Out of this, however, he drew the consolation that he was a Jew and that a Jew suffered. But gradually, as the long and terrible week drew to a close, he regained his composure and some idea of purpose in life: to go on as planned. Although he was imperfect, the ideal was not. As for his quest of a bride, the thought of continuing afflicted him with anxiety and heartburn, yet perhaps with this new knowledge of himself he would be more successful than in the past. Perhaps love would now come to him and a bride to that love. And for this sanctified seeking who needed a Salzman?

The marriage broker, a skeleton with haunted eyes, returned that very night. He looked, withal, the picture of frustrated expectancy—as if he had steadfastly waited the week at Miss Lily Hirschorn's side for a telephone call that never came.

Casually coughing, Salzman came immediately to the point: "So how did you like her?"

Leo's anger rose and he could not refrain from chiding the matchmaker: "Why did you lie to me, Salzman?"

Salzman's pale face went dead white, the world had snowed on him.

"Did you not state that she was twenty-nine?" Leo insisted.

"I give you my word—"

"She was thirty-five, if a day. *At least* thirty-five."

"Of this don't be too sure. Her father told me—"

"Never mind. The worst of it was that you lied to her."

"How did I lie to her, tell me?"

"You told her things about me that weren't true. You made me out to be more, consequently less than I am. She had in mind a totally different person, a sort of semi-mystical Wonder Rabbi."

"All I said, you was a religious man."

"I can imagine."

Salzman sighed. "This is my weakness that I have," he confessed. "My wife says to me I shouldn't be a salesman, but when I have two fine people that they would be wonderful to be married, I am so happy that I talk too much." He smiled wanly. "This is why Salzman is a poor man."

Leo's anger left him. "Well, Salzman, I'm afraid that's all."

The marriage broker fastened hungry eyes on him.

"You don't want any more a bride?"

"I do," said Leo, "but I have decided to seek her in a different way. I am no longer interested in an arranged marriage. To be frank, I now admit the necessity of premarital love. That is, I want to be in love with the one I marry."

"Love?" said Salzman, astounded. After a moment he remarked, "For us, our love is our life, not for the ladies. In the ghetto they—"

"I know, I know," said Leo. "I've thought of it often. Love, I have said to myself, should be a by-product of living and worship rather than its own end. Yet for myself I find it necessary to establish the level of my need and fulfill it."

Salzman shrugged but answered, "Listen, rabbi, if you want love, this I can find you also. I have such beautiful clients that you will love them the minute your eyes will see them."

Leo smiled unhappily. "I'm afraid you don't understand."

But Salzman hastily unstrapped his portfolio and withdrew a manila packet from it.

"Pictures," he said, quickly laying the envelope on the table.

Leo called after him to take the pictures away, but as if on the wings of the wind, Salzman had disappeared.

March came. Leo had returned to his regular routine. Although he felt not quite himself yet—lacked energy—he was making plans for a more active social life. Of course it would cost something, but he was an expert in cutting corners; and when there were no corners left he would make circles rounder. All the while Salzman's pictures had lain on the table, gathering dust. Occasionally as Leo sat studying, or enjoying a cup of tea, his eyes fell on the manila envelope, but he never opened it.

The days went by and no social life to speak of developed with a member of the opposite sex—it was difficult, given the circumstances of his situation. One morning Leo toiled up the stairs to his room and stared out the window at the city. Although the day was bright his view of it was dark. For some time he watched the people in the street below hurrying along and then turned with a heavy heart to his little room. On the table was the packet. With a sudden relentless gesture he tore it open. For a half-hour he stood by the table in a state of excitement, examining the photographs of the ladies Salzman had included. Finally, with a deep sigh he put them down. There were six, of varying degrees of attractiveness, but look at them long enough and they all became Lily Hirschorn: all past their prime, all starved behind bright smiles, not a true personality in the lot. Life, despite their frantic yoohooings, had passed them by; they were pictures in a brief case that stank of fish. After a while, however, as Leo attempted to return the photographs into the envelope, he found in it another, a snapshot of the type taken by a machine for a quarter. He gazed at it a moment and let out a cry.

Her face deeply moved him. Why, he could at first not say. It gave him the impression of youth—spring flowers, yet age—a sense of having been used to the bone, wasted; this came from the eyes, which were hauntingly familiar, yet absolutely strange. He had a vivid impression that he had met her before, but try as he might he could not place her although he could almost recall her name, as if he had read it in her own handwriting. No, this couldn't be; he would have remembered her. It was not, he affirmed, that she had an extraordinary beauty—no, though her face was attractive enough; it was that *something* about her moved him. Feature for feature, even some of the ladies of the photographs could do better; but she leaped forth to his heart—had *lived,* or wanted to—more than just wanted, perhaps regretted how she had lived—had somehow deeply suffered: it could be seen in the depths of those reluctant eyes, and from the way the light enclosed and shone from her, and within her, opening realms of possibilities: this was her own. Her he desired. His head ached and eyes narrowed with the intensity of his gazing, then as if an obscure fog had blown up in the mind, he experienced fear of her and was aware that he had received an impression, somehow, of evil. He shuddered, saying softly, it is thus with us all. Leo brewed some tea in a small pot and sat sipping it without sugar, to calm himself. But before he had finished drinking, again with excitement he examined the face and found it good: good for Leo Finkle. Only such a one could understand him and help him seek whatever he was seeking. She might, perhaps, love him. How she had happened to be among the discards in Salzman's barrel he could never guess, but he knew he must urgently go find her.

Leo rushed downstairs, grabbed up the Bronx telephone book, and searched for Salzman's home address. He was not listed, nor was his office. Neither was he in the Manhattan book. But Leo remembered having written down the address on a slip of paper after he had read Salzman's advertisement in the "personals" column of the *Forward.* He ran up to his room and tore through his papers, without luck. It was exasperating. Just when he needed the matchmaker he was nowhere to be found. Fortunately Leo remembered to look in his wallet. There on a card he found his name written and a Bronx address. No phone number was listed, the reason—Leo now recalled—he had originally communicated with Salzman by letter. He got on his coat, put a hat on over his skull cap and hurried to the subway station. All the way to the far end of the Bronx he sat on the edge of his seat. He was more than once tempted to take out the picture and see if the girl's face was as he remembered it, but he refrained, allowing the snapshot to remain in his inside coat pocket, content to have her so close. When the train pulled into the station he was waiting at the door and bolted out. He quickly located the street Salzman had advertised.

The building he sought was less than a block from the subway, but it was not an office building, nor even a loft, nor a store in which one could rent office space. It was a very old tenement house. Leo found Salzman's name in pencil on a soiled tag under the bell and climbed three dark flights to his apartment. When he knocked, the door was opened by a thin, asthmatic, gray-haired woman, in felt slippers.

"Yes?" she said, expecting nothing. She listened without listening. He could have sworn he had seen her, too, before but knew it was an illusion.

"Salzman—does he live here? Pinye Salzman," he said, "the matchmaker?"

She stared at him a long minute. "Of course."

He felt embarrassed. "Is he in?"

"No." Her mouth, though left open, offered nothing more.

"The matter is urgent. Can you tell me where his office is?"

"In the air." She pointed upward.

"You mean he has no office?" Leo asked.

"In his socks."

He peered into the apartment. It was sunless and dingy, one large room divided by a half-open curtain, beyond which he could see a sagging metal bed. The near side of a room was crowded with rickety chairs, old bureaus, a three-legged table, racks of cooking utensils, and all the apparatus of a kitchen. But there was no sign of Salzman or his magic barrel, probably also a figment of the imagination. An odor of frying fish made Leo weak to the knees.

"Where is he?" he insisted. "I've got to see your husband."

At length she answered, "So who knows where he is? Every time he thinks a new thought he runs to a different place. Go home, he will find you."

"Tell him Leo Finkle."

She gave no sign she had heard.

He walked downstairs, depressed.

But Saltzman, breathless, stood waiting at his door.

Leo was astounded and overjoyed. "How did you get here before me?"

"I rushed."

"Come inside."

They entered. Leo fixed tea, and a sardine sandwich for Salzman. As they were drinking he reached behind him for the packet of pictures and handed them to the marriage broker.

Salzman put down his glass and said expectantly, "You found somebody you like?"

"Not among these."

The marriage broker turned away.

"Here is the one I want." Leo held forth the snapshot.

Salzman slipped on his glasses and took the picture into his trembling hand. He turned ghastly and let out a groan.

"What's the matter?" cried Leo.

"Excuse me. Was an accident this picture. She isn't for you."

Salzman frantically shoved the manila packet into his portfolio. He thrust the snapshot into his pocket and fled down the stairs.

Leo, after momentary paralysis, gave chase and cornered the marriage broker in the vestibule. The landlady made hysterical outcries but neither of them listened.

"Give me back the picture, Salzman."

"No." The pain in his eyes was terrible.

"Tell me who she is then."

"This I can't tell you. Excuse me."

He made to depart, but Leo, forgetting himself, seized the matchmaker by his tight coat and shook him frenziedly.

"Please," sighed Salzman. *"Please."*

Leo ashamedly let him go. "Tell me who she is," he begged. "It's very important for me to know."

"She is not for you. She is a wild one—wild, without shame. This is not a bride for a rabbi."

"What do you mean wild?"

"Like an animal. Like a dog. For her to be poor was a sin. This is why to me she is dead now."

"In God's name, what do you mean?"

"Her I can't introduce to you," Salzman cried.

"Why are you so excited?"

"Why, he asks," Salzman said, bursting into tears. "This is my baby, my Stella, she should burn in hell."

Leo hurried up to bed and hid under the covers. Under the covers he thought his life through. Although he soon fell asleep he could not sleep her out of his mind. He woke, beating his breast. Though he prayed to be rid of her, his prayers went unanswered. Through days of torment he endlessly struggled not to love her; fearing success, he escaped it. He then concluded to convert her to goodness, himself to God. The idea alternately nauseated and exalted him.

He perhaps did not know that he had come to a final decision until he encountered Salzman in a Broadway cafeteria. He was sitting alone at a rear table, sucking the bony remains of a fish. The marriage broker appeared haggard, and transparent to the point of vanishing.

Salzman looked up at first without recognizing him. Leo had grown a pointed beard and his eyes were weighted with wisdom.

"Salzman," he said, "love has at last come to my heart."

"Who can love from a picture?" mocked the marriage broker.

"It is not impossible."

"If you can love her, then you can love anybody. Let me show you some new clients that they just sent me their photographs. One is a little doll."

"Just her I want," Leo murmured.

"Don't be a fool, doctor. Don't bother with her."

"Put me in touch with her, Salzman," Leo said humbly. "Perhaps I can be of service."

Salzman had stopped eating and Leo understood with emotion that it was now arranged.

Leaving the cafeteria, he was, however, afflicted by a tormenting suspicion that Salzman had planned it all to happen this way.

Leo was informed by letter that she would meet him on a certain corner, and she was there one spring night, waiting under a street lamp. He appeared, carrying a small bouquet of violets and rosebuds. Stella stood by the lamp post, smoking. She wore white with red shoes, which fitted his expectations, although in a troubled moment he had imagined the dress red, and only the shoes white. She waited uneasily and shyly. From afar he saw that her eyes—clearly her father's—were filled with desperate innocence. He pictured, in her, his own redemption. Violins and lit candles revolved in the sky. Leo ran forward with flowers outthrust.

Around the corner, Salzman, leaning against a wall, chanted prayers for the dead.

SAUL BELLOW (1915-   )

At the thematic center of Jewish-American writing is the quality of suffering; at the heart of Saul Bellow's work is this same characteristic, made a matter of self-conscious choice. Suffering leads Bellow's leading figures—one can scarcely call them heroes—to a comic affirmation, which is a form of dignity that triumphs over their torment. The quality of suffering and the verbal form it takes stem from Bellow's poverty-stricken Jewish childhood in Montreal and the Jewishness which he has made a part of his adult vision of the world.

Saul Bellow was born on July 10, 1915, in Lachine, Quebec, and grew up in a slum of Montreal. As a child he learned four languages— English, Hebrew, Yiddish, and French—and his training in the Old Testament was extensive. When he was nine years old, the family moved to Chicago. He studied at the University of Chicago and North-western University, where he was influenced by the noted anthropologist, Melville Jean Herskovitz. Bellow went to the graduate school at the University of Wisconsin but found that he was more interested in writing than in anthropology. "Every time I worked on my thesis," he has remarked, "it turned out to be a story." Toward the end of the war he published his first novel, Dangling Man (1944), and followed it with six others: The Victim (1947), The Adventures of Augie March (1953), Seize the Day (1956), Henderson the Rain King (1959), Herzog (1964), and Mister Sammler's Planet (1970). He has also written a play, The Last Analysis, which did not do well when it opened on Broadway in 1964 but which had a more successful run when it reappeared in an off-Broadway theater in 1971.

Although The Victim is a novel that deals directly with the theme of anti-Semitism and though other works by Bellow have strong elements of his Jewishness, no book so clearly captures his personal point of view and the sense of his own Jewish attitudes as Herzog. The following selection recreates Herzog's memory of his father when Herzog himself was a boy.

HERZOG

As for my late unlucky father, J. Herzog, he was not a big man, one of the small-boned Herzogs, finely made, round-headed, keen, nervous, handsome. In his frequent bursts of temper he slapped his sons swiftly with both hands. He did everything quickly, neatly, with skillful Eastern European flourishes: combing his hair, buttoning his shirt, stropping his bone-handled razors, sharpening pencils on the ball of his thumb, holding a loaf of bread to his breast and slicing toward himself, tying parcels with tight little knots, jotting like an artist in his account book. There each canceled page was covered with a carefully drawn X. The 1s and 7s carried bars and streamers. They were like pennants in the wind of failure. First Father Herzog failed in Petersburg, where he went through two dowries in one year. He had been importing onions from Egypt. Under Pobedonostsev the police caught up with him for illegal residence. He was convicted and sentenced. The account of the trial was published in a Russian journal printed on thick green paper. Father Herzog sometimes unfolded it and read aloud to the entire family, translating the proceedings against Ilyona Isakovitch Herzog. He never served his sentence. He got away. Because he was nervy, hasty, obstinate, rebellious. He came to Canada, where his sister Zipporah Yaffe was living.

In 1913 he bought a piece of land near Valleyfield, Quebec, and failed as a farmer. Then he came into town and failed as a baker; failed in the dry-goods business; failed as a jobber; failed as a sack manufacturer in the War, when no one else failed. He failed as a junk dealer. Then he became a marriage broker and failed—too short-tempered and blunt. And now he was failing as a bootlegger, on the run from the provincial Liquor Commission. Making a bit of a living.

In haste and defiantly, with a clear tense face, walking with mingled desperation and high style, a little awkwardly dropping his weight on one heel as he went, his coat, once lined with fox, turned dry and bald, the red hide cracking. This coat sweeping open as he walked, or marched his one-man Jewish march, he was saturated with the odor of the Caporals he smoked as he covered Montreal in his swing—Papineau, Mile-End, Verdun, Lachine, Point St. Charles. He looked for business opportunities—bankruptcies, job lots, mergers, fire sales, produce—to rescue him from illegality. He could calculate percentages mentally at high speed, but he lacked the cheating imagination of a successful businessman. And so he kept a little still in Mile-End, where goats fed in the empty lots. He traveled on the tramcar. He sold a bottle here and there and waited for his main chance. American rum-runners would buy the stuff from you at the border, any amount, spot cash, if you could get it there. Meanwhile he smoked cigarettes on the cold platforms of streetcars. The Revenue was trying to catch him. Spotters were after him. On the roads to the border were hijackers. On Napoleon Street he had five mouths to feed. Willie and Moses were sickly. Helen studied the piano. Shura was fat, greedy, disobedient, a plotting boy. The rent, back rent, notes due, doctors' bills to pay, and he had no English, no friends, no influence, no trade, no assets but his still—no help in all the world. His sister Zipporah in St. Anne was rich, very rich, which only made matters worse.

Grandfather Herzog was still alive, then. With the instinct of a Herzog for the grand thing, he took refuge in the Winter Palace in 1918 (the Bolsheviks allowed it for a while). The old man wrote long letters in Hebrew. He had lost his precious books in the upheaval. Study was impossible now. In the Winter Palace you had to walk up and down all day to find a *minyan*. Of course there was hunger, too. Later, he predicted that the Revolution would fail and tried to acquire Czarist currency, to become a millionaire under the restored Romanoffs. The Herzogs received packets of worthless rubles, and Willie and Moses played with great sums. You held the glorious bills to the light and you saw Peter the Great and Catherine in the watermarked rainbow paper. Grandfather Herzog was in his eighties but still strong. His mind was powerful and his Hebrew calligraphy elegant. The letters were read aloud in Montreal by Father Herzog—accounts of cold, lice, famine, epidemics, the dead. The old man wrote, "Shall I ever see the faces of my children? And who will bury me?" Father Herzog approached the next phrase two or three times, but could not find his full voice. Only a whisper came out. The tears were in his eyes and he suddenly put his hand over his mustached mouth and hurried from the room. Mother Herzog, large-eyed, sat with the children in the primitive kitchen which the sun never entered. It was like a cave with the ancient black stove, the iron sink, the green cupboards, the gas ring.

Mother Herzog had a way of meeting the present with a partly averted face. She encountered it on the left but sometimes seemed to avoid it on the right. On this withdrawn side she often had a dreaming look, melancholy, and seemed to be seeing the Old World—her father the famous *misnagid,* her tragic mother, her brothers living and dead, her sister, and her linens and servants in Petersburg, the dacha in Finland (all founded on Egyptian onions). Now she was cook, washerwoman, seamstress on Napoleon Street in the slum. Her hair turned gray, and she lost her teeth, her very fingernails wrinkled. Her hands smelled of the sink.

Herzog was thinking, however, how she found the strength to spoil her children. She certainly spoiled me. Once, at nightfall, she was pulling me on the sled, over crusty ice, the tiny glitter of snow, perhaps four o'clock of a short day in January. Near the grocery we met an old baba in a shawl who said, "Why are you pulling him, daughter!" Mama, dark under the eyes. Her slender cold face. She was breathing hard. She wore the torn seal coat and a red pointed wool cap and thin button boots. Clusters of dry fish hung in the shop, a rancid sugar smell, cheese, soap —a terrible dust of nutrition came from the open door. The bell on a coil of wire was bobbing, ringing. "Daughter, don't sacrifice your strength to children," said the shawled crone in the freezing dusk of the street. I wouldn't get off the sled. I pretended not to understand. One of life's hardest jobs, to make a quick understanding slow. I think I succeeded, thought Herzog.

Mama's brother Mikhail died of typhus in Moscow. I took the letter from the postman and brought it upstairs—the long latchstring ran through loops under the banister. It was washday. The copper boiler steamed the window. She was rinsing and wringing in a tub. When she read the news she gave a cry and fainted. Her lips turned white. Her arm lay in the water, sleeve and all. We two were alone in the house. I was terrified when she lay like that, legs spread, her long hair undone, lids brown, mouth bloodless, deathlike. But then she got up and went to lie down. She wept all day. But in the morning she cooked the oatmeal nevertheless. We were up early.

My ancient times. Remoter than Egypt. No dawn, the foggy winters.

In darkness, the bulb was lit. The stove was cold. Papa shook the grates, and raised an ashen dust. The grates grumbled and squealed. The puny shovel clinked underneath. The Caporals gave Papa a bad cough. The chimneys in their helmets sucked in the wind. Then the milkman came in his sleigh. The snow was spoiled and rotten with manure and litter, dead rats, dogs. The milkman in his sheepskin gave the bell a twist. It was brass, like the winding-key of a clock. Helen pulled the latch and went down with a pitcher for the milk. And then Ravitch, hung-over, came from his room, in his heavy sweater, suspenders over the wool to keep it tighter to the body, the bowler on his head, red in the face, his look guilty. He waited to be asked to sit.

The morning light could not free itself from gloom and frost. Up and down the street, the brick-recessed windows were dark, filled with darkness, and schoolgirls by twos in their black skirts marched toward the convent. And wagons, sledges, drays, the horses shuddering, the air drowned in leaden green, the dungstained ice, trails of ashes. Moses and his brothers put on their caps and prayed together,

"*Ma tovu ohaleha Yaakov. . . .*"
"How goodly are thy tents, O Israel."

Napoleon Street, rotten, toylike, crazy and filthy, riddled, flogged with harsh weather—the bootlegger's boys reciting ancient prayers. To this Moses' heart was attached with great power. Here was a wider range of human feelings than he had ever again been able to find. The children of the race, by a never-failing miracle, opened their eyes on one strange world after another, age after age, and uttered the same prayer in each, eagerly loving what they found. What was wrong with Napoleon Street? thought Herzog. All he ever wanted was there. His mother did the wash, and mourned. His father was desperate and frightened, but obstinately fighting. His brother Shura with staring disingenuous eyes was plotting to master the world, to become a millionaire. His brother Willie struggled with asthmatic fits. Trying to breathe he gripped the table and rose on his toes like a cock about to crow. His sister Helen had long white gloves which she washed in thick suds. She wore them to her lessons at the conservatory, carrying a leather music roll. Her diploma hung in a frame, *Mlle. Hélène Herzog . . . avec distinction.* His soft prim sister who played the piano.

On a summer night she sat playing and the clear notes went through the window into the street. The square-shouldered piano had a velveteen runner, mossy green as though the lid of the piano were a slab of stone.

From the runner hung a ball fringe, like hickory nuts. Moses stood behind Helen, staring at the swirling pages of Haydn and Mozart, wanting to whine like a dog. Oh, the music! thought Herzog. He fought the insidious blight of nostalgia in New York—softening, heart-rotting emotions, black spots, sweet for one moment but leaving a dangerous acid residue. Helen played. She wore a middy and a pleated skirt, and her pointed shoes cramped down on the pedals, a proper, vain girl. She frowned while she played—her father's crease appeared between her eyes. Frowning as though she performed a dangerous action. The music rang into the street.

Aunt Zipporah was critical of this music business. Helen was not a genuine musician. She played to move the family. Perhaps to attract a husband. What Aunt Zipporah opposed was Mama's ambition for her children, because she wanted them to be lawyers, gentlemen, rabbis, or performers. All branches of the family had the caste madness of *yichus*. No life so barren and subordinate that it didn't have imaginary dignities, honors to come, freedom to advance.

Zipporah wanted to hold Mama back, Moses concluded, and she blamed Papa's failure in America on these white gloves and piano lessons. Zipporah had a strong character. She was witty, grudging, at war with everyone. Her face was flushed and thin, her nose shapely but narrow and grim. She had a critical, damaging, nasal voice. Her hips were large and she walked with wide heavy steps. A braid of thick glossy hair hung down her back.

Now Uncle Yaffe, Zipporah's husband, was quiet-spoken, humorously reserved. He was a small man but strong. His shoulders were wide, and he wore a black beard like King George V. It grew tight and curly on his brown face. The bridge of his nose was dented. His teeth were broad, and one was capped with gold. Moses had smelled the tart flavor of his uncle's breath as they played checkers. Over the board, Uncle Yaffe's broad head with short black twisted hair, a bit bald, was slightly unsteady. He had a mild nervous tremor. Uncle Yaffe, from the past, seemed to find out his nephew at this very instant of time and to look at him with the brown eyes of an intelligent, feeling, satirical animal. His glance glittered shrewdly, and he smiled with twisted satisfaction at the errors of young Moses. Affectionately giving me the business.

In Yaffe's junkyard in St. Anne the ragged cliffs of scrap metal bled rust into the puddles. There was sometimes a line of scavengers at the gate. Kids, greenhorns, old Irishwomen, or Ukrainians and redmen from the Caughnawaga reservation, came with pushcarts and little wagons, bringing bottles, rags, old plumbing or electrical fixtures, hardware, paper, tires, bones to sell. The old man, in his brown cardigan, stooped, and his strong trembling hands, sorted out what he had bought. Without straightening his back he could pitch pieces of scrap where they belonged—iron here, zinc there, copper left, lead right, and Babbitt metal by the shed. He and his sons made money during the War. Aunt Zipporah bought real estate. She collected rents. Moses knew that she carried a bankroll in her bosom. He had seen it.

"Well, *you* lost nothing by coming to America," Papa said to her.

Her first reply was to stare sharply and warningly at him. Then she said, "It's no secret how we started out. By labor. Yaffe took a pick and shovel on the CPR until we saved up a little capital. But you! No, you were born in a silk shirt." With a glance at Mama, she went on, "You got used to putting on style, in Petersburg, with servants and coachmen. I can still see you getting off the train from Halifax, all dressed up among the greeners. *Gott meiner!* Ostrich feathers, taffeta skirts! *Greenhorns mit strauss federn!* Now forget the feathers, the gloves. Now—"

"That seems like a thousand years ago," said Mama. "I have forgotten all about servants. I am the servant. *Die dienst bin ich.*"

"Everyone must work. Not suffer your whole life long from a fall. Why must your children go to the conservatory, the Baron de Hirsch school, and all those special frills? Let them go to work, like mine."

"She doesn't want the children to be common," said Papa.

"My sons are not common. They know a page of *Gemara,* too. And don't forget we come from the greatest Hasidic rabbis. Reb Zusya! Herschele Dubrovner! Just remember."

"No one is saying . . ." said Mama.

To haunt the past like this—to love the dead! Moses warned himself not to yield so greatly to this temptation, this peculiar weakness of his character. He was a depressive. Depressives cannot surrender childhood —not even the pains of childhood. He understood the hygiene of the matter. But somehow his heart had come open at this chapter of his life and he didn't have the strength to shut it. So it was again a winter day in St. Anne, in 1923—Aunt Zipporah's kitchen. Zipporah wore a crimson crepe de Chine wrapper. Discernible underneath were voluminous yellow bloomers and a man's undershirt. She sat beside the kitchen oven, her face flushing. Her nasal voice often rose to a barbed little cry of irony, of false dismay, of terrible humor.

Then she remembered that Mama's brother Mikhail was dead, and she said, "Well—about your brother—what was the matter?"

"We don't know," said Papa. "Who can imagine what a black year they're making back home." (It was always *in der heim,* Herzog reminded himself.) "A mob broke into his house. Cut open everything, looking for *valuta*. Afterwards, he caught typhus, or God knows what."

Mama's hand was over her eyes, as though she were shading them. She said nothing.

"I remember what a fine man he was," said Uncle Yaffe. "May he have a *lichtigen Gan-Eden*."

Aunt Zipporah, who believed in the power of curses, said, "Curse those Bolsheviks. They wanted to make the world *horav*. May their hands and feet wither. But where are Mikhail's wife and children?"

"No one knows. The letter came from a cousin—Shperling, who saw Mikhail in the hospital. He barely recognized him."

Zipporah said a few more pious things, and then in a more normal manner she added, "Well, he was an active fellow. Had plenty of money, in his time. Who knows what a fortune he brought back from South Africa."

"He shared with us," said Mama. "My brother had an open hand."

"It came easily," said Zipporah. "It's not as if he had to work hard for it."

"How do you know?" said Father Herzog. "Don't let your tongue run away with you, my sister."

But Zipporah couldn't be restrained now. "He made money out of those miserable black Kaffirs! Who knows how! So you had a dacha in Shevalovo. Yaffe was away in the service, in the Kavkaz. I had a sick child to nurse. And you, Yonah, were running around Petersburg spending two dowries. Yes! You lost the first ten thousand rubles in a month. He gave you another ten. I can't say what else he was doing, with Tartars, gypsies, whores, eating horsemeat, and God only knows what abominations went on."

"What kind of malice is in you?" said Father Herzog, angry.

"I have nothing against Mikhail. He never harmed me," Zipporah said. "But he was a brother who gave, so I am a sister who doesn't give."

"No one said it," Father Herzog said. "But if the shoe fits, you can wear it."

Engrossed, unmoving in his chair, Herzog listened to the dead at their dead quarrels.

"What do you expect?" said Zipporah. "With four children, if I started to give, and indulged your bad habits, it would be endless. It's not my fault you're a pauper here."

"I am a pauper in America, that's true. Look at me. I haven't got a copper to bless my naked skin. I couldn't pay for my own shroud."

"Blame your own weak nature," said Zipporah. "*Az du host a schwachen natur, wer is dir schuldig?* You can't stand alone. You leaned on Sarah's brother, and now you want to lean on me. Yaffe served in the Kavkaz. *A finsternish!* It was too cold for dogs to howl. Alone, he came to America and sent for me. But you—you want *alle sieben glicken.* You travel in style, with ostrich feathers. You're an *edel-mensch.* Get your hands dirty? Not you."

"It's true. I didn't shovel manure *in der heim.* That happened in the land of Columbus. But I did it. I learned to harness a horse. At three o'clock in the morning, twenty below in the stable."

Zipporah waved this aside. "And now, with your still? You had to escape from the Czar's police. And now the Revenue? And you have to have a partner, a *goniff.*"

"Voplonsky is an honest man."

"Who—that *German?*" Voplonsky was a Polish blacksmith. She called him a German because of his pointed military mustaches and the German cut of his overcoat. It hung to the ground. "What have you in common with a blacksmith? You, a descendant of Herschel Dubrovner! And he, a Polisher *schmid* with red whiskers! A rat! A rat with pointed red whiskers and long crooked teeth and reeking of scorched hoof! Bah! Your partner. Wait and see what he does to you."

"I'm not so easy to take in."

"No? Didn't Lazansky swindle you? He gave it to you in the real Turkish style. And didn't he beat your bones also?"

That was Lazansky, in the bakery, a giant teamster from the Ukraine. A huge ignorant man, an *amhoretz* who didn't know enough Hebrew to bless his bread, he sat on his narrow green delivery wagon, ponderous, growling "Garrap" to his little nag and flicking with the whip. His gross voice rolled like a bowling ball. The horse trotted along the bank of the Lachine Canal. The wagon was lettered

LAZANSKY—PATISSERIES DE CHOIX

Father Herzog said, "Yes, it's true he beat me."

He had come to borrow money from Zipporah and Yaffe. He did not want to be drawn into a quarrel. She had certainly guessed the purpose of this visit and was trying to make him angry so that she might refuse him more easily.

"Ai!" said Zipporah. A brilliantly shrewd woman, her many gifts were cramped in this little Canadian village. "You think you can make a fortune out of swindlers, thieves, and gangsters. You? You're a gentle creature. I don't know why you didn't stay in the Yeshivah. You wanted to be a gilded little gentleman. I know these hooligans and *razboiniks*. They don't have skins, teeth, fingers like you but hides, fangs, claws. You can never keep up with these teamsters and butchers. Can you shoot a man?"

Father Herzog was silent.

"If, God forbid, you had to shoot . . ." cried Zipporah. "Could you even hit someone on the head? Come! Think it over. Answer me, *gazlan*. Could you give a blow on the head?"

Here Mother Herzog seemed to agree.

"I'm no weakling," said Father Herzog, with his energetic face and brown mustache. But of course, thought Herzog, all of Papa's violence went into the drama of his life, into family strife, and sentiment.

"They'll take what they like from you, those *leite*," said Zipporah. "Now, isn't it time you used your head? You do have one—*klug bist du*. Make a legitimate living. Let your Helen and your Shura go to work. Sell the piano. Cut expenses."

"Why shouldn't the children study if they have intelligence, talent," said Mother Herzog.

"If they're smart, all the better for my brother," said Zipporah. "It's too hard for him—wearing himself out for spoiled princes and princesses."

She had Papa on her side, then. His craving for help was deep, bottomless.

"Not that I don't love the children," said Zipporah. "Come here, little Moses, and sit on your old *tante*'s knee. What a dear little *yingele*." Moses on the bloomers of his aunt's lap—her red hands held him at the belly. She smiled with harsh affection and kissed his neck. "Born in my arms, this child." Then she looked at brother Shura, who stood beside his mother. He had thick, blocky legs and his face was freckled. "And you?" said Zipporah to him.

"What's wrong?" said Shura, frightened and offended.

"Not too young to bring in a dollar."

Papa glared at Shura.

"Don't I help?" said Shura. "Deliver bottles? Paste labels?"

Papa had forged labels. He would say cheerfully, "Well, children, what shall it be—White Horse? Johnnie Walker?" Then we'd all call out our favorites. The paste pot was on the table.

In secret, Mother Herzog touched Shura's hand when Zipporah turned her eyes on him. Moses saw. Breathless Willie was scampering outside with his cousins, building a snow fort, squeaking and throwing snowballs. The sun came lower and lower. Ribbons of red from the horizon wound over the ridges of glazed snow. In the blue shadow of the fence, the goats were feeding. They belonged to the seltzer man next door. Zipporah's chickens were about to roost. Visiting us in Montreal, she sometimes brought a fresh egg. One egg. One of the children might be sick. A fresh egg had a world of power. Nervous and critical, with awkward feet and heavy hips, she mounted the stairs on Napoleon Street, a stormy woman, a daughter of Fate. Quickly and nervously she kissed her fingertips and touched the mezuzah. Entering, she inspected Mama's housekeeping. "Is everybody well?" she said. "I brought the children an egg." She opened her big bag and took out the present, wrapped in a piece of Yiddish newspaper (*Der Kanader Adler*).

A visit from Tante Zipporah was like a military inspection. Afterwards, Mama laughed and often ended up by crying, "Why is she my enemy! What does she want? I have no strength to fight her." The antagonism, as Mama felt it, was mystical—a matter of souls. Mama's mind was archaic, filled with old legends, with angels and demons.

Of course Zipporah, that realist, was right to refuse Father Herzog. He wanted to run bootleg whisky to the border, and get into the big time. He and Voplonsky borrowed from moneylenders, and loaded a truck with cases. But they never reached Rouses Point. They were hijacked, beaten up, and left in a ditch. Father Herzog took the worse beating because he resisted. The hijackers tore his clothes, knocked out one of his teeth, and trampled him.

He and Voplonsky the blacksmith returned to Montreal on foot. He stopped at Voplonsky's shop to clean up, but there was not much he could do about his swollen bloody eye. He had a gap in his teeth. His coat was torn and his shirt and undergarment were bloodstained.

That was how he entered the dark kitchen on Napoleon Street. We were all there. It was gloomy March, and anyway the light seldom reached that room. It was like a cavern. We were like cave dwellers. "Sarah!" he said. "Children!" He showed his cut face. He spread his arms so we could see his tatters, and the white of his body under them. Then he turned his pockets inside out—empty. As he did this, he began to cry, and the children standing about him all cried. It was more than I could bear that anyone should lay violent hands on him—a father, a sacred being, a king. Yes, he was a king to us. My heart was suffocated by this horror. I thought I would die of it. Whom did I ever love as I loved them?

Then Father Herzog told his story.

"They were waiting for us. The road was blocked. They dragged us from the truck. They took everything."

"Why did you fight?" said Mother Herzog.

"Everything we had . . . all I borrowed!"

"They might have killed you."

"They had handkerchiefs over their faces. I thought I recognized . . ."

Mama was incredulous. "*Landtsleit?* Impossible. No Jews could do this to a Jew."

"No?" cried Papa. "Why not! Who says not! Why shouldn't they!"

"Not Jews! Never!" Mama said. "Never. Never! They couldn't have the heart. Never!"

"Children—don't cry. And poor Voplonsky—he could barely creep into bed."

"Yonah," said Mama, "you must give up this whole thing."

"How will we live? We have to live."

He began to tell the story of his life, from childhood to this day. He wept as he told it. Put out at four years old to study, away from home. Eaten by lice. Half starved in the Yeshivah as a boy. He shaved, became a modern European. He worked in Kremenchug for his aunt as a young man. He had a fool's paradise in Petersburg for ten years, on forged papers. Then he sat in prison with common criminals. Escaped to America. Starved. Cleaned stables. Begged. Lived in fear. A *baal-chov*—always a debtor. Shadowed by the police. Taking in drunken boarders. His wife a servant. And this was what he brought home to his children. This was what he could show them—his rags, his bruises.

Herzog, wrapped in his cheap paisley robe, brooded with clouded eyes. Under his bare feet was a small strip of carpet. His elbows rested on the fragile desk and his head hung down. He had written only a few lines to Nachman.

I suppose, he was thinking, that we heard this tale of the Herzogs ten times a year. Sometimes Mama told it, sometimes he. So we had a great schooling in grief. I still know these cries of the soul. They lie in the breast, and in the throat. The mouth wants to open wide and let them out. But all these are antiquities—yes, Jewish antiquities originating in the Bible, in a Biblical sense of personal experience and destiny. What happened during the War abolished Father Herzog's claim to exceptional suffering. We are on a more brutal standard now, a new terminal standard, indifferent to persons. Part of the program of destruction into which the human spirit has poured itself with energy, even with joy. These personal histories, old tales from old times that may not be worth remembering. I remember. I must. But who else—to whom can this matter? So many millions—multitudes—go down in terrible pain. And, at that, moral suffering is denied, these days. Personalities are good only for comic relief. But I am still a slave to Papa's pain. The way Father Herzog spoke of himself! That could make one laugh. His *I* had such dignity.

"You must give it up," Mama cried. "You must."

"What should I do, then! Work for the burial society? Like a man of seventy? Only fit to sit at deathbeds? *I*? Wash corpses? *I*? Or should I go to the cemetery and wheedle mourners for a nickel? To say *El malai rachamim. I*? Let the earth open and swallow me up!"

"Come, Yonah," said Mama in her earnest persuasive way. "I'll put a compress on your eye. Come, lie down."

"How can I?"

"No, you must."

"How will the children eat?"

"Come—you must lie down awhile. Take off that shirt."

She sat by the bed, silent. He lay in the gray room, on the iron bedstead, covered with the worn red Russian blanket—his handsome forehead, his level nose, the brown mustache. As he had from that dark corridor, Moses now contemplated those two figures.

Nachman, he began again to write, but stopped. How was he to reach Nachman with a letter? He would do better to advertise in the *Village Voice.* But, then, to whom would he send the other letters he was drafting?

He concluded that Nachman's wife was dead. Yes, that must be it. That slender, thin-legged girl with the dark brows that rose high and recurved again beside her eyes, and the wide mouth which curved down at the corners—she had committed suicide, and Nachman ran away because (who could blame him) he would have had to tell Moses all about it. Poor thing, poor thing—she too must be in the cemetery.

ARTHUR MILLER (1915–   )

Arthur Miller is considered by many as America's most important living dramatist. Since the production of All My Sons *in 1947, he has written a series of plays which constitute a modern form of tragedy and which explore Miller's favorite themes: ambition, responsibility, and justice. For Miller tragedy seemed to be "the only form [of drama] there was. The rest of it was all either attempts at it, or escapes from it. But tragedy was the basic pillar. . . . it's got so we've lost the technique of grappling with the world that Homer had, that Aeschylus had, that Euripides had. And Shakespeare. How amazing it is that people who adore the Greek drama fail to see that these great works are works of a man confronting his society, the illusions of the society, the faiths of the society. They're social documents, not little piddling private conversations."*

Arthur Miller was born on October 17, 1915, in the Harlem section of Manhattan. His father was a well-to-do manufacturer. He attended the University of Michigan, where he studied playwriting and where he achieved his first modest success. Returning to New York after college, he wrote more plays, radio scripts, and the novel Focus. *His first real success was* All My Sons *(1947), which won the New York Drama Critics Award in 1947. His next play,* Death of a Salesman *(1949), won the Critics Circle Award and the Pulitzer Prize for Drama and has proved to be his most popular single work. His other dramas include* The Crucible *(1953).* A View from the Bridge *(1955),* After the Fall *(1963),* Incident at Vichy *(1964), and* The Price *(1968). Miller's one collection of stories is* I Don't Need You Any More *(1967).*

"I care about all of my plays," Miller has said, "but the only story I like is Monte Sant' Angelo, *published in* Harper's *and* Prize Short Stories *of 1951." Miller has not been centrally concerned with his short stories, which have been written for his "own pleasure," but which nevertheless are, in certain cases, extremely effective. He has not drawn upon his Jewishness for much of his work, but two of his plays—*After the Fall *and* Incident at Vichy—*as well as the short story, "Monte Sant' Angelo," do use Jewish subjects and reveal aspects of the author that are particularly interesting.*

Monte Sant' Angelo

THE DRIVER, who had been sitting up ahead in perfect silence for nearly an hour as they crossed the monotonous green plain of Foggia, now said something. Appello quickly leaned forward in the back seat and asked him what he had said. "That is Monte Sant' Angelo before you." Appello lowered his head to see through the windshield of the rattling little Fiat. Then he nudged Bernstein, who awoke resentfully, as though his friend had intruded. "That's the town up there," Appello said. Bernstein's annoyance vanished, and he bent forward. They both sat that way for several minutes, watching the approach of what seemed to them a comically situated town, even more comic than any they had seen in the four weeks they had spent moving from place to place in the country. It was like a tiny old lady living on a high roof for fear of thieves.

The plain remained as flat as a table for a quarter of a mile ahead. Then out of it, like a pillar, rose the butte; squarely and rigidly skyward it towered, only narrowing as it reached its very top. And there, barely visible now, the town crouched, momentarily obscured by white clouds, then appearing again tiny and safe, like a mountain port looming at the end of the sea. From their distance they could make out no road, no approach at all up the side of the pillar.

"Whoever built that was awfully frightened of something," Bernstein said, pulling his coat closer around him. "How do they get up there? Or do they?"

Appello, in Italian, asked the driver about the town. The driver, who had been there only once before in his life and knew no other who had made the trip—despite his being a resident of Lucera, which was not far away—told Appello with some amusement that they would soon see how rarely anyone goes up or comes down Monte Sant' Angelo. "The donkeys will kick and run away as we ascend, and when we come into the town everyone will come out to see. They are very far from everything. They all look like brothers up there. They don't know very much either," He laughed.

"What does the Princeton chap say?" Bernstein asked.

The driver had a crew haircut, a turned-up nose, and a red round face with blue eyes. He owned the car, and although he spoke like any Italian when his feet were on the ground, behind his wheel with two Americans riding behind him he had only the most amused and superior attitude toward everything outside the windshield. Appello, having translated for Bernstein, asked him how long it would take to ascend. "Perhaps three quarters of an hour—as long as the mountain is," he amended.

Bernstein and Appello settled back and watched the butte's approach. Now they could see that its sides were crumbled white stone. At this closer vantage it seemed as though it had been struck a terrible blow by some monstrous hammer that had split its structure into millions of seams. They were beginning to climb now, on a road of sharp broken rocks.

"The road is Roman," the driver remarked. He knew how much Americans made of anything Roman. Then he added, "The car, however, is from Milan." He and Appello laughed.

And now the white chalk began drifting into the car. At their elbows the altitude began to seem threatening. There was no railing on the road, and it turned back on itself every two hundred yards in order to climb again. The Fiat's doors were wavering in their frames; the seat on which they sat kept inching forward onto the floor. A fine film of white talc settled onto their clothing and covered their eyebrows. Both together began to cough. When they were finished Bernstein said, "Just so I understand it clearly and without prejudice, will you explain again in words of one syllable why the hell we are climbing this lump of dust, old man?"

Apello laughed and mocked a punch at him.

"No kidding," Bernstein said, trying to smile.

"I want to see this aunt of mine, that's all." Appello began taking it seriously.

"You're crazy, you know that? You've got some kind of ancestor complex. All we've done in this country is look for your relatives."

"Well, Jesus, I'm finally in the country. I want to see all the places I came from. You realize that two of my relatives are buried in a crypt in the church up there? In eleven hundred something."

"Oh, is this where the monks came from?"

"Sure, the two Appello brothers. They helped build that church. It's very famous, that church. Supposed to be Saint Michael appeared in a vision or something."

"I never thought I'd know anybody with monks in his family. But I still think you're cracked on the whole subject."

"Well, don't you have any feeling about your ancestors? Wouldn't you like to go back to Austria or wherever you came from and see where the old folks lived? Maybe find a family that belongs to your line, or something like that?"

Bernstein did not answer for a moment. He did not know quite what he felt and wondered dimly whether he kept ragging his friend a little because of envy. When they had been in the country courthouse where Appello's grandfather's portrait and his great-grandfather's hung—both renowned provincial magistrates; when they had spent the night in Lucera where the name Appello meant something distinctly honorable, and where his friend Vinny was taken in hand and greeted in that intimate way because he was an Appello—in all these moments Bernstein had felt left out and somehow deficient. At first he had taken the attitude that all the fuss was childish, and yet as incident after incident, landmark after old landmark, turned up echoing the name Appello, he gradually began to feel his friend combining with this history, and it seemed to him that it made Vinny stronger, somehow less dead when the time would come for him to die.

"I have no relatives that I know of in Europe," he said to Vinny. "And if I had they'd have all been wiped out by now."

"Is that why you don't like my visiting this way?"

"I don't say I don't like it," Bernstein said and smiled by will. He wished he could open himself as Vinny could; it would give him ease and strength, he felt. They stared down at the plain below and spoke little.

The chalk dust had lightened Appello's black eyebrows. For a fleeting moment it occurred to Appello that they resembled each other. Both were over six feet tall, both broad-shouldered and dark men. Bernstein was thinner, quite gaunt and long-armed. Appello was stronger in his arms and stooped a little, as though he had not wanted to be tall. But their eyes were not the same. Appello seemed a little Chinese around the eyes, and they glistened black, direct, and, for women, passionately. Bernstein gazed rather than looked; for him the eyes were dangerous when they could be fathomed, and so he turned them away often, or downward, and there seemed to be something defensively cruel and yet gentle there.

They liked each other not for reasons so much as for possibilities; it was as though they both had sensed they were opposites. And they were lured to each other's failings. With Bernstein around him Appello felt diverted from his irresponsible sensuality, and on this trip Bernstein often had the pleasure and pain of resolving to deny himself no more.

The car turned a hairpin curve with a cloud below on the right, when suddenly the main street of the town arched up before them. There was no one about. It had been true, what the driver had predicted—in the few handkerchiefs of grass that they had passed on the way up the donkeys had bolted, and they had seen shepherds with hard mustaches and black shakos and long black cloaks who had regarded them with the silent inspection of those who live far away. But here in the town there was no one. The car climbed onto the main street, which flattened now, and all at once they were being surrounded by people who were coming out of their doors, putting on their jackets and caps. They did look strangely related, and more Irish than Italian.

The two got out of the Fiat and inspected the baggage strapped to the car's roof, while the driver kept edging protectively around and around the car. Appello talked laughingly with the people, who kept asking why he had come so far, what he had to sell, what he wanted to buy, until he at last made it clear that he was looking only for his aunt. When he said the name the men (the women remained at home, watching from the windows) looked blank, until an old man wearing rope sandals and a knitted skating cap came forward and said that he remembered such a woman. He then turned, and Appello and Bernstein followed up the main street with what was now perhaps a hundred men behind them.

"How come nobody knows her?" Bernstein asked.

"She's a widow. I guess she stays home most of the time. The men in the line died out here twenty years ago. Her husband was the last Appello up here. They don't go much by women; I bet this old guy remembered the name because he knew her husband by it, not her."

The wind, steady and hard, blew through the town, washing it, laving its stones white. The sun was cool as a lemon, the sky purely blue, and the clouds so close their keels seemed to be sailing through the next street. The two Americans began to walk with the joy of it in their long strides. They came to a two-story stone house and went up a dark corridor and knocked. The guide remained respectfully on the sidewalk.

There was no sound within for a few moments. Then there was— short scrapes, like a mouse that started, stopped, looked about, started again. Appello knocked once more. The doorknob turned, and the door opened a foot. A pale little woman, not very old at all, held the door wide enough for her face to be seen. She seemed very worried.

"Ha?" she asked.

"I am Vincent Georgio."

"Ha?" she repeated.

"Vicenzo Giorgio Appello."

Her hand slid off the knob, and she stepped back. Appello, smiling in his friendly way, entered, with Bernstein behind him closing the door. A window let the sun flood the room, which was nevertheless stone cold. The woman's mouth was open, her hands were pressed together as in prayer, and the tips of her fingers were pointing at Vinny. She seemed crouched, as though about to kneel, and she could not speak.

Vinny went over to her and touched her bony shoulder and pressed her into a chair. He and Bernstein sat down too. He told her their relationship, saying names of men and women, some of whom were dead, others whom she had only heard of and never met in this sky place. She spoke at last, and Appello could not understand what she said. She ran out of the room suddenly.

"I think she thinks I'm a ghost or something. My uncle said she hadn't seen any of the family in twenty or twenty-five years. I bet she doesn't think there are any left."

She returned with a bottle that had an inch of wine at the bottom of it. She ignored Bernstein and gave Appello the bottle. He drank. It was vinegar. Then she started to whimper and kept wiping the tears out of her eyes in order to see Appello. She never finished a sentence, and Appello kept asking her what she meant. She kept running from one corner of the room to another. The rhythm of her departures and returns to the chair was getting so wild that Appello raised his voice and commanded her to sit.

"I'm not a ghost, Aunty. I came here from America—" He stopped. It was clear from the look in her bewildered, frightened eyes that she had not thought him a ghost at all, but what was just as bad—if nobody had ever come to see her from Lucera, how could anybody have so much as thought of her in America, a place that did exist, she knew, just as heaven existed and in exactly the same way. There was no way to hold a conversation with her.

They finally made their exit, and she had not said a coherent word except a blessing, which was her way of expressing her relief that Appello was leaving, for despite the unutterable joy at having seen with her own eyes another of her husband's blood, the sight was itself too terrible in its associations, and in the responsibility it laid upon her to welcome him and make him comfortable.

They walked toward the church now. Bernstein had not been able to say anything. The woman's emotion, so pure and violent and wild, had scared him. And yet, glancing at Appello, he was amazed to see that his friend had drawn nothing but a calm sort of satisfaction from it, as though his aunt had only behaved correctly. Dimly he remembered himself as a boy visiting an aunt of his in the Bronx, a woman who had not been in touch with the family and had never seen him. He remembered how forcefully she had fed him, pinched his cheeks, and smiled and smiled every time he looked up at her, but he knew that there was nothing of this blood in that encounter; nor could there be for him now if on the next corner he should meet a woman who said she was of his family. If anything, he would want to get away from her, even though he had always gotten along with his people and hadn't even the usual snobbery about them. As they entered the church he said to himself that some part of him was not plugged in, but why he should be disturbed about it mystified him and even made him irritated with Appello, who now was asking the priest where the tombs of the Appellos were.

They descended into the vault of the church, where the stone floor was partly covered with water. Along the walls, and down twisting corridors running out of a central arched hall, were tombs so old no candle could illuminate most of the worn inscriptions. The priest vaguely remembered an Appello vault but had no idea where it was. Vinny moved from one crypt to another with the candle he had bought from the priest. Bernstein waited at the opening of the corridor, his neck bent to avoid touching the roof with his hat. Appello, stooped even more than usual, looked like a monk himself, an antiquary, a gradually disappearing figure squinting down the long darkness of the ages for his name on a stone. He could not find it. Their feet were getting soaked. After half an hour they left the church and outside fought off shivering small boys selling grimy religious postcards, which the wind kept taking from their fists.

"I'm sure it's there," Appello said with fascinated excitement. "But you wouldn't want to stick out a search, would you?" he asked hopefully.

"This is no place for me to get pneumonia," Bernstein said.

They had come to the end of a side street. They had passed shops in front of which pink lambs hung head down with their legs stiffly jutting out over the sidewalk. Bernstein shook hands with one and imagined for Vinny a scene for Chaplin in which a monsignor would meet him here, reach out to shake his hand, and find the cold lamb's foot in his grip, and

Chaplin would be mortified. At the street's end they scanned the endless sky and looked over the precipice upon Italy.

"They might even have ridden horseback down there, in armor—Appellos." Vinny spoke rapidly.

"Yeah, they probably did," Bernstein said. The vision of Appello in armor wiped away any desire to kid his friend. He felt alone, desolate as the dried-out chalk sides of this broken pillar he stood upon. Certainly there had been no knights in his family.

He remembered his father's telling of his town in Europe, a common barrel of water, a town idiot, a baron nearby. That was all he had of it, and no pride, no pride in it at all. Then I am an American, he said to himself. And yet in that there was not the power of Appello's narrow passion. He looked at Appello's profile and felt the warmth of that gaze upon Italy and wondered if any American had ever really felt like this in the States. He had never in his life sensed so strongly that the past could be so peopled, so vivid with generations, as it had been with Vinny's aunt an hour ago. A common water barrel, a town idiot, a baron who lived nearby. . . . It had nothing to do with *him*. And standing there he sensed a broken part of himself and wondered with a slight amusement if this was what a child felt on discovering that the parents who brought him up were not his own and that he entered his house not from warmth but from the street, from a public and disordered place. . . .

They sought and found a restaurant for lunch. It was at the other edge of the town and overhung the precipice. Inside, it was one immense room with fifteen or twenty tables; the front wall was lined with windows overlooking the plain below. They sat at a table and waited for someone to appear. The restaurant was cold. They could hear the wind surging against the windowpanes, and yet the clouds at eye level moved serenely and slow. A young girl, the daughter of the family, came out of the kitchen, and Appello was questioning her about food when the door opened and a man came in.

For Bernstein there was an abrupt impression of familiarity with the man, although he could not fathom the reason for his feeling. The man's face looked Sicilian, round, dark as earth, high cheekbones, broad jaw. He almost laughed aloud as it instantly occurred to him that he could converse with this man in Italian. When the waitress had gone, he told this to Vinny, who now joined in watching the man.

Sensing their stares, the man looked at them with a merry flicker of his cheeks and said, "*Buon giorno.*"

"*Buon giorno,*" Bernstein replied across the four tables between them, and then to Vinny, "Why do I feel that about him?"

"I'll be damned if I know," Vinny said, glad now that he could join his friend in a mutually interesting occupation.

They watched the man, who obviously ate here often. He had already set a large package down on another table and now put his hat on a chair, his jacket on another chair, and his vest on a third. It was as though he were making companions of his clothing. He was in the prime of middle age and very rugged. And to the Americans there was something mixed up about his clothing. His jacket might have been worn by a local man; it was tight and black and wrinkled and chalk-dust-covered. His trousers were dark brown and very thick, like a peasant's, and his shoes were snubbed up at the ends and of heavy leather. But he wore a black hat, which was unusual up here where all had caps, and he had a tie. He wiped his hands before loosening the knot; it was a striped tie, yellow and blue, of silk, and no tie to be bought in this part of the world, or worn by these people. And there was a look in his eyes that was not a peasant's inward stare; nor did it have the innocence of the other men who looked at them on the streets here.

The waitress came with two dishes of lamb for the Americans. The man was interested and looked across his table at the meat and at the strangers. Bernstein glanced at the barely cooked flesh and said, "There's hair on it."

Vinny called the girl back just as she was going to the newcomer and pointed at the hair.

"But it's lamb's hair," she explained simply.

They said, "Oh," and pretended to begin to cut into the faintly pink flesh.

"You ought to know better, signor, than to order meat today."

The man looked amused, and yet it was unclear whether he might not be a trifle offended.

"Why not?" Vinny asked.

"It's Friday, signor," and he smiled sympathetically.

"That's right!" Vinny said although he had known all along.

"Give me fish," the man said to the girl and asked with intimacy about her mother, who was ill these days.

Bernstein had not been able to turn his eyes from the man. He could not eat the meat and sat chewing bread and feeling a rising urge to go over to the man, to speak to him. It struck him as being insane. The whole place—the town, the clouds in the streets, the thin air—was turning into a hallucination. He knew this man. He was sure he knew him. Quite clearly that was impossible. Still, there was a thing beyond the impossibility of which he was drunkenly sure, and it was that if he dared he could start speaking Italian fluently with this man. This was the first moment since leaving America that he had not felt the ill-ease of traveling and of being a traveler. He felt as comfortable as Vinny now, it seemed to him. In his mind's eye he could envisage the inside of the kitchen; he had a startlingly clear image of what the cook's face must look like, and he knew where a certain kind of soiled apron was hung.

"What's the matter with you?" Appello asked.

"Why?"

"The way you're looking at him."

"I want to talk to him."

"Well, talk to him." Vinny smiled.

"I can't speak Italian, you know that."

"Well, I'll ask him. What do you want to say?"

"Vinny—" Bernstein started to speak and stopped.

"What?" Appello asked, leaning his head closer and looking down at the tablecloth.

"Get him to talk. Anything. Go ahead."

Vinny, enjoying his friend's strange emotionalism, looked across at the man, who now was eating with careful but immense satisfaction. "*Scusi,* signor."

The man looked up.

"I am a son of Italy from America. I would like to talk to you. We're strange here."

The man, chewing deliciously, nodded with his amiable and amused smile and adjusted the hang of his jacket on the nearby chair.

"Do you come from around here?"

"Not very far."

"How is everything here?"

"Poor. It is always poor."

"What do you work at, if I may ask?"

The man had now finished his food. He took a last long drag of his wine and got up and proceeded to dress and pull his tie up tightly. When he walked it was with a slow, wide sway, as though each step had to be conserved.

"I sell cloth here to the people and the stores, such as they are," he said. And he walked over to the bundle and set it carefully on a table and began untying it.

"He sells cloth," Vinny said to Bernstein.

Bernstein's cheeks began to redden. From where he sat he could see the man's broad back, ever so slightly bent over the bundle. He could see the man's hands working at the knot and just a corner of the man's left eye. Now the man was laying the paper away from the two bolts of cloth, carefully pressing the wrinkles flat against the table. It was as though the brown paper were valuable leather that must not be cracked or rudely bent. The waitress came out of the kitchen with a tremendous round loaf of bread at least two feet in diameter. She gave it to him, and he placed it flat on top of the cloth, and the faintest feather of a smile curled up on Bernstein's lips. Now the man folded the paper back and brought the string around the bundle and tied the knot, and Bernstein uttered a little laugh, a laugh of relief.

Vinny looked at him, already smiling, ready to join the laughter, but mystified. "What's the matter?" he asked.

Bernstein took a breath. There was something a little triumphant, a new air of confidence and superiority in his face and voice. "He's Jewish, Vinny," he said.

Vinny turned to look at the man. "Why?"

"The way he works that bundle. It's exactly the way my father used to tie a bundle—and my grandfather. The whole history is packing bundles and getting away. Nobody else can be as tender and delicate with bundles. That's a Jewish man tying a bundle. Ask him his name."

Vinny was delighted. "Signor," he called with that warmth reserved in his nature for members of families, any families.

The man, tucking the end of the string into the edge of the paper, turned to them with his kind smile.

"May I ask your name, signor?"

"My name? Mauro di Benedetto."

"Mauro di Benedetto. Sure!" Vinny laughed, looking at Bernstein. "That's Morris of the Blessed Moses."

"Tell him I'm Jewish," Bernstein said, a driving eagerness charging his eyes.

"My friend is Jewish," Vinny said to the man, who now was hoisting the bundle onto his shoulder.

"Heh?" the man asked, confused by their sudden vivacity. As though wondering if there were some sophisticated American point he should have understood, he stood there smiling blankly, politely, ready to join in this mood.

"*Judeo*, my friend."

"*Judeo*?" he asked, the willingness to get the joke still holding the smile on his face.

Vinny hesitated before this steady gaze of incomprehension. "*Judeo*. The people of the Bible," he said.

"Oh, yes, yes!" The man nodded now, relieved that he was not to be caught in ignorance. *"Ebreo,"* he corrected. And he nodded affably to Bernstein and seemed a little at a loss for what they expected him to do next.

"Does he know what you mean?" Bernstein asked.

"Yeah, he said, 'Hebrew,' but it doesn't seem to connect. Signor," he addressed the man, "why don't you have a glass of wine with us? Come, sit down."

"Thank you, signor," he replied appreciatively, "but I must be home by sundown and I'm already a little late."

Vinny translated, and Bernstein told him to ask why he had to be home by sundown.

The man apparently had never considered the question before. He shrugged and laughed and said, " I don't know. All my life I get home for dinner on Friday night, and I like to come into the house before sundown. I supposed it's a habit; my father—you see, I have a route I walk, which is this route. I first did it with my father, and he did it with his father. We are known here for many generations past. And my father always got home on Friday night before sundown. It's a manner of the family I guess."

"Shabbas begins at sundown on Friday night," Bernstein said when Vinny had translated. "He's even taking home fresh bread for the Sabbath. The man is a Jew, I tell you. Ask him, will you?"

"Scusi, signor." Vinny smiled. "My friend is curious to know whether you are Jewish."

The man raised his thick eyebrows not only in surprise but as though he felt somewhat honored by being identified with something exotic. "Me?" he asked.

"I don't mean American," Vinny said, believing he had caught the meaning of the man's glance at Bernstein. *"Ebreo,"* he repeated.

The man shook his head, seeming a little sorry he could not oblige Vinny. "No," he said. He was ready to go but wanted to pursue what obviously was his most interesting conversation in weeks. "Are they Catholics? The Hebrews?"

"He's asking me if Jews are Catholics," Vinny said.

Bernstein sat back in his chair, a knotted look of wonder in his eyes. Vinny replied to the man, who looked once again at Bernstein as though wanting to investigate this strangeness further, but his mission drew him up and he wished them good fortune and said good-by. He walked to the kitchen door and called thanks to the girl inside, saying the loaf would warm his back all the way down the mountain, and he opened the door and went out into the wind of the street and the sunshine, waving to them as he walked away.

They kept repeating their amazement on the way back to the car, and Bernstein told again how his father wrapped bundles. "Maybe he doesn't know he's a Jew, but how could he not know what Jews are?" he said.

"Well, remember my aunt in Lucera?" Vinny asked. "She's a school-teacher, and she asked me if you believed in Christ. She didn't know the first thing about it. I think the ones in these small towns who ever heard of Jews think they're a Christian sect of some kind. I knew an old Italian once who thought all Negroes were Jews and white Jews were only converts."

"But his name . . ."

" 'Benedetto' is an Italian name too. I never heard of 'Mauro' though. 'Mauro' is strictly from the old sod."

"But if he had a name like that, wouldn't it lead him to wonder if . . . ?"

"I don't think so. In New York the name 'Salvatore' is turned into 'Sam.' Italians are great for nicknames; the first name never means much. 'Vicenzo' is 'Enzo,' or 'Vinny' or even 'Chico.' Nobody would think twice about 'Mauro' or damn near any other first name. He's obviously a Jew, but I'm sure he doesn't know it. You could tell, couldn't you? He was baffled."

"But, my God, bringing home a bread for *Shabbas!*" Bernstein laughed, wide-eyed.

They reached the car, and Bernstein had his hand on the door but stopped before opening it and turned to Vinny. He looked heated; his eyelids seemed puffed. "It's early—if you still want to I'll go back to the church with you. You can look for the boys."

Vinny began to smile, and then they both laughed together, and Vinny slapped him on the back and gripped his shoulder as though to hug him. "Goddam, now you're starting to enjoy this trip!"

As they walked briskly toward the church the conversation returned always to the same point, when Bernstein would say, "I don't know why, but it gets me. He's not only acting like a Jew, but an Orthodox Jew. And doesn't even know—I mean it's strange as hell to me."

"You look different, you know that?" Vinny said.

"Why?"

"You do."

"You know a funny thing?" Bernstein said quietly as they entered the church and descended into the vault beneath it. "I feel like—at home in this place. I can't describe it."

Beneath the church, they picked their way through the shallower puddles on the stone floor, looking into vestibules, opening doors, searching for the priest. He appeared at last—they could not imagine from where—and Appello bought another candle from him and was gone in the shadows of the corridors where the vaults were.

Bernstein stood—everything was wet, dripping. Behind him, flat and wide, rose the stairway of stones bent with the tread of millions. Vapor steamed from his nostrils. There was nothing to look at but shadow. It was dank and black and low, an entrance to hell. Now and then in the very far distance he could hear a step echoing, another, then silence. He did not move, seeking the root of an ecstasy he had not dreamed was part of his nature; he saw the amiable man trudging down the mountains, across the plains, on routes marked out for him by generations of men, a nameless traveler carrying home a warm bread on Friday night—and kneeling in church on Sunday. There was an irony in it he could not name. And yet pride was running through him. Of what he should be proud he had no clear idea; perhaps it was only that beneath the brainless crush of history a Jew had secretly survived, shorn of his consciousness but forever caught by that final impudence of a Saturday Sabbath in a Catholic country; so that his very unawareness was proof, a proof as mute as stones, that a past lived. A past for me, Bernstein thought, astounded by its importance for him, when in fact he had never had a religion or even, he realized now, a history.

He could see Vinny's form approaching in the narrow corridor of crypts, the candle flame flattening in the cold draft. He felt he would look differently into Vinny's eyes; his condescension had gone and with it a certain embarrassment. He felt loose, somehow the equal of his friend—and how odd that was when, if anything, he had thought of himself as superior. Suddenly, with Vinny a yard away, he saw that his life had been covered with an unrecognized shame.

"I found it! It's back there!" Vinny was laughing like a young boy, pointing back toward the dark corridor.

"That's great, Vinny," Bernstein said. "I'm glad."

They were both stooping slightly under the low, wet ceiling, their voices fleeing from their mouths in echoed whispers. Vinny held still for an instant, catching Bernstein's respectful happiness, and saw there that his search was not worthless sentiment. He raised the candle to see Bernstein's face better, and then he laughed and gripped Bernstein's wrist and led the way toward the flight of steps that rose to the surface. Bernstein had never liked anyone grasping him, but from this touch of a hand in the darkness, strangely, there was no implication of a hateful weakness.

They walked side by side down the steep street away from the church. The town was empty again. The air smelled of burning charcoal and olive oil. A few pale stars had come out. The shops were all shut. Bernstein thought of Mauro di Benedetto going down the winding, rocky road, hurrying against the setting of the sun.

DELMORE SCHWARTZ (1913–1966)

Delmore Schwartz was born in Brooklyn, New York, on December 8, 1913. He studied at the University of Wisconsin, New York University, and Harvard University, and received his B.A. from N.Y.U. in 1935. In 1939 he published In Dreams Begin Responsibilities, *and followed this collection of stories and poems with a verse play,* Shenandoah *(1941); an autobiographical poem,* Genesis, Book I *(1943); a group of short stories,* The World is a Wedding *(1948);* Vaudeville for a Princess and Other Poems *(1950);* Summer Knowledge: New and Selected Poems 1938–1958 *(1959), which received the Bollingen Prize in Poetry and the Shelley Memorial Prize in 1960; and* Successful Love, and Other Stories *(1961). Schwartz served as editor and associate editor of* New Republic *from 1955–1957. Finally paranoid, he died on July 11, 1966. Schwartz taught at a number of universities: Harvard (1940–1947), Princeton, and Syracuse University (1962–1966).*

An extraordinarily prolific and varied writer, Schwartz was deeply concerned with his Jewish middle-class background, which informs much of his fiction and poetry.

AMERICA! AMERICA!

WHEN BELMONT WEISS the muscian returned from Paris in 1934, he found that he had very little to do. He was unable to work with the great fluency and excitement he had enjoyed when he was younger, and something had happened to the people he had known before going to Europe. The depression had happened to them; the full sense of it had, after years, wholly modified their hopes and desires. The boys with whom he had gone to college not only no longer lived in the same neighborhood, but in addition they saw little of each other and were embarrassed when they met. What impressed Belmont most of all was the modification of the sense of humor which had prevailed among them. After a few visits, Belmont gave up his effort to renew the old friendships; for he saw that they no longer existed.

However, he was not bored. He wished very much that he were back in Paris again, and he hoped to be able to go back again next year, foolishly enough as it turned out. Meanwhile he was taking it easy, as his mother said. He was enjoying an ease, an indolence, a sense of relaxation which seemed unwarranted and peculiar to him. But he had done so much work during the previous year that a period of inactivity seemed unavoidable. Or so, at least, he told himself, in facile self-consolation.

He would sleep late every morning and then sit for a long time at the breakfast table and listen to his mother's endless conversation while she went about her household tasks. It was simple for Belmont to alternate his attention between his mother's inexhaustible talk and the morning newspaper. The sunlight made the kitchen's whiteness pleasant, the apartment was well heated, the newspaper was interesting, and Belmont would take another cup of coffee and turn the page when he saw that his mother was about to tell her nominal audience the story of one of her friends, a subject she enjoyed more than any other except for the story of her own life.

One morning, however, Belmont had begun to feel somewhat uneasy about his enjoyment of these two hours of breakfast. He had done nothing, he had not even listened to music for a week, and as he explained in a letter, "when I am not working, I begin to feel 'unreal.' " But on this morning, his mother's story began to interest him very much. Indeed her conversation had come to interest him more and more, although she always talked of people who did not interest him in the least, relatives, old family friends, neighbors of ten years back. Mrs. Weiss had begun to tell her younger son of her friends, the Baumanns. She would have preferred her older son, who was a lawyer, and the substantial son, as her audience. But it really did not matter, since she was ironing yesterday's wash, and conversation was not only a delight in itself, but made one forget the repetitive monotony of ironing.

The Baumanns, Mrs. Weiss reminded Belmont, had been the ones who gave Belmont a silver spoon when he was born. She brought forth the spoon from one of the drawers under the cupboard where she kept the dishes and showed Belmont his initials engraved in twining letters upon the top of the spoon which was now twenty-five years old. The acquaintance of the Baumanns and the Weisses, which intermittently involved years of close friendship, dated back many years to a period just before the turn of the century. Belmont's father, who was now dead, had been a young man of twenty-two when he had gone into what was then called the insurance *game* (the word rang in Belmont's mind when his mother used it, for she had a fine aural memory for the speech she had heard other people employ). Mr. Baumann had already established himself in this field of endeavor with a moderate amount of success. In fact, the insurance business was ideally suited to Mr. Baumann's temperament.

Belmont's mother proceeded to explain in great detail just why the field of insurance provided so genial a medium for a man of Mr. Baumann's tastes and inclinations. Insurance involved the important matter of finding one's way into the homes and the confidences of those who were going to be insured. Insurance could not be sold as a grocer or druggist sells his *goods* (Belmont was moved again) by waiting for the customer to come to you. Nor could you, like the book salesman, go from house to house, plant one foot in the doorway, and start talking before the housewife had a chance to shut the door in your face. For insurance, it was necessary to become friendly with a great many people, who would come to know you and like you and trust you, who would listen with respect to you and take your advice. You had to join various lodges and societies of your own class and race.

This necessity worked no hardship on Mr. Baumann, for he enjoyed groups and gatherings of all kinds; he enjoyed them intensely. In his youth he had belonged to the societies of people who had come from the old country, and upon his marriage, he had joined his wife's association. Then he had joined a Masonic lodge, and besides this, he participated in the social life of the neighborhood synagogue, though he was actually an admirer of Ingersoll. In this way, he had come to know a great many people, and he visited them with unfailing devotion to his love of sociability. To visit a friend was an involved activity for him. It required that he come into the house with much amiability (telling his host that he had been thinking and talking about him the other day) and announce that he had only *dropped* in for a few moments. Only after protestations of a predictable formality would he permit himself to be seated for a cup of tea. Once seated, said Mrs. Weiss (imposing from time to time her own variety of irony upon the irony which sang in Belmont's mind at every phase of her story), once seated it was hours before Mr. Baumann arose from the dining-room table on which a fresh tablecloth had been laid, and from which the lace cover and the cut-glass had been withdrawn.

Mr. Baumann drank tea in the Russian style, as he often explained. He drank it, that is to say and as he often said, from a glass, not from a cup; a cup was entirely out of the question. And while he drank and ate, he discoursed inimitably and authoritatively upon every subject, but especially upon Judaism, the private life of European royalty, and the new discoveries of science, for these were his favorite subjects. A silent amazement would sometimes grow among his auditors at the sheer length of time that he could continue to eat and drink, while talking; until at last, since there was little else left upon the table, he would absent-mindedly take up the crumbs on the tablecloth.

Even as a young man (Mrs. Weiss had not known him until he was in his forties), it was said of him that he looked like a banker. As he grew older and became quite plump, this impression was emphasized. He took to pince-nez glasses and handsome vests delicately lined at the top with white, the whole view enhanced by gold watch and chain, and resembling, as Belmont remembered, certain photographs of the first J. P. Morgan. His friends were generally delighted by most aspects of his being, but particularly impressed by his appearance. They could be shamed, often enough, into allowing him to *write* some insurance for them. It was a time of general prosperity for these people. They were rising in the world, most of them, after having come to America as grown children, and they could afford an insurance policy, just as they could afford to look down on newcomers to America and on their own selves in earlier years, a state of being for which the special term, *greenhorn,* had been created. But most of all, they liked Mr. Baumann. They were flattered by his company. When he paid a visit, he conferred upon the household a tone of being well informed, even of intellectuality, which pleased the husband because of what it implied to the wife, the implication being that although he, the husband, was too busy a man in the dress business to know much of these worldly matters, yet he was capable of having as a friend and *bringing into the house,* this friendly and cultivated man who spoke English with a Russian accent which was undoubtedly *refined.*

After a time in the insurance business there is no urgent need to acquire new customers and new policies. One can live comfortably on the commissions due one as the premiums continue to be paid from year to year. It is true that one must keep up one's acquaintance with the policy-holder and see to it that the stress of hard times does not make him foolish enough to give up his policy and cease to pay the premiums. But this need of assuring your clients, urging or cajoling them into continuing their policies, does not, or did not in those days interfere with the habit of sleeping late in the morning and making one's breakfast the occasion for the most painstaking scrutiny of the morning newspaper. Indeed, one can go for vacations in the Catskills or at Lakewood whenever one pleases, and this Mr. Baumann and his family often did. They went at least four times a year, usually during the high holy days, during Passover, sometimes in the summer, and during the week between Christmas and New Year's. In fact, Mr. Baumann had quite frequently written some of his best policies during the general high spirits which are the rule during vacations and at resorts. He was undoubtedly at his best during such times and amid such circumstances.

At this point, Belmont recognized in his mother's tone the resentment she had always felt toward those who lived well and permitted nothing to interfere with their enjoyment of life. It was the resentment of one who felt no inclination, herself, to live well, and regarded it as unjustified except on the part of the very rich or during vacations.

An insurance man, however, has one urgent duty, the necessity of putting in an appearance at the funerals of those he has known even very slightly. This attendance is a perfect way in which to pay tribute to one of the irreducible facts upon which the insurance business is based. Moreover, it provides a basis for useful conversation. "Yes," Mr. Baumann would say, "I was at L——'s funeral today." His tone implied the authoritative character of his presence. "Yes!" He would reiterate emphatically, "We all have to go, sooner or later!" And as he squeezed the lemon into his tea, he dwelt upon various aspects of the funeral, the children's lack of understanding, the widow's hysterical weeping, the lifelike appearance of the corpse. "He looked," Mr. Baumann would say, "just like he was taking a nap." However, apart from *doing business*, Mr. Baumann enjoyed funerals for their own sake. They were representative meetings of people with whom he had everything in common and to whom he was a very interesting and well-informed man, and even, so he seemed to himself at times, a sage without rabbinical trappings.

Mrs. Weiss finished ironing a tablecloth with the greatest precision and neatness. She folded it carefully, placed it with the other garments already ironed, and took a new piece, permitting herself no pause in her monologue.

Mrs. Baumann, she continued, was the one person who was unable to take Mr. Baumann with the seriousness he expected and received in all quarters. She preferred the rabbi of the neighborhood synagogue whenever there was a need for neighborhood sages. She and her husband shared so many interests that there was naturally a good deal of antagonism between them. Whatever gentleman happened to be occupying the rabbinical position in the neighborhood surpassed her husband at his own game, so far as she was concerned, surpassed him in unction, suavity, and fecundity of opinion.

Mrs. Baumann was small, almost tiny next to her large and heavy husband, and nervous, fussy, anxious, while he was always assured and in company merely moved to smile when she attacked him with ironic remarks and told him that he was talking too much. Really, however, they loved the same things, and her resentment sprang from his being free to pursue a social life while she was burdened with the ceaseless activities involved in bringing up three children. Toward her children, toward her friends, toward all things Jewish, she directed an inexhaustible charity and indulgence and interest, so much so that she neglected her own household because she spent so much time visiting, like her husband, and telling in patient detail endless stories of her children, of friends, and of Jewish activities. In this period a short time before the World War, Freud and Bergson were chronicled in the Jewish newspapers as Jews who had made a great success in the wide world, and Mrs. Baumann relished their fame to the extent of making out, mistakenly enough, the nature of their doctrines. In this way, Belmont's father, who visited the Baumann household very often before his marriage, learned of the doctrines of Freud and passed them on to the salesmen who worked for him in the real estate business.

There was only one thing which Mrs. Baumann enjoyed more than finding out that a successful inventor or musician was Jewish; and that was to hear of some new fad, especially if it had to do with food. She herself often spoke of herself as having a new *fad* and believing that everyone should have fads; for the word pleased her and its full connotation had escaped her when she first heard of it. She said often that she wished she were a vegetarian.

Belmont became nervous as he listened. He was not sure at any given moment whether the cruelty of the story was in his own mind or his mother's tongue. And his own thoughts, which had to do with his own life, and seemed to him to have nothing to do with these people, began to trouble him.

As the Baumann children grew up, they seemed to gain a great deal from the intensive social life of the household. For the small apartment near Eastern Parkway where they lived came in the end to be a kind of community center on Sunday nights, and all whom Mr. Baumann met in his leisurely round of business were invited there. Both husband and wife knew very well how glad lonely people are to have a house to come to when they have been thrown from the old country into the immense alienation of metropolitan life. And the Baumanns knew too, although they would never have wished to express the belief, that it was very important to have something to eat amid the talk, for people do not continue very long without the desire to eat; besides, the conversations, the stories, the jokes, the comments, are heightened, improved in quality, excited by the food and beverages, and the food one gets in another's household seems *exceptionally appetizing*.

Belmont, listening, tried to go back by means of imagination to the lives of those people. Certainly there were times in the old country when food was very scarce, so that one of the most wonderful things about America was the abundance of food. It was impossible, however, for Belmont, who had always been well fed, to convince himself that he knew what their states of mind in regard to food could have been. He returned to his mother who was still painting scenes of the Baumanns' social life on Sunday nights.

The Baumann children grew up amid these pleasant circumstances of much sociability and *company*. Each of them acquired social talents which earned gratifying applause from the visitors, who were expected, in any case, by an unseen, unspoken understanding, to make much of the children of any household they visited socially. Dick, the oldest, learned to play the piano very cleverly and to recite limericks and parodies. Sidney, the youngest, was enchanted by the Sunday nights and went so far as to bring the neighborhood cronies, the boys who lived on the same *block*, to the house. This was something most children avoided out of a general shame that their parents spoke broken English. Sidney showed much less talent than his brother, but was well liked by all partly because he was small and *cute*; partly because he was so fond of the company. Martha, the girl, suffered from the intense aversions and shames and frustrations of girlhood, and as her father said, she took it out on the piano, playing romantic music day and night. She was very *smart* and clever, and her remarks, when she was no more than fifteen, were sometimes so biting that she would be scolded helplessly and vainly, but tirelessly by her mother. Outsiders, however, were charmed, not annoyed, when she was *fresh*. When she was older, she defended herself by saying that she had learned her wit at the Sunday night school of gossip, when the whole company devoted itself to analyses of the failings of their absent friends. Nevertheless, despite her bitter remarks and comments on whatever went on in the household, she loved its whole regime very much, although she was annoyed to find that she depended upon it so much for her day-to-day food and drink of the spirit.

It was about the time that the two older children, Dick and Martha, were getting old enough to need jobs that Belmont's father and Mr. Baumann went into partnership in the real estate business. Belmont's father had been in this business for some time and he had made a good deal of money. But at this time his need of capital (which he could have procured elsewhere) and his fondness for the company of the Baumanns, had made him offer Mr. Baumann a partnership. It was an offer made in a moment of weakness, when he had just enjoyed a good dinner at the Baumann household. Whenever Belmont's father was very pleased and had enjoyed himself, he suffered from such generous impulses, which did not, however, prevent him from repairing the evil consequences of his act with an equally characteristic ruthlessness when it became clear that his generosity had not only been costly (for in that case, he could forget it), but would be of continuing costliness.

This is what happened very soon with the partnership. Mr. Baumann and Dick soon showed Belmont's father that their habits of living were not going to be altered by the fact that they were members of a *going concern*. Father and son arrived at the office an hour before noon, which gave them time to go through the mail before going out for an unhurried lunch. Both of them drew handsome salaries from the business, which troubled Belmont's father more than anything else. When it was a question of selling a plot of land or a house to a customer, Mr. Baumann often allowed his interests of the moment, which were usually international in scope, to make him forget entirely the need of persuading the customer to make *the deal*. He ingratiated himself with the prospective customer all the time; but that very process ingratiated the customer with Mr. Baumann, a situation in which the mutual bloom of friendship soon made business matters either unimportant or a question of tact and delicacy. Dick followed in his father's footsteps and took customers to the ball game, which was well enough except that he too forgot the ulterior purpose of such expenditures of time, energy, and the firm's money. In three short months, Belmont's father appreciated his error and spent a week of bad half-sleepless nights trying to figure out the easiest way to free himself of his pleasure-loving partner and son. Finally, and as always, he solved this problem in the most brutal way by sending them a letter informing them of his grievances and dissolving the partnership. This summary dismissal ended the friendship between the two families for a time. But Mr. Baumann was really unable to sustain a grudge, although his wife certainly could and did in fact pester him about his weakness in forgetting the injuries done to him by his ostensible friends.

Dick could not manage to hold down any job for any length of time and as yet he showed few signs of making his way in the world. But he did seem to make an immense number of friends everywhere and to be in request all over Brooklyn because he was literally always the life of the party. It was at one such party that he met his future wife, a beautiful girl who had already begun to make a good living by running her own beauty parlor. She was the only child of a mother who had been deserted by her husband and she had never been so charmed before as she was by Dick's various activities in company, his parodies, imitations, songs, pranks, and his fine air of well-being and happiness. Somewhat perplexed by the girl's adoring looks, Dick had invited her to the Baumann ménage, where Mrs. Baumann immediately fell in love with her. Dick was nothing if not suggestible, and arranged matters in a variety of ways and after a certain amount of urging upon her part, all parties involved recognized the inevitability of the marriage. But Dick had first to make a living; his wife had her handsome business, which she *ran* with a cousin of hers. But this situation offended Mrs. Baumann's sense of propriety. She expected and expressed her expectation that it would end very soon. She insisted that it must end before the two were married. She could not tolerate the idea that her daughter-in-law not only worked for a living, but also that she made more money than her son did, and she would not countenance the marriage until Susan gave up her business. Dick, however, was in no particular hurry to get married. He did want to please his mother, for this was one aspect of his desire to please everyone, the whole world. But he enjoyed being *single* from morning to night and did not conceive of his marriage as enforcing any change in his habits. It meant merely another addition to his wide circle of acquaintances.

Belmont listened to his mother's account with increasing absorption, but again and again his own thoughts intervened and he reflected on his separation from these people. It seemed, and it seemed sad and unfortunate, that he was a thousand miles away from them in every sense. He was separated from any kind of life from which he could draw satisfaction and gain recognition and dignity. His interests belonged only to himself and a few other widely dispersed people like himself. When he had satisfied his objectives, no one or almost no one would be pleased, essentially. These people of whom he was hearing—not for the first or last time—should have been his genuine relatives and friends, for he had lived surrounded by their lives since the day of his birth. But he was an artist and an artist of the kind that could only be a monster to them in every actual way, although they would be pleased when his name and picture appeared in the newspaper. This particular lower middle class from which he came produced opposites of itself, sheer perversions of all that it had worked for and wanted, children contemptuous of every aspect of their parents. These thoughts had occurred to him often enough before, and he had dismissed them each time as he was now going to, by supposing that he dramatized the matter, and by assuring himself that the situation had little to do with his true work as a musician.

His mother had gone up to the roof to take some more wash down from the line. She told Belmont that it was time he was getting dressed (he had been sitting at the table garbed in dressing gown and pajamas), but before he had a chance to reply, she resumed her story.

The *engagement* of Dick and Susan protracted itself and after two years the couple began to take their intermediate state almost for granted. Mrs. Baumann would mention proudly to her friends that Susan *practically* lived with them. It was by no means unusual for Susan to spend every week-day evening at the Baumann home. Dick would read the sport pages, while his mother interrupted his perusal from time to time, demanding that he admire the profile of his fiancée, who would be sewing. Susan was indeed very good-looking, and her business prospered exceedingly, while Dick went from one job to another, wholly unperturbed by the fact that a girl was waiting for him, a fact to which his mother sometimes summoned his attention.

Finally Mrs. Baumann arranged that the marriage should occur at the outset of one of Dick's business ventures, as if she were afraid to await the outcome. This new business was a small jewelry store in downtown New York near Wall Street, the capital being provided by Mr. Baumann. Within eight months Dick had to give up the business in order to avoid bankruptcy, and Susan had to go back to work as an assistant in a beauty parlor, a humiliation which disillusioned her with regard to her mother-in-law *once and for all*. The two never again managed to get along very well together, despite Mrs. Baumann's imperturbable admiration for her daughter-in-law. Mrs. Baumann could not understand her son's inability to make a living and provide for his wife. No one failed to be delighted by his charm and his intelligence; and he always seemed to acquire a great deal of information about whatever business he was engaged in; but somehow he could not be successful nor make anything *pay*.

After his marriage, Dick was as much a habitué of his parents' household as before, for he and his bride had taken an apartment nearby in order to please Mrs. Baumann. And when it was necessary for Susan to go back to work again, it became convenient for the young married couple to have dinner every night with the whole Baumann family, a course which Susan came to resent more and more, though she was of a divided heart, for she often enjoyed the atmosphere of the family circle as much as before her marriage. One topic prevailed above all others in that household, the wonders of America. This was a subject which many of the foreign-born—for example, Belmont's grandmother—loved to discuss; but in the Baumann household it was discussed with a scope, intensity, subtlety, and appreciative gusto such as could seldom have been equaled elsewhere. This was partly because Mr. Baumann was very much interested in science and partly because he was so pleased with America. When the first plane flight was made, when apartment houses with elevators became common, when the new subway was built, someone or other in the Baumann household would mention the event, looking up from the newspaper where it was stated, and saying: "You see: America!" When the toiletbowl flushed like Niagara, when a suburban homeowner killed his whole family, and when a Jew was made a member of President Theodore Roosevelt's cabinet, the comment was: "America! America!" The expectations of these people who had come in their youth to the brave new world had not been fulfilled in the least. They had expected to be rich, above all, and they had had a very different image of what their new life would be. But something else had happened to their expectations. They had been amazed to the point where they saw that their imaginations were inadequate to the immense developments which were occurring in the world of their time. They expected, of course, that all the wonders would continue and multiply, and Mr. Baumann had the weird idea that his grandchildren would come home from business by a means of transportation which resembled the cash carriers which flew in tubes from place to place in the department stores. Mrs. Baumann's conceptions of the future were of a less mechanical-scientific character. She dreamed that her sons would be millionaires and her grandsons rabbis and philosophers.

The youngest child, Sidney, had arrived at the age where it was expected that he too should make a living for himself. But the disappointments occasioned by Dick's career were as nothing to the difficulties which Sidney created. The older son had been an indifferent student. Sidney, however, flatly refused to continue school at all after a certain time, and he displayed an unheard-of finickiness with regard to the jobs which were obtained for him through Mr. Baumann's many friends. He left one job as a shipping clerk because he did not like *the class* of people with whom he had to work. He refused to take jobs during July and August on the basis of the ill effects of working during the summer heat, a reason with which he had been fortified by the countless family discussions of health and food and exercise. His mother always defended and humored him, saying that his health was delicate; but Sidney usually made his father furious and sometimes almost insanely angry. Mrs. Baumann would point out that Sidney was to be admired, after all, for his sensitivity to the finer things of life. Mr. Baumann, however, became very much concerned because this was the second example of impracticality in his children. When angered, he blamed this lack on his wife and his wife's family, but came to Belmont's father to discuss the matter with him, the two having been long ago reconciled.

"I'll tell you what to do," said Belmont's father, "but you won't do it. Ship Sidney out into the world. Make him stand on his own two feet. As long as he has a home to come to, and a mother to give him something to eat, and a lot of company in the house from morning to night, he's not going to worry about losing a job."

"But if a boy does not have ambition, is that enough?" Mr. Baumann replied. "I always say, it all depends on the individual. His home has nothing to do with it. It is always the character of the person that counts."

"Sure it depends on character," Belmont's father argued, "but he only finds out that he has to make his own way in the world when he has no home to come back to and no one to give him cigarette money. Why, if I were your son," said Belmont's father, flattered by being asked his advice and wishing to return the compliment, "I would quit work myself and just sit around and enjoy the pleasant evenings."

This advice was taken a year later. Sidney was sent to Chicago to be on his own, although not without first being given the names of numerous relatives and friends of the family in Chicago. In three months he had returned, having exhausted his funds and quarreled with his boss over working hours. He was received back in the bosom of his family with great joy, and though Mr. Baumann grumbled, and Martha addressed habitual ironic remarks to her brother as *a captain of industry,* no one had failed to feel his absence keenly and to be pleased deeply by his return. "Well: you can try in New York as well as Chicago," said Mr. Baumann. "A smart boy like you is bound to get started sooner or later." Mrs. Baumann believed that he would one day fall in love and that would be the turning point. Either, that is, he would find a rich girl attracted by his indubitably fine personality; or he would meet some poor girl and his desire to marry her would be the needed spur to ambition. In America, people were always or almost always successful. Mrs. Baumann had seen too many ignorant and poorly brought-up fools make out very well to believe otherwise.

By this time Belmont's mind had been so much absorbed by all that he had heard from his voluble mother through this long morning, that he began to remember all the occasions in which he had, in one way or another, heard about, seen, and talked with the members of the Baumann family. He had been born during his father's partnership with Mr. Baumann (that was the reason for the silver spoon they had given him) and the chief occasions of the Weiss family life, weddings, funerals, *affairs,* had always been marked by the presence of the Baumanns. For each fact which Belmont's mother afforded him, his own mind spontaneously contributed another one. From time to time he would interrupt his mother and remind her of what he remembered. Then the flow of her conversation would seize upon his suggestion and move in the new direction with renewed vigor and fullness of detail.

Some time before Sidney's trip to Chicago, Martha had suffered a brief and successfully overcome attack of spinal meningitis, which left her, however, with a curvature of the spine which made it unlikely that she would ever be able to have children. Martha concluded that this lack, together with her plainness of appearance (which disappeared in her natural vivacity and wit) would prevent her from getting a husband and leave her one of the accursed species of *old maids,* the greatest shame which could occur to a girl from the point of view of any Jewish mother. Her belief that she would not be able to get married heightened Martha's daring wit and *nerve.* She was the one who continued her father's intellectual interests. As he upon occasion would cite the authors he had read in Russia as a young man, Pushkin, Tolstoy, Lermontov; so she was very much taken up with Bernard Shaw and H. G. Wells, and spoke with bitter passion about woman's suffrage. And then, to everyone's amazement, a young doctor who had frequented the household, a very shy fellow who was already quite successful, and who had, moreover, a big family of his own to support, asked Martha to marry him, afraid above all that she would launch out at him with her famous sharpness and scorn. When she told him that he would have to go through life without children, he replied with a fine simplicity that he loved her and expected her to make a home for him which would be like her mother's household.

Their marriage was the greatest satisfaction of the Baumanns' life, although it did not compensate for the inability of the two sons to support themselves. Mrs. Baumann tirelessly praised her son-in-law, never ceased to marvel at his magnanimity in marrying a girl who could not bear him children, and took especial pride in the fact that he was so good a doctor, a fact which not only impressed all other women of her acquaintance, whose hope was so often for a son or son-in-law who was a doctor, but also was linked with her passionate interest in everything that had to do with health.

Martha's harshness and sharpness were merely increased by her marriage, and she was especially relentless with her brothers, while her husband, Maurice, stood by, gently protesting because she had again called both of them failures. Maurice had an admiration for the arts from which he gained the usual independence of business values. He would try to argue with Martha that she was very conventional in this respect and accepting conventional notions of success. With her brutality of tongue, Martha would assert that there was one thing at which the Baumanns were wonderfully successful, and that was marriage. They made excellent marriages. In saying this, she referred not only to her own husband's prosperity and generosity, but also to Susan, who had started her own beauty shop once more and for a number of years supported her husband and herself and also provided him with the capital for each new enterprise to which he was spurred by his mother's anguish at the whole situation. Martha's impatience with her family increased yearly and she wished to see less and less of them, but her husband soothed the hurt feelings of the parents and gently insisted on paying the weekly visit, although the couple had moved to a well-to-do suburb on Long Island.

America! America! The expression began to recur in Belmont's mind, like a phrase of a piece of music which he had heard too often the day before. He was moved, and his mother was also, in her own way, by the fact that Martha, the family rebel, the one who had freed herself from the family circle, should have been the one to make out well with her life. It seemed to Belmont's mother (and this perception amazed him) that the two sons were unsuccessful just because they were so much like their father, who had, however, been successful enough, from every point of view. The sons had taken over the father's attitudes and way of life wholly; but for some reason which was not clear, it no longer worked.

Belmont remembered now the last visit of Mrs. Baumann to his mother just a month before he had left for Paris. It was an afternoon in late fall; Belmont was working very hard in his room and the sounds at the door which indicated visitors annoyed him because he knew he would have to stop work and come from his room in his shirt-sleeves and abstracted look to greet his mother's friends. Mrs. Baumann had come with a woman of her own age, and when he came into the living room, Mrs. Baumann, whose volubility was only equaled by his mother's, told him in a rush the story of her friendship with this woman. They had come to America together in the year 1888 as young girls. They had met on shipboard and this made them *shipsisters*. But although their friendship had continued in a mild way for some years, one day at a picnic of their old country's society, a sudden storm had come to disturb the fine summer Sunday, everyone had run for cover, and they had not seen each other again for the next nineteen years. For that was in 1911 and it was now 1930. The two old women, Mrs. Baumann and her shipsister, continued drinking their tea, and telling the young musician of their feelings in regard to what had come of their lives, and Belmont, suddenly tired and relaxed because he had stopped working, listened and drank tea also. Mrs. Baumann told him that in her sixty-five years of life she had known perhaps as many as a thousand people well, and when she tried to sleep at night, all those faces came back to her so clearly that she believed she could draw their pictures if she were an artist. She was sickened and horrified by this plenitude of memory, although it was not wholly clear why she should have been utterly appalled by the past. And the result was that she could not sleep at night and nothing was more pleasant than the sound of the milkman's wagon which indicated that the darkness would soon be at an end, and she could get up and make breakfast for her family. She told Belmont that sometimes she thought she ought to go to see a psychoanalyst like Freud, a reference he could not at first understand because she pronounced the name to rhyme with food. Her companion offered advice at this juncture and said that she believed that everyone ought to have a hobby; her hobby was knitting and it seemed to her that if she did not have her knitting to do in the morning, she would certainly *go crazy*. From his mother, Belmont learned later that this woman's daughter had married a *Gentile* and the result was that she was allowed to visit her only child only upon carefully arranged monthly dates when the husband had been asked to absent himself by his wife. Her one longing, and one which would not, she knew, be satisfied, was to go back to the old country for a visit; she thought of Belmont's imminent journey in terms of her own desire to return and advised him to visit the Roumania from which she had come as a young girl. Listening to the two old women, Belmont tried to call images to his mind of their trip to the new world, their arrival at Ellis Island, and their first impressions of New York City. But he could not; there was nothing in his own experience which he could feel as comparable to that great displacement of the body and spirit which their coming to America must have been.

Belmont's mother had almost finished ironing her wash, but she was far from done with her story. There was no attribute of the family which she was not capable of illustrating with any number of examples, and each example itself provoked fresh memories and new ideas about these people she had known for thirty years. What she said bloomed in Belmont's mind into shapes which would have astonished and angered her; her words descended into the marine world of his mind and were transformed there as the swimmers and divers seen in the movie, moving underwater through new pressures and compulsions, bubbling, and raising heavy arms to free themselves from the dim and dusky green weight of the water.

Belmont's mother had arrived at the twenties, by which time the most bitter animosity had come to exist between Mr. Baumann and his son, Sidney. Whenever Sidney was criticized by his father for his indolence, lack of initiative, and inability to keep any job, he would point out to his father the fact that many of his father's friends had made or were making fortunes. Few of them had the bearing and personality of Mr. Baumann, but they were able to give their sons a start in life. Sidney was an avid reader of newspapers, like his mother, and he had acquired a host of examples of immigrants who had become millionaires; the whole movie industry constituted, for Sidney, a standing example of his father's ineptitude. It was true that it was unfair to go beyond the family's circle of friends in order to make such comparisons; but Sidney was merciless when criticized. Mr. Baumann was left helpless by Sidney's attack. He felt that there was something wrong not only with the contrast which was made by his son, but also with the repeated assertion that his life had not been successful. He himself was satisfied. He had always provided for his wife and his children and kept them in comfort. It was true that he did not work very hard, but that was unnecessary, since he had an income from the commissions of insurance policies he had written for thirty years, when the premiums were paid or when the policy was renewed. Sidney, however, brushed aside these answers as obvious admissions of weakness. He pointed out that other sons of their class of people had a ten dollar bill to spend on a girl on a Saturday night, but he did not. The more unsuccessful he was, the more outrageous became his verbal assault upon his father for not being a millionaire. Usually, it is true, he was provoked to these attacks by the attempts to get him to work by insulting him and bringing forward as examples other young men of his age who were doing very well, and who as a matter of fact, would soon be wealthy men in their own right, although they came from households and had parents who were really *common*.

After Belmont's father had left his mother early in the twenties, the Baumanns and Belmont's mother became better friends than ever. Mrs. Baumann and Belmont's mother would often discuss the fate of the Baumann children during frequent visits, although their friendship was somewhat handicapped by the fact that Mrs. Baumann was twenty years older than Mrs. Weiss. Belmont's mother remembered now that she had once given Mrs. Baumann some advice which she still regarded as very good. She had told her friend that the salvation of the family would have been to go into the summer-hotel business, as they had once come very near doing. No one, Belmont's mother had said and now reiterated, would have been better equipped for that business than the Baumanns.

When his mother said such things, Belmont suffered from the illusion, for the moment at any rate, that she had a greater understanding than he did of most of the difficulties of life. And it seemed to him at such times that the ignorance he took for granted in her was a sign of his own ignorance. Her understanding simply worked in different, less theoretical terms than his. She had clearly seen, he was sure, the necessity of a relationship he was always meeting in music, the necessity that the individual musician find the medium suitable to his own special gifts.

One could hardly doubt that the summer hotel would have been the proper medium for the undeniable gifts of the Baumanns.

What Mrs. Baumann could not understand at all and discussed most often with Belmont's mother was the paradox that her sons, who had a much better bringing-up than other young men of her circle and class, had made out so poorly in comparison with them. She wished to know where the responsibility lay and the head start she attributed to her children made matters even more perplexing. She was worried about her husband's accusation that it was her own humoring and *babying* and *indulging* of the two boys which made them lacking in self-reliance and initiative and ambition. Mr. Baumann remembered the advice given him by Belmont's father, that the children would be more ambitious if they had no home to come to, and distorted it into this explanation which blamed Mrs. Baumann for pampering her sons. Mrs. Baumann would present the problem to Belmont's mother again and again, anxious to be told that on the contrary she had always been a wonderful mother. Belmont's mother was always ready to blame someone for everything that happened, but she had a vaguely general interest in the matter which left her free of her usual prepossessions. She observed that one trouble was that the Baumann sons were not willing to go from door to door, for the sake of getting some business; they had not been brought up to expect *hard knocks* and unfriendliness, and it was precisely here that boys who had been brought up in meaner families had the advantage over them. It was a strange and sad thing, both women agreed, that a certain refinement—nothing like the Four Hundred, you understand, but merely a simple taste of the usual good things of life—should be a severe and even a fatal handicap. But worst of all, Mrs. Weiss would say, the greatest handicap of all had been their fine home and family surroundings which had weakened the boys for a career in a world where you had to fight for everything you wanted and you had to fight to keep whatever you had. Belmont's mother would say to Mrs. Baumann that this was a *cut-rate, cut-throat world* (an expression as popular with her as: *dog eat dog*), and the best way to be prepared for such a world, as her own experience had shown her, was to be born into a family of thirteen children in which there was never enough for everyone to eat.

After 1929, when all the people who had been so successful lost so much, Sidney achieved new heights of scorn. There had been times before 1929 when he had been contemptuous of *the system,* but now that no one was able to make out well, he took the country-wide depression as a personal vindication. Every banker or broker who had been caught in some kind of dishonesty was one more instance to Sidney of his own integrity. He would say that if he had been prepared to do the things they had done, he too might have been as successful as they. But now Mr. Baumann was unable to support an idle son very well. With the hard times, many people had abandoned their insurance, or, what was worse, borrowed on it. The father's difficulties and the son's arrogance made the quarrels between them of a desperate character. Mr. Baumann had been dressing to pay a visit one Saturday night and he had been unable to find the pair of shoes he wanted. He was as always concerned about how he was going to be dressed and he became very irritated about not being able to find his shoes. He came into his son's bedroom to ask him if he had seen the shoes, and Sidney, outstretched upon his bed reading and smoking, had been annoyed at the interruption and told him that he ought not to be so concerned about such a cheap pair of shoes. The shoes were not cheap, in any case, and this characteristic judgment of his taste by his son, who used canons derived from his jobs at Christmas in clothing stores patronized by the rich, infuriated Mr. Baumann. He struck Sidney and only the screaming entrance of Mrs. Baumann prevented the continuance of a fist fight. The next day Sidney had a black eye which he vainly tried to hide with powder. It was a Sunday and the Baumanns were going for a visit. Sidney wished to go along, being incapable of enduring any solitude at any time and having nowhere to go that afternoon. But he was reminded of his black eye by his mother and his father added that he had no clothes, particularly no shoes, suitable for the people they were going to visit. When the Baumanns returned late in the evening they found an emergency wagon and the police in front of the apartment house. Sidney had attempted to kill himself by turning on the gas in the kitchen; there had been an explosion and he had not even been seriously injured. Sidney was taken to Bellevue and kept there for a number of months. When his mother visited him, he told her that it was his father, *she should remember,* who had driven him to insanity. Mr. Baumann, when told of this, retaliated by saying that his son had not been able to be anything but a failure even at suicide, and he told everybody that at the asylum Sidney could not be persuaded to engage in the forms of occupational therapy; it seemed an epitome to him that even in the insane asylum, his son should refuse to do anything *remotely resembling work.* Nothing could make Mr. Baumann forget what Sidney had said to him during the early years of the depression when Mr. Baumann's income was sharply curtailed. He had told his father that *the old oil* no longer worked, and when his father had asked him, *what oil, what is this oil?,* the son had said, *banana oil!* laughing with his whole body at his own witticism and then going on to explain to his father that he could no longer expect to persuade anyone that insurance was anything but *a gyp* by the old methods of striking up a friendship and paying long visits and acting like a sage of the neighborhood.

Sidney remained under observation. Dick had for some years assisted his wife in her thriving beauty parlor. He had a child now, a grandchild of whom Mrs. Baumann made much, until she was forbidden to see the child more than twice a week by her daughter-in-law. Martha and her husband prospered more than the rest of the family combined; for the practice of medicine was not so closely attached to the prosperity of the rest of the world as was such a business as insurance. Martha, after an operation and much nervousness, had also had a child. Both grandchildren were daughters, which was disappointing, but which was, at any rate, an indication that not all disappointments resulted from financial matters. (Dick would often say that *money was not everything.*)

The whole family was ashamed of Sidney's *smash-up*, as Dick called it, but this did not keep them from discussing the whole matter with all their many friends. Mr. Baumann at seventy was still able to eke out a living for his wife and himself. But he was a disappointed and a disillusioned man. He blamed everything on the individual, on the lack of *will power* on the part of his sons. Mrs. Baumann, however, would say to Belmont's mother that *you see: this is what we came to America for forty-five years ago, for this.*

Belmont was tired of his mother's story and tired of having remained seated in one place for three hours. He was sick and tired of the mood in which he had heard the story, the irony and contempt with which he had listened for the most part. He had listened from such a distance that what he saw was an outline and thus a caricature. How different the picture would be if he had been able to see those lives from the inside, looking out.

His mother asked him whether he wanted his lunch now, and he told her that he would go for a walk first. But instead he went into the bedroom he was sharing for a time with his older brother and sat down in the armchair by the window, trying to free himself of the conflicting emotions which the narrative had created in him. The bedroom window looked out on a back courtyard, which was empty except for a clothesline and one hanging aerial which had been loosened from its place by the wind. His gaze was directly out of the window at nothing at all. He recognized the blindness involved, the self-concern and the revery which always kept him from seeing what surrounded him.

It now seemed to him that he had seen nothing of his connections with all these people. The separation and the alienation from them which he felt keenly at times was actual enough, but coexisted with the immense unity between his own life and the lives of these people. As the air was full of the radio's voices, so it was also full of intimations of the countless habits, activities, desires and memories which united him to the people from whom he had come, not only his own family and not only their friends, but the age in which they had lived and the conditions which had moved them. He had for a long time seen himself as *different*, because he was an artist and because they regarded him as different and because art had no important part in their lives. That was what his separation and his difference amounted to; it was an aspect of the whole context in which he existed as a product of those people and their lives.

The relationship which he now recognized did not seem a pleasant matter to him. He did not feel any allegiance, whatever that could be, to these people; and he certainly did not feel that he would want to spend his time with them, nor did he feel that he would resent any less the fact that they would never *understand* his music. But every quality of the Baumann family which his mother had displayed with her sharp tongue he now saw as corresponding to some quality in himself, modified by the change of circumstances, by the fact that he belonged to the third generation. The contemptuous mood which had governed him as he listened and with which he had enveloped everything his mother said was really self-contempt.

His emotion took the new form of a kind of profound uneasiness, for he now began to see himself within the whole context of those lives and from the distant perspective he had adopted all morning. Looked at from that perspective, his own life, past and present, invited the same irony. He turned his mind deliberately from this prospect, as from the memory of an occasion of great embarrassment, of gaucheness and lack of tact. The impression was pathetic. It made actual the curious omniscience one gains in looking at an old photograph in which the posing faces and the old-fashioned clothes and the moment itself seem ridiculous, ignorant, and wholly unaware of the period quality, which is actually there, and the subsequent revelation of failure and waste. Lifting one's gaze from the photograph, it might occur to one to recognize that the very moment of looking has or will have, in its time, the same character. As he thought of this limitation of vision, Belmont kept himself from looking at it too closely, though he promised himself that he would do so later. When Belmont's mother had concluded by saying that it was a peculiar but assured fact that many people seem to be ruined by their finest qualities,

Belmont had been shocked, for her observation became a generalization about the usual fate of human beings, and his own fate. He saw the sources of his being in these lives and the fact presented him with a kind of incipient terror, such as he could feel at any moment if he imagined himself hanging by his hands from the window ledge of their fifth-floor apartment. And now it seemed to him that all those lives inhabited the air he breathed and would be present wherever he was. Their America would always be present in him.

1940

GRACE PALEY (1922–   )

Born in New York on December 11, 1922, Grace Paley grew up in New York and studied at Hunter College (1938–1939). She has taught at Columbia University, Syracuse University, and Sarah Lawrence. Her stories have appeared in leading journals and the best of them have been collected in The Little Disturbances of Man (1959).

The Loudest Voice

There is a certain place where dumb-waiters boom, doors slam, dishes crash; every window is a mother's mouth bidding the street shut up, go skate somewhere else, come home. My voice is the loudest.

There, my own mother is still as full of breathing as me and the grocer stands up to speak to her. "Mrs. Abramowitz," he says, "people should not be afraid of their children."

"Ah, Mr. Bialik," my mother replies, "if you say to her or her father 'Ssh,' they say, 'In the grave it will be quiet.'"

"From Coney Island to the cemetery," says my papa. "It's the same subway; it's the same fare."

I am right next to the pickle barrel. My pinky is making tiny whirl-pools in the brine. I stop a moment to announce: "Campbell's Tomato Soup. Campbell's Vegetable Beef Soup. Campbell's S-c-otch Broth . . ."

"Be quiet," the grocer says, "the labels are coming off."

"Please, Shirley, be a little quiet," my mother begs me.

In that place the whole street groans: Be quiet! Be quiet! but steals from the happy chorus of my inside self not a tittle or a jot.

There, too, but just around the corner, is a red brick building that has been old for many years. Every morning the children stand before it in double lines which must be straight. They are not insulted. They are waiting anyway.

I am usually among them. I am, in fact, the first, since I begin with "A."

One cold morning the monitor tapped me on the shoulder. "Go to Room 409, Shirley Abramowitz," he said. I did as I was told. I went in a hurry up a down staircase to Room 409, which contained sixth-graders. I had to wait at the desk without wiggling until Mr. Hilton, their teacher, had time to speak.

After five minutes he said, "Shirley?"

"What?" I whispered.

He said, "My! My! Shirley Abramowitz! They told me you had a particularly loud, clear voice and read with lots of expression. Could that be true?"

"Oh yes," I whispered.

"In that case, don't be silly; I might very well be your teacher some-day. Speak up, speak up."

"Yes," I shouted.

"More like it," he said. "Now, Shirley, can you put a ribbon in your hair or a bobby pin? It's too messy."

"Yes!" I bawled.

"Now, now, calm down." He turned to the class. "Children, not a sound. Open at page 39. Read till 52. When you finish, start again." He looked me over once more. "Now, Shirley, you know, I suppose, that Christmas is coming. We are preparing a beautiful play. Most of the parts have been given out. But I still need a child with a strong voice, lots of stamina. Do you know what stamina is? You do? Smart kid. You know, I heard you read 'The Lord is my shepherd' in Assembly yester-day. I was very impressed. Wonderful delivery. Mrs. Jordan, your teacher, speaks highly of you. Now listen to me, Shirley Abramowitz, if you want to take the part and be in the play, repeat after me, 'I swear to work harder than I ever did before.' "

I looked to heaven and said at once, "Oh, I swear." I kissed my pinky and looked at God.

"That is an actor's life, my dear," he explained. "Like a soldier's, never tardy or disobedient to his general, the director. Everything," he said, "absolutely everything will depend on you."

That afternoon, all over the building, children scraped and scrubbed the turkeys and the sheaves of corn off the schoolroom windows. Good-bye Thanksgiving. The next morning a monitor brought red paper and green paper from the office. We made new shapes and hung them on the walls and glued them to the doors.

The teachers became happier and happier. Their heads were ringing like the bells of childhood. My best friend Evie was prone to evil, but she did not get a single demerit for whispering. We learned "Holy Night" without an error. "How wonderful!" said Miss Glacé, the student teacher. "To think that some of you don't even speak the language!" We learned "Deck the Halls" and "Hark! The Herald Angels". . . . They weren't ashamed and we weren't embarrassed.

Oh, but when my mother heard about it all, she said to my father: "Misha, you don't know what's going on there. Cramer is the head of the Tickets Committee."

"Who?" asked my father. "Cramer? Oh yes, an active woman."

"Active? Active has to have a reason. Listen," she said sadly, "I'm surprised to see my neighbors making tra-la-la for Christmas."

My father couldn't think of what to say to that. Then he decided: "You're in America! Clara, you wanted to come here. In Palestine the Arabs would be eating you alive. Europe you had pogroms. Argentina is full of Indians. Here you got Christmas. . . . Some joke, ha?"

"Very funny, Misha. What is becoming of you? If we came to a new country a long time ago to run away from tyrants, and instead we fall into a creeping pogrom, that our children learn a lot of lies, so what's the joke? Ach, Misha, your idealism is going away."

"So is your sense of humor."

"That I never had, but idealism you had a lot of."

"I'm the same Misha Abramovitch, I didn't change an iota. Ask anyone."

"Only ask me," says my mama, may she rest in peace. "I got the answer."

Meanwhile the neighbors had to think of what to say too.

Marty's father said: "You know, he has a very important part, my boy."

"Mine also," said Mr. Sauerfeld.

"Not my boy!" said Mrs. Klieg. "I said to him no. The answer is no. When I say no! I mean no!"

The rabbi's wife said, "It's disgusting!" But no one listened to her. Under the narrow sky of God's great wisdom she wore a strawberry-blond wig.

Every day was noisy and full of experience. I was Right-hand Man. Mr. Hilton said: "How could I get along without you, Shirley?"

He said: "Your mother and father ought to get down on their knees every night and thank God for giving them a child like you."

He also said: "You're absolutely a pleasure to work with, my dear, dear child."

Sometimes he said: "For God's sakes, what did I do with the script? Shirley! Shirley! Find it."

Then I answered quietly: "Here it is, Mr. Hilton."

Once in a while, when he was very tired, he would cry out: "Shirley,

I'm just tired of screaming at those kids. Will you tell Ira Pushkov not to come in till Lester points to that star the second time?"

Then I roared: "Ira Pushkov, what's the matter with you? Dope! Mr. Hilton told you five times already, don't come in till Lester points to that star the second time."

"Ach, Clara," my father asked, "what does she do there till six o'clock she can't even put the plates on the table?"

"Christmas," said my mother coldly.

"Ho! Ho!" my father said. "Christmas. What's the harm? After all, history teaches everyone. We learn from reading this is a holiday from pagan times also, candles, lights, even Chanukah. So we learn it's not altogether Christian. So if they think it's a private holiday, they're only ignorant, not patriotic. What belongs to history, belongs to all men. You want to go back to the Middle Ages? Is it better to shave your head with a secondhand razor? Does it hurt Shirley to learn to speak up? It does not. So maybe someday she won't live between the kitchen and the shop. She's not a fool."

I thank you, Papa, for your kindness. It is true about me to this day. I am foolish but I am not a fool.

That night my father kissed me and said with great interest in my career, "Shirley, tomorrow's your big day. Congrats."

"Save it," my mother said. Then she shut all the windows in order to prevent tonsillitis.

In the morning it snowed. On the street corner a tree had been decorated for us by a kind city administration. In order to miss its chilly shadow our neighbors walked three blocks east to buy a loaf of bread. The butcher pulled down black window shades to keep the colored lights from shining on his chickens. Oh, not me. On the way to school, with both my hands I tossed it a kiss of tolerance. Poor thing, it was a stranger in Egypt.

I walked straight into the auditorium past the staring children. "Go ahead, Shirley!" said the monitors. Four boys, big for their age, had already started work as propmen and stagehands.

Mr. Hilton was very nervous. He was not even happy. Whatever he started to say ended in a sideward look of sadness. He sat slumped in the middle of the first row and asked me to help Miss Glacé. I did this, although she thought my voice too resonant and said, "Show-off!"

Parents began to arrive long before we were ready. They wanted to make a good impression. From among the yards of drapes I peeked out at the audience. I saw my embarrassed mother.

Ira, Lester, and Meyer were pasted to their beards by Miss Glacé.

She almost forgot to thread the star on its wire, but I reminded her. I coughed a few times to clear my throat. Miss Glacé looked around and saw that everyone was in costume and on line waiting to play his part. She whispered, "All right . . ." Then:

Jackie Sauerfeld, the prettiest boy in first grade, parted the curtains with his skinny elbow and in a high voice sang out:

> "Parents dear
> We are here
> To make a Christmas play in time.
> It we give
> In narrative
> And illustrate with pantomime."

He disappeared.

My voice burst immediately from the wings to the great shock of Ira, Lester, and Meyer, who were waiting for it but were surprised all the same.

"I remember, I remember, the house where I was born . . ."

Miss Glacé yanked the curtain open and there it was, the house—an old hayloft, where Celia Kornbluh lay in the straw with Cindy Lou, her favorite doll. Ira, Lester, and Meyer moved slowly from the wings toward her, sometimes pointing to a moving star and sometimes ahead to Cindy Lou.

It was a long story and it was a sad story. I carefully pronounced all the words about my lonesome childhood, while little Eddie Braunstein wandered upstage and down with his shepherd's stick, looking for sheep. I brought up lonesomeness again, and not being understood at all except by some women everybody hated. Eddie was too small for that and Marty Groff took his place, wearing his father's prayer shawl. I announced twelve friends, and half the boys in the fourth grade gathered round Marty, who stood on an orange crate while my voice harangued. Sorrowful and loud, I declaimed about love and God and Man, but because of the terrible deceit of Abie Stock we came suddenly to a famous moment. Marty, whose remembering tongue I was, waited at the foot of the cross. He stared desperately at the audience. I goaned, "My God, my God why hast thou forsaken me?" The soldiers who were sheiks grabbed poor Marty to pin him up to die, but he wrenched free, turned again to the audience, and spread his arms aloft to show despair and the end. I murmured at the top of my voice, "The rest is silence, but as everyone in this room, in this city—in this world—now knows, I shall have life eternal."

That night Mrs. Kornbluh visited our kitchen for a glass of tea.

"How's the virgin?" asked my father with a look of concern.

"For a man with a daughter, you got a fresh mouth, Abramovitch."

"Here," said my father kindly, "have some lemon, it'll sweeten your disposition."

They debated a little in Yiddish, then fell in a puddle of Russian and Polish. What I understood next was my father, who said, "Still and all, it was certainly a beautiful affair, you have to admit, introducing us to the beliefs of a different culture."

"Well, yes," said Mrs. Kornbluh. "The only thing . . . you know Charlie Turner—that cute boy in Celia's class—a couple others? They got very small parts or no part at all. In very bad taste, it seemed to me. After all, it's their religion."

"Ach," explained my mother, "what could Mr. Hilton do? They got very small voices; after all, why should they holler? The English language they know from the beginning by heart. They're blond like angels. You think it's so important they should get in the play? Christmas . . . the whole piece of goods . . . they own it."

I listened and listened until I couldn't listen any more. Too sleepy, I climbed out of bed and kneeled. I made a little church of my hands and said, "Hear, O Israel . . ." Then I called out in Yiddish, "Please, good night, good night. Ssh." My father said, "Ssh yourself," and slammed the kitchen door.

I was happy. I fell asleep at once. I had prayed for everybody: my talking family, cousins far away, passersby, and all the lonesome Christians. I expected to be heard. My voice was certainly the loudest.

NORMAN MAILER (1923–   )

The *"warrior, presumptive general, ex-political candidate, embattled aging enfant terrible of the literary world, wise father of six children, radical intellectual, existential philosopher, hard-working author, champion of obscenity, husband of four battling sweet wives, amiable bar drinker, and much exaggerated street fighter, party giver, hostess insulter . . . had . . . a fatal taint, a last remaining speck of the one personality he found absolutely insupportable—the nice Jewish boy from Brooklyn."*

*Why Mailer should find this aspect of his multifaceted personality insupportable is suggested by the remark that follows. "Something in his adenoids gave it away—he had the softness of a man early accustomed to mother-love." The very fact that Mailer should isolate his Jewishness dramatizes the difficulties he has—unlike Emerson, Twain, Howells, Eliot, or Hemingway in previous generations—of being the representative writer of our time. Clearly, as Richard Gilman points out, "he long ago made it out of niceness and Jewishness and Brooklyn"; but there is the residue of that "softness" which distinguishes him from Hemingway or Robert Lowell. Some of Mailer's best work—*The Naked and the Dead, *"The Man who Studied Yoga," and "A Time of Her Time"—is expressive, at least in part, of his Jewishness; it could be written by no author other than one who stood a litte outside, and even felt intimidated by, the Protestant tradition in our literature which ended with World War II. He knows, as he writes in* Armies of the Night, *that as one of "the grandsons of the immigrants," he has a special kind of "love affair with America."*

Norman Mailer was born in Long Branch, New Jersey, in 1923, grew up in Brooklyn, and was graduated from Harvard in 1943. During the war he served as a rifleman in Leyte, Luzon, and Japan; he was "very gentle, shy, quiet," in the words of a novelist who served with him in the Philippines, "not at all aggressive." When Mailer returned from the war he wrote his war novel, The Naked and the Dead (1948), *and in the next twenty years followed it with four other novels:* Barbary Shore (1951), *concerned with socialism;* The Deer Park (1955), *an exploration of the movie industry;* An American Dream (1965), *a treatment of the loss of the heroic ideal in American society; and* Why Are We in Vietnam? (1967), *a bitter attack on the violent sensibility that caused the Vietnam war. Mailer's essays and confessional writings have become increasingly important and the best of them contain profound perceptions into American society:* Advertisements for Myself (1959),

The Presidential Papers (*1963*), Cannibals and Christians (*1966*), The Armies of the Night (*1968*), *and* Miami and the Siege of Chicago (*1968*). *His most recent publications include* Of a Fire on the Moon (*1971*) *and* The Prisoner of Sex (*1971*).

The Marshal and the Nazi

THEY PUT HIM in the rear seat of a Volkswagen camper and he welcomed the opportunity to relax. Soon they would drive him, he guessed, to some nearby place where he would be arraigned, fined, and released. He kept searching the distance for sight of Lowell and Macdonald whom he assumed would be following any minute. The thought that they might not have been picked up was depressing, for he could only guess at the depth of Lowell's dejection if he had botched his arrest, and now, with each twenty seconds, he became more gloomily certain that Lowell and Macdonald had been turned back, had failed to get arrested, and blamed himself now for the rush with which he had set out—he should have warned them the arrest might not be automatic, that one might have to steal it—he felt somehow incompetent at not having properly prepared them.

Now a new man entered the Volkswagen. Mailer took him at first for a Marshal or an official, since he was wearing a dark suit and a white motorcycle helmet, and had a clean-cut stubborn face with short features. But he was carrying something which looked like a rolled-up movie screen over five feet long, and he smiled in the friendliest fashion, sat down next to Mailer, and took off his helmet. Mailer thought he was about to be interrogated and he looked forward to that with this friendly man, no less! (Of course the prisoner often looks forward to his interrogation) but then another man carrying a clipboard came up to them, and leaning through the wide double door of the camper, asked questions of them both. When Mailer gave his name, the man with the clipboard acted as if he had never heard of him, or at least pretended

never to have heard of him, the second possibility seeming possible since
word traveled quickly from reporters.

"How do you spell it?"

"M.A.I.L.E.R."

"Why were you arrested, Mr. Miller?"

"For transgressing a police line as a protest against the war in Vietnam."

The Clipboard then asked a question of the man sitting next to him.
"And why were *you* arrested?"

"As an act of solidarity with oppressed forces fighting for liberty
against this country in Southeast Asia."

The Clipboard nodded drily, as if to say, "Yeah, we're all crazy here."
Then he asked, pointing to the object which looked like a rolled-up
movie screen. "You want that with you?"

"Yessir," said the man next to Mailer. "I'd like to take it along."

The Clipboard gave a short nod, and walked off. Mailer would never
see him again. If the History has therefore spent a pointless exchange
with him, it is to emphasize that the first few minutes of an arrest such
as this are without particular precedent, and so Mailer, like a visitor
from Mars, or an adolescent entering polite society, had no idea of what
might be important next and what might not. This condition of innocence was not, however, particularly disagreeable since it forced him to
watch everything with the attention, let us say, of a man like William
Buckley spending his first hour in a Harlem bar—no, come! things are
far safer for Mailer at the Pentagon.

He chatted with his fellow prisoner, Teague, Walter Teague was the
name, who had been in the vanguard of the charge Mailer had seen
from the parking lot. But before any confused impressions were to be
sorted, they were interrupted by the insertion of the next prisoner put
into the Volkswagen, a young man with straight blond hair and a Nazi
armband on his sleeve. He was installed in the rear, with a table between, but Mailer was not happy, for his eyes and the Nazi's bounced
off each other like two heads colliding—the novelist discovered he was
now in a hurry for them to get this stage of the booking completed. He
was also privately indignant at the U.S. Army (like a private citizen,
let us say, who writes a letter to his small-town newspaper) at the incredible stupidity of putting a Nazi in the same Volkswagen camper
with Pentagon demonstrators—there were two or three other cars available, at least!—next came the suspicion that this was not an accident,
but a provocation in the making. If the Nazi started trouble, and there
was a fight, the newspaper accounts would doubtless state that Norman

Mailer had gotten into an altercation five minutes after his arrest. (Of course, they would not say with whom.) This is all doubtless most paranoid of Mailer, but then he had had nearly twenty years of misreporting about himself, and the seed of paranoia is the arrival of the conviction that the truth about oneself is never told. (Mailer might have done better to pity the American populace—receiving misinformation in systematic form tends to create mass schizophrenia: poor America—Eddie and Debbie are True Love.)

Now they were moved out of the camper and over to an Army truck. There was Teague, and the novelist, and another arrestee—a tall Hungarian who quickly told Mailer how much he liked his books and in much the same breath that he was a Freedom Fighter—there was also a new U.S. Marshal, and the Nazi. The prisoners climbed one by one over the high tailgate, Mailer finding it a touch awkward for he did not wish to dirty his dark blue pinstripe suit, and then they stood in the rear of the truck, a still familiar 2½ ton 6-by of a sort which the novelist hadn't been in for twenty-one years, not since his Army discharge.

Standing in the truck, a few feet apart from each other, all prisoners regarding one another, the Nazi fixed on Mailer. Their eyes locked like magnets coming into line, and for perhaps twenty seconds they stared at each other. Mailer looked into a pair of yellow eyes so compressed with hate that back of his own eyes he could feel the echo of such hatred ringing. The Nazi was taller than Mailer, well-knit, and with neatly formed features and a shock of blond hair, would have been handsome but for the ferocity of his yellow eyes which were sunk deep in their sockets. Those eyes made him look like an eagle.

Yet Mailer had first advantage in this eye-staring contest. Because he had been prepared for it. He had been getting into such confrontations for years, and rarely lost them, even though he sometimes thought they were costing him eyesight. Still, some developed instinct had made him ready an instant before the Nazi. Every bit of intensity he possessed— with the tremors of the March and the Marshall's arm still pent in him —glared forth into the other's eyes: he was nonetheless aghast at what he saw. The American Nazis were all fanatics, yes, poor mad tormented fanatics, their psyches twisted like burning leaves in the fire of their hatreds, yes, indeed! but this man's conviction stood in his eyes as if his soul had been focused to a single point of light. Mailer could feel violence behind violence rocking through his head. If the two of them were ever alone in an alley, one of them might kill the other in a fight— it was not unlike holding an electric wire in the hand. And the worst of it was that he was not even feeling violent himself—whatever violence he possessed had gone to his eyes—by that route had he projected himself on the Nazi.

After the first five seconds of the shock had passed, he realized he might be able to win—the Nazi must have taken too many easy contests, and had been too complacent in the first moment, yes it was like wrestlers throwing themselves on each other: one knuckle of one finger a little better able to be worked on a grip could make the difference —now he could feel the hint of force ebbing in the other's eyes, and could wonder at his own necessity to win. He did not hate the Nazi nearly so much as he was curious about him, yet the thought of losing had been intolerable as if he had been *obliged* not to lose, as if the duty of his life at this particular moment must have been to look into that Nazi's eye, and say with his own, "You claim you have a philosophical system which comprehends all—you know nothing! My eyes encompass yours. My philosophy contains yours. You have met the wrong man!" And the Nazi looked away, and was hysterical with fury on the instant.

"You Jew bastard," he shouted. "Dirty Jew with kinky hair."

They didn't speak that way. It was too corny. Yet he could only answer, "You filthy Kraut."

"Dirty Jew."

"Kraut pig."

A part of his mind could actually be amused at this choice—he didn't even hate Germans any more. Indeed Germans fascinated him now. Why they liked his books more than Americans did. Yet here he could think of nothing better to return than "Kraut pig."

"I'm not a Kraut," said the Nazi, "I'm a Norwegian." And then as if the pride of his birth had tricked him into communication with an infidel, thus into sacrilege, the Nazi added quickly, "Jew bastard red," then cocked his fist. "Come here, you coward," he said to Mailer, "I'll kill you."

"Throw the first punch, baby," said Mailer, "you'll get it all."

They were both absolutely right. They had a perfect sense of the other. Mailer was certainly not brave enough to advance on the Nazi— it would be like springing an avalanche on himself. But he also knew that if the Nazi jumped him, one blond youth was very likely to get massacred. In retrospect, it would appear not uncomic—two philosophical monomaniacs with the same flaw—they could not help it, they were counterpunchers.

"Jew coward! Red bastard!"

"Go fuck yourself, Nazi baby."

But now a tall U.S. Marshal who had the body and insane look of a very good rangy defensive end in professional football—that same hard high-muscled build, same coiled spring of wrath, same livid conviction that everything opposing the team must be wrecked, sod, turf, grass, uniforms, helmets, bodies, yes even bite the football if it will help—now leaped into the truck and jumped between them. "Shut up," he said, "or I'll wreck both of you." He had a long craggy face somewhere in the physiognomical land between Steve McQueen and Robert Mitchum, but he would never have made Hollywood, for his skin was pocked with the big boiling craters of a red lunar acne, and his eyes in Cinemascope would have blazed an audience off their seat for such gray-green flame could only have issued from a blowtorch. Under his white Marshal's helmet, he was one impressive piece of gathered wrath.

Speaking to the Marshal at this point would have been dangerous. The Marshal's emotions had obviously been marinating for a week in the very special bile waters American Patriotism reserves for its need. His feelings were now caustic as a whip—too gentle the simile!—he was in agonies of frustration because the honor of his profession kept him from battering every prisoner's head to a Communist pulp. Mailer looked him over covertly to see what he could try if the Marshal went to work on him. All reports: negative. He would not stand a chance with this Marshal—there seemed no place to hit him where he'd be vulnerable; stone larynx, leather testicles, ice cubes for eyes. And he had his Marshal's club in his hand as well. Brother! Bring back the Nazi!

Whether the Marshal had been once in the Marine Corps, or in Vietnam, or if half his family were now in Vietnam, or if he just hated the sheer Jew York presumption of that slovenly, drug-ridden weak contaminating America-hating army of termites outside this fortress' walls, he was certainly any upstanding demonstrator's nightmare. Because he was full of American rectitude and was fearless, and savage, savage as the exhaust left in the wake of a motorcycle club, gasoline and cheap perfume were one end of his spectrum, yeah, this Marshal loved action, but he was also in that no man's land between the old frontier and the new ranch home—as they, yes *they*—the enemies of the Marshal—tried to pass bills to limit the purchase of hunting rifles, so did *they* try to kill America, inch by inch, all the forces of evil, disorder, mess and chaos in the world, and *cowardice!* and city ways, and slick shit, and despoliation of national resources, all the subtle invisible creeping paralyses of Communism which were changing America from a land where blood was red to a land where water was foul—yes in this Marshal's mind— no lesser explanation could suffice for the Knight of God light in the flame of his eye—the evil was without, America was threatened by a foreign disease, and the Marshal was threatened to the core of his sanity by any one of the first fifty of Mailer's ideas which would insist that the evil was within, that the best in America was being destroyed by what in itself seemed next best, yes American heroism corrupted by American know-how—no wonder murder stood out in his face as he looked at the novelist—for the Marshal to lose his sanity was no passing psychiatric affair: think rather of a rifleman on a tower in Texas and a score of his dead on the street.

But now the Nazi began to play out the deepest of ceremonies. The truck standing still, another Marshall at the other end of the van (the one indeed who had arrested Mailer) and Teague and the Hungarian to different sides, everyone had their eyes on the Norwegian. He now glared again at Mailer, but then whipped away his eyes before a second contest could begin, and said, "All right, Jew, come over here if you want a fight."

The Marshall took the Nazi and threw him against the side-wall of the truck. As he bounced off, the Marshal gave him a rap below the collarbone with the butt of his club. "I told you to shut up. Now, just shut up." His rage was intense. The Nazi looked back at him sullenly, leaned on the butt of the club almost defiantly as if the Marshal didn't know what foolish danger he was in to treat the Nazi so, the Nazi had a proud curved hint of a smile, as if he were recording the features of this Marshal forever in the history of his mind, the Nazi's eyes seemed to say to the Marshal, "You are really on my side although you do not admit it—you would like to beat me now because in the future you know you will yet kiss my boots!" And the Marshall traveling a high edge of temper began to slam the Nazi against the wall of the truck with moderate force, but rhythmically, as if he would pacify them both by this act, bang, and bang, step by step, the imaginary dialogue of the Marshal to the Nazi now sounding in Mailer's ear somewhat like this, "Listen, Nazi, you're nothing but a rat fart who makes my job harder, and gives the scum around me room to breathe, cause they look at you and feel righteous. You just keep me diverted from the real danger."

And the Nazi looked back with a full sullen pouting defiance as if from deep in himself he was all unconsciously saying to the Marshal, "You know I am beautiful, and you are frightened of me. I have a cause, and I am ready to die for it, and you are just ready to die for a uniform. Join me where the real war is. Already the strongest and wildest men in America wear our symbol on their motorcycle helmets."

And the Marshal, glaring back at the Nazi, butt of his club transfixing him against the wall of the van, gave a contemptuous look, as if to drop him with the final unspoken word. "Next to strong wild men, you're nothing but a bitch."

Then the truck began to move, and the Marshal calmer now, stood silently between Mailer and the Nazi; and the Nazi also quiet now, stood in place looking neither at the Marshal nor Mailer. Some small storm of hysteria seemed to have worked itself out of the van.

HERBERT GOLD (1924–   )

"The American Jewish community is most important to me as a writer," Herbert Gold *has written, "because it is a mirror in which the rest of America can be seen. Like all mirrors, it invites distortion."* Gold's *work is broad in scope, sophisticated in tone, and free from any parochial view of Judaism; but certain stories, like* "The Heart of the Artichoke" *and* "Aristotle and the Hired Thugs," *do reveal a special point of view that can be attributed to his Jewishness.*

Born in Cleveland, Ohio, on March 9, 1924, Gold studied at Columbia University from 1943–1946. His novels include Birth of a Hero *(1951),* The Prospect Before Us *(1954),* The Man Who Was Not With It *(1956),* The Optimist *(1959),* Therefore Be Bold *(1960), and* Salt. Love and Like *(1960) and* The Magic Will *(1971) are volumes of short stories;* The Age of Happy Problems *(1962),* First Person Singular: Essays of the Sixties *(1963) are collections of essays. He has taught at Western Reserve (1951–1953) and Wayne State University (1954–1956), and as a Visiting Professor at Cornell, Berkeley, and Harvard.*

" 'Aristotle and the Hired Thugs' is partly a tribute to my real father," Gold *has said, "partly an urging upon myself of the necessity to survive in a time of personal shipwreck, partly another retreat to childhood to find what I can learn from it and thus give over to mastery as an adult. We ransom the present with booty illicitly carried from an imaginary past. I regret the brutal crudeness of the story, which has been attacked for its criticism of the Jewish tradition of nonviolence, but I would regret even more being destroyed as were six million other Jews."*

Aristotle and the Hired Thugs

In 1933 my father had two mighty enemies. Against one of them he struggled all the long fruit-and-vegetable day, hoisting the crates and loading a top-heavy truck in early morning, at dawn, in his sheepskin jacket, then meeting the customers until evening in a store built narrow and dark in the alleyway between a bakery and a Peerless showroom. Against the other enemy he fought all night, tossing and groaning in his sleep, fierce with that strange nightmare which allows an angry man to be pursued without ever retreating.

His daytime adversary was one shared by most other Americans—the Great Depression. The one of his nights was that beast clanking and roaring in the streets of fantastic Deutschland. "Hitler!" he said at breakfast, shaking the sleep from his head. "I'm almost ashamed to be human. The other strawberries don't like the rotten strawberry, they blush rotten red if you don't pluck him out—"

"Have another cup of Wheatena for the strength in it," chanted my mother, grieving with him like a good wife because of the need for strength on a troubled planet.

"Sorry, no time—look at the clock!" He hadn't meant to complain; it was the only earth he knew. "The lettuce is in already, and the pascal comes with it." And standing up, jacketed in sheepskin, shod in Army-Navy boots, he drained his coffee, dropped the cup in the sink, and was off to the market downtown near the flats of Cleveland. Before light on a May morning, he fought the battered reconditioned motor of his third-hand truck, cursed, lifted the hood, wiped the wires and plugs. Mother opened the kitchen window to watch. Then fits and coughs, then action. Mother watched him go, and waved. *Action*—his pockets filled with knives, hammers, dollars, a deck of cards, and funny pictures to show his friends in the chill damp of a spring morning. Down the suburban streets, up the suburban highway he rattled; and through the sleeping city where the street lights abruptly died in the dawn; and only rare bedroom lamps and kitchen noises greeted him on his way.

But the Central Farmers' Market was a city in full life. Carloads of vegetables steamed with the haggle and babble of selling under corrugated zinc roofs and no roofs at all. Hot fat soup was sold from great tureens by farmers' wives—nickel soup for before the sale, coffee and steaming pies for later, ten cents, to be wolfed down whole by desperate eaters who could not remember whether this was their second or their third breakfast. My father paced the aisles of lettuce and tender peas, the green corridors of spinach, deep into silent back parlors of early fruit off the railway cars. Private, at one with food, he sniffed gratefully, at his ease, homely, taking the pleasures of business on his tongue and in his deep-breathing lungs. He went to the produce market as to worship—putting Hitler and bank holidays behind him in the glory of America's bounty. He squeezed a plum until the wine spurted. He wiped his eyes.

Joe Rini surprised him in his shadowy lair. "What you doing here, Sam?"

"Same as you! Good, eh?"

"But can we sell it? I still got last week's plums left over."

My father shrugged, the sheepskin ruffling against a crate. "They get soggy in the cooler. What else can we do?"

"Nothing—and these look like prime. Here, let me taste."

"Taste, go on. Me, I'd like to buy."

The fruitmen rivalled, of course, for the favor of the farmers, who were of another breed, not washing in those days as a protest against the cost of living. Their best produce many times rotted in the fields, and the farmers often suffered terrible bellyaches from the hopeless eating of an unbought crop. Even striated beefsteak tomatoes, warmed by sun and dusted with salt, can be too many! The farmers suffered from mortgages, skin diseases, unrepaired fences, chronically pregnant wives. Regularly removed from their lonely land to confront a crazy urban cackle, and perhaps returning without the profit of seed and fertilizer, they passed cards among themselves.

The immigrant Italian and Jewish fruitmen, with their occasional Greek and Negro colleagues, exchanged printed jokes and dirty pictures. They first competed and argued, then huddled for eat and gossip, sharing each other's hard times in the pleasure and intimacy of these early mornings. They left dawn with regret, jamming their trucks into gritty day.

The farmers' wives, bundled and red and unfragrant as men, dipped up the last coffee and watched without a word. Drops of fat cream whirled round like crazy fishlets in the tin cups. The farmers too had their whispered consultations, but these never ended in a burst of laughter as they got the point. Their little cards were other dreams, dreams of riding and hunting, gothic fantasies of ritual, celebration, and chastisement. The Black Legion haunted the countryside around Cleveland. It made contact with the Klan in Parma and the Bund in Lakewood, and there were histories of drilling in open fields, the youngsters standing guard with broomsticks. Their cards made them members together for sacred order and vengeance. Cousins who rarely came out saw each other on Sunday after church to listen to screaming harangues from the platforms of pickups. During the dark winter of 1933, some farmers discovered that they had the call—or at least as much a one as the man in blue serge sent down from Jackson, Michigan.

Al Flavin was a farmer with whom my father had dealt for almost ten years. They had never been friends, but my father gave as good a price as anyone and Flavin took good care of his lettuce; they met in commerce. An angry man who had sometimes wrestled at country fairs, a giant with magnificent hairy paws, he began to know glory for the first time since abandoning his boyish victories on sweaty canvas. Men listened to him. He became a Commander or a Knight or a Dragon, whatever the Black Legion name for it was. He could not pay off the loan on his greenhouse, but he could gather the legionnaires in before-dawn consultations at the edge of town.

It must have made Al feel distant from himself to break up the meeting, give the mystic handshake, crushing the wrists of men less mighty than he, climb into a truck with a load strapped on, and then go meekly off to do business with Sam Stein.

"All right, make it eleven crates for ten," my father said.

"Ten crates," Al repeated stubbornly.

"Eleven. Or ten and my last price."

"No. Ten crates. My price."

"Al, listen to me," my father said. "You *know* I can't buy it your way. Joe Rini will undersell me, he'll throw circulars on all the porches, and then where will I be? You got to make sense in business."

"You heard me."

"What's the matter, you don't feel good today, Al? Something hurting?"

"Joe Rini don't buy from me. I bring in first quality stuff."

"I know, I *know*, that's why I stand here and argue with you. I *want* your stuff, Al. I like it."

My father rocked, smiling. Al Flavin stood behind his barricade of lettuce. Patience, patience—the soul is tried on earth. At last they were agreed, some place between demand and offer, and then joining in the traditional aftermath of successful negotiation, the two of them completed their deal by hoisting the produce into my father's truck. Hot and sighing when this was done, the cash changing hands, usually they came to a moment of benevolent treaty, and the plump fruitman would light up with the burly, brooding farmer. Al Flavin was busy behind his squeezed-shut eyes trying to remember who he is, who other people are.

"Okay, Al," my father said, "have a cigar."

Now he remembered. He felt his card and sorted my father out: "*Kike!*"

"Wh-wh-wh," said my father.

Flavin's shoulder caught my father and halfspun him around as the man stamped off in the flapping galoshes which he wore almost into summer. My father stammered, wh-wh-wh, meaning *What?* and *Why?* First amazed, then stooped and solemn, pouting with thought. It was well past dawn now, but suddenly the nightmare toppled onto his daytime dream, and he was standing in the sad, crooked streets of old Nuremberg.

My father stopped dealing with Al Flavin. This did not put an end to it. He heard Flavin's word every market-day morning, first whispered, then called after him, twice a week. The single note grated on his nerves. The market is supposed to be a pleasure. My mother made him promise not to fight. Flavin, huge, profligate with his wrestler's flesh, yearning to brawl, would crush him in his paws. It was policy. Flavin was a Commander. He hoped to convert the waverers by rolling with Sam Stein in the running wash of the market gutters.

"I'd get him with the peen of my hammer first!" my father yelled.

"Sam, Sam, we don't want trouble."

"I'll break his head with the claw!"

Mother petted him, stroked him. "Think of your business. You got a family, Sam, you got to count them."

"I'll Kill Him, Bella!"

"Shush, you're making noise, the neighbors. You got to count me, too. No trouble, please, for your kids' sake."

"No, no, no." His eyes were red with sleepless thinking. There was an angry scratch in the tender eye-flesh. He breathed as if he were struggling for air. "No, you're right, Bella. But if he touches me one more time—"

That time came, however, on a morning during the dog days of July, when even at early market hours the men panted and sweated under the blood-eyed sun before it reared up onto the exhausted city. Ice trickled through the crates of lettuce, rustling, and evaporated on cement still hot from the day before. The overfed market rats loped along on seared paws. Flavin sprang from behind a heap of crates, pretending to be in a hurry, and struck my father with his knee at the belly, so that he lost his balance and stumbled like a drunk. He grunted. He tried but could not quite sob out his breath. It was caught, trapped, exterminated some place within, and he lay sprawled on the soft market refuse while the little world of pain in his belly spun faster than the earth's turning, and only a moment later, when the hurtling agony at the center of his being slowed down to weakness, and the weakness to a sour sickness that drained into his mouth, did he remember again who he was. It's an assault against life that brings this gnawing, liver-eating agony upon a man gasping for his breath with his head against a crate of lettuce. The blood shrieked like eagles in his ears. It's a wish of murder—extermination. It's a terrible pain that makes a man forget he is Sam Stein.

Flavin roared, pushed the laughter forward with all his weight, and stood with his huge arms welcoming. Once taciturn, he had learned the tricks of oratory: "Looks drunk, don't he? Ain't he a rummy? Never did run into a rummy kike before, did you ever, boys?"

An offering of laughter. The rest would gather when the rich noise of brawling crashed out. Flavin was in boots, kicking free of a broken crate, ready.

Sam Stein pained badly in the gut. He climbed up dizzily and shook his head clear. He felt for the silver-pronged crating hammer in his back pocket. Flavin crouched, his long jaw twitching with desire. The buttons of his pants were stretched and a tab of shirt came out his fly. Flavin could wait another moment to find and make himself real. The usual hubbub of commercial dispute hid them now; the life of the market swirled unknowing about the two men, food rising in great

towers and vaults above them, around them, and only a couple of farmers watched. Joe Rini, terrified, blowing saliva, also watched.

My father had promised my mother.

He loved life and the right *to win*.

Flavin might kill him.

My father walked away rapidly, hunched, turning red for shame
and white for planning, and grabbed Joe Rini by the sleeve and took
him with him. "Joe, Joe," he said, "I got to talk to you. I know you got
friends. I got to talk to them, too."

"What you got to say, Sam?"

"Oh maybe I could kill him, but then again maybe not. It wouldn't
be so good if he gave me a beating. Those other cossacks would feel
too nice about it. Or worse. A bad precedent. No justice in that. So. . . ."

Eagerly Rini talked into the void. "So you know how they drink.
They're drunkards. So don't raise your blood pressure." My father's eye
made him stop. Rini agreed. My father decided slowly:

"The way things are going on the market now, Joe, it won't be safe
for any of us soon."

"What you thinking, Sam?" Rini asked.

He was thinking, but in his own words: precedent, morale, example.
This was a political question to be answered in the impure, compromising way of politics. A passionate answer—Sam Stein's face bloodied, a
crowd secretly smiling over Sam Stein's fallen body, an inflamed Al
finding his dream of power fulfilled—this was the worst possibility which
my father's furious body had almost given him. The philosophical thing
to do was to master that hot inner twitch, and then, only then, to think
out how to discourage the cossack mob.

Job and Noah had patience; yet Job was permitted his anger. Not an
educated man, my father knew that the patriarchs had even spoken for
passion on earth, properly used. And he knew no other place for justice
except here below, on earth, where he hoped to have more children.

He breathed deeply once, twice, again, that's better, and then
thanked God for giving him a sense of responsibility. He thanked the
Lord of Creation that his healthy, willing, complaining wife had come to
mind. Wistfully he thanked the Almighty for prudence—and also for
his friend Joe Rini. He said to Joe Rini: "You're going to help me now."

That very night Joe found the three young friends whom he had in
mind and brought them to the house. My father wanted to meet them
. . . "make your acquaintance." How formal we become under embarrassment. For fifty dollars he could buy a beating with any refinements

he named. Except nothing vicious, of course—what do you think, they were queers? They were mere administrators.

"No, *no!*" my mother cried. "So then he'll kill you next, and what's the good? We can't afford it."

"We can't afford not to," my father said stonily. "We're going to do what the Frenchies won't do. When he makes his noise, we march into the Rhineland and stop it good. You don't have to listen to that noise. You stop it the best way you can. You stop it. You *stop* it."

"Sam, O Sam, it's dangerous, it's fifty dollars."

"It's the cost of living, Bella."

Joe Rini's friends, three young chaps with slicked-down hair, nervous hands, and old jokes, were very sociable. They jiggled and dandled and played beanbag with me, as if I were a baby, although I was eight years old already. They took time over the business because my father likes business. Also he wanted to be certain. Mother served liver *with,* the rich slabs covered by curly, glistening onions. How can businessmen discuss serious matters without keeping up their strength? Mugs of strong black coffee, too.

"For fifty dollars, Mr. Stein," said the leader of the group, "we can maybe kill him for you. It's no extra. We'll be working anyway. His truck has got to stop for a light on the edge of town, and there we are."

"No, no," my father said. "Put him in the hospital, that's all."

"Mr. Rini says he used to work in the commission house with you. He says you're buddies from way back. It's no trouble at all."

"No!" my father said. "The man has a wife and kids, just like me. His big boy is too dumb to run a farm by himself—"

"We got smart kids," my mother interrupted, smiling, politely patting with a napkin, pleased by their appetites. "My big boy, he gets such marks from his teacher—"

"Bella, shush. Go call up somebody on the telephone if you got to talk. Listen."

The businessmen shrugged apologetically, being brought up in a tradition which favors mothers, and turned regretfully back to hear out my father and his scrupling. They were unaccustomed to fine distinctions, but they came of devoted families: they enjoyed a mother's pride.

"So don't do that what you said there," my father repeated. "I just want him to learn a little, have time to think a little. The hospital."

"Okay," the leader of the trio said reluctantly, "you're the boss. You get a hold of us if you change your mind, will you? To you the price remains the same."

"The hospital," my father repeated, making them promise.

"Let us worry about the details, Mr. Stein. Fifty goes a long way these days."

My father arose angrily, sending his cup ringing against a platter. "*I said the hospital!*"

"The hospital, hospital," they intoned mournfully, and filed out.

The next morning Flavin did not show up at the market. It was so easy to follow him from the country in a flivver, stop with him at a red light, get rid of the cigarettes, and pile quickly onto his truck. So instead of Flavin, a weary, hardworking young thug appeared and nodded to Dad, saying that they had been careful, just as he said. But it would have been no extra trouble, in fact, the reverse.

My father was undelighted. By his veiled eyes he signalled regret at the weight of the world: he was obliged to send Flavin down to defeat without earning the kiss of victory. Life had provided him—as it does everyone—with one more little blemish on the ideal of brave perfection. He found it a necessary business, nothing more, a merely rational victory, and he foresaw the possibility of being ambushed in his turn by a man who might not bother to think of his wife and children. Nevertheless, reason consoled him.

"What if he does it to you now, Sam? Where will I and the kids be? Where will *you* be if you're dead?"

"Well, it's a risk. But in this life you have to take chances and defend yourself like you can. And now let me answer your question: If I'm dead, I'm no place."

He sent Flavin a five-dollar bouquet of flowers, followed the next morning by a two-dollar plant with thick wet leaves and a decorative sprinkle of spangles. Joe Rini approved. A friend who went to see Flavin in the hospital reported that they were the only flowers he received.

The moral which my father drew was one which he wanted to teach England and France in 1933 and after. Still strong and capable, Flavin came quietly to work in his bandages about ten days later. He sold tomatoes to my father, and they haggled like gentlemen over the price. They mistered each other warily. There was further talk of the Black Legion, but not a gesture from Flavin. In a few years even the talk passed.

Sometimes my father thought that he might be beat up, but it never happened, although once he was robbed. That was not Flavin's work.

Flavin had taken instruction well, administered according to Aristotelean principles, with moderation, by a man whose fundamental passionate mildness led him to a reasonable strictness: the hospital for Flavin, nothing worse. Nightmares go on, but they have answers—albeit risky, rational, incomplete, and not ideally valorous. Poor Flavin, unused to surprises—he was discouraged.

And my mother was consoled. Dad made another fifty dollars to replace the ones spent in good works.

PHILIP ROTH (1933–   )

It seems clear, now that Philip Roth has arrived at a point in his career when his work can be sharply defined, that his finest writing concentrates on the tensions he has experienced as a Jew in America. The impressive stories collected in Goodbye, Columbus *were followed by* Letting Go *(whose best portions involved, once again, Jewish characters) and* When She Was Good; *but these novels did not have the satiric sting and the deeply personal conflict of Roth's early work or of his most accomplished novel,* Portnoy's Complaint. *Through the complaint that Roth has waged against the psychologically damaging effects of the Jewish tradition on a young Jew, he has made a broad criticism of American culture at large.*

Philip Roth was born in Newark, New Jersey, on March 19, 1933. He was educated at Bucknell University, where he received his B.A. in 1954, and at the University of Chicago, where he was awarded his M.A. in 1955 and later served as an instructor. While at the University of Chicago, Roth began to publish the short stories included in Goodbye, Columbus. *In general these stories—"Eli, the Fanatic," "The Conversion of the Jews," "Epstein," "Defender of the Faith"—concern the conflict between traditional values and the newly found prosperity of middle- and upper-middle-class Jews. The book won the National Book Award in 1959. Roth followed these stories with his first full-length novel,* Letting Go *(1962), which deals with the tensions resulting from a mixed marriage in which reason and emotion are at odds with each other;* When She Was Good *(1967), which traces the self-righteous fanaticism of a Midwestern housewife;* Portnoy's Complaint *(1969), which dramatizes the conflict between generations of Jews and which underscores a young Jew's attempt to free himself of the moral inhibitions imposed upon him by his religion; and* Our Gang *(1971), a satire of Richard Nixon. Roth's latest novel is* The Great American Novel. *For Alex Portnoy, pursuit of sexual freedom is naturally filled with the sort of tortured guilt that is very much an ingredient in the writing of Jews. Roth is fully conscious of the significance of guilt as a theme in his work: "Not until I had got hold of guilt, you see, as a comic idea, did I begin to feel myself lifting free and clear of my last book and my old concerns."*

Portnoy's Complaint

. . . I AM so small I hardly know what sex I am, or so you would imagine. It is early in the afternoon, spring of the year Four. Flowers are standing up in purple stalks in the patch of dirt outside our building. With the windows flung open the air in the apartment is fragrant, soft with the season—and yet electric too with my mother's vitality: she has finished the week's wash and hung it on the line; she has baked a marble cake for our dessert tonight, beautifully bleeding—there's that blood again! there's that knife again!—anyway expertly bleeding the chocolate in and out of the vanilla, an accomplishment that seems to me as much of a miracle as getting those peaches to hang there suspended in the shimmering mold of jello. She has done the laundry and baked the cake; she has scrubbed the kitchen and bathroom floors and laid them with newspapers; she has of course dusted; needless to say, she has vacuumed; she has cleared and washed our luncheon dishes and (with my cute little assistance) returned them to their place in the *milchiks* cabinet in the pantry—and whistling like a canary all the morning through, a tuneless melody of health and joy, of heedlessness and self-sufficiency. While I crayon a picture for her, she showers—and now in the sunshine of her bedroom, she is dressing to take me downtown. She sits on the edge of the bed in her padded bra and her girdle, rolling on her stockings and chattering away. Who is Mommy's good little boy? Who is the best little boy a mommy ever had? Who does Mommy love more than anything in the whole wide world? I am absolutely punchy with delight, and meanwhile follow in their tight, slow, agonizingly delicious journey up her legs the transparent stockings that give her flesh a hue of stirring dimensions. I sidle close enough to smell the bath powder on her throat—also to appreciate better the elastic intricacies of the dangling straps to which the stockings will presently be hooked (undoubtedly with a flourish of trumpets). I smell the oil with which she has polished the four gleaming posts of the mahogany bedstead, where she sleeps with a man who lives with us at night and on Sunday afternoons. My father they say he is. On my fingertips, even though she has washed each one of those little piggies with a warm wet cloth, I smell my lunch, my tuna fish salad. Ah, it might be cunt I'm sniffing. Maybe it is! Oh, I want to growl with pleasure. Four years old, and yet I sense in my blood—uh-huh, again with the blood—how rich with passion is the moment, how dense with possibility. This fat person with the long hair whom they call my sister is away at school. This man, my father, is off somewhere making money, as best he is able. These two are gone, and who knows, maybe I'll be lucky, maybe they'll never come back . . . In the meantime, it is afternoon, it is spring, and for me and me alone a woman is rolling on her stockings and singing a song of love. Who is going to stay with Mommy forever and ever? *Me.* Who is it who goes with Mommy wherever in the whole wide world Mommy goes? *Why me, of course. What a silly question—but don't get me wrong, I'll play the game!* Who had a nice lunch with Mommy, who goes downtown like a good boy on the bus with Mommy, who goes into the big store with Mommy . . . and on and on and on . . . so that only a week or so ago, upon my safe return from Europe, Mommy had this to say—

"Feel."

"*What?*"—even as she takes my hand in hers and draws it toward her body—"Mother—"

"I haven't gained five pounds," she says, "since you were born. Feel," she says, and holds my stiff fingers against the swell of her hips, which aren't bad . . .

And the stockings. More than twenty-five years have passed (the game is supposed to be over!), but Mommy still hitches up the stockings in front of her little boy. Now, however, he takes it upon himself to look the other way when the flag goes fluttering up the pole—and out of concern not just for his own mental health. That's the truth, I look away not for me but for the sake of that poor man, my father! Yet what preference does Father really have? If there in the living room their grown-up little boy were to tumble all at once onto the rug with his mommy, what would Daddy do? Pour a bucket of boiling water on the raging, maddened couple? Would he draw *his* knife—or would he go off to the other room and watch television until they were finished? "What are you looking away—?" asks my mother, amused in the midst of straightening her seams. "You'd think I was a twenty-one-year-old girl; you'd think I hadn't wiped your backside and kissed your little tushy for you all those years. Look at him"—this to my father, in case he hasn't been giving a hundred percent of his attention to the little floor show now being performed—"look, acting like his own mother is some sixty-year-old beauty queen."

But you *are* a Jew, my sister says. You are a Jewish boy, more than you know, and all you're doing is making yourself miserable, all you're doing is hollering into the wind . . . Through my tears I see her patiently explaining my predicament to me from the end of my bed. If I am fourteen, she is eighteen, and in her first year at Newark State Teacher's College, a big sallow-faced girl, oozing melancholy at every pore. Sometimes with another big, homely girl named Edna Tepper (who has, however, to recommend her, tits the size of my head), she goes to a folk dance at the Newark Y. This summer she is going to be crafts counselor in the Jewish Community Center day camp. I have seen her reading a paperback book with a greenish cover called A Portrait of the Artist as a Young Man. All I seem to know about her are these few facts, and of course the size and smell of her brassiere and panties. What years of confusion! And when will they be over? Can you give me a tentative date, please? When will I be cured of what I've got!

Do you know, she asks me, where you would be now if you had been born in Europe instead of America?

That isn't the issue, Hannah.

Dead, she says.

That isn't the issue!

Dead. Gassed, or shot, or incinerated, or butchered, or buried alive. Do you know that? And you could have screamed all you wanted that you were not a Jew, that you were a human being and had nothing whatever to do with their stupid suffering heritage, and still you would have been taken away to be disposed of. You would be dead, and I would be dead, and

But that isn't what I'm talking about!

And your mother and your father would be dead.

But why are you taking their side!

I'm not taking anybody's side, she says. I'm only telling you he's not such an ignorant person as you think.

And she isn't either, I suppose! I suppose the Nazis make everything she says and does smart and brilliant too! I suppose the Nazis are an excuse for everything that happens in this house!

Oh, I don't know, says my sister, maybe, maybe they are, and now she begins to cry too, and how monstrous I feel, for she sheds her tears for six million, or so I think, while I shed mine only for myself. Or so I think.

IRVIN FAUST

Irvin Faust is a young writer whose work is primarily concerned with life in urban America. Born in Brooklyn, Faust was educated at the City College of New York and Teachers College, Columbia University, where he received his doctorate. He has published widely in journals like The Paris Review *and* The Sewanee Review. *His most recent publication is the novel,* Willy Remembers.

Jake Bluffstein and Adolf Hitler

THE WORST THING about it was that Mr. Bluffstein was a good Jew. If he weren't, it might have been understandable. Or even bearable. But it was like rubbing salt in the wound when that feeling had to come over him in *temple*. On Friday night yet.

Throughout the service he had watched the three refugees—Moscovitz, Steiner and Levy—off by themselves in a corner, as he had been watching with almost a fascination for several months. Like always they were hunched over as if they were hiding, like always they were moaning crazily into the *minyan,* when the idea shot into his head and just like that, so natural he didn't even think, he said to himself, no *wonder* they got the business, and all of a sudden he felt the shivers busting around inside of him . . .

With the prayer book in his hand, feeling the *tallis* around his neck like an iron collar, he bent his knees deeper and bobbed his head harder. With the Torah staring down at him. With the *Kaddish* mumbling through his lips, for his brother and sister, dead in Belsen, they should rest in peace. And when the ordeal of the service was over at last and he murmured good *shabbas* to the rabbi and everyone else except the refugees, he hurried out into the snow before anyone should see his upset. He was all the way to Amsterdam Avenue, listening to his feet crunching down the snow—even the way the great boots crunched through Paris and Warsaw and Lidice—before he let himself think on it a little . . .

For four years now, he realized, since the end of the war, he had been uneasily conscious of an excitement missing from the world, and so from his life. A zetz, a danger, a chance you took when you got up in the morning that by nighttime it would all be changed. And so with the risk—for Jake was always a gambler—each day was bearable. But since the big blast it was just the poison mushroom and that's all, one blow-up and nothing. A big zero. No tingle. A whole different set-up now. And so out of a clear blue sky he began to carry around inside him this steady drawing, like a sty coming to a head. Like hell a sty, he thought. Like a . . . *homesickness* . . .

He went straight to the apartment and all through the soup and beef flanken he was very quiet, and when Sarah asked him about the services he shrugged and said like always, services. Then she got the quiet, suffering look and he felt a terrible annoyance, like he used to feel when he watched the girls on Seventh Avenue and then came home and compared. But he said nothing. Instead he found himself thinking—without even trying—suffering, *always* the suffering. Just like the refs.

Very quickly he went to the magazine rack and picked out *Newsweek* and for the rest of the evening he carefully read every article, and then with the *Jahrzeit* candles quietly flickering, went to bed, like he had each night for thirty years. But when he lay next to Sarah he could only stare at the light outlining the shades and listen to the buses rumbling past, he felt so funny, with a lightness in the head, like he was just taking off in an aeroplane for a crazy, roaring ride, who the hell knew where. It might even be, he thought uneasily, change of life, except that deep down underneath the breastbone, where the heartburn was, he knew he had enough charge in him for *all* the chickens in the office . . . Then he heard Sarah wheeze throatily and before he could stop the plane it took off. He pushed it down and it pushed back up. He gave in a little and it swept through his body. It swept through how *they* coveted Jewish women, and for the first time in years he felt a rippling thrill as in the dangerous night he ran his hand softly along her thick *verboten* flank.

All day Saturday he was deep in thought. On the long walk down Riverside Drive and back as the ice, cracking apart up the Hudson, floated down to the bay. Just as he had floated all these years.

Hell, for thirty-five years Jake Bluffstein had lived and breathed a hundred percent American Jew. *American* first. Three Navy Es his plant had earned, turning out more skivvies than Acme and Schorr's put together, and the hell with cost plus. After that he'd collected up and down Seventh Avenue for UJA and for all he gave didn't declare a nickel. They had a pine tree in Haifa with his name on it, "Jacob Aaron Bluffstein," and in summer he loved the thought of his leafy arms cooling off the parched Jewish sand . . .

He passed Grant's Tomb and walked faster. Directly east was Jewish Theological. Faster yet he walked.

At 140th Street he sat down and stared across at the Palisades and upriver at the gorgeous hills sweeping off behind the George Washington Bridge. It was a scene that always refreshed him; some of his biggest deals he had cooked up here. In his relaxation he thought about what Sy, his nephew, had told him. Here the Hudson looked like the Rhine, Sy said. Sy, with the face of an Aryan, who had crossed at Remagen and swept all over Bavaria, through the Black Forest and into Kassel, Worms, Regensberg, Munich, Wiesbaden, the Sudeten. *Berchtesgaden* . . . Bluffstein trembled and leaned his head back, blowing his smoking breath out over the stone wall that lined the sidewalk.

He got up and shook his head. He must be *mishugah*. Jake Bluffstein had sent packages for twenty-five years to Posen and Cracow. Underwear, shoes, Campell soup, cigarettes, vitamin pills. And felt good and right about each package. He trembled again. Oh yeah? What were you really thinking, Bluffstein, with each fancy box? Think. Poor, sorry *schnorrers*, you were thinking, having to get clothes and what to eat from practically a stranger. Begging, you thought. And what else, Mr. Yankee Doodle Dandy? How about the picture in front of your eyes, clear as a snapshot, of the storm trooper opening the last package and stamping "Address Unknown." Exciting words, hah Jake Bluffstein!

Enough! It was too much already on one person's head. He began walking back . . . Brothers and sisters melted down in the ovens so even Blood and Guts Patton had to puke. Sy had told him. And he, like a *schmuck*, a bleeding heart for a bunch of goons, jailbirds, cokies. Fags! Read it in the books, it's all there . . . Oi, but the wild, ecstatic discipline, the torchlight parades, miles of black shirts and stamped on each one's middle, "GOTT MITT UNS" . . . GOTT MITT MURDERERS . . . He stopped on the 130th Street viaduct and leaned over. Below was a drop of a hundred feet. He forced his mind over the pictures Sy had brought back, of the concentration camps, men who weren't men, the shiny interlacing of bones and teeth, showerheads of death and the big fat chimneys . . . The question slugged him and sent him reeling back from the edge, pins and needles all over from the logic: HOW ELSE YOU GONNA ESTABLISH RACIAL PURITY? . . .

When he got home, Sarah already had his favorite noodle and mondel soup ready. He ate silently while she hummed around him, talking all kinds of nonsense. "Bluffstein, a little more salad. The tea is strong enough? . . . Have another cookie, Bluffstein . . . *Ess*, Bluffstein." . . . Bluffstein. For years it's Jake. Now all of a sudden he's a strong, young *paskudnyak,* like in the beginning, as if they were once more partners. Her hair was wet and sitting crazy in a ball on one side, her face was powdered like a chop in flour dust. As if after last night Sally Rand was expecting encores. He hunched over his glass of tea while she carried on. It was disgusting the way she had given in and squirmed all over (even if it was the first time since he got *shikkah* V-E Day). Like putting out for a stranger and loving it. Strength through joy, he thought bitterly.

He didn't go to temple that night.

By Monday lunchtime he was back to himself again, almost. Wheeling and dealing and using the telephone like a built-in extension to his arm. Cracking wise all over the office, so the red in Shirley the switchboard's face peaked up to the platinum streak in her hair, and the packing room almost forgot the coffee break from laughing with the boss. He ate dairy with the boys at Steinberg's and coaxed thirty gross pleated dickies out of Hy Weissman over the strudel and tossed double or nothing for the check and won. He was old Seventh Avenue Jake. But Jake, the pro, the coldfish operator knew a difference. All day a back door to his brain kept swinging open and dumping *chazerai* out before he could slam the door shut. And all the while a voice needled him like he was a pilot on TWA with his own private earphones. He would talk big markdown on a new lot of dirndls—a real spring leader—and the control tower, of all the infuriating, *mishugenah* things in the world, says Hindenberg was a real *schmuck,* he never had a chance. As if it was red hot news! . . . Ever so calmly he would walk to his own bathroom, wash his hands and look down *his* Seventh Avenue to Acme and United and the Flatiron Building and . . . Thuringia, Wilhelmstrasse. ADOLPHHITLERPLATZ.

Back, very very slowly to the cluttered desk and the invoices, controlling every movement, while his head spins and one name keeps sliding in and out of the earphones, while he plays "Bluffstein Brothers, Notions, Frocks and Young Ideas . . ." All morning, in and out the voice. Harry . . . Hymie . . . Hesh . . . On the tip of his tongue, he could almost bite it off. And then, over cancan petticoats, ahhh the relief . . . *Hershel.* Hershel Grynzpan. The crazy little bastard who knocked off the SS colonel in Paris in 1937. He leaned against his hands and closed his eyes and savored the front page of the *Times.* He could almost reach out and touch the mobs winding up like Carl Hubbell and throwing bricks through the store windows . . . Hershel. He should have been an SS himself, he had the guts of a burglar. That wasn't the act of a Jew, murder. God forbid they should hit the police blotter! That was their trouble. More murders they needed instead of wailing. Blood oaths and parades and fires. This they needed instead of the thinking. Why shouldn't a Jew have the pleasure of a little persecution? Of a Grynzpan popping the colonel. A Reichtag fire. Ahh the fire. Bluffstein surrendered to the excitement, the terror and awe of those wild first days, the signs of madness to come. The whole world tantalized when every so often the mysterious door cracked open and the blackness shot out and jumped back. The years swept over him, setting off a wild, empty yearning, leading to nowhere except pleasure, like the way he felt when Shirley bent far over the file. He was dizzy with a longing to go back, as though it were Passover and the lure of the Concord was on him again.

He stopped. "*Petzl,* what are you doing, tearing yourself to pieces!" With a tremendous toss of his head, like a great old bull throwing off the pics, he wrenched free of the *New York Times* and the pitching mobs; he forced fresh air into his head and ripped off the earphones. "Lippman," he called to his head errand boy. "I'm packing in, you check up," and he left without even a look down Shirley's dress . . .

He knew exactly where he should go. Across 34th Street by bus and a transfer to the Second Avenue line, all the way down to Avenue A. There he got off and walked around, in and out the familiar streets, studying the stores and the three floors above them. *His* little old New York, straight out of the World's Fair. Georgie Jessel in his knickers could easy step out and telephone mama. Jake bucked up. All right, Bluffstein, he challenged, you got a fight on your hands. So let's draw the line and start belting back; a fighter you've always been, *Yakov,* and if you got a poison in you, you drink dishwater and vomit it up!

He thought of calling Sarah, saying he would be late, and instead had a lox and creamcheese at Rapoport's. He stared hard into the windows of Moskowitz and Lupowitz, at the giant pastramis and the strudels and he walked to the Second Avenue Theater where he forced a study of the pictures of Aaron Lebedeff. He smiled; screw Emil Jannings, he told himself. A soft voice sneaked in: Max Schmeling—you bet on Louis and *really* rooted for Schmeling. *Max Baer,* with the *Mogen David* on the trunks was his *true* hero, he answered back and hurried on. In every appetizing store window, every tailor shop, he fought for nostalgia, for the old feeling. But all he could feel was tired. He got so tired he thought for a crazy moment of going to Rabbi Berliner and coming clean, but he was disgusted with such a thought. Like a Catholic at confession, hah Bluffstein, he mocked, to a psychiatrist you'll go first, *ahbenit!*

So he kept looking for himself, the faraway Jake Bluffstein, up and down, in and out, from Houston to Fourteenth Street. Feeling like a spy with his *shlemazel.* Until he couldn't avoid it any longer and walked almost sideways up to the two-story taxpayer on Avenue C. Still there like he feared, no project standing in its dust. Tante Riva and Uncle Wolff. Skullcaps and sweaty black dresses. Even the lousy little store downstairs. A pizza. Could he see yet under all the years, "Bluffstein Brothers?" God, not still. Him and Abie and a couple of boards for a counter. Poor, mushy little Abiela, never had the guts and in two years pushed out. Abie, you were a loser. So why should you ask for me at the end? Still kissing the boot! And where do you come off to have a beautiful kid like Sy? . . . Aaaach it was a mistake coming. All he looked for was impure. Pizzas and burger heavens and spik sharpies. The plunging in had revived not the livewire Jake with the world opening up for him, but back alleys and dirty houses squeezing back from the sun and everybody old and accepting and so goddam happy because the Kaiser and Franz Yussel were good to the Yids. *They* had the right idea; could you respect such an element? Kick me a little easier and I'll love you. He was suddenly nauseous . . .

He flagged a taxi and rode to the Seventh Avenue Subway to prove he had really left it all behind and tipped the driver a dollar he shouldn't think he was a cheap Jew bastard.

It was very late when he got off the IRT at 103rd Street. It was cold and Broadway was still and empty, even of the dogwalkers. There was a mystery and a hush in the dark that he finally had all to himself. He clicked off block after block, catching a piece of the river down the side streets, gleaming in pink and blue curlicues from the giant neons on the Jersey side. Store fronts were quiet, Loew's marquee was cold and peaceful. It was a time for a man to relax at last, to let the mind out a couple of notches, let it soar out in all the loneliness . . . Across rooftops and down into cellars . . . Was that a screech in the distance, a muffled jumping down, a quick scuffle and a truck gunning through the streets? . . .

He stopped. There, corner a Hundred Third, pushing back between Jompole's Haberdashery and Miss Millie's Lingerie. Moscovitz's, the ref butcher. Small and grimy, with the neon tubes in the window spelling kosher in Hebrew and grey-cold. He tiptoed up to the window, cupped his hands and looked inside. A few thin briskets, ribs showing like their owner's, hung dark red, behind the block . . . Bluffstein shook his head. His hand fumbled through his pocket and pulled out a piece of marking

chalk. The chalk lifted and his hand began to move and he moved behind it, feeling an excitement that carried a brand-new dimension. Like
Jake Bluffstein was *young* again.

Again and again his hand slashed against the glass and the storefront
came alive—

JUDE

Then with a burst of energy, like a thin little kid, he sprinted away
into the dark.

The next day he called in sick and went straight downtown to 42nd
Street. Purposefully he walked to the Public Library and feeling as grim
as the lions on guard, went inside and directly to the central file. There
he looked up the cards he wanted under O, L, T and S, filled out his
slips and walked to the big reading room. His number flashed and out
came his books on the Ogaypayu, Lenin, Trotsky and Stalin. Grimly he
walked to a crowded table, sat down, opened the books and studied. For
two hours he read. He tried. Finally he had to sigh and lean back.
Nothing.

All along he had known it, but he had to make sure. For it wasn't
the first time he had tried. Now it was final; they just didn't have it, the
commies, no zing, no *tam*. Like a second love affair, but not even. Purges,
trials, executions, confessions. *Phooey*. No excitement, no imagination.
Like Russian Jews, dull and heavy. So OK he'd made a legitimate effort
to balance out the odds. Nobody, not even the kibitzing earphones
(which were getting to be like old friends) could say he didn't try. OK.
He returned the books and his obligation met, hurried to the back-news-
paper files.

He plunged into the old days like they were a Turkish bath. He
turned pages as if he were reading *Berlin Diary* again, or *Rommel*, and
magic headlines jumped out at him: "Maginot Line Breached," "Seyss-
Inquhart Forms Cabinet," "Dollfuss," "Anschluss," "Rhineland." *Gott*,
"Hershel Grynzpan!" He charged backward to the time when the whole
shooting match teetered deliciously on the edge . . . Then he asked
himself the sneaky little questions he had never listened to. The sharp
little knives. Was it maybe *Rosenfeld* after all, and not Roosevelt? Or
at least maybe an international deal? . . . Was Father Coughlin *all*
wrong? . . . Were the Protocols *all* phony? If—listen good now—if there
were no Jews, would there have been a war?

Ah there it is Bluffstein, after ten years. The *real* Jewish problem. Like who killed Jesus AND NO CRAP . . .

It was the rush hour when he got on the subway, his big ball of knowledge swelling inside him like the growing head of a baby, an inch of clothing away from a stiff-looking broad with a girdle and a detached type in a homburg and a pack of ordinaries staring into each other's eyes. He smelled garlic and Juicy Fruit and cooking fat, but it was comfortable being hemmed in. And exciting, too, with his secret. He looked into the stiff broad's eyes and drew a blank. He tried the homburg. The homburg was looking at the *Mirror* and Bluffstein leaned over his shoulder. There staring at him as if were looking in a mirror was Moscovitz's store and a cop pointing. His hand tingled. At that moment the homburg looked at him, just a bare flick and then turned to the advertising cards. But Jake caught it in that look. It had clicked between them. And Jake knew why.

The guy was a Nazi!

He looked around. All over the car he saw the flashing look and the acknowledgement. The car was loaded with them. And *he* could spot them. And he could spot something else, too. All the others, including the stiff broad, they were the JEWS . . . and in that particular car, at that moment they were all waiting, the Jews to get the business and the Nazis, with all their hidden power and explosiveness, marking time, waiting for someone to pull it all together.

When he got home, Sarah was reading *Peace of Soul* again. Peace, her whole mental outlook, as if life were one *tsuris* after another. She wore the sad, puffy, putting up with everything look again, as if to accuse him forever. Only *this* time he was reinforced under his belt and he wasn't buying.

"Why don't you read something educational?" he said. "Don't you know they're a racket, these books?"

No answer. She was hoping, of course, that he wouldn't start up.

"Do you know the world you live in?" he said in a reasonable voice. "Do you wanna know? No."

A sigh.

"The size of a pea is your brain."

Deeper the sigh.

"People like you started the war. You know that? You Sarah Margolis, started the war. With your sighing . . ."

She put the book on her lap. Her eyes were big and watery; the nose would soon start to run. "Jackie, why are you torturing me?" she said. "For three days you're torturing. Something is wrong at the place?"

He was suddenly furious. "No nothing is wrong at the *place*," he mimicked. She sighed and picked up the book and he almost choked with anger.

"I'm torturing you, hah? All I want you should be a little educated so we can carry on an intelligent conversation and *I'm* torturing."

Her nose started and he felt the anger turn to satisfaction. Only at these times did Mr. Bluffstein feel relieved. Before these moments there was always doubt, a questioning. That with her silence she might throw everything up to him from the first day—the first minute—like a bank account she was saving and always adding interest for the big withdrawal . . . Two huge tearballs rolled down the puffed cheeks and he felt an edge . . . All right so he told Levinson, the marriage broker, it had to be a girl with a little money, was that a crime? This you throw up? *He* should throw up. How her mother and father pushed him in, a good-looking ox, right off the boat. But no, love it should be. Who was she anyhow, Norma Shearer? . . . The pinochle games . . . to his dying day she wouldn't forget waiting up all night. Put that into the account. So who told her to wait? What should he do, right way knock her up? What were they, strict Catholics? No, when he saw his way clear and he was good and ready . . . He felt a terrible heartburn . . . Mark, she had named him. *It.* Mark, a name for a *mensch. Gott!* A poor terrible thing with a head like a watermelon, he couldn't even hold up and she nursed him and *kvetched* over him like he was Sy . . . Until he put him away and each week she visited and came back with that silent, puffy look. And one Sunday she stopped visting . . . And the peace books started. And only when he was *shikkah* could he touch her . . . So it was his fault? NO, it was the Tribe. Trapping him wherever he turned. Like screwing poor Abie—if he didn't somebody else would—and Abie turns around and has a Sy. Play it safe and an idiot son you get. Why not, Jews have the highest rate of mental sickness, look it up in the encyclopedia. And T.B. also . . . All right so he left momma and poppa—what else, join the emperor's army? So all the refs have to come over and torture him with the old country. And her putting up with every goddam thing, like they *always* put up, never once telling him go shit in his hat.

"Aaah what's the use talking," he said. "In a thousand years you'll never understand what it's all about."

She came over to him and her face had two jagged lines where the tears had run through the powder. "Jackie," she said, "you should let me help you a little bit. Don't keep in so much. The war is over, you don't have to keep on killing yourself. Jackella, let me help you with your crisis."

He looked up suddenly. "What kind of *drek?* I ain't got pneumonia." He forced a smile and a calmness into his voice. "Forget forget, go back to your book. First give me to eat, hah? . . ."

After the boiled tripe and rice pudding he went for a walk and brooded over all the silent complications crisscrossing like underground rivers in Howe Caverns beneath his skin. For over an hour he thought and then walked home. Sure enough, there was Rabbi Berliner, looking very cheerful, like a big coincidence. And Sarah looking too innocent.

"Well hello, Jacob," the rabbi said, a happy smile spread over his smooth face. Berliner was all head, like Mark, but he was no idiot. He was one of the new rabbis, from Cleveland or Toledo, very American. He wore neat, single-breasted suits and tab collars. Congregation Beth Shomar was very proud to get him. "I was hoping I'd find you in," the rabbi said.

"I been out for a walk."

"That's excellent for the system. I had an incipient duodenal ulcer once, in the seminary in Ohio while I was working to make both ends meet, and they said I should exercise after eating to use up all that acid. That's what tears up the stomach lining."

"Yeah, I like a little walk when I feel gassy."

"Well well, so how have you been, Jacob?"

"I been ok, Rabbi, and you?"

"Up to my ears. With the building fund and the afternoon center, never a dull moment."

"Well you just fill in my blank check anytime, Rabbi."

"I know, oh I know that. I know I can always count on my Jacob. Therefore I'm—ah—a little concerned when I don't see him in the synagogue for a few days."

Jake looked at Sarah. The book was already up.

"I been working so late I ain't had time for *shul,*" he said carefully. "It's inventory."

"Of course," Berliner smiled. "Only don't forget God's inventory."

"I won't forget, Rabbi."

"I thought maybe . . . if you had some kind of problem, I might be of assistance." He folded his hands across his stomach.

Jake thought he could laugh right in his face. He remembered thirty years ago and the help old Berkowitz, with his black suit, like a priest, gave them with the baby. "It's your burden, *Yakov,* your trial. God picked you because you're strong." He wanted to yell, what did being a good Jew get *me.*

Smiling back he said, "No problem, Rabbi. Just invoices." Berliner nodded and unlaced his fingers and tapped the ends together like they were cigarettes. "Well *I* got a problem, Jacob," he said, leaning forward confidentially. "We had a . . . incident . . . lately, with a member of the congregation . . . A little anti-Semitic business I reported immediately to B'nai B'rith. Maybe you heard."

Jake looked straight in his face. "No, I didn't. That's a shame. You need a couple of dollars for anything?"

"Oh, that's very kind, so typical. You have such a good heart. No, with thanks. I thought really, the biggest help would be if you came regularly again to temple. You were always such a pillar of strength, Jacob."

"Sure sure Rabbi, why not."

He was all at once sick and tired of the conversation, as if he'd played around long enough with a manufacturer. "So while you're here, Rabbi, have a little drink," he said and without waiting he went to the kitchen and took down the muscatel and three glasses. He came back and poured for each of them. The rabbi raised his glass. "*L'Chayem,*" he said.

"We should only live and be healthy," Sarah murmured.

"*L'Chayem,*" Jake said. He looked over his glass and the rabbi looked back. He had stopped smiling; his face had a knowhow, a strength. He nodded and his octagonal, rimless glasses flashed. And in that instant Jake knew. Like in the subway. Under the Middle West and the ivy suits, underneath all the fancy business, *the rabbi was a Nazi, too.*

When he got to the Synagogue, he could hear the voices of the *minyan;* above the scattered chorus, the three refs were wailing. It was still early, but that made it even more exciting. The chalk slid out and with big, bold strokes he zigzagged over the wall, right above the date, 1929–5690. Across—down—across. Down—across—down.

He felt an explosive freedom in his chest, a total clearing, as if every piece of phlegm that had ever choked up his life was spilling out at last.

All day, every day, Jake was on the go. One night he spent at the Hotel St. George in Brooklyn, sweating out all the impurities in the steam room. Then to the 34th Street Y, then the Mills Hotel on 19th. Down to the Central Plaza in the Village, the Salvation Army on the

Bowery; he sat around lobbies or walked the streets, always watching and studying, finding out things and marking it all up in a mental ledger. An excitement was building up under him, like 1912 again, only with no blocks or detours, everything wide open in front of him. Better than 1912 because now he had a maturity and a wisdom, an X ray in his head that let him look inside a man and tell the basics. If he were one or the other. It all boiled down; you had to be either one . . .

Nobody could snow him. He could break down the busboys in the Automat, the nickel sprayers behind the counter, the winos in the soup kitchens and the lady soul-savers, shipping clerks and bosses, the rush-hour crowd, the losers watching the newsreels, the wanderers. It made everything pure and simple and neat; no underground rivers. It was a knowhow *they* must have had in Munich and Essen and Cologne.

The time was over for reading and meditation; he was finding them everywhere—parks, subways, buses, department stores, all hours, day and night. The city was lousy with them. And in the discovering, he found that something was transforming in him. He was leaving behind Jake Bluffstein, shaking him off like he never happened; and as if he were making great, clean knife cuts through thick baloney, he was slicing loose of Abie and Mark and momma and poppa and grandmomma and grandpoppa and Sarah and her side and his side and the whole *mishpucha* and all the others, hanging on and choking the life out of him. Even Hershel, jumping out of little side streets and wanging away, and a cruddy couple acres and a thousand years of pushing on top one another and tearing your heart out by the roots. All this he was kissing off.

He felt like Columbus.

After just one week he walked boldly up to his place at two in the morning and wrecked his office. It gave him a genuine pleasure . . . So who could understand? Crazy hah?

Like a fox.

In the papers, underneath the by-lines, a good seventy-five percent of the reporters—make it eighty-five—would nod their heads in satisfaction. There would be contacts all over the city—that was the important thing—who, reading, would get the message and nod all at once, together. A deep, silent, knowing OK. Like the way they tsked-tsked over the swastikas and underneath smiled. Or made every housewife on her own bed with Sonny Wisecarver, pulled every heist with Dillinger and brodied off every ledge. All that communing he felt inside him.

He had fallen into something BIG.

Two Saturdays went by. On the third, Synagogue Beth Shomar was bright and busy and over half filled up, including a fine turnout in the ladies' section. On the new dais, Rabbi Berliner, resplendent in a great, white *tallis,* that draped his shoulders like a mantle of snow on Mount Sinai, intoned much deeper and richer than he did during the week, his Hebrew tinged with a delicate refined English accent. The service ran with a smoothness, a precision the rabbi could feel and control, like his dictaphone that he could speed up, slow down, reverse, or stop. Beneath him the congregation was following like a good child. Over in the corner, the three refugees, like one man, were bobbing and ducking, crying into the service with a heavy accent, just a little too loudly, but this was the way with foreigners, so in his mind the rabbi excused them. In the ladies' section, to his great satisfaction, was Sarah Bluffstein, obviously getting relief. Looking sad and weighted with great suffering and the least little bit contented around her red, puffy eyes. He had been so afraid for her, that maybe she couldn't find her way after recent events, but here she was, he had met her needs and she was pulling through beautifully, as if in fact a great understanding had come to her in her ordeal . . . Maybe, he thought, raising his hands to the ceiling, when all was said and done it was for the best. *Yakov,* with all his generosity, always had a dangerous kind of all-knowing smartness about him, like so many New York Jews. He raised higher. Thank heaven he had kept his congregation membership out of the papers. There was enough trouble in the world. If only they could hold off a little longer, until it blew over. He lowered his hands and opened his eyes. Things were going so well; all around Sarah were brand new faces; the attendance drive was really beginning to roll . . .

At ten o'clock, just as he gathered himself for the sermon in English, when the temple was busiest with prayer, there came a break in the precision. A skipping of a beat. The rabbi felt a ripple starting in the back of the temple and passing row on row right up to him. He looked out. In the last row, next to Harry Markman, sat Jake Bluffstein.

He wore his double-breasted, navy-blue overcoat; his color was good, his body filled out the entire seat. His arms were folded like the same old Jake.

Instantly Rabbi Berliner clasped his hands together and bent forward and let the goodness of the world rise from the depths of his chest. All around him he could feel a flying out of hearts to Sara Bluffstein filling his temple.

Jake Bluffstein had come a long way. From Forest Hills, out on the Island. And before that Greenpoint. And before that Staten Island and

Inwood and Fordham and the Village. On subways, buses, ferryboats he had traveled. He had been very busy. But now he sat with a calmness on his face, looking straight ahead.

Jake didn't quite know why he was here, but he knew this was the place to be. The sun shining through the stained-glass windows told him, and the rich candelabra and the crouching, golden lions. It was the kind of setting he had prepared for.

Then the moment came when the rabbi, in his saddest voice, said, "To all who mourn the loss of loved ones . . ." and Jake felt his time. He rose. He did not say the *Kaddish* as he had for years past; it did not enter his mind. He stepped into the aisle and walked forward, past the people standing and murmuring for the dead and he walked up to the dais. The rabbi smiled, clasped his shoulder, nodded his head reassuringly and stepped back. The murmurs stopped and the heads turned up. Jake smiled at the rabbi, turned to the congregation, stood against the railing and began to speak.

He spoke so effortlessly. The words rolled out like a waterfall dropping from his mouth. They poured out in Yiddish and German and Hebrew, even Russian. And the people listened. He told the faces beneath him all the things they longed to hear. Of the great injustices in their lives and the crimes committed against them. Of their enemies pressing from every side, choking the life out of them. His body grew taut and he gripped the rail and saw the passion in their eyes. They were leaning toward him from every seat, giving in to him. The woman with the white face and blue hair looked like she could kiss his feet, the three bone-thin men with the caved-in faces were ready for orders. A layer had been stripped from all of them and they were wide open.

He gave it to them. He told them who to blame. He brought it out in the open.

Then he switched on them. He reassured them. He spoke of their future. He spoke of their greatness, their destiny; they ate it up. He spoke of perfection, of purity, of *beauty;* they loved it. They were with him a hundred percent. He struck the rail for emphasis and the rhythm of his pounding carried his words beyond the building, to the thousands who were waiting all over the city, from the Unter den Linden to the Brandenburg Gate.

He rose up to ecstasy and he let them share with him; their faces were in his hands. He was the artist, moulding them into anything he pleased, joy, terror, hope, power. His arms swung wide and his words were no longer words he recognized, but *they* recognized and the message flowed out like honey. Every problem was being handled on this balcony.

So when he saw the men in uniform marching toward him, he was ready. He turned off the words suddenly and stiffened his entire body. The exaltation flowed through every nerve and muscle and gathered in a ball under his arm, then thrust his arm out so it stood like a shaft of lightning. Power and nobility rippled up and down, to the tips of his straining fingers.

He saw a great sea of faces, miles and miles of faces. "SIEG," he roared and the uniformed men marching toward him from the faces, raised their arms for all the millions behind them and roared back, "HEIL."

He was free at last.

ELIE WIESEL (1928–   )

Elie Wiesel is one of the most exceptional writers to have survived the concentration camps at Auschwitz and Buchenwald. Born on September 30, 1928, Wiesel grew up in Sighet, Roumania. In the Spring of 1944, he, his parents, and three sisters were taken to the death camp at Auschwitz, Poland. His father was murdered before his eyes and his mother and youngest sister exterminated. In 1945, Wiesel was transferred to Buchenwald. As a consequence of these inhuman experiences, Wiesel grew obsessed with the central theme that informs his fiction: the attempt to reconcile a benevolent God with the existence of evil in the world.

After the war, Elie Wiesel lived in Paris for a number of years and then immigrated into the United States. In 1957, he began to write for the Jewish Daily Forward; *in 1963 he became an American citizen. From the time of the traumatic events in the concentration camps, Wiesel wanted to become a writer. His first novel,* Night *(1960), is autobiographical and records the experiences at Auschwitz and Buchenwald of a fifteen-year-old boy. His other books include* Dawn *(1961),* The Accident *(1962),* The Town Beyond the Wall *(1964),* The Gates of the Forest *(1966),* The Jews of Silence; a Personal Report *(1966),* Zalmen; or, The Madness of God *(1968),* Legends of Our Time *(1968), and* A Beggar in Jerusalem *(1968).*

Yom Kippur: The Day Without Forgiveness

WITH A LIFELESS LOOK, a painful smile on his face, while digging a hole in the ground, Pinhas moved his lips in silence. He appeared to be arguing with someone within himself and, judging from his expression, seemed close to admitting defeat.

I had never seen him so downhearted. I knew that his body would not hold out much longer. His strength was already abandoning him, his movements were becoming more heavy, more chaotic. No doubt he knew it too. But death figured only rarely in our conversations. We preferred to deny its presence, to reduce it, as in the past, to a simple allusion, something abstract, inoffensive, a word like any other.

"What are you thinking about? What's wrong?"

Pinhas lowered his head, as if to conceal his embarrassment, or his sadness, or both, and let a long time go by before he answered, in a voice scarcely audible: "Tomorrow is Yom Kippur."

Then I too felt depressed. My first Yom Kippur in the camp. Perhaps my last. The day of judgment, of atonement. Tomorrow the heavenly tribunal would sit and pass sentence: "And like unto a flock, the creatures of this world shall pass before thee." Once upon a time—last year—the approach of this day of tears, of penitence and fear, had made me tremble. Tomorrow, we would present ourselves before God, who sees everything and who knows everything, and we would say: "Father, have pity on your children." Would I be capable of praying with fervor again? Pinhas shook himself abruptly. His glance plunged into mine.

"Tomorrow is the Day of Atonement and I have just made a decision: I am not going to fast. Do you hear? I am not going to fast."

I asked for no explanation. I knew he was going to die and suddenly I was afraid that by way of justification he might declare: "It is simple, I have decided not to comply with the law anymore and not to fast because in the eyes of man and of God I am already dead, and the dead can disobey the commandments of the Torah." I lowered my head and made believe I was not thinking about anything but the earth I was digging up under a sky more dark than the earth itself.

We belonged to the same Kommando. We always managed to work side by side. Our age difference did not stop him from treating me like a friend. He must have been past forty. I was fifteen. Before the war, he had been *Rosh-Yeshiva,* director of a rabbinical school somewhere in Galicia. Often, to outwit our hunger or to forget our reasons for despair, we would study a page of the Talmud from memory. I relived my childhood by forcing myself not to think about those who were gone. If one of my arguments pleased Pinhas, if I quoted a commentary without distorting its meaning, he would smile at me and say: "I should have liked to have you among my disciples."

And I would answer: "But I am your disciple, where we are matters little."

That was false, the place was of capital importance. According to the law of the camp I was his equal; I used the familiar form when I addressed him. Any other form of address was inconceivable.

"Do you hear?" Pinhas shouted defiantly. "I will not fast."

"I understand. You are right. One must not fast. Not at Auschwitz. Here we live outside time, outside sin. Yom Kippur does not apply to Auschwitz."

Ever since Rosh Hashana, the New Year, the question had been bitterly debated all over camp. Fasting meant a quicker death. Here everybody fasted all year round. Every day was Yom Kippur. And the book of life and death was no longer in God's hands, but in the hands of the executioner. The words *mi yichye umi yamut,* "who shall live and who shall die," had a terrible real meaning here, an immediate bearing. And all the prayers in the world could not alter the *Gzar-din,* the inexorable movement of fate. Here, in order to live, one had to eat, not pray.

"You are right, Pinhas," I said, forcing myself to withstand his gaze. "You *must* eat tomorrow. You've been here longer than I have, longer than many of us. You need your strength. You have to save your strength, watch over it, protect it. You should not go beyond your limits. Or tempt misfortune. That would be a sin."

Me, his disciple? I gave him lessons, I gave him advice, as if I were his elder, his guide.

"That is not it," said Pinhas, getting irritated. "I could hold out for one day without food. It would not be the first time."

"Then what is it?"

"A decision. Until now, I've accepted everything. Without bitterness, without reservation. I have told myself: 'God knows what he is doing.' I have submitted to his will. Now I have had enough, I have reached my limit. If he knows what he is doing, then it is serious; and it is not any less serious if he does not. Therefore, I have decided to tell him: 'It is enough.' "

I said nothing. How could I argue with him? I was going through the same crisis. Every day I was moving a little further away from the God of my childhood. He had become a stranger to me; sometimes, I even thought he was my enemy.

The appearance of Edek put an end to our conversation. He was our master, our king. The Kapo. This young Pole with rosy cheeks, with the movements of a wild animal, enjoyed catching his slaves by surprise and making them shout with fear. Still an adolescent, he enjoyed possessing such power over so many adults. We dreaded his changeable moods, his sudden fits of anger: without unclenching his teeth, his eyes half-closed, he would beat his victims long after they had lost consciousness and had ceased to moan.

"Well?" he said, planting himself in front of us, his arms folded. "Taking a little nap? Talking over old times? You think you are at a resort? Or in the synagogue?"

A cruel flame lit his blue eyes, but it went out just as quickly. An aborted rage. We began to shovel furiously, not thinking about anything but the ground which opened up menacingly before us. Edek insulted us a few more times and then walked off.

Pinhas did not feel like talking anymore, neither did I. For him the die had been cast. The break with God appeared complete.

Meanwhile, the pit under our legs was becoming wider and deeper. Soon our heads would hardly be visible above the ground. I had the weird sensation that I was digging a grave. For whom? For Pinhas? For myself? Perhaps for our memories.

On my return to camp, I found it plunged in feverish anticipation: they were preparing to welcome the holiest and longest day of the year. My barracks neighbors, a father and son, were talking in low voices. One was saying: "Let us hope the roll-call does not last too long." The other added: "Let us hope that the soup is distributed before the sun sets, otherwise we will not have the right to touch it."

Their prayers were answered. The roll-call unfolded without incident, without delay, without public hanging. The section-chief hurriedly distributed the soup; I hurriedly gulped it down. I ran to wash, to purify myself. By the time the day was drawing to a close, I was ready.

Some days before, on the eve of Rosh Hashana, all the Jews in camp—Kapos included—had congregated at the square where roll was taken, and we had implored the God of Abraham, Isaac, and Jacob to end our humiliation, to change sides, to break his pact with the enemy. In unison we had said *Kaddish* for the dead and for the living as well. Officers and soldiers, machine guns in hand, had stood by, amused spectators, on the other side of the barbed wire.

Now, we did not go back there for *Kol Nidre*. We were afraid of a selection: in preceding years, the Day of Atonement had been turned into a day of mourning. Yom Kippur had become *Tisha b'Av*, the day the Temple was destroyed.

Thus, each barracks housed its own synagogue. It was more prudent. I was sorry, because Pinhas was in another block.

A Hungarian rabbi officiated as our cantor. His voice stirred my memories and evoked that legend according to which, on the night of Yom Kippur, the dead rise from their graves and come to pray with the living. I thought: "Then it is true; that is what really happens. The legend is confirmed at Auschwitz."

For weeks, several learned Jews had gathered every night in our block to transcribe from memory—by hand, on toilet paper—the prayers for the High Holy Days. Each cantor received a copy. Ours read in a loud voice and we repeated each verse after him. The *Kol Nidre*, which releases us from all vows made under constraint, now seemed to me anachronistic, absurd, even though it had been composed in similar circumstances, in Spain, right near the Inquisition stakes. Once a year the converts would assemble and cry out to God: "Know this, all that we have said is unsaid, all that we have done is undone." *Kol Nidre?* A sad joke. Here and now we no longer had any secret vows to make or to deny: everything was clear, irrevocable.

Then came the *Vidui*, the great confession. There again, everything rang false, none of it concerned us anymore. *Ashamnu*, we have sinned. *Bagadnu*, we have betrayed. *Gazalnu*, we have stolen. What? Us? *We* have sinned? Against whom? by doing what? *We* have betrayed? Whom? Undoubtedly this was the first time since God judged his creation that victims beat their breasts accusing themselves of the crimes of their executioners.

Why did we take responsibility for sins and offenses which not one of us could ever have had the desire or the possibility of committing? Perhaps we felt guilty despite everything. Things were simpler that way. It was better to believe our punishments had meaning, that we had deserved them; to believe in a cruel but just God was better than not to believe at all. It was in order not to provoke an open war between God and his people that we had chosen to spare him, and we cried out: "You are our God, blessed be your name. You smite us without pity, you shed our blood, we give thanks to you for it, O Eternal One, for you are determined to show us that you are just and that your name is justice!"

I admit having joined my voice to the others and implored the heavens to grant me mercy and forgiveness. At variance with everything my lips were saying, I indicted myself only to turn everything into derision, into farce. At any moment I expected the Master of the universe to strike me dumb and to say: "That is enough—you have gone too far." And I like to think I would have replied: "You, also, blessed be your name, you also."

Our services were dispersed by the camp bell. The section-chiefs began to yell: "Okay, go to sleep! If God hasn't heard you, it's because he is incapable of hearing."

The next day, at work, Pinhas joined another group. I thought: "He wants to eat without being embarrassed by my presence." A day later, he returned. His face even more pale, even more gaunt than before. Death was gnawing at him. I caught myself thinking: "He will die because he did not observe Yom Kippur."

We dug for several hours without looking at each other. From far off, the shouting of the Kapo reached us. He walked around hitting people relentlessly.

Toward the end of the afternoon, Pinhas spoke to me: "I have a confession to make."

I shuddered, but went on digging. A strange, almost child-like smile appeared on his lips when he spoke again: "You know, I fasted."

I remained motionless. My stupor amused him.

"Yes, I fasted. Like the others. But not for the same reasons. Not out of obedience, but out of defiance. Before the war, you see, some Jews rebelled against the divine will by going to restaurants on the Day of Atonement; here, it is by observing the fast that we can make our indignation heard. Yes, my disciple and teacher, know that I fasted. Not for love of God, but against God."

He left me a few weeks later, victim of the first selection.

He shook my hand: "I would have liked to die some other way and elsewhere. I had always hoped to make of my death, as of my life, an act of faith. It is a pity. God prevents me from realizing my dream. He no longer likes dreams."

Nonetheless, he asked me to say *Kaddish* for him after his death, which, according to his calculations, would take place three days after his departure from camp.

"But why?" I asked, "since you are no longer a believer?"

He took the tone he always used when he explained a passage in the Talmud to me: "You do not see the heart of the matter. Here and now, the only way to accuse him is by praising him."

And he went, laughing, to his death.

Once and for All

Delmore Schwartz

Once, when I was a boy,
Apollo summoned me
To be apprenticed to the endless summer of light and
    consciousness,
And thus to become and be what poets often have been,
A shepherd of being, a riding master of being, holding the
    sun-god's horses, leading his sheep, training his eagles,
Directing the constellations to their stations, and to each
    grace of place.
But the goat-god, piping and dancing, speaking an un-
    known tongue or the language of the magician,
Sang from the darkness or rose from the underground,
    whence arise
Love and love's drunkenness, love and birth, love and death,
    death and rebirth
Which are the beginning of the phoenix festivals, the tragic
    plays in celebration of Dionysus,
And in mourning for his drunken and fallen princess, the
    singers and sinners, fallen because they are, in the end,
Drunken with pride, blinded by joy.

And I followed Dionysus, forgetting Apollo. I followed him
    far too long until I was wrong and chanted:

For a biographical note on Delmore Schwartz see p. 254.

"One cannot serve both gods. One must choose to win and
   lose."
But I was wrong and when I knew how I was wrong I
   knew
What, in a way, I had known all along.
This was the new world, here I belonged, here I was wrong
   because
Here every tragedy has a happy ending, and any error
   may be
A fabulous discovery of America, of the opulence hidden in
   the dark depths and glittering heights of reality.

The Would-Be Hungarian

Delmore Schwartz

Come, let us meditate upon the fate of a little boy who
    wished to be
Hungarian! Having been moved with his family to a new
    suburb, having been sent to a new school, the only
    Catholic school in the new suburb,
Where all the other children were Hungarian,

He felt very sad and separate on the first day, he felt more
    and more separated and isolated
Because all the other boys and girls pitied and were sorry
    for him since he was not
Hungarian! Hence they pitied and were sorry for him so
    much they gave him handsome gifts,
Presents of comic books, marbles and foreign coins, pepper-
    mints and candy, a pistol, and also their devoted sym-
    pathy, pity and friendship

Making him sadder still since now he saw how all Hun-
    garians were very kind and generous, and he was not

Hungarian! Hence he was an immigrant, an alien: he was
    and he would be,
Forever, no matter what, he could never become Hungarian!
Hungarian! Hence he went home on the first day, bearing

his gifts and telling his parents how much he wished
   to be
Hungarian: in anguish, in anger,
Accusing them of depriving him, and misusing him: amus-
   ing them,
So that he rose to higher fury, shouting and accusing them

—Because of you I am a stranger, monster, orang-outang!
Because of you (his hot tears say) I am an orang-outang!
   and not
Hungarian! Worse than to have no bicycle, no shoes . . .
        Behold how this poor boy, who wished so passion-
           ately to be Hungarian
        Suffered and knew the fate of being American.
                Whether on Ellis Island, Plymouth Rock,

Or in the secret places of the mind and heart
This is America—as poetry and hope
This is the fame, the game and the names of our fate:
This we must suffer or must celebrate.

MURIEL RUKEYSER (1913–   )

Muriel Rukeyser's poetry is deeply subjective, although it is closely related to the historical and social forces of the moment. In her early work of the 1930's, she first assumed that radical political posture which is present in all her writing. During World War II, she identified strongly with the suffering Jews of Europe and her poetry of this period is the most powerful and impressive of her career; her intense emotion, which at times can be excessive, found an objective correlative in the persecution of Jews.

Muriel Rukeyser was born on December 15, 1913, and was educated at Vassar College. She has taught at Sarah Lawrence College and has won numerous prizes for her poetry, including the Yale Series of Younger Poets Award in 1935, the National Institute Award in 1942, and the Levinson Prize in 1947. Her books include Theory of Flight (1935); A Turning Wind (1939); The Green Wave (1948); Selected Poems (1951); Elegies (1957); Poems Selected and New (1961); and Waterlily Fire: Poems 1935–1962 (1962).

The Blood Is Justified

Beat out continuance in the choking veins
before emotion betrays us, and we find
staring behind our faces, accomplices of death.
Not to die, but slowly to validate our lives   :
simply to move, lightly burdened, alone,
carrying in this brain survival, carrying
within these ribs, history,
the past deep in the bone.

    Unthread time till its empty needle prick your flesh
    sewing your scars with air, treating the wounds
    only by laceration   and the blood is fresh
    blood on our skin on our lips over our eyes.

Living they move on a canvas of centuries
restored from death in artful poses, found
once more by us, descendants, foraging,
ravelling time back over American ground.
How did they wish, grandparents of these wars,
what cataracts of ambition fell across their brains?   :

The heavy boots kicked stones down Wisconsin roads,
Augusta Coller danced her début at Oshkosh   :
they spoke these names   :   Milwaukee, Waukesha,
the crackle and drawl of Indian strange words.

Jungle-savage the south
raw green and shining branches, the crying
of parakeets, the painted stone,
the altars stained with oil   :
Mexico   :   and Canada wheaten and polar with
snow halfway up the sky   :
all these unknown.

What treason to their race has fathered us?
They walked in the towns, the men selling clothing etc.
the women tatting and boiling down grape jelly.
If they were asked this, surely they did not answer.
Over the country, Wisconsin, Chicago, Yonkers,
I was begotten, American branch no less because
I call on the great names of other countries.
I do not say   :   Forgive, to my kindred dead,
only   :   Understand my treason, See I betray you kissing,
I overthrow your milestones weeping among your tombs.

From out your knowing eyes I sprang, child of your distant
      wombs,
of your full lips.   Speaking allegiance, I turn,
steadfastly to destroy your hope.   Your cargo in me
swings to ports hostile to your old intent.

In us recurrences.   :   My generation feeds
the wise assault on your anticipation,
repeating historic sunderings, betraying our fathers,
all parricidal in our destinies.
How much are we American?   Not knowing
those other lands, being
blood wrung from your bone, our pioneers,
we call kindred to you, we claim links, speaking
your tongue, although we pass, shaking
your dream with revolution since we must.
By these roads shall we come upon our country.
Pillowed upon this birthright, we may wake
strong for such treason, brave with your fallen dust.

O, we are afflicted with these present evils,
they press between the mirror and our eyes,

obscuring your loaned mouths and borrowed hair.
We focus on our times, destroying you, fathers
in the long ground   :   you have given strange birth
to us who turn against you in our blood
needing to move in our integrity, accomplices
of life in revolution, though the past
be sweet with your tall shadows, and although
we turn from treasons, we shall accomplish these.

To Be a Jew in the Twentieth Century

To be a Jew in the twentieth century
Is to be offered a gift. If you refuse,
Wishing to be invisible, you choose
Death of the spirit, the stone insanity.
Accepting, take full life. Full agonies:
Your evening deep in labyrinthine blood
Of those who resist, fail, and resist; and God
Reduced to a hostage among hostages.

The gift is torment. Not alone the still
Torture, isolation; or torture of the flesh.
That may come also. But the accepting wish,
The whole and fertile spirit as guarantee
For every human freedom, suffering to be free.
Daring to live for the impossible.

KARL SHAPIRO (1913–   )

In the foreword to Five Young American Poets (1941), *which contains his early poetry, Karl Shapiro offers a statement of his poetic aims which has held true for all his later work: "The reader will see that I write about myself, my house, my street, and my city, and not about America, the word that is the chief enemy of modern poetry." Shapiro's concrete approach to his subject is reflected in his "Jewish" poetry. He is self-consciously Jewish—one of his books is entitled* Poems of a Jew (1958)*—and the poems he writes form specific images of Jewish life, as their titles suggest: "The Synagogue," "Shylock," "Jew," "The Alphabet," "The Confirmation," "The Jew at Christmas Eve," "The Murder of Moses."*

Karl Shapiro was born on November 10, 1913, in Baltimore, Maryland, and was educated at the University of Virginia (1932–1937) and Johns Hopkins University (1936–1939). He has taught at Johns Hopkins University, the University of Nebraska, Chicago Circle Campus of the University of Illinois, and the University of California at Davis. He was editor of Poetry: A Magazine of Verse *from 1950 to 1956 and* The Prairie Schooner *from 1956 to 1966. In 1945 he was awarded the Pulitzer Prize for* V-Letter and Other Poems *and in 1946 was appointed Consultant in Poetry at the Library of Congress. His books include* Person, Place, and Thing (1942); V-Letter and Other Poems (1944); Essay on Rime (1945); Poems of a Jew (1958); In Defense of Ignorance (1960); The Bourgeois Poet (1964); Selected Poems *and* White-Haired Lover (1968).

Shylock

Ho, no, no, no, no, my meaning in saying he
is a good man is to have you understand me,
that he is sufficient.—THE MERCHANT OF
VENICE

Home from the court he locked the door and sat
In the evil darkness, suddenly composed.
The knife shone dimly on the table and his eyes
Like candles in an empty room
Shone hard at nothing. Yet he appeared to smile.

Then he took up his talith and his hat
And prayed mechanically and absently closed
His fingers on the knife. If he could realize
His actual defeat or personal doom
He must die or change or show that he was vile.

Nevertheless he would remain and live,
Submit to baptism, pay his fines,
Appear in the Rialto as early as tomorrow,
Not innocently but well aware
That his revenge is an accomplished fact.

And poverty itself would help to give
Humility to his old designs.
His fallen reputation would help borrow
A credit of new hate; for nothing will repair
This open breach of nature, cruel and wracked.

His daughter lies with swine, and the old rat
Tubal will be obsequious

To buy off his disgrace and bargain on his shame.
Despair can teach him nothing at all:
Gold he hates more than he hates Jesus' crown.

The logic of Balthasar will fall flat
On heaven's hearing. Incurious
As to the future, totally clear of blame,
He takes his ledgers out of the wall
And lights them with a taper and sits down.

JEW

The name is immortal but only the name, for the rest
Is a nose that can change in the weathers of time or persist
Or die out in confusion or model itself on the best.

But the name is a language itself that is whispered and hissed
Through the houses of ages, and ever a language the same,
And ever and ever a blow on our heart like a fist.

And this last of our dream in the desert, O curse of our
    name,
Is immortal as Abraham's voice in our fragment of prayer
Adonai, Adonai, for our bondage of murder and shame!

And the word for the murder of God will cry out on the air
Though the race is no more and the temples are closed of
    our will
And the peace is made fast on the earth and the earth is
    made fair;

Our name is impaled in the heart of the world on a hill
Where we suffer to die by the hands of ourselves, and to kill.

The Murder of Moses

By reason of despair we set forth behind you
And followed the pillar of fire like a doubt,
To hold to belief wanted a sign,
Called the miracle of the staff and the plagues
Natural phenomena.

We questioned the expediency of the march,
Gossiped about you. What was escape
To the fear of going forward and Pharaoh's wheels?
When the chariots mired and the army flooded
Our cry of horror was one with theirs.

You always went alone, a little ahead,
Prophecy disturbed you, you were not a fanatic.
The women said you were meek, the men
Regarded you as a typical leader.
You and your black wife might have been foreigners.

We even discussed your parentage; were you really a Jew?
We remembered how Joseph had made himself a prince,
All of us shared in the recognition
Of his skill of management, sense of propriety,
Devotion to his brothers and Israel.

We hated you daily. Our children died. The water spilled.
It was as if you were trying to lose us one by one.
Our wandering seemed the wandering of your mind,
The cloud believed we were tireless,
We expressed our contempt and our boredom openly.

At last you ascended the rock; at last returned.
Your anger that day was probably His.

343

HOWARD NEMEROV (1920–   )

Howard Nemerov was born in New York City on March 1, 1920. He was educated at Harvard University (B.A., 1941). After serving in the Royal Canadian Air Force and the United States Army Air Force during World War II, he taught for a short time at Hamilton College in Clinton, New York, and then at Bennington College in Vermont (1948–1966) and Brandeis University. His books include Image and the Law (1947), a collection of poetry; The Melodramatists (1949), a novel; Guide to the Ruins (1950), poetry; Federigo, or the Power of Love (1954), The Salt Garden (1955), and The Homecoming Game (1957), novels; Mirrors and Windows (1958), a book of poems; A Commodity of Dreams, and Other Stories (1959); New and Selected Poems (1960); The Next Room of the Dream (1962), which contains, in addition to forty-five poems, two verse plays; Poetry and Fiction (1964), a collection of essays and reviews; and Journal of the Fictive Life (1965). In 1963 Nemerov served as consultant in poetry to the Library of Congress.

Nemerov, as M. L. Rosenthal has pointed out, has an "urban-centered mind, nervously alive, morally centered, but self-mocking." These qualities are particularly evident in the small body of writing which Nemerov has devoted to Jewish themes.

One Forever Alien

When I become the land, when they will build
Blast furnaces over me, and lay black asphalt
For hundreds of miles across my ribs, and wheels
Begin to bounce interminably on the bone;
When I enter, at last, America, when I am
Part of her progress and a true patriot,
And the schoolchildren sing of my sacrifice,
Remembering the burial day of my birth—
Then even the efficient will have to forgive me,
And those that harden their hearts welcome me home.

Then, in that day, my countrymen,
When I shall come among you fleeced as the lamb
And in the diaper of the grave newly arrayed,
The Adam Qadmon, the greenhorn immigrant,
Shall pass the customs at the port of entry
Where the Guardian Lady lifts her flaming sword.
Forgiven the original sin of his origin,
He comes as a bond redeemed, as newly negotiable,
    To be as a soybean before you.

Debate with the Rabbi

You've lost your religion, the Rabbi said.
    It wasn't much to keep, said I.
You should affirm the spirit, said he,
And the communal solidarity.
    I don't feel so solid, I said.

We are the people of the Book, the Rabbi said.
    Not of the phone book, said I.
Ours is a great tradition, said he,
And a wonderful history.
    But history's over, I said.

We Jews are creative people, the Rabbi said.
    Make something, then, said I.
In science and in art, said he,
Violinists and physicists have we.
    Fiddle and physic indeed, I said.

Stubborn and stiff-necked man! the Rabbi cried.
    The pain you give me, said I.
Instead of bowing down, said he,
You go on in your obstinacy.
    We Jews are that way, I replied.

ALLEN GINSBERG (1926–   )

The bardic, oral tradition in American poetry, represented by Walt Whitman in the nineteenth century, finds its twentieth-century exponent in Allen Ginsberg. Appearing as an Old Testament prophet, Ginsberg travels the world like the wandering Jew, preaches sexual liberty, reads his mantras as though they are Hebrew prayers, and speaks for the youth and oppressed minorities of America. Ginsberg calls himself a "Buddhist Jew," and perhaps that is as good a description of his religious temperament as any other. He is certainly in the tradition of prophetic poets whose work is essentially religious. His early affiliation with the Beat generation and Zen Buddhism; his later attraction to holy men in India, to Martin Buber, and to mystics in general—these tendencies point to a religious quest that he has made since his earliest poetry.

Allen Ginsberg was born in Newark, New Jersey, on June 3, 1926. His father was a poet and a high-school teacher; his mother, a Russian immigrant, suffered from paranoia, and her mental breakdown had a profound effect on Ginsberg, which he recorded in Kaddish for Naomi Ginsberg (1961). In Newark, during the Depression, Ginsberg grew up in poverty.

Ginsberg came to Columbia University in 1943 and was dismissed in 1945 when he was accused of scribbling an anti-Semitic obscenity on the dust of his dormitory window. Diana Trilling, in "The Other Night at Columbia," interpreted Ginsberg's remark as a denial of his middle-class Jewish background; but Ginsberg himself claimed that he had wished only to shock an anti-Semitic Irish cleaning woman who worked for the college. He succeeded, for the woman reported the comment to a dean who quickly expelled Ginsberg. In 1945 Ginsberg returned to the college and received his B.A. in 1948. During this period, he became friendly with Jack Kerouac and William Burroughs; through Burroughs, he discovered other writers who influenced him: Spengler, Yeats, Rimbaud, Korzybski, Proust, and Celine. Increasingly Ginsberg turned to mysticism as a way of resolving his own quarrel with modern society.

In 1951 Ginsberg went to San Francisco as a market research consultant. In a short while, under the influence of therapy, he left his routine life and devoted his full time to writing poetry. He became a leading figure in the San Francisco renaissance and published his poetic manifesto, Howl and Other Poems (1956). "Howl," the title poem, is one of the best known works of the Beat generation. This volume was followed by Kaddish and Other Poems (1961). Ginsberg traveled widely in the 1960's—to India and the East, to Cuba, and to Eastern Europe—, preaching yoga, meditation, and the use of drugs. His earliest poems were *published under the titles,* Empty Mirror (*1962*) *and* Reality Sandwiches (*1963*). *Other books of poetry include* T. B. Baby Poems, Planet News, 1961–1967 (*1968*), Ankor Wat (*1969*), *and* Indian Journals (*1970*).

Kaddish for Naomi Ginsberg 1894-1956

Strange now to think of you, gone without corsets & eyes, while
    I walk on the sunny pavement of Greenwich Village.
downtown Manhattan, clear winter noon, and I've been up all
    night, talking, talking, reading the Kaddish aloud, listen-
    ing to Ray Charles blues shout blind on the phonograph
the rhythm the rhythm—and your memory in my head three
    years after—And read Adonais' last triumphant stanzas
    aloud—wept, realizing how we suffer—
And how Death is that remedy all singers dream of, sing,
    remember, prophesy as in the Hebrew Anthem, or the
    Buddhist Book of Answers—and my own imagination of
    a withered leaf—at dawn—
Dreaming back thru life, Your time—and mine accelerating
    toward Apocalypse,
the final moment—the flower burning in the Day—and what
    comes after,
looking back on the mind itself that saw an American city
a flash away, and the great dream of Me or China, or you and
    a phantom Russia, or a crumpled bed that never existed—
like a poem in the dark—escaped back to Oblivion—
No more to say, and nothing to weep for but the Beings in the
    Dream, trapped in its disappearance,
sighing, screaming with it, buying and selling pieces of
    phantom, worshipping each other,

worshipping the God included in it all—longing or inevitability?—while it lasts, a Vision—anything more?

It leaps about me, as I go out and walk the street, look back
over my shoulder, Seventh Avenue, the battlements of
window office buildings shouldering each other high under
a cloud, tall as the sky an instant—and the sky above—
an old blue place.

or down the Avenue to the South, to—as I walk toward the
Lower East Side—where you walked 50 years ago, little
girl—from Russia, eating the first poisonous tomatoes of
America—frightened on the dock—

then struggling in the crowds of Orchard Street toward what?
—toward Newark—

toward candy store, first home-made sodas of the century,
hand-churned ice cream in backroom on musty brownfloor-
boards—

Toward education, marriage, nervous breakdown, operation,
teaching school, and learning to be mad, in a dream—
what is this life?

Toward the Key in the window—and the great Key lays its
head of light on top of Manhattan, and over the floor,
and lays down on the sidewalk—in a single vast beam,
moving, as I walk down First toward the Yiddish Theater
—and the place of poverty

you knew, and I know, but without caring now—Strange to
have moved thru Paterson, and the West, and Europe and
here again,

with the cries of Spaniards now in the doorstoops doors and
dark boys on the street, fire escapes old as you

—Tho you're not old now, that's left here with me—

Myself, anyhow, maybe as old as the universe—and I guess
that dies with us—enough to cancel all that comes—
What came is gone forever every time—

That's good! That leaves it open for no regret—no fear radia-
tors, lacklove, torture even toothache in the end—

Though while it comes it is a lion that eats the soul—and the
lamb, the soul, in us, alas, offering itself in sacrifice to
change's fierce hunger—hair and teeth—and the roar of
bonepain, skull bare, break rib, rot-skin, braintricked
Implacability.

Ai! ai! we do worse! We are in a fix! And you're out, Death

let you out, Death had the Mercy, you're done with your
century, done with God, done with the path thru it—
Done with yourself at last—Pure—Back to the Babe dark
before your Father, before us all—before the world—

There, rest. No more suffering for you. I know where you've
gone, it's good.

No more flowers in the summer fields of New York, no joy now,
no more fear of Louis,

and no more of his sweetness and glasses, his high school
decades, debts, love, frightened telephone calls, conception
beds, relatives, hands—

No more of sister Eleanor,—she gone before you—we kept it
secret—you killed her—or she killed herself to bear with
you—an arthritic heart—But Death's killed you both—
No matter—

Nor your memory of your mother, 1915 tears in silent movies
weeks and weeks—forgetting, agrieve watching Marie
Dressler address humanity, Chaplin dance in youth,

or Boris Godinov, Chaliapin's at the Met, halling his voice of a
weeping Czar—by standing room with Elanor & Max—
watching also the Capitalists take seats in Orchestra,
white furs, diamonds,

with the YPSL's hitch-hiking thru Pennsylvania, in black baggy
gym skirts pants, photograph of 4 girls holding each other
round the waste, and laughing eye, too coy, virginal
solitude of 1920

all girls grown old, or dead, now, and that long hair in the
grave—lucky to have husbands later—

You made it—I came too—Eugene my brother before (still
grieving now and will gream on to his last stiff hand, as
he goes thru his cancer—or kill—later perhaps—soon
he will think—)

And it's the last moment I remember, which I see them all
thru myself, now—tho not you

I didn't foresee what you felt—what more hideous gape of
bad mouth came first—to you—and were you prepared?

To go where? In that Dark—that—in that God? a radiance?
A Lord in the Void? Like an eye in the black cloud in a
dream? Adonoi at last, with you?

Beyond my remembrance! Incapable to guess! Not merely the
yellow skull in the grave, or a box of worm dust, and

a stained ribbon—Deathshead with Halo? Can you believe
    it?
Is it only the sun that shines once for the mind, only the flash
    of existence, than none ever was?
Nothing beyond what we have—what you had—that so pitiful
    —yet Triumph.
to have been here, and changed, like a tree, broken, or flower—
    fed to the ground—but mad, with its petals, colored,
    thinking Great Universe, shaken, cut in the head, leaf-
    stript, hid in an egg crate hospital, cloth wrapped, sore
    —freaked in the moon brain, Naughtless.
No flower like that flower, which knew itself in the garden, and
    fought the knife—lost
Cut down by an idiot Snowman's icy—even in the Spring—
    strange ghost thought—some Death—Sharp icicle in his
    hand—crowned with old roses—a dog for his eyes—cock
    of a sweatshop—heart of electric irons.
All the accumulations of life, that wear us out—clocks, bodies,
    consciousness, shoe, breasts—begotten sons—your Com-
    munism—'Paranoia' into hospitals.
You once kicked Elanor in the leg, she died of heart failure
    later, You of stroke. Asleep? within a year, the two of
    you, sisters in death. Is Elanor happy?
Max grieves alive in an office on Lower Broadway, lone large
    mustache over midnight Accountings, not sure. His life
    passes—as he sees—and what does he doubt now? Still
    dream of making money, or that might have made money,
    hired nurse, had children, found even your Immortality,
    Naomi?
I'll see him soon. Now I've got to cut through—to talk to you
    —as I didn't when you had a mouth.
Forever. And we're bound for that, Forever—like Emily Dickin-
    son's horses—headed to the End.
They know the way—These Steeds—run faster than we think
    —it's our own life they cross—and take with them.

Magnificent, mourned no more, marred of heart, mind
behind, married dreamed, mortal changed—Ass and face done
with murder.
    In the world, given, flower maddened, made no Utopia,

shut under pine, almed in Earth, blamed in Lone, Jehovah, accept.

Nameless, One Faced, Forever beyond me, beginningless, endless, Father in death. Tho I am not there for this Prophecy, I am unmarried, I'm hymnless, I'm Heavenless, headless in blisshood I would still adore

Thee, Heaven, after Death, only One blessed in Nothingness, not light or darkness, Dayless Eternity—

Take this, this Psalm, from me, burst from my hand in a day, some of my Time, now given to Nothing—to praise Thee —But Death

This is the end, the redemption from Wilderness, way for the Wonderer, House sought for All, black handkerchief washed clean by weeping—page beyond Psalm—Last change of mine and Naomi—to God's perfect Darkness—Death, stay thy phantoms!

Only to have not forgotten the beginning in which she drank
    cheap sodas in the morgues of Newark,
only to have seen her weeping on grey tables in long wards of
    her universe
only to have known the weird ideas of Hitler at the door, the
    wires in her head, the three big sticks
rammed down her back, the voices in the ceiling shrieking out
    her ugly early lays for 30 years,
only to have seen the time-jumps, memory lapse, the crash of
    wars, the roar and silence of a vast electric shock,
only to have seen her painting crude pictures of Elevateds
    running over the rooftops of the Bronx
her brothers dead in Riverside or Russia, her lone in Long
    Island writing a last letter—and her image in the sun-
    light at the window
The key is in the sunlight at the window in the bars the key
    is in the sunlight.
only to have come to that dark night on iron bed by stroke when
    the sun gone down on Long Island
and the vast Atlantic roars outside the great call of Being to
    its own
to come back out of the Nightmare—divided creation—with
    her head lain on a pillow of the hospital to die

—in one last glimpse—all Earth one everlasting Light in the
    familiar blackout—no tears for this vision—
But that the key should be left behind—at the window—the
    key in the sunlight—to the living—that can take
that slice of light in hand—and turn the door—and look
    back see
Creation glistening backwards to the same grave, size of
    universe,
size of the tick of the hospital's clock on the archway over the
    white door—

O mother
what have I left out
O mother
what have I forgotten
O mother
farewell
with a long black shoe
farewell
with Communist Party and a broken stocking
farewell
with six dark hairs on the wen of your breast
farewell
with your old dress and a long black beard around the vagina
farewell
with your sagging belly
with your fear of Hitler
with your mouth of bad short stories
with your fingers of rotten mandolines
with your arms of fat Paterson porches
with your belly of strikes and smokestacks
with your chin of Trotsky and the Spanish War
with your voice singing for the decaying overbroken workers
with your nose of bad lay with your nose of the smell of the
    pickles of Newark
with your eyes
with your eyes of Russia
with your eyes of no money
with your eyes of false China
with your eyes of Aunt Elanor

with your eyes of starving India
with your eyes pissing in the park
with your eyes of America taking a fall
with your eyes of your failure at the piano
with your eyes of your relatives in California
with your eyes of Ma Rainey dying in an ambulance
with your eyes of Czechoslovakia attacked by robots
with your eyes going to painting class at night in the Bronx
with your eyes of the killer Grandma you see on the horizon
        from the Fire-Escape
with your eyes running naked out of the apartment screaming
        into the hall
with your eyes being led away by policemen to an ambulance
with your eyes strapped down on the operating table
with your eyes with the pancreas removed
with your eyes of appendix operation
with your eyes of abortion
with your eyes of ovaries removed
with your eyes of shock
with your eyes of lobotomy
with your eyes of divorce
with your eyes of stroke
with your eyes alone
with your eyes
with your eyes
with your Death full of Flowers

Caw caw caw crows shriek in the white sun over grave stone
        in Long Island
Lord Lord Lord Naomi underneath this grass my halflife and
        my own as hers
caw caw my eye be buri'd in the same Ground where I stand
        in Angel
Lord Lord great Eye that stares on All and moves in a black
        cloud
caw caw strange cry of Beings flung up into sky over the waving
        trees
Lord Lord O Grinder of giant Beyonds my voice in a boundless
        field in Sheol

Caw caw the call of Time rent out of foot and wing an instant
in the universe
Lord Lord an echo in the sky the wind through ragged leaves
the roar of memory
caw caw all years my birth a dream caw caw New York the big
the broken shoe the vast highschool caw caw all Visions
of the Lord
Lord Lord Lord caw caw caw Lord Lord Lord caw caw caw
Lord

LIONEL TRILLING (1905–   )

Lionel Trilling is one of the important critics of the twentieth century. His period of greatest achievement was in the 1940's and 1950's, when he wrote a series of essays and books that explored the relationship between society and literature and that urged a revival of the liberal tradition in American culture.

Born in 1905 in New York, Trilling studied at Columbia University and was awarded his Ph.D. in 1938. He taught briefly at the University of Wisconsin and Hunter College; since 1932 he has been associated with Columbia College. His books include Matthew Arnold *(1938) and* E. M. Forster *(1943), critical studies which have defined the significance of these authors for modern readers;* The Middle of the Journey *(1947), a political novel;* The Liberal Imagination *(1950),* The Opposing Self *(1955),* Authenticity and Sincerity *(1972) and* Beyond Culture *(1965), collections of essays which have had an extensive influence on subsequent critics.*

Although his important work ranges freely through Western culture, Trilling has written certain essays—"Wordsworth and the Rabbis" and the introduction to Isaac Babel's fiction—which derive their significance from the blending of a muted Jewishness and a sophisticated secular education. His comments on the relationship of the Jew to American society, part of a symposium for the Contemporary Jewish Record, *are especially interesting, for they were made at the end of World War II, after Trilling had published his book on Matthew Arnold and was at the threshold of writing his most important essays.*

Under Forty

It is never possible for a Jew of my generation to "escape" his Jewish origin. In order to be sure of this I have only to remember how, when I was a child beginning to read for pleasure, certain words would leap magnetically to my eye from the page before I had reached them in the text. One such word was "snake"; others were words of such sexual explicitness as a child is likely to meet in his reading; and there was the word "Jew." These were words, that is, which struck straight to the unconscious, where fear, shame, attraction and repulsion are indistinguishable. Yet there was no dramatic or even specific reason why the word "Jew" should produce (as it still produces) so deep, so visceral, a reverberation. I was never a victim of prejudice or persecution. My family was fairly well established; although my parents were orthodox in the form of their religion they had a strong impulse to partake of the general life and to want it for me. My childhood was spent in a comfortable New York suburb where a Jewish group formed around the synagogue an active community large enough to be both interesting and protective; at the same time we Jewish children were perfectly at home in the pleasant public school. Those were days in which Jews lived with an ampler hope than now; yet even then the word "Jew" could have for a Jewish child an emotional charge as strong as I have described.

A childhood feeling so intense obviously does not disappear. It is clear to me that my existence as a Jew is one of the shaping conditions of my temperament, and therefore I suppose it must have its effect on my intellect. Yet I cannot discover anything in my professional intellectual life which I can specifically trace back to my Jewish birth and rearing. I do not think of myself as a "Jewish writer." I do not have it in mind to serve by my writing any Jewish purpose. I should resent it if a critic of my work were to discover in it either faults or virtues which he called Jewish.

In what I might call my life as a citizen my being Jewish exists as a point of honor. The phrase is grandiloquent although I do not mean it to be. I can have no pride in seeing a long tradition, often great and heroic, reduced to this small status in me, for I give only a limited respect to points of honor: they are usually mortuary and monumental, they have being without desire. For me the point of honor consists in feeling that I would not, even if I could, deny or escape being Jewish. Surely it is at once clear how minimal such a position is—how much it hangs upon only a resistance (and even only a passive one) to the stupidity and brutality which make the Jewish situation so bad as it is.

The position I have described as mine is perhaps the position of most American writers of Jewish birth. It creates no surprise and no resentment until it is formulated. And when it is formulated it has, I suppose, a certain gracelessness—if only because millions of Jews are suffering simply because they have the heritage that I so minimize in my own intellectual life. I do not want to "answer" this conformation —to do so, except at great length and with many modulations, could only make the position appear more graceless than it must seem to some. I would say, however, that we are on all sides required to imagine the unimaginable sufferings of masses of men and that while the most common failure of the imagination will certainly be insensibility, there is also the failure of merely symbolic action, of mere guilty gesture.

But the position I have described brings with it no feeling of guilt toward the American Jewish community. I hope I have enough knowledge and sympathy to understand what has led this community to its impasse of sterility, but understanding does not mitigate the perception of the unhappy fact. If what I have called my "point of honor" is minimal and even negative, if, that is, it does not *want* enough and is nothing more than a resistance to an external force, it seems to me that the position of the American Jewish community is to be described in much the same way. There is, I know, much show and talk of affirmation, but only to the end that the negative, or neuter, elements may be made more acceptable. As I see it, the great fact for American Jews is their exclusion from certain parts of the general life and every activity of Jewish life seems to be a response to this fact.

Jewish religion is, I am sure, very liberal and intelligent and modern.

Its function is to provide, chiefly for people of no strong religious impulse, a social and rational defense against the world's hostility. A laudable purpose surely, but not a sufficient basis for a religion; and one has only to have the experience of modern Judaism trying to deal with a death ritual to have the sense of its deep inner uncertainty, its lack of grasp of life which must eventually make even its rational social purpose quite abortive. Modern Jewish religion at its best may indeed be intelligent and soaked in university knowledge, but out of it there has not come a single voice with the note of authority—of philosophical, or poetic, or even of rhetorical, let alone of religious, authority.

Of Jewish cultural movements I know something at first hand, for I once served as a minor editor of a notable journal of Jewish culture. The effort this journal represented was, it even now seems to me, a generous one; but its results were sterile at best. I was deep in—and even contributed to—the literature of Jewish self-realization of which Ludwig Lewisohn was the best-known exponent. This was a literature which attacked the sin of "escaping" the Jewish heritage; its effect, it seems to me, was to make easier the sin of "adjustment" on a wholly neurotic basis. It fostered a willingness to accept exclusion and even to intensify it, a willingness to be provincial and parochial. It is in part accountable for the fact that the Jewish social group on its middle and wealthy levels—that is, where there is enough leisure to allow a conscious consideration of social and spiritual problems—is now one of the most self-indulgent and self-admiring groups it is possible to imagine.

To describe this situation is almost to account for it. And to account for it is, in one sense, to forgive it. But in one sense only: for history does not forgive the results of the unfortunate conditions it brings, and, contrary to the popular belief, suffering does not confer virtue. As the Jewish community now exists, it can give no sustenance to the American artist or intellectual who is born a Jew. And so far as I am aware, it has not done so in the past. I know of writers who have used their Jewish experience as the subject of excellent work; I know of no writer in English who has added a micromillimetre to his stature by "realizing his Jewishness," although I know of some who have curtailed their promise by trying to heighten their Jewish consciousness.

Under Forty

Delmore Schwartz

To be the child of immigrants from Eastern Europe is in itself a special kind of experience; and an important one to an author. He has heard two languages through childhood, the one spoken with ease at home, and the one spoken with ease in the streets and at school, but spoken poorly at home. Students of speech have explained certain kinds of mispronunciation in terms of this double experience of language. To an author, and especially to a poet, it may give a heightened sensitivity to language, a sense of idiom, and a sense of how much expresses itself through colloquialism. But it also produces in some a fear of mispronunciation; a hesitation in speech; and a sharpened focus upon the characters of the parents. And in some, especially if they are interested in the teaching of literature, the cultivation of a fantastic precision of speech and an accent which is more English than the English accent: nothing is more pathetic and comic than the pride which the parents suffer from when they hear the eloquent son speak in accents worthy of an Oxford don: how can they know that this would be regarded as a caricature by a true don?

To be a Jewish child of immigrants is much modified, if one's childhood has been lived in New York City. It is then possible and it is even likely that one knows only Jews as intimate friends, or intimate friends of one's parents; and hears about anti-Semitism from time to time, but it is merely something heard about. It is an interesting abstraction, or it is part of the barbarous past. Anti-Semitic episodes occur,

For a biographical note on Delmore Schwartz see p. 254.

361

but they are not frequent enough to be understood, even when the parents seek to explain them and refer to the horror of persecution in the old country. But this is almost certainly a condition peculiar to New York, and perhaps peculiar to the period between 1920 and 1933, when "Abie's Irish Rose" was an unparalleled hit. A true knowledge of what it is to be a Jew is obscured by this, by the easy contempt for all kinds of immigrants which dominates the national humor, and by the Jewish jokes that the parents tell. Perhaps a further qualification is necessary, and one should say that this kind of blunting of the fact of Jewishness is peculiar to the lower middle class, where there is little social aspiration, and where, on the other hand, the tenement house or slum has not produced the rage of the street gangs.

And then, so far as a positive inheritance of the Jewish heritage is concerned, it is directed, in the lower middle class at least, to the day of confirmation, which for the child is likely to be only the most important of birthday parties, the one for which he must go to Hebrew school (this is the phrase), and learn by rote from teachers who speak broken English certain passages in a dead language. The contrast between the authority of the public school teachers and the weakness of the Hebrew school teacher is one which makes the child wonder what reason can justify the emphasis upon Jewishness. I remember my own extreme admiration for the rabbi who spoke to us on Sundays. It seemed to me that he could prove or disprove anything, and that he could find a profound meaning in any story or incident. But I took this to be a personal gift; he was a very wise man; he seemed more intelligent than any of the teachers in public school. But then I merely wondered why he limited himself to what we then called the temple, and I had no way of knowing that his dialectical and interpretative skills were an inheritance.

So far I have spoken of what I take to be an experience which is common to a Jew in New York, of the lower middle class and in a family of immigrants from Eastern Europe. I do not know how typical this account is, but I cannot suppose that it is peculiar to myself.

For myself I should say that the fact of Jewishness was a matter of naive and innocent pride, untouched by any sense of fear. This was the consequence of ignorance, and it was this pure pride which continued until I went to a school which was not in New York City. There too, however, my ignorance of the character of anti-Semitism was increased, in a way, by a personal weakness, namely, the weakness of supposing that when anyone did not like me, the reason was my personal character and behavior. The habit of supposing that much of the quality of one's experience is chiefly personal in origin is a great weakness; and yet a weakness which protects one, and which, once it is surmounted, becomes a source of strength. If one is regarded as *peculiar* and if one is *left out* of the social life only by Christian boys and girls, then one is tempted to be impersonal and to be sure that each time it is the consequence of being a Jew. But by contrast, if one is regarded as peculiar and if one is also left out of the social life by Jews, if this experience is one which one finds in one's family also, then one is ignorant of the distinction between the two kinds of being left out. Thus it was the revival of political anti-Semitism which illuminated for me the difference between being left out by Christians and by Jews. It was then that I was able to understand the social anti-Semitism which had always been part of my experience without my understanding that it was certainly present. It was also then possible to understand the important distinction between social anti-Semitism and the political kind to which so much attention has been drawn in recent years.

All of this ignorance and growing recognition has been important to me as an author. For I would like to think that my chief motive as an author is an effort to understand the causes of my experiences; I would like to understand more and more what has happened to me. My ignorance, my weakness of being too personal, my self-concern— each of these traits in itself an evil—helped me to regard my own experience with other human beings as a common and universal thing, and not local or regional or racial. And this was a good thing for a time, although if it had continued, the evil effects of ignorance would have been an increasing weakness. And then, when I knew enough to distinguish between the different kinds of alienation, this knowledge illuminated my own mind for me in the most fruitful way, fruitful at least in terms of what my aims have been. I understood my own personal squint at experience; and the fact of being a Jew became available to me as a central symbol of alienation, bias, point of view, and certain other characteristics which are the peculiar marks of modern life, and as I think now, the essential ones. And thus I have to say (with gratitude and yet diffidence because it has been so different for other Jews, different to the point of death) that the fact of Jewishness has been nothing but an ever-growing good to me, and it seems clear to me now that it can be, at least for me, nothing but a fruitful and inexhaustible inheritance.

"Under Forty"

Muriel Rukeyser

I was born in New York, and I always loved the city. I remember an association test in school; the name 'New York' was given, and the others responded 'stone,' 'big,' 'crowds,' 'high.' I thought 'home.' But home did not mean ease and a cottage. It meant clash and growth. My father is a business man—a salesman really, the member of a group that shifts in society according to the period—and during my childhood and adolescence he was in the building business, sharing responsibility in the fierce skyscrapers whose stone climbed up the frames of steel, where short fire was flung and caught by the riveters—sharing excitement in the implacable cranes that dug sand, in the roads leaping out from the city, even in the horrible little real estate developments whose jerry-built walls would lean before a strong wind. I thought of my father as a builder. He was helping to make New York. Even the sidewalk I played on, in front of an apartment house like a huge trunk, was partly made by him.

It is true that we have to reckon the generations of the Jews according to their wanderings. Most of the younger Jewish writers in America are the children of immigrants, and I am not representative of that generation. It has the qualities which Margaret Mead points out as 'second-generation'—split with the parent culture, leaning over backward to be 'American' at its most acceptable. My father's cousin recently stood up at a Town Hall meeting and said, needlessly, "I am an *American*."

For a biographical note on Muriel Rukeyser see p. 334.

My parents did not migrate from Europe, but from America. My father came to New York from Wisconsin, where his grandfather had gone in 1848. He was brought up among the Western stories—Hill putting the railroads through, Juneau who went to Alaska. His mother had gone to a parochial school before there were any secular schools. His family was large, with many cousins as well as brothers and sisters, and he made most of his friends inside the family, but left as soon as he could. My mother came from Yonkers, which was then a rather English town on the Hudson, and had not yet become an industrial offshoot of New York. Her sisters and brothers, and she herself, were going through an anti-religious reaction against their studious and improvident father. The young man my father and the young woman my mother had no cultural resources to strengthen them. There was not a trace of Jewish culture that I could feel—no stories, no songs, no special food—but then there was not *any* cultural background that could make itself felt. My father had reacted even further from religion after an early tragedy, and art seemed not to mean anything to him. *Julius Caesar* was the only written work he ever mentioned. His friends were of several religions, and so were his business associates. His partner in business was an Italian, an enthusiastic pioneer for fascism here and in Italy.

There was no mark of Judaism in my childhood home except for a silver ceremonial goblet, handed down from a great-grandfather who had been a cantor, and a legend that my mother's family was directly descended from Akiba.

I went to religious school automatically. Once there, I was excited, not by the digests and easy versions of Jewish history or by the smattering of prayer book Hebrew, but by the Bible itself in English. And all this time, I had no idea of what a Christian was. I knew that our maids were Christian, and all the governesses my sister and I ever had were Christian. I did not know what a Jew was, nor that the term could be used in contempt. Once it had been shouted, but to a bunch of us who were ringing doorbells and running, and we knew we could expect scolding if we were caught at that. I was told never to say the name 'Jesus'; I knew there was something about Christians that had color and tenderness and a child in it, and that suffering of some sort was bound up with all of that. But what I knew of my religion was confined to the trip on Sunday morning across the Park to where the Temple stood, its pale green copper dome rising over the little round lake where other children sailed boats, and where the trees flowered pink in Spring.

Then, suddenly, out of a need or sadness of her own, my mother
turned to religion. She cannot be said to have turned back, for she had
never known anything like this impulse and response. There was a
sudden new insistence, and its force was sharply felt in my family. I
began to go to Temple with my mother, instead of to the Museum,
and I went every Saturday for seven years. They were years in which
I was learning through hostility. I was having a 'sheltered' childhood,
and the fact that I played with street-gangs and knew about the prostitutes on the Drive and the house across the street and the chauffeur's
private life were breaches which escaped my parents. There were a
few sets of books at home, but after I had gone through these, I read
whatever the maids recommended. This was the sheltered life, this
was a life of comfort. All I knew was that it was not comfortable to me.
I was beginning to care about a set of values which poetry was giving
me. School could back up some of this; but there was nothing at home
or in the Temple to answer me.

I think that many people brought up in reformed Judaism must
go starving for two phases of religion: poetry and politics. The sermons
I heard were pale and mechanically balanced talks. I grew up among a
group of Jews who wished, more than anything else, I think, to be
invisible. They were playing possum. They shrank away from the
occasional anger of the rabbi, and said that such a man ought not be
in that pulpit; they were the people who read Sokolsky's column at
breakfast, and agreed with him every time he said that Jews should
be quiet and polite, and should never protest; they were the people
who felt that Hitler would be all right if he would only leave the Jews
alone; they were, later, the people who told van Paassen he was crazy
to worry about the Jews in Germany and Poland. They supported big
charities. They gave generously of their money. Some of the women
even gave their time. But they wanted a religion of reassurance; they
listened to the muted organ, and refused to be involved in suffering
that demanded resistance, and refused to acknowledge evil. If they
had a mission as a responsible and inspired people, they did not want
it. It was enough to be Jewish. Charity was about the most they could
give; not struggle; they would neither approach the source nor make
the connections.

There was one place where this was done, for me; and that was in
the Bible. I sat under the shadowy dome during the drone of the
watered-down sermon and the watered-down liturgical music, and I read
the Bible. Its clash and poetry and nakedness, its fiery vision of conflict
resolved only in God, were true to me, no matter what I was coming

to believe about the reality of the world or power or divinity or death or love. The Bible was closer to the city than anything that was going on or could possibly go on in the Temple.

Now it is much later, and I am being asked questions about my heritage and my writing. But it is not late enough; it is more than ten years since that time, and I have begun to come a little closer to the source and the connections. But just begun. I have moved around this country some, South a few times, west to California, north into Canada. I have lived in the Middle West and Mexico, and once I went to Europe. I have seen Scottsboro and Gauley Bridge, had good years at College, and looked for my first jobs in the middle of the depression. I crossed the frontier into Spain on the first day of the war, and stayed long enough to see Catalonia win its own war and make peace, a peace that could not be held. I have had a government job in wartime, with a division that was undermined from the beginning, making war posters for American distribution. And all the time I have been writing poems, and after each trip I have come back to New York.

I do not know how far I am representative of any group in Jewish life. I was brought up without any reason to be proud of being Jewish, and then was told to be proud; without any reason for shame, and then saw that people were ashamed. I was a fat child, and hated that condition until I grew up and grew into my skin. I saw people feeling toward their Jewishness as I felt toward my size. But I never had that. I saw my religion sharply divided into three divisions: there was the dogma, the ethic, with which I wrestled; there was the poetry and fire, a deepening source of power to me; and there was the organized church, which I saw as torpid and conservative, and which I repudiated. The chief pressures against me, and against what was coming to be my work and belief, came from torpor and conservatism—or from fear, from active reaction, as in the person, again, of my father's cousin, who began to want me to change my name, so that it would not so much resemble his own. But these people were narrow, on the side of narrowness; whatever grew from the fact that I was Jewish, I would have to live, I knew, for the other side.

My themes and the use I have made of them have depended on my life as a poet, as a woman, as an American and as a Jew. I do not know what part of that is Jewish; I know I have tried to integrate these four aspects, and to solve my work and my personality in terms of all four. I feel that I am at the beginning of that attempt, too. Jewish references have come into some of my poems—the strong cry of the *Shema*, the raw, primitive blast of the *Shofar*, the Friday candles, the tragic migrations, modern tortures and the Warsaw ghetto, Joel and Ezekiel (in terms of John Brown), images started in me by the poetry of the prophets in the English Bible. I have already accepted the fact that the treatment of minorities is a good test of democracy, or any other system; I do not believe that is a particularly Jewish idea. I have wanted Jews, and everyone else, to have social equality anywhere in the world. On the way out of adolescence, I searched, as others do, for ancestors. I felt, then and now, that if one is free, freedom can extend to a certain degree into the past, and one may choose one's ancestors, to go on with their wishes and their fight. But I do not think that Jews are any more responsive to any of these ideas than are Christians. I am not afraid of allies in anything I may undertake, and I would work for my few beliefs with anyone who is willing to work for them.

To live as poet, woman, American, and Jew—this chalks in my position. If the four come together in one person, each strengthens the others. Red-baiting, undercuts at the position of women, anti-intellectual and anti-imaginative drives such as Congress has recently been conducting— these are on the same level as the growing storm of anti-Semitism.

One questions oneself when all these attacks arrive; and one looks at the Jews. The Jews I knew as a child, the Jewish professionals who were able to get out of Europe and come here as refugees, the Jews who could put up with fascism as long as it left them alone, the Jews who objected to a poster against discrimination because it mentioned Jews and Negroes together. The Jews that so many Christians, fighting fascism and all its implications, look sideward at. And then one thinks of the men and women in the Warsaw ghetto, standing as the Loyalists stood in Spain, weaponless against what must have seemed like the thunder and steel of the whole world; one thinks of the men and women, Jews moving freely in Russia; one thinks of the men and women, planting Palestine and taking a fierce oath never to put down their arms.

To me, the value of my Jewish heritage, in life and in writing, is its value as a guarantee. Once one's responsibility as a Jew is really assumed, one is guaranteed, not only against fascism, but against many kinds of temptation to close the spirit. It is a strong force in oneself against many kinds of hardness which may arrive in the war—the idea that when you throw off insight, you travel light and are equipped for fighting; the idea that it is impractical to plan and create, and that concrete construction and invention are the only practical things, apart from killing. Organized religion has not been able to take a strong stand about these things, any more than it has been able to stand with the Jews in Warsaw, or against the disguised Fascists at home.

But the conflict enlarges and grows, with one's own life and writing swept up in it. And the imagination moves, the spirit opens, one knows again what it is to be Jewish; and what it will always be at its best in one's life and one's writing: memory and fire and poetry and the wandering spirit that never changes in its love of man.

PHILIP RAHV (1908–   )

As an editor of Partisan Review from 1934 until 1969, Philip Rahv held a role of considerable importance in the literary world. Together with William Phillips, Rahv founded the magazine and guided it until it became, in T. S. Eliot's words, "America's leading literary magazine." Rahv has also been a literary critic of considerable distinction, stressing the social and historical forces which have influenced art.

Philip Rahv was born in Kupin in the Ukraine on March 10, 1908. His family settled in Providence, Rhode Island in 1922, but Rahv rebelled against his provincial background and went to New York, where he soon became an important left-wing journalist and reviewer. He joined the John Reed Club, the official sponsor of Partisan Review, and during the thirties and forties he continued to publish not only important polemics but literary criticism of the highest order. Some of his best essays, dealing with Hawthorne, James, Tolstoy, and Kafka, were included in Image and Idea (1949). He has edited numerous volumes—The Great Short Stories of Henry James (1944), The Bostonians (1945), The Short Novels of Tolstoy (1946), Discovery of Europe: The Story of the American Experience in the Old World (1947)—and has taught at New York University, Indiana University, and Brandeis University. Recently he has created a new journal, entitled Modern Occasions.

"Introduction" to *A Malamud Reader*

That Bernard Malamud is one of the very few writers of stature to emerge on our literary scene since the last war is now scarcely open to question. The author of four novels and two volumes of short stories, he has received several national prizes and his due measure of recognition from critics and reviewers. But he has also been frequently extolled for the wrong reasons, by critics who do not properly sort out or define with precision the imaginative qualities peculiar to him that make up his creative individuality; and sometimes he has been appraised as a special sort of genre-writer, dealing with the "laughter through tears," the habits of life, exotic to outsiders, of immigrant Jews, an ethnic group considered to stand in a marginal relation to American society at large. Generally speaking, he has been assimilated all too readily to the crowd of American-Jewish writers who have lately made their way into print. The homogenization resulting from speaking of them as if they comprised some kind of literary faction or school is bad critical practice in that it is based on simplistic assumptions concerning the literary process as a whole as well as the nature of American Jewry, which, all appearances to the contrary, is very far from constituting a unitary group in its cultural manifestations. In point of fact, the American-Jewish writers do not in the least make up a literary faction or school. And in the case of Malamud, the ignorant and even malicious idea that such a school exists has served as a way of confusing him with other authors with whom (excepting his Jewish ancestry) he has virtually nothing in common.

The truth is that many writers are Jewish in descent without being in any appreciable way "Jewish" in feeling and sensibility; and I am noting this not in criticism of anyone in particular but simply by way of stating an obvious fact usually overlooked both by those who "celebrate" the arrival of American Jews on the literary scene and by those who deplore it. It is one thing to speak factually of a writer's Jewish extraction and it is something else again to speak of his "Jewishness," which is a very elusive quality and rather difficult to define. In this respect Norman Mailer may well serve as a conspicuous example. Mailer's consciousness of himself as a Jew is, I would say, quite unimportant to him as a writer, if not wholly negative. Among the protagonists of his fiction his favorite alter ego appears to be a character called Sergius O'Shaugnessy—a name not without significance. Other American-Jewish writers either back away from their Jewishness or adopt an attitude towards it which is empty of cultural value; it is only in their bent for comic turns that they call to mind some vestigial qualities of their ethnic background. In any case, what is mostly to be observed among these writers is ambivalence about Jewishness rather than pride or even simple acceptance. Malamud differs, however, from such literary types in that he fills his "Jewishness" with a positive content. I mean that "Jewishness," as he understands and above all feels it, is one of the principal sources of value in his work as it affects both his conception of experience in general and his conception of imaginative writing in particular. One can see this in the very few instances when his characters touch on literature in their extremely articulate but "broken" speech. Thus in the one-act play "Suppose a Wedding" (not included in this volume), the retired Yiddish actor Feuer tangles with a young man who can only speak of tragedy in terms of Aristotle's theory of catharsis. Feuer says:

> Don't quote me your college books. A writer writes tragedy so people don't forget they are human. He shows us the conditions that exist. He organizes for us the meaning of our lives so it is clear to our eyes. That's why he writes it, that's why we play it. My best roles were tragic roles. I enjoyed them the most though I was also marvelous in comedy. "Leid macht auch lachen."

The last sentence is a saying in Yiddish which means that suffering also makes for laughter. If you are looking for Malamud's "poetics," it is in such speeches of his characters that you will locate it, not in any explicit critical pronouncements. Another equally revealing passage is to be found in his novel *The Assistant,* when Helen Bober, the Jewish girl so pathetically aspiring in her dreams of a college education, is on the verge of becoming involved with the unlettered Italian clerk in her father's grocery. They meet in the branch library of their neighborhood:

He asked her what she was reading.
"*The Idiot*. Do you know it?"
"No. What's it about?"
"It's a novel."
"I'd rather read the truth."
"It is the truth."

Malamud's conception of literature, as a mode of truth-saying, undercuts all our old and new debates about the role of the aesthetic motive in our lives. For in his context of profound commitment to the creative word the very term "aesthetic," with the compartmentalization of the human faculties that it suggests, seems almost out of place, if not frivolous; and it strongly reminds us of Kafka's moral earnestness in his approach to the making of literature, of which he conceived as a sacred expenditure of energy, an effort at communion with his fellow men, the reflected splendor of religious perception.

Malamud's "Jewishness" is also connected with a certain stylization of language we find in his fiction, a deliberate linguistic effort at once trenchantly and humorously adapting the cool Wasp idiom of English to the quicker heartbeats and greater openness to emotion of his Jewish characters; and it is particularly in the turns and twists of their dialogue that this effort is most apparent and most successful. These people are emotionally highly charged and desperate in their urgency to make themselves heard. Malamud insists on giving them their head, on letting them speak out of their genuine fervor—and to achieve this authenticity of speech he refuses to censor their bad, even laughable grammar, distorted syntax, and vivid yet comical locutions that sound like apt imitations of Yiddish. In this regard, any one of his narratives—such as "Take Pity," "The Mourners," "The Magic Barrel," "Idiots First," etc.—in which "Old World" Jewish types predominate can serve as a case in point.

Another "Jewish" trait in Malamud, as I read him, is his feeling for human suffering on the one hand and for a life of value, order, and dignity on the other. Thus he is one of the very few contemporary writers who seems to have escaped the clutch of historical circumstance that has turned nihilism into so powerful a temptation; nihilistic attitudes, whether of the hedonistic or absurdist variety, can never be squared with Malamud's essentially humanistic inspiration. The feeling for human suffering is of course far from being an exclusively "Jewish" quality. It figures even more prominently in Dostoevsky. The Russian novelist, however, understands suffering primarily as a means of purification and of eventual salvation, whereas in Malamud suffering is not idealized: suffering is not what you are looking for but what you are likely to get.

Malamud is seldom concerned with the type of *allrightnik* Jews who lend themselves to satirical treatment (as in Philip Roth's *Goodbye, Columbus*); his chief concern is rather with the first-generation, poor hardworking immigrants, whose ethos is not that of prosperity but that of affliction and endurance. Hence he is at times inclined to speak of suffering as the mark of the Jew and as his very fate. Leo Finkle, who is among the major characters of that extraordinary story "The Magic Barrel," draws out of his very discomfiture the consolation "that he was a Jew and a Jew suffered." Frank Alpine in *The Assistant,* thinking of what it means to be a Jew, explains it to himself as follows: "That's what they live for . . . to suffer. And the one who has got the biggest pain in the gut and can hold onto it longest without running to the toilet is the best Jew. No wonder they got on his nerves." This is of course an outsider's point of view, and it remains for Morris Bober, the unlucky and impoverished owner of the grocery store, to correct his Italian clerk's assertion that Jews like to suffer:

"If you live, you suffer. Some people suffer more, but not because they want. But I think if a Jew don't suffer for the Law, he will suffer for nothing."

"What do you suffer for, Morris?" Frank said.

"I suffer for you," Morris said calmly.

Frank laid his knife down on the table. His mouth ached. "What do you mean?"

"I mean you suffer for me."

The clerk let it go at that.

Here Malamud transcends all sectarian understanding of suffering, seeing it as the fate of the whole of mankind, which can only be mitigated when all men assume responsibility for each other. The contrast between Jew and Gentile is thus resolved on the level of feeling and direct intuition, and what this resolution suggests is an affinity with the Dostoevskyan idea of universal brotherhood and mutual responsibility. Yet Dostoevsky's correlative idea that "we're all cruel, we're all monsters" (as Dmitri Karamazov phrases it) is quite alien to Malamud. Frank Alpine is the guilty one when he takes Helen Bober against her will just as she has begun learning to love him. After the violation she cries: "Dog— uncircumcised dog." What restitution can Alpine possibly make for abusing Helen's trust? After much brooding and many incidents Alpine enters a symbolic death and rebirth, and his decision is made without Helen's knowledge or prompting. "One day in April Frank went to the hospital and had himself circumcised. For a couple of days he dragged himself around with a pain between his legs. The pain enraged and inspired him. After Passover he became a Jew." So *The Assistant* ends, with the sentences I have quoted. Frank Alpine's act is not to be understood as a religious conversion. Within the context of the novel, what Frank's singular act stands for is the ultimate recognition by this former hold-up man and thief of the humanity that he had so long suppressed within himself.

Along with the theme of suffering, one finds in Malamud the theme of the meaningful life, which is the antithesis of "the unlived life" against which his leading characters are always contending. The college teacher S. Levin, in *A New Life,* becomes involved in what threatens to become a sordid affair with Pauline, another man's wife. But when she probes him for what he thinks life offers at its best, his reply is: "Order, value, accomplishment, love." Levin, who is at times prone to consider himself "his own pathetic fallacy," struggles to discover an authentic self amidst the circumstances that surround him; nor is he likely either to overestimate or underestimate himself. "Why must Levin's unlived life put him always in peril? He had no wish to be Faust, or Gatsby; or St. Anthony of Somewhere who to conquer his torment nipped off his balls. Levin wanted to be himself, at peace in present time." And again: "He left to Casanova or Clark Gable the gourmandise, the blasts and quakes of passion." Levin comes to a state of the Far West looking for welcome and a chance of organizing his existence anew. He begins as S. Levin, a half-anonymous *schlemiel,* and in the last chapters he has turned into a *mensch* called Seymour Levin, who against all odds had become a husband to Pauline and the father of her children.

But the irony of the *schlemiel* turning *mensch* pervades the book, tempering the exaltation of the last pages. Levin's first lovemaking to Pauline takes place in a forest glade, and "he was throughout conscious of the marvel of it—in the open forest, nothing less, what triumph!" And when he first kisses her, "he was humbly grateful. . . . They were standing under a tree and impulsively kissed. . . . They kissed so hard his hat fell off." The displaced hat is an ironic counterpoint—the signature of reality inscribed in a romantic pastoral. An identical irony is to be encountered in many of Malamud's stories. In "The Last Mohican," Fidelman, "a self-conscious failure as a painter," gets off the train in Rome and soon discovers the remains of the Baths of Diocletian. "Imagine," he muttered. "Imagine all that history." He confronts history as Levin confronts nature in Marathon, Cascadia (Oregon?). Fidelman likes to wander in the old sections of Rome near the Tiber. "He had read that here, under his feet, were the ruins of Ancient Rome. It was an inspiring business, he, Arthur Fidelman, after all born a Bronx boy, walking around in all this history." But Fidelman, for all the thrills that history provides him, is a person lacking in genuineness—cautious, withdrawn, self-centered. It takes Susskind, the starving and demanding refugee, a nuisance to Fidelman, to supply him with the revelation he so badly needs. Susskind steals the briefcase containing the first chapter of Fidelman's scholarly work on Giotto—the only chapter he had managed to write. The last paragraphs of the story are wonderfully conceived and written: a model of economy in expression. After much importunity, Susskind returns the briefcase.

> Fidelman savagely opened it, searching frenziedly in each compartment, but the bag was empty. The refugee was already in flight.
> With a bellow the student started after him.
> "You bastard, you burned my chapter."
> "Have mercy," cried Susskind, "I did you a favor."
> "I'll do you one and cut your throat."
> "The words were there but the spirit was missing."
> In a towering rage Fidelman forced a burst of speed, but the refugee, light as the wind in his marvelous knickerbockers, his green coattails flying, rapidly gained ground.

It is only then that Fidelman, moved by all "he had lately learned, had a triumphant insight." Half sobbing, he shouts: "Susskind, come back . . . All is forgiven." So the spirit missing in his life and studies finally descends upon the hapless Fidelman.

Of all Malamud's stories, surely the most masterful is "The Magic Barrel," perhaps the best story produced by an American writer in recent decades. It belongs among those rare works in which meaning and composition are one and the same. Who can ever forget the matchmaker Salzman, "a commercial Cupid," smelling "frankly of fish which he loved to eat," who looked as if he were about to expire but who somehow managed, by a trick of his facial muscles, "to display a broad smile"? The pictures of prospective brides that the matchmaker shows the rabbinical student Finkle, intent on matrimony, prove very discouraging—all these girls turn out to be either old maids or cripples. But Salzman contrives to leave one picture in Finkle's room by which his imagination is caught as in a trap. The description of the picture is full of mystery, yet admirably concrete; it is as good as, if not better than, the description of the picture of Nastasya Filippovna which makes so much for the vitality of the first part of *The Idiot*.

Caught, Finkle in turn must now pursue Salzman, who has suddenly become elusive. When tracked down, he swears that he had inadvertently left the fatal picture in Finkle's room. "She's not for you. She is a wild one, wild, without shame. . . . Like an animal, like a dog. For her to be poor was a sin. This is why to me she is dead now. . . . This is my baby, my Stella, she should burn in hell." But Finkle will not relent. It is Stella he must see, and Salzman arranges their meeting "on a certain street corner." The last sentences of this tale are like a painting by Chagall come to life.

He appeared, carrying a small bouquet of violets and rosebuds. Stella stood by the lamp, smoking. She wore white with red shoes, which fitted his expectations, although in a troubled moment he had imagined the dress red, and only the shoes white. She waited uneasily and shyly. From afar he saw that her eyes—clearly her father's—were filled with desperate innocence. He pictured, in her, his own redemption. Violins and lit candles revolved in the sky. Leo ran forward with flowers outthrust.

Around the corner, Salzman, leaning against a wall, chanted prayers for the dead.

Thus the rabbinical student who, as he confesses, had come to God not because he loved Him but precisely because he did not, attempts to find in the girl from whose picture "he had received, somehow, an impression of evil" the redemption his ambiguous nature demands.

It seems to me that "The Magic Barrel," a story rooted in a pathology that dares to seek its cure in a thrust towards life, sums up many of the remarkable gifts of insight and expressive power that Malamud brings to contemporary literature.

ISAAC ROSENFELD (1912–1956)

Isaac Rosenfeld was an important essayist and reviewer of the 1940's and 1950's who possessed, in Saul Bellow's words, "one of those ready, lively, clear minds that see the relevant thing immediately." Born and brought up in Chicago, Rosenfeld attended high school and the University of Chicago with Bellow. He studied for his Ph.D. in the early 1940's, but he soon abandoned academic life for a position with The New Republic. His reputation as a literary journalist grew quickly.

Rosenfeld taught sporadically at New York University, the University of Minnesota, and Chicago University at the same time as he wrote a wide variety of reviews and articles on contemporary literature. The best of his work has been included in a volume (An Age of Enormity [1962] edited by Theodore Solotaroff, which indicates Rosenfeld's sensible appreciation of writers as different as Sholom Aleichem and Richard Wright. He wrote to no critical formula and as Solotaroff points out, if he can be said to have had a method it "was mainly Saint-Beuve's principle that criticism is 'justness of characterization'."

"Under Forty"

ALL DISCUSSIONS pertaining to the Jews must begin with some very gloomy observations. The Jews are, everywhere, a minority group, and it is a particular misfortune these days to be a minority group in the United States. A conscious member of such a group is necessarily over-conscious: he is distracted by race and religion, distressed by differences which in a healthy society would be considered healthful. The very simple state of being a Jew—and it should occupy no more of a man's attention than any ordinary fact of his history—has created traumas, fears of violence, defenses against aggression. These are about the worst con-ditions under which an artist could seek to carry on his work. An artist should first of all have the security of a dignified neutrality. He should be able to consider himself a *mensch mit alle menschen gleich*—that is, an equal, a man among men, a representative even if extraordinary individual. But a Jewish writer unconsciously feels that he may at any time be called to account not for his art, nor even for his life, but for his Jewishness. Only a brave man can be a brave artist, let alone a good one, in a hostile world. It is therefore clear to me that whatever contribution Jewish writers may make to American literature will depend on matters beyond their control as writers.

But the position of Jewish writers—artists and intellectuals in gen-eral—is not entirely an unfortunate one. For the most part the young Jewish writers of today are the children of immigrants, and as such—not completely integrated in society and yet not wholly foreign to it—they enjoy a critical advantage over the life that surrounds them. They are bound to observe much that is hidden to the more accustomed native eye.

The insight available to most Jewish writers is a natural result of their position in American life and culture. Jews are marginal men. As marginal men, living in cities and coming from the middle classes they are open to more influences than perhaps any other group. I vaguely recall a Yiddish proverb to the effect that bad luck always knows where to find a Jew; and as a barometer of political calamity the Jews in this country are second only to the Negroes. But even gentler influences, short of fatality, know where to find Jews—in the middle, in the over-lapping area where events converge. And the middle position has its cultural correlate, that of being centrally exposed to all movements in art and in thought. This position of cultural exposure gives the Jewish writer the advantage of access. (There is much more to be said about this point—more than I have the space or the knowledge to disclose. But, generally speaking, the position of Jewish writers illustrates one of the strangest phenomena of modern life. Since modern life is so complex that no man can possess it in its entirety, the outsider often finds himself the perfect insider.)

Close as they are to the main developments in America, some Jewish writers may retain more than a little of European culture. Either through their position in the Jewish community, their childhood, or the influence of their immigrant parents, they may possess a sense of reference to an earlier community. I don't know how widespread this old world feeling is among Jewish writers. But if it is at all common, I should say it is a valuable thing. Jews in America have relatively little contact with coun-try life, with small town folk and farmers. But through cultural retention, through a subliminal orientation to more primitive surroundings, they may still find in themselves access to rural life, understanding of its character and traditions.

But it is one thing to consider the Jewish writer's social equipment, and quite another to regard his actual position in society. As a member of an international insecure group he has grown personally acquainted with some of the fundamental themes of insecurity that run through modern literature. He is a specialist in alienation (the one international banking system the Jews actually control). Alienation puts him in touch with his own past traditions, the history of the Diaspora; with the present predicament of almost all intellectuals and, for all one knows, with the future conditions of civilized humanity. Today nearly all sensibility—thought, creation, perception—is in exile, alienated from the society in which it barely managed to stay alive.

But alienation from society, like the paradox of the outsider, may function as a condition of entrance into society. Surely it is not a condition for the Jew's re-entrance into the world that has rejected him. But persecution may lead him, as it has in the past, to a further effort to envisage the good society. No man suffers injustice without learning, vaguely but surely, what justice is. The desire for justice, once it passes beyond revenge, becomes the deepest motive for social change. Out of their recent sufferings one may expect Jewish writers to make certain inevitable moral discoveries. These discoveries, enough to indict the world, may also be crucial to its salvation.

I do not want to make too much of alienation. It is the only possible condition, the theme we have to work with, but it is undesirable, for it falls short of the full human range. Besides, in every society, in every group, there are what Saul Bellow has called "colonies of the spirit." Artists create their colonies. Some day these may become empires.

David Levinsky: The Jew
as American Millionaire

I HAD LONG AVOIDED *The Rise of David Levinsky* because I imagined it was a badly written account of immigrants and sweatshops in a genre which—though this novel had practically established it—was intolerably stale by now. It is nothing of the kind. To be sure, it is a genre piece, and excellence of diction and sentence structure are not among its strong points; but it is one of the best fictional studies of Jewish character available in English, and at the same time an intimate and sophisticated account of American business culture, and it ought to be celebrated as such.

The story is a simple one and fundamentally Jewish in conception, as it consists of an extended commentary on a single text, somewhat in the manner of Talmud. This text is presented in the opening paragraph:

> Sometimes, when I think of my past . . . the metamorphosis I have gone through strikes me as nothing short of a miracle. I was born and reared in the lowest depths of poverty and I arrrived in America—in 1885—with four cents in my pocket. I am now worth more than two million dollars and recognized as one of the two or three leading men in the cloak-and-suit trade in the United States. *And yet . . . my inner identity . . . impresses me as being precisely the same as it was thirty or forty years ago. My present station, power, the amount of worldly happiness at my command, and the rest of it, seem to be devoid of significance.*

I have set in italics what I take to be the key sentences. These express Levinsky's uniquely Jewish character, as they refer to the poor days of his childhood and early youth ("my inner identity") when, supported by his mother, he devoted himself to the study of the Jewish Law. Nothing in a man's life could be more purely Jewish, and his constant longing, through all his later years, for the conditions of his past confirms him in an unchanging spirit. But the remarkable thing about this theme, as the late Abraham Cahan developed it, is that it is, at the same time, an exemplary treatment of one of the dominant myths of American capitalism—that the millionaire finds nothing but emptiness at the top of the heap. It is not by accident that Cahan, for forty years and until his death the editor of the *Jewish Daily Forward,* and identified all his life with Jewish affairs and the Yiddish language, wrote this novel in English (it has only recently been translated into Yiddish). He was writing an American novel par excellence in the very center of the Jewish genre.

It seems to me that certain conclusions about the relation between Jewish and American character should be implicit in the fact that so singularly Jewish a theme can so readily be assimilated to an American one. I am not suggesting that Jewish and American character are identical, for the Levinsky who arrived in New York with four cents in his pocket was as unlike an American as anyone could possibly be; but there is a complementary relation between the two which, so far as I know, no other novel has brought out so clearly.

David Levinsky was born in the Russian town of Antomir in 1865. His father died when David was three, and he lived with his mother in one corner of a basement room that was occupied by three other families. "The bulk of the population [of Antomir]," writes Cahan, "lived on less than . . . twenty-five cents . . . a day, and that was difficult to earn. A hunk of rye bread and a bit of herring or cheese constituted a meal. [With] a quarter of a copeck (an eighth of a cent) . . . one purchased a few crumbs of pot cheese or some boiled water for tea. . . . Children had to nag their mothers for a piece of bread." But Levinsky's mother, who "peddled pea mush [and did] odds and ends of jobs," was kind to him and indulgent, "because God has punished you hard enough as it is, poor orphan mine."

At the usual early age, Levinsky was sent to *cheder,* where he was made to feel very keenly the disadvantages of poverty, as his teachers risked nothing in punishing a poor boy. His mother would intervene for him (this impulse was to prove fatal) and fought with many a *melamed* for laying hands on her David. In spite of the humiliations and hardships, she maintained him in *cheder,* and after his Bar Mitzvah sent him to Yeshiva (Talmudic seminary) at an even greater sacrifice, as it meant he would not be in a position to relieve her distress by learning a trade. She was determined that he devote his life to God, and he showed great aptitude for holy study. He soon distinguished himself as a student, but his sexual instincts began to distract his mind. His contacts with women, as was the case with all Yeshiva students, were extremely limited. It was considered "an offense to good Judaism" for a pious man to seek feminine company, attend dances, dress in worldly fashion, or in any other way to behave as a "Gentile." Naturally, these restraints only multiplied Levinsky's temptations. He would do penance, undergo a period of religious exaltation, and again fall into sin (in his mind).

The next great event in his life was the death of his mother. Levinsky, in earlocks and black caftan, was attacked by Gentile boys on his way from the Yeshiva. When he came home bruised and bleeding, his mother, against his entreaties and those of their friends and neighbors, ran to the Gentile quarter to avenge him. This was the last time he saw her alive. She was brought back with a broken head.

It is a credit to Cahan's economy as a writer and to his grasp of character that at this point, in the sixty-odd pages which I have summarized, he has already drawn so convincing a picture of Levinsky, including all essential details, that Levinsky's subsequent adventures in the old country and America, his further encounters with poverty and with women, the rest of his intellectual development, and his ultimate transformation into a millionaire, have all been fully prepared. I will therefore cut off the exposition and attempt some generalizations which may serve the understanding of the whole of Levinsky's character and perhaps help explain how the old-world Yeshiva student is essentially an American in ethos.

Levinsky's character was formed by hunger. The individual experiences of his life—poverty, squalor, orphanage, years of religious study and sexual restraint, the self-sacrificing love of his mother and her violent death—all these experiences contain, as their common element, a core of permanent dissatisfaction. This dissatisfaction expresses itself in two ways: first, as a yearning for fulfillment, where it operates to win for him all the goods and values he has been deprived of—wealth, dignity, a "father principle" as well as a substitute for his father (as shown in his passionate attachment to Red Sender, with whom he studied at the Yeshiva), the pleasures of intellectual liberty that attend his break with Orthodoxy, the pleasures of sex, and unrestrained access to the society of women, though he goes among them mainly to find a substitute for his mother. (These are the positive "Americanizing" tendencies of his discontent.) At the same time, dissatisfaction has become an organic habit, a form which determines his apprehension of experience in general, and actually directs the flow of experience his way, so that he is not merely the result of what has happened to him, but on the contrary, the events in his life are predetermined, in large measure, by what he has already become. In the second sense, dissatisfaction is unending; instead of providing the urge to overcome privation, it returns every fulfillment, by a way no matter how roundabout, to the original tension, so that no satisfaction is possible.

Thus Levinsky is a man who cannot feel at home with his desires. Because hunger is strong in him, he must always strive to relieve it; but precisely because it is strong, it has to be preserved. It owes its strength to the fact that for so many years everything that influenced Levinsky most deeply—say, piety and mother love—was inseparable from it. For hunger, in this broader, rather metaphysical sense of the term that I have been using, is not only the state of tension out of which the desires for relief and betterment spring; precisely because the desires are formed under its sign, they become assimilated to it, and convert it into the prime source of all value, so that the man, in his pursuit of whatever he considers pleasurable and good, seeks to return to his yearning as much as he does to escape it.

Levinsky's entire behavior is characterized by this duality. In love, he is drawn to women he cannot have. They are either hopelessly above his rank in wealth, sophistication, and culture, or married and faithful mother-surrogates, or simply not interested. The women who do find him attractive fail to move him. He goes to prostitutes, one frustration feeding the other.

His accumulation of wealth, which he wins through perseverance, ingenuity, and luck, is also of this pattern—it, too, represents a loss, a virtual impoverishment. Before he turned to business enterprise, Levinsky had entertained serious academic ambitions. Though he had broken away from Orthodoxy, shaved his beard, adopted American dress, and gone to night school to learn English, he had retained his Talmudic intellectuality and love of scholarship. He took a job in the garment industry only as a means of sending himself through college. The event to which he attributes his becoming a businessman fell on a day when he was having his lunch in the factory. A bottle of milk slipped out of his hands as he was trying to open it and spilled on some silks. His employer, Jeff Manheimer, who witnessed the accident, broadly made fun of his clumsiness and called him a lobster. The humiliation festered, and that very day Levinsky decided to steal the boss's designer and go into business for himself. This is the reason he gives, but it is a rationalization. He would never have entered business and gone on to wealth had it not been necessary to sacrifice something—in this case his desire for learning. And when he obtains great wealth, it makes a circle, joining the pattern of his love life by condemning him to loneliness, as he suspects all women who smile on him want only his money.

So with everything. All things in Levinsky's life are divided, alienated from themselves, and simplicity is impossible. But no matter how many transformations it undergoes, his hunger remains constant. He longs for his wretched boyhood (which appeals to him "as a sick child does to its mother") from which, were he able to reenter it, he would again be driven in an endless yearning after yearning.

Now this is a profoundly Jewish trait, our whole history is marked by this twist. The significant thing about the structure I have been describing is that it is not confined to single personalities like Levinsky, but is exactly repeated on an impersonal and much larger scale in Jewish history, religion, culture—wherever our tradition and its spirit find expression. Consider *Galut,* the Diaspora, through the centuries in which it has dominated Jewish life: the theme of the Return, of yearning for Eretz Israel, to which are linked Cabala and Messianism, modes of prayer and worship as well as modern political and social movements, so that the whole becomes a compendium of Jewish activity per se—the yearning for Israel runs through the Diaspora in no simple sense, as of a fixed desire for a fixed object. It is a reflexive desire, turning on itself and becoming its own object. This is the meaning of the passage: "If I forget Thee O Jerusalem. . . ." The yearning is itself Jerusalem, as in the words ". . . if I prefer not Jerusalem above my chief joy," and it is to this yearning that the good Jew remains faithful. Otherwise, why the proscription of temporizing in *Galut,* of making any compromise with desire, no matter how small, even down to the obdurate and seemingly ridiculous prohibition of shaving the beard? The hunger must be preserved at all cost. This theme is taken up and elaborated all through Yiddish literature, receiving its ultimate ironic sanctification in the work of Sholom Aleichem, where squalor, suffering, and persecution become the "blessings of poverty," signs and stigmata of the condition of being Chosen, "for which the whole world envies us." The character of David Levinsky, therefore, does not stand alone, nor does he come, with his four cents, unattended to the American shore. He drags the whole past after him, being himself the Diaspora Man.

But what is so American about this? Nothing directly, especially if I am right in calling Levinsky the essential Jewish type of the Dispersion. And yet in the character of the American businessman and in the surrounding culture that his figure dominates, there is also such a twist, a similar play on striving and fulfillment. We worship success; all the same it is on process and origin that we place the emphasis of gratification, seldom on the attainment as such. The value of the successful man's career lies in "rags to riches," it is defined in our saying, "He worked himself up." Of those who are born to wealth we say, "Poor little rich boy." Now this, I am aware, is folklore, and there is a great deal of irony in it, too. Nevertheless, our favorite representation of the rich is of a class that doesn't know what to do with its money. It has brought them no real accretion of happiness, and the process of accumulation, on which the emphasis falls, is manifestly a self-destructive one, as it never can be stopped in time: the successful man faces the futility of retirement. He, too, loves to dream about his boyhood in an unreal *askesis,* having for the most part been ashamed of the ascetic impulse (poverty, we protest too much, is no disgrace) which he has concealed under a conspicuous acquistion; and yet he is not enough a materialist to enjoy his goods as they come to him and welcome the spiritual consolations that worldly pleasures bestow. "Money isn't everything," he will say, making more, and he says this to preserve an air of disconsolateness, as though virtue were impossible without a sour face. He does all this for show, but unconsciously his affectations hit upon the truth. All his life he is at loose ends, and expert only in ennui, which Tolstoy defined as the desire for desire, cousin to Levinsky's yearning. And even if none of this is true, and there is (as I strongly suspect) a direct gratification in wealth as such, it is still significant that most of us profess it to be true, clinging to a protective disenchantment.

Whatever the case with our much disputed and still, I suppose, amorphous American, Levinsky, the Diaspora Man, had relatively little to overcome (speaking inwardly) to grow into the typical American of fortune. Only the environment was alien to him, but its inner loneliness was anticipated in his own, for one loneliness is much like another; and the very fact that the American environment was alien, and would remain so, to his Jewishness, enabled him to make good in it on his own peculiar terms—to satisfy everything but hunger. To be sure, his is only a single career, a single example of the Jew as American, but it draws our attention to the considerable structural congruity that must underlie the character and culture of the two peoples. And if Levinsky's career is understood in its essentially Jewish aspect, it may explain why the Jews, as an immigrant group, were among the first to achieve a virtually flawless Americanization.

I have purposely refrained from treating David Levinsky as a fictional character and have spoken of the novel as though it were the actual memoir of an American Jew, in tribute to Cahan's power of characterization. Such immediacy of revelation is the novel's strongest quality, and Levinsky is made to talk about himself not only with an authentic accent, but with a motive in disclosure verging on something sly—precisely as such a man would talk. This well known and widely respected businessman tells the truth about himself, his love affairs, his efforts to outsmart the unions, the way other men tell lies—to see if he can get away with it! But as fiction, Cahan's writing lacks continuity: his transitions from subject to subject tend to be abrupt, with a perseveration in the linking of sex and economics. Thus when he describes Levinsky's broken engagement (the cause was his falling in love with another woman), Cahan devotes less than twenty lines to the scene, and opens his very next paragraph (after a line space, but this may have been the typographer's doing) with the words, "Our rush season had passed. . . ." Often the trains of thought collide within the single paragraph, business plowing into everything else. True, Levinsky's mind would work this way, and the habit would also serve him the purpose of saying, "I may not be doing so well with the girls—but think of the money I'm making." (Though business is meaningless to Levinsky, one of the most touching insights of the novel is provided by Cahan's showing how he succumbs to a businessman's vulgarity of tone and manner, and berates himself for the weakness.) Yet it is not always possible to distinguish character from author, and this failure in detachment, the consequence of an imperfectly developed ear for nuances in language, becomes noticeable and sometimes quite confusing when there is no lucky congruity to justify it, as in the matter of the abrupt transitions from pleasure to business.

But these flaws, as I have already indicated, are of minor account. So much so, that I wonder what the critical reception and, no doubt, misunderstanding, of *The Rise of David Levinsky* must have been, that it should languish in the status of an "undiscovered" book, a standard footnote or paragraph in surveys of American Jewish literature, and not be known for the remarkable novel it is.

ALFRED KAZIN (1915–   )

"From my first conscious moments," Alfred Kazin has written, "I was absorbed in the most intimate problems of the working class, in the fire and color of immigrant life—and perhaps most of all, thanks in part to my parents' quaint, old-fashioned socialism and to my own traditionalism, in the historic Jewish effort to realize the kingdom of God in this world." Kazin established his fame on the basis of a literary criticism strongly committed to social forces. He is always sensitive to the aesthetic problems involved in a work of art, but he approaches them with a deep awareness of their relationship to social history; his dedication of Contemporaries *to Edmund Wilson indicates his allegiance to that form of criticism which strikes a balance between history and art. Like Wilson, he has been attentive to the work of his contemporaries and has written some of the finest criticism of postwar fiction. Kazin's work is eclectic, his essays ranging from Melville and Dreiser to Thomas Mann and James Baldwin; but he has also been extremely sensitive to his Jewish background. His autobiography,* A Walker in the City, *is a moving portrait of the development of a Jewish boy in an immigrant family.*

Alfred Kazin was born on June 5, 1915, in the Brownsville section of Brooklyn. His parents had emigrated from Czarist Russia, and his youth in Brownsville as well as his young manhood in New York literary circles is recorded in A Walker in the City *(1951) and* Starting Out in the Thirties *(1965). He went to the City College of New York and, in his senior year, began his career as a literary critic for* The New Republic. *In 1935 he received his Master's degree from Columbia University and soon after began to write* On Native Grounds, *which appeared in 1942. Since* On Native Grounds, *Kazin has devoted himself primarily to the writing of essays, collected in* The Inmost Leaf *(1955) and* Contemporaries *(1962). He has taught at many different universities and is presently on the faculty of the State University at Stonybrook.*

.

"Under Forty"

WHEN I THINK of Jews for whom the word meant and means something, I think of Sholem Aleichem and Peretz, the scholars of Vilna, the great hearts of the Jewish Socialist Bund who helped to defend Warsaw. I think of the Hasidim, of some of the people in the stories of I. J. Singer. Of the people who have tried to build a co-operative, not a purely Jewish, culture in certain Palestine communities. Of Bialik and Marc Chagall, of Ernest Bloch; and because of the quality of their "emancipation," of the Nello Roselli who was to be murdered by Mussolini, but not before he had told Fascist Italy "why I cannot be a Zionist"; and Rosa Luxemburg. What I admire in the Jewish tradition, and in certain Jews whom I know, is the texture of a genuine and received Hebrew culture; an indestructible belief in the spiritual foundations of a human life; the feeling for the book; the kind of universal curiosity which springs out of so profound a sense of nationality (not nationalism) that it lives on the illumination its sources provide, as in the wit of Sholem Aleichem, or in Marc Chagall's bitter fantasy of the Jewish Jesus on the cross, with the prayer-shawl around his loins and angelic rabbis in mourning above him.

I admire these; I have been influenced as a writer and as a person by the idea of them—I only wish I knew how much. But I have never seen much of what I admire in American Jewish culture, or among Jewish writers in America generally. The American Jew can get into such an unhappy limbo—neither completely lost from what he thinks his ancestors had, nor found in what he wants; with an occasional ritual gesture that is like the rigor mortis of an Elk convention. Who is he? What is Jewish in him? What does he believe, especially in these terrible years, that separates him at all from our national habits of acquisitiveness, showiness, and ignorant brag? I do not ask for superior virtue on his part, and honestly no longer expect it. But what a pity that he should feel "different," when he believes so little; what a stupendous moral pity, historically, that the fascist cutthroats should have their eyes on him, too, when he asks for so little—only to be safe, in all the Babbitt-warrens. When even his suffering may be so sterile, as his fears can be so selfish.

"They are spectators no longer but full participants in the cultural life of the country." I wonder. I think it is about time we stopped confusing the experience of being an immigrant, or an immigrant's son, with the experience of being Jewish. When I read a novel by an American Jew that is at least as grounded in the life it rejects as Farrell's *Studs Lonigan* or Dreiser's *Sister Carrie,* I shall believe in the empirical fact of our participation. But that participation can come only through a quality of understanding and love. I do not see it now—I see the Broadway boys making the over-eager jokes of our self-defense; and the music of Tin Pan Alley and Hollywood; and the sickening plays of the George S. Kaufmans. And those who know so very well what being Jewish means, and then proceed to speak for me. Those who speak with such familiarity —and such easy verbal love—of Jewish qualities, of the Jewish soul, and even of Jewish wretchedness.

The American Jewish writers I admire are scholars and critics—it is so easy, a Rabbi said, for us to be interpreters; and a few poets who may occasionally (as in Karl Shapiro's new poems from Australia) write with great purity and irony on historic Jewish symbols which they have meditated. Most of the playwrights, scenario writers, popular novelists and lecturers, especially the kind who cry into their literary beer, I would like to shoot. Or the popular book-reviewer, a veritable national personality, who just wants to hate Germans—all Germans. What degradation there, and what naïveté.

Yet the sources of influence are plain, and the loyalties are fascinated with symbols. I think that I have been most deeply influenced by my struggle against a merely imposed faith; and against a sentimental chauvinism. I know how easy it is for the American Jew, at least in my circumstances and of my generation, to confuse his timidity with devotion, his parochialism (or suspiciousness, grounded in the self-driven life of the Pale) with a conscious faith. My parents are Jews—not particularly devout, not particularly conscious of being insincere in their occasional devotion; but Jews for whom the symbols have had a direct and tender meaning, and for whom the code had a plain integrity. I had no such luck. I learned that Jews were "different"—but different, as I had to suppose, only because the ones I knew were always poor and usually scared. I was taught that it was proper to be confirmed—but I never learned what the texts meant: only to repeat them. I went to Jewish religious clubs and met Tammany politicians; to Zionist clubs, and encountered only a dreary middle-class chauvinism. I have never found chauvinism any more attractive in Jews than in anyone else (and I do know the prime cause, and always feel it). Or lack of imagination and sympathy, or the foolish pride that Uzbeks have in those who are only Uzbeks.

I learned long ago to accept the fact that I was Jewish without being a part of any meaningful Jewish life or culture. I have tried to be dignified in my knowledge of it and even to hope that I could be appreciative. But I learned what was more important for me in my apprenticeship as a writer—to follow what I really believed in, not that which would merely move me through associations or naive community feelings. The writing I have been most deeply influenced by—Blake, Melville, Emerson, the seventeenth-century English religious poets, and the Russian novelists— has no direct associations in my mind with Jewish culture; it has every association, of course, with the fact that, like many another American, I have had to make my own culture. When Blake says, "Truth cannot be so uttered as to be understood without being believed," I know the deep sources of that faith in the Hebrew prophets. But the directness of that insight interests me now, not a fact in history which my mind knows as it knows that Szigetti is Jewish, and Einstein, and the woman who stepped on my foot in the bus and hates Negroes.

The Jew as Modern American Writer

EMMA LAZARUS, who wrote those lines inscribed on the base of the Statue of Liberty ("Give me your tired, your poor . . . Your huddled masses, yearning to breathe free"), was the first Jew whom Ralph Waldo Emerson ever met. Emerson's daughter Ellen, an old Sunday-school teacher, noted how astonishing it was "to get a real unconverted Jew (who had no objections to calling herself one, and talked freely about 'our Church' and 'we Jews'), and to hear how Old Testament sounds to her, and find she has been brought up to keep the Law, and the Feast of the Passover, and the day of Atonement. The interior view was more interesting than I could have imagined. She says her family are outlawed now, they no longer keep the Law, but Christian institutions don't interest her either."

Emma Lazarus had been sending Emerson her poems for years; he responded with uncertain praise, for they were excessively literary and understandably raised questions in the mind of so subtle a critic. But although she was not to become a consciously "Jewish" poet until the Russian pogroms aroused her, her being a Jew had certainly distinguished her in the literary world of Victorian America. She was that still exotic figure, that object of Christian curiosity, "the Jew"—and to descendants of the New England Puritans, straight out of their Bible.

Proust was to say that in every Jew "there is a prophet and a bounder." Emma Lazarus was still the "prophet" when she visited Concord. This was in 1876, when Jews in this country were getting known as "bounders." General Grant in a Civil War order had said "Jew" when he meant peddler, but impoverished farmers in the West now said "Jew" when they meant Wall Street financier. New England writers like James Russell Lowell and Henry Adams became obsessed with Jews and "the Jewish question" as soon as there were real Jews on the American scene. The "prophet" figure that literary New England had always known from books had become the "bounder"—and, worse, the ragged *shtetl* Jew whom Adams examined with such loathing from a Russian railway car and in New York when he heard him speaking "a weird guttural Yiddish." Henry James, returning to his native downtown streets, announced that "the deᵢizens of the New York Ghetto, heaped as thick as the splinters on the table of a glass-blower, had each, like the fine glass particle, his or her individual share of the whole hard glitter of Israel." The Jew in New York was an instance of alienness, an object to be studied. James would have been astonished to think of a writer coming out of this milieu. And, to do him justice, not many immigrant Jews saw themselves as writers in English. Henry Adams' sometime protégé, Bernard Berenson, who had come here from Lithuania, was to find himself only as an art historian in Italy.

William Dean Howells, now a Socialist in New York, praised Abraham Cahan's *Yekl: A Tale of the New York Ghetto.* But Howells was predisposed to Russian literature, Cahan was a "Russian" realist in English, and Howells, like so many Westerners enjoying or soon to enjoy New York's "Europeanness," was also a democratic idealist, naturally friendly to all these new peoples in New York. His friend Mark Twain said that Jews were members of the human race; "that is the worst you can say about them." But this easy Western humor was still very far from the creative equality that Jewish and non-Jewish writers were some day to feel. Mark Twain, like Maxim Gorky in Russia, protested against pogroms and was friendly to Jews; but as late as 1910, when he died, there was no significant type of the Jewish writer in this country. The older German-Jewish stock had produced many important scholars and publicists; it was to produce an original in Gertrude Stein. But the positive, creative role of the Jew as modern American, and above all as a modern American writer, was in the first years of this century being prepared not in the universities, not even in journalism, but in the vaudeville theaters, music halls, and burlesque houses where the pent-up eagerness of penniless immigrant youngsters met the raw urban scene on its own terms. It was not George Jean Nathan, Robert Nathan, or Ludwig Lewisohn any more than it was Arthur Krock, David Lawrence, Adolph Ochs, or Walter Lippmann who established the Jew in the national consciousness as a distinctly American figure; it was the Marx Brothers, Eddie Cantor, Al Jolson, Fannie Brice, George Gershwin. Jewish clowns, minstrels, song-writers helped to fit the Jew to America, and America to the Jew, with an élan that made for future creativity in literature as well as for the mass products of the "entertainment industry."

Proust, with his artist's disengagement from both "prophet" and "bounder"; Henry Adams, with his frivolous hatred of the immigrant ("five hundred thousand Jews in New York eating kosher, and saved from the drowning they deserve"), had never conceived of the Jew as a representative national entertainer. But in the naturalness and ease with which the Jewish vaudevillian put on blackface, used stereotypes, and ground out popular songs, in the avidity with which the public welcomed him, was the Jew's share in the common experience, the Jew's average-ness and typicality, that were to make possible the Jew-as-writer in this country. In Western Europe, Jewish "notables" had been a handful—as odd as the occasional prime minister of Italy or Britain; in Eastern Europe, where the Jews were a mass, it was their very numbers that was so disturbing to anti-Semites in office, who even in Soviet Russia were to keep Jews down because the thought of too many Jews being allowed to exercise their talents at once could obviously be viewed as a threat to their own people. As Mikoyan was to say some years ago to a Jewish delegation, "We have our own cadres now." But in this country the very poverty and cultural rawness of the Jewish immigrant masses, the self-assertive egalitarianism of the general temper, and the naturalness with which different peoples could identify with each other in the unique halfway house that was New York (without New York it would no doubt all have been different, but without New York there would have been no immigrant epic, no America) gave individual performers the privilege of representing the popular mind. Never before had so numerous a mass of Jews been free citizens of the country in which they lived, and so close to the national life. And although many a genteel young literatus now analyzing Nathanael West and Saul Bellow shudders at his connection with Potash and Perlmutter, Eddie Cantor, and Fannie Brice, it is a fact that this "vulgar culture," proceeding merrily to the irreverent genius of the Marx Brothers (whose best movies were written by S. J. Perelman, the college chum and brother-in-law of Nathanael West), helped to found, as a natural habitat for the Jews in this country, the consciously grotesque style of parody that one finds in Perelman, West, Odets, Bellow, in many Broadway-Hollywood satirists, and even in an occasional literary critic, like Isaac Rosenfeld and Harold Rosenberg, impatient with the judicial tone that comes with the office. The Jewish writer, a late arrival in this country and admittedly of uncertain status, had to find his model in the majority culture, and although this had some depressing consequences in the mass, it was on the whole fortunate, for the sharply independent novelists, poets, and critics to come, that they were influenced more by the language of the street than by the stilted moralism that has always been a trap for the Jewish writer.

But of course the popular culture was invigorating and even liberating so long as it was one of many cultures operating simultaneously on the Jewish writer's mind. Ever since the legal emancipation of the Jews in Western Europe, there had been two principal cultures among the Jews— the orthodox, religious tradition, pursuing its own way often magnificently indifferent to the issues shaking European thought; and the newly secularistic culture of the "Jewish intellectuals," who found in the cause of "progressive humanity," in philosophic rationalism, in socialism, and cultural humanism, their sophisticated equivalent of Judaism. In Western Europe, for the most part, these two cultures no longer irritated each other. But among the Yiddish-speaking Jews of Eastern Europe, "enlightenment" did not appear until late in the 19th century; while in Western Europe the medieval ghettos were a barely tolerated memory, in Russia the Jewish Pale of Settlement, restricting most Jews to certain areas and restricting the intensity of their existence to the *shtetl* and its religious customs, remained a searing memory in the lives of immigrants and their children. The "dark" ages and the "modern" age, the ghetto and the revolutionary movement, persecution and free human development, were conjoined in the Jewish mind. The tension and ardor with which the two cultures of modern Jewry were related, in individual after individual, helps to explain the sudden flowering of painters among Russian Jews in the first years of this century, the extraordinary spiritual energy invested in the idea of socialism, the "twist" that Isaac Babel liked to give his Russian sentences, the general passion for "culture" and "cultural advancement," the revolutionary zeal with which former yeshiva boys turned political commissars spoke of the great new age of man.

Babel wrote of ex-seminarists riding away with the Red Cavalry from their "rotted" Bibles and Talmuds, Chagall's *rebbes* sprouted wings over the thatched roofs of Vitebsk and sang the joys of the flesh. The force of some immense personal transformation could be seen in the conscious energy of Trotsky's public role in the Russian Revolution. These revolutionaries, writers, scientists, painters were the "new men," the first mass secularists in the long religious history of the Jews, yet the zeal with which they engaged themselves to the "historic" task of desacralizing the European tradition often came from the profound history embedded in Judaism itself—it certainly did not come from the experience of Jews with other peoples in Eastern Europe. These "new men" had a vision of history that, as their critics were to tell them, was fanatically all of one piece, obstinately "Jewish" and "intellectual"—a vision in which some subtle purposiveness to history always managed to reassert itself in the face of repeated horrors. But what their critics could not recognize was that this obstinate quest for "meaning" was less a matter of conscious thought than a personal necessity, a requirement of survival, the historic circumstance that reasserted itself in case after case among the Jews, many of whom had good reason to believe that their lives were a triumph over every possible negation, and who, with the modesty of people for whom life itself is understandably the greatest good, found it easy to rejoice in the political and philosophical reasoning that assured them civic respect, civic peace, and the life of the mind.

"Excess of sorrow laughs," wrote Blake in *The Marriage of Heaven and Hell.* "Excess of joy weeps." For Jews in this country, who had triumphed over so much, remembered so much, were in such passionate relations with the two cultures—of religion and "modernity" that many believed in simultaneously—their conscious progress often became something legendary, a drama rooted in the existential fierceness of life lived and barely redeemed every single day. There was an intensity, a closeness to many conflicting emotions, that often seemed unaccountably excessive to other peoples. The need to explain himself to himself, to put his own house in order, was a basic drive behind many a Jewish writer. People to whom existence has often been a consciously fearful matter, who have lived at the crossroads between the cultures and on the threshold between life and death, naturally see existence as tension, issue, and drama, woven out of so many contradictions that only a work of art may appear to *hold* these conflicts, to compose them, to allow the human will some detachment. Surely never in history has a whole people had to endure such a purgation of emotions as took place at the Eichmann trial. It was this that led Harold Rosenberg to show the cruel dramatic necessity behind the trial—the need of the Jews to tell their story, to relive the unbearable, the inadmissible, the inexpressible. The Jew who has lived through the age of Hitler cannot even say, with Eliot, "After such knowledge, what forgiveness?" For he has to live with his knowledge if he is to live at all, and this "knowledge" enforces itself upon him as a fact both atrocious and dramatic, a mockery of the self-righteous Christianity that has always surrounded him, a parody of the Orthodox Judaism that has sought to justify the ways of God to man, a drama founded on the contrast between the victims and all those who remained spectators when the Jews were being slaughtered.

There are experiences so extreme that, after living them, one can do nothing with them *but* put them into words. There are experiences so terrible that one can finally do nothing with them but not forget them. This was already the case with many of the young Jewish writers just out of the city ghettos, who began to emerge in significant numbers only in the early 30's. Looking back on this emergence, one can see that it needed the peculiar crystallization of ancient experiences, and then the avidity with which young writers threw themselves on the American scene, to make possible that awareness of the Jew as a new force that one sees in such works of the 30's as Henry Roth's *Call It Sleep,* Michael Gold's *Jews Without Money,* Daniel Fuchs's *Summer in Williamsburg,* Albert Halper's *The Chute,* Odet's *Awake and Sing,* Meyer Levin's *The Old Bunch,* and even in West's *Miss Lonelyhearts,* whose hero is not named a Jew but who is haunted by the indiscriminate pity that was to mark the heroes of Bernard Malamud and Edward Wallant. In the 20's there had been several extraordinarily sensitive writers, notably Paul Rosenfeld and Waldo Frank, out of the older, German-Jewish stock; but on the whole, it needed the turbulent mixing of the ghetto and the depression to make possible the wild flurry of strong new novels and plays in the 30's.

Yet the social realists of the 30's were often boxed in, mentally, by the poverty and hopelessness of their upbringing and the bitterness, deprivations, and anti-Semitism of depression America. The extraordinary brevity of so many literary careers in America is a social fact that any account of the Jewish writer in America must contend with as an omen for the future. Although the aborted career is common enough in American writing and was particularly marked among writers of the 30's—many were shipwrecked by the failure of their political hopes, and many crippled as artists by the excessive effort it took to bring out their non-selling books—it is also a fact that writers from the "minorities" have a harder time getting started, and tend, as a group, to fade out more easily, than those writers from the older stocks whose literary culture was less deliberately won and is less self-conscious. A historian of the Negro novel in this country says that most Negroes who have published one book have never published another—and one might well wonder what, until the sudden fame of James Baldwin, would have induced any Negro writer in this country to keep at it except the necessity of telling his own story. Thinking of the family situation portrayed in *Call It Sleep,* one can see why, having written *that* up, to the vast indifference of the public in the 30's, the author should have felt that he was through. The real drama behind most Jewish novels and plays, even when they are topical and revolutionary in feeling, is the contrast between the hysterical tenderness of the Oedipal relation and the "world"; in the beginning there was the

Jewish mother and her son, but the son grew up, he went out into the world, he became a writer. That was the beginning of his career and usually the end of the novel. Jews don't believe in original sin, but they certainly believe in the original love that they once knew in the *shtetl*, in the kitchen, in the Jewish household—and after *that* knowledge, what forgiveness? In this, at least, the sentimental author of *Jews Without Money* parallels the master of childhood in *Call It Sleep*.

What saved Jewish writing in America from its innate provincialism, what enabled it to survive the moral wreckage of the 30's, was the coming of the "intellectuals"—writers like Delmore Schwartz, Saul Bellow, Lionel Trilling, Karl Shapiro, Harold Rosenberg, Isaac Rosenfeld, Lionel Abel, Clement Greenberg, Bernard Malamud, Irving Howe, Philip Rahv, Leslie Fiedler, Robert Warshow, Paul Goodman, Norman Mailer, Philip Roth, William Phillips. It was these writers, and younger writers in their tradition, who made possible intellectual reviews like *Partisan Review* and serious, objective, unparochial magazines like *Commentary*— a magazine which has emphasized general issues and regularly included so many writers who are not Jews. *Commentary*, founded in November 1945, was hospitable to this new maturity and sophistication among Jewish writers in America; it established itself on the American scene easily, and with great naturalness, exactly in those years immediately after the war when American Jews began to publish imaginative works, and intellectual studies of distinction—*Dangling Man, The Victim, The Middle of the Journey, The Liberal Imagination, Death of a Salesman, The Naked and the Dead, The World Is a Wedding, The Lonely Crowd, The Natural, The Adventures of Augie March, The Mirror and the Lamp, The Tradition of the New*.

From a gifted writer outside this group, Salinger, contemptuous of its ideologies, was an "intellectual" writing about "intellectuals." Even a middlebrow sullenly critical of its preoccupations, Herman Wouk, did it the honor of "exposing" an intellectual in *The Caine Mutiny*. Whether they were novelist or just intellectual pundits at large, what these writers all had in common was the ascendancy of "modern literature," which has been more destructive of bourgeois standards than Marxism, was naturally international-minded, and in a culture bored with middle-class rhetoric upheld the primacy of intelligence and the freedom of the imagination. The heroes of these "intellectuals" were always Marx, Freud, Trotsky, Eliot, Joyce, Valéry; the "intellectuals" believed in the "great enlighteners," because their greatest freedom was to be enlighteners of all culture themselves, to be the instructors and illuminati of the modern spirit. Unlike so many earlier writers, who had only their hard story to tell and then departed, the Jewish "intellectuals" who emerged in the 40's found shelter under the wide wings of the "modern movement," and so showed an intellectual spirit that Jews had not always managed in the great world.

Commentary has, more than any other "Jewish" magazine known to me, been a symbol of and a home for this intellectual spirit. I remember that as the first issues began to appear at the end of that pivotal year of 1945, I was vaguely surprised that it dealt with so many general issues in so subtly critical and detached a fashion, regularly gave a forum to non-Jewish writers as well as to Jewish ones. Like many Jewish intellectuals of my time and place, brought up to revere the universalism of the Socialist ideal and of modern culture, I had equated "Jewish" magazines with a certain insularity of tone, subject matter, writers' names—with mediocrity. To be a "Jewish writer"—I knew several, and knew of many more, who indefatigably managed this by not being any particular kind of writer at all—was somehow to regress, to strike attitudes, to thwart the natural complexities of truth. There were just too many imprecisions and suppressions in the parochially satisfied "Jewish" writer. It was enough to be a Jew *and* a writer. "Jewish" magazines were not where literature could be found, and certainly not the great world. "Jewish" magazines worried over the writer's "negative" attitude toward his "Jewishness," nagged you like an old immigrant uncle who did not know how much resentment lay behind his "Jewishness."

But *Commentary,* to the grief of many intellectual guardians of the "Jewish" world, marked an end to that, which is why its interest for a large intellectual public has been so significant. It has always been natural for Protestant Americans to believe, in the words of John Jay Chapman, that "the heart of the world is Jewish." But after 1945 and the unparalleled, inexpressible martyrdom of the Jewish people in Europe, it was natural for non-Jews everywhere to believe, as Jews now had more reasons than ever to believe, that Jewish survival and Jewish self-determination related to everything in the world. The particular distinction of *Commentary* among Jewish magazines has been to articulate and to support this many-sided relatedness. As one can see from the extraordinary opening section of this anthology—"The Holocaust and After"—the Jewish writer after 1945 had particular reason to feel that this most terrible of all events in Jewish history bound him more closely to every fundamental question of human nature and historic failure involved in Europe's self-destruction. As the late Solomon Bloom showed in his detached and heart-rending study of Mordechai Chaim Rumkowski, the "Dictator of the Lodz Ghetto" who sent so many of his own people to death, the Jewish historian had materials more atrocious than any in modern literature for the recognition of how squalid and self-deluded human nature could be. Yet, as this anthology goes on to show, the Jewish art critic, essayist, economist, political observer, psychoanalyst, sociologist had only to take up aspects of contemporary experience in general to show the relevance to all this experience of his native, obstinate, questing spirit as a Jew. One can cite from this brilliant anthology, virtually at random, materials so various and fascinating as George Lichtheim's "Reflections on Trotsky," Hannah Arendt's stark notes on the German scene, David Daiches' examination of the new Biblical scholarship, Leslie Farber's " 'I'm Sorry, Dear.' " And where else would the non-Jewish writer and our common American problems come together so happily as in Dwight Macdonald's "By Cozzens Possessed," James Baldwin's "Equal In Paris," Edmund Wilson's "Paul Rosenfeld: Three Phases"?

Of course the prosperity that began with the war encouraged the new Jewish writers to feel that the country was theirs. Immediately after the war, indeed, some of them embraced this newfound land, their America, with an enthusiasm made slightly hysterical by the need to cast off Marxist ideology. Yet this new liveliness could be attributed in the greatest part to the closing up of a time-lag, to the sudden eruption of writers whose time had come—and who had often been brought up in old-fashioned ways that impressed the dizzyingly complex new world upon their minds with special vividness. Jean-Paul Sartre says in *Les Mots* of the grandfather who brought him up—"Between the first Russian Revolution and the first World War, fifteen years after Mallarmé's death . . . a man of the 19th century was foisting upon his grandson ideas that had been current under Louis Philippe. . . . Ought I to complain? . . . In our bustling societies, delays sometimes give a head start." Many a Jewish writer has been brought up on his grandfather's ideas, and now engages the last third of the 20th century with special eagerness. Generally speaking, the Jewish intellectuals who since the 40's have exercised so much influence on American culture started very far back. If the young man from the provinces, as Lionel Trilling named him, typifies the encounter with the great world in 19th-century novels, it was significantly the Jewish intellectual who was now to write the key book on Matthew Arnold, the definitive biographies of Henry Adams, Henry James, James Joyce, who was to become the theoretician of action painting, the most resourceful American novelist of the postwar period, the editor of the leading cultural review, the Reichian *enfant terrible* of the universities, the novelist of orgiastic high life in Palm Springs, Las Vegas, Hollywood, and the Waldorf Towers. Often enough graduates of the old revolutionary movement, with its intellectual ardor, its internationalism, its passion for political complexities, and its taste for action, these Jewish intellectuals combined an American belief in the "tradition of the new" with their own moral tradition and their passion for the Europe of the great thinkers, their driving personal ambition with the knowledge that they were exceptions, "survivors," as Moses Elkanah Herzog said, of the age that had seen their brethren slaughtered like cattle in the abattoirs that the Nazis had made of Eastern Europe. Just as it was Southern writers, with their knowledge of defeat and their instinctive irony, who in the 40's spoke to the chastened American mind, so it is Jewish writers who now represent to many Americans the unreality of their prosperity and the anxiety of their condition. In situations of inestimable complexity, requiring the most "sophisticated" and "expert" "analysis" of the "complex factors," it was often enough Jews, born and pushed to be intellectuals, who became the connoisseurs of the new chaos, the mental elite of the power age. Never was interpretation, explanation, commentary, a vital new *midrash,* so much needed as in the period, starting with the war, when the world was so much compressed and subtilized by the new technological revolution—and never were there so many Jewish intellectuals prepared to do the explaining. The ragged old "prophet" was not much in evidence, and the Jew-as-bounder was not to be thought of, but the age of the intellectuals was in full swing.

All the writers were intellectuals now, the best writers as well as the most conformists—novelists like Saul Bellow and Norman Mailer dealt in the drama of concepts, had heroes who lived by concepts, and suffered for them. The world seemed suspended on concepts, and in the mass magazines as in the universities and publishing houses, a mass of indistinguishable sophisticates genuflected to the modern idols and talked the same textbook formulae about Joyce, James, Eliot, Faulkner, Picasso, Stravinsky. The Sunday book supplements were soon all as apocalyptic as a Jewish novelist after a divorce, and one could regularly read footnotes to the absurdity of the human condition, the death of tragedy, and the end of innocence by pseudo-serious minds who imitated Bellow, Mailer, Fiedler, Ginsberg, Goodman as humorlessly as teen-age girls copied hair styles from the magazines.

Definitely, it was now the thing to be Jewish. But in Western universities and small towns many a traditional novelist and professor of English felt out of it, and asked, with varying degrees of self-control, if there was no longer a good novel to be written about the frontier, about Main Street, about the good that was in marriage? Was it possible, these critics wondered aloud, that American life had become so deregionalized and lacking in local color that the big power units and the big cities had pre-empted the American scene, along with the supple Jewish intellectuals who were at home with them? Was it possible that Norman Mailer had become the representative American novelist?

It was entirely possible, and certainly the thought would not have astonished Mailer, just as the power of his example for other novelists did not astonish Saul Bellow. Whatever pain this ascendancy might cause to writers who felt out of it because they lived in Montana or in the wrong part of California, it was a fact that there were now Jewish novelists who, as writers, had mastered the complex resources of the modern novel, who wrote English lovingly, possessively, masterfully, for whom the language and the form, the intelligence of art, had become as natural a way of living as the Law had been to their grandfathers. Literature had indeed become their spiritual world, their essential personal salvation, in a world where all traditional markers were fast disappearing. But in the frothy turbulent "mix" of America in the 60's, with its glut, its power drives, its confusion of values, the Jewish writer found himself so much read, consulted, imitated, that he knew it would not be long before the reaction set in—and in fact the decorous plaint of the "Protestant minority" has been succeeded by crudely suggestive phrases about the "Jewish Establishment," the "O.K. writers and the Poor Goy," "The Jewish-American Push." Yet it is plainly a certain success that has been resented, not the Jew. And if the Jew has put his distinct mark on modern American writing, it is surely because, in a time when the old bourgeois certainties and humanist illusions have crumbled, the Jew is practiced in what James called "the imagination of disaster" and "does indeed see life as ferocious and sinister." The contemporary literary temper is saturnine, panicky, black in its humor but adroit in shifting the joke onto the shoulders of society. And the Jewish writer, with his natural interest in the social fact, has been particularly quick to show the lunacy and hollowness of so many present symbols of authority. Anxiety hangs like dry electricity in the atmosphere of modern American life, and the stimulus of this anxiety, with all its comic overtones, is the realized subject in the novels of Joseph Heller, Bruce Jay Friedman, Richard Stern, Jeremy Larner, the plays of Jack Gelber and Arthur Kopit. There is real madness to modern governments, modern war, modern moneymaking, advertising, science, and entertainment; this madness has been translated by many a Jewish writer into the country they live in, the time that offers them everything but hope. In a time of intoxicating prosperity, it has been natural for the Jewish writer to see how superficial society can be, how pretentious, atrocious, unstable—and comic. This, in a secular age when so many people believe in nothing but society's values, is the significance to literature of the Jewish writer's being a Jew.

LESLIE FIEDLER (1917–   )

Leslie Fiedler's chief importance as a writer is represented by his literary criticism and particularly by his lengthy study, Love and Death in the American Novel (1960). In that work, anticipated by an essay entitled, "Come Back to the Raft Ag'in, Huck Honey," Fiedler studies American society in terms of depth psychology and anthropology and explores the myths and archetypes of our literature. American fiction, he demonstrates, has been gothic rather than realistic, haunted by masochism and sadism, death, innocent homosexuality, miscegenation, and incest; in their escape from reality and from adult heterosexuality, great American writers have searched the underworld of their imagination and produced apocalyptic works. Although his most significant criticism is concerned with the traditional classics of American literature, Fiedler has also written most perceptively of Jewish-American writing.

Leslie Fiedler was born on March 8, 1917, in Newark, New Jersey. He received his B.A. from New York University in 1938 and his Ph.D. from the University of Wisconsin in 1941. Fiedler has served on the faculties of Montana State University, from 1947–1963, and the University of Buffalo, from 1963 until the present day. He has also taught at the Universities of Bologna, Rome, Venice, Athens, Sussex, Princeton, Columbia, Vermont, and Vincennes. Fiedler's books include An End to Innocence: Essays in Culture and Politics (1960), Love and Death in the American Novel (1959), No in Thunder: Essays on Myth and Literature (1960), Waiting for the End (1964), The Last Jew in America (1966), and Being Busted (1969). He has also written fiction: Pull Down Vanity (1962), The Second Stone: a Love Story (1963), and Back to China (1965).

Zion as Main Street

CERTAINLY, we live at a moment when, everywhere in the realm of prose, Jewish writers have discovered their Jewishness to be an eminently marketable commodity, their much vaunted alienation to be their passport into the heart of Gentile American culture. It is, indeed, their quite justified claim to have been *first* to occupy the Lost Desert at the center of the Great American Oasis (toward which every one now races, Coca-Cola in one hand, Martin Buber in the other), which has made certain Jewish authors into representative Americans, even in the eyes of State Department officials planning cultural interchanges. The autobiography of the urban Jew whose adolescence coincided with the Depression, and who walked the banks of some contaminated city river with tags of Lenin ringing in his head, who went forth (or managed not to) to a World War in which he could not quite believe, has come to seem part of the mystical life history of a nation.

Even in the realm of poetry, writers of Jewish origin are beginning, for the first time, not only to project the most viable images of what it means to be an American, but to determine the cadences with which we glorify or deplore that condition. The very lines inscribed on the base of the Statue of Liberty are, to be sure, by Emma Lazarus, who called one collection of her poems *Songs of a Semite;* but it was not until the appearance of Delmore Schwartz and Karl Shapiro, in the years just before and after World War II, that Jewish-American poets succeeded in producing verse capable of living in libraries and the hearts of other poets, rather than on monuments and in the mouths of politicians. And only within the last decade has a poet as Jewish in his deepest memories (whatever his current allegiances) as Allen Ginsberg been able to stand at the head of a new poetic movement.

Yet the moment of triumph for the Jewish writer in the United States has come just when his awareness of himself as a Jew is reaching a vanishing point, when the gesture of rejection seems his last possible connection with his historical past; and the popular acceptance of his alienation as a satisfactory symbol for the human condition threatens to turn it into an affectation, a fashionable cliché. Indeed, the recent recognition of even the most serious Jewish-American writers seems somehow less an event in literary history than an incident in the development of middlebrow taste, part of the minor revolution which has made Harry Golden into a modern prophet and has enabled newspapers to build circulation by running serializations of the latest pseudo-books of Leon Uris. Surely, a kind of vicarious shame at the monstrosities practiced against the Jews of Germany by the Nazis has something to do with revolution; and the establishment of the State of Israel has tended to give even the Jews in exile a less ambiguous status, while the struggle against Great Britain leading to that establishment has lent them a certain sentimental cachet, ranking them, in the minds of American Anglophobes, with the Irish and the mythical revolutionary ancestors of us all.

But it is chiefly the resurgence of "intergroup understanding," the tidal wave of toleration that has flowed into the vacuum left by the disappearance of zeal and the attenuation of faith among churchgoers, which has carried the Jews along with it. And they have benefited, too, by the canonization of support for "little people" among the pieties of yesterday's liberalism which have become the orthodoxy of today's New Deal-New Frontier conservatism. Armenians, Greeks, Chinese, Cubans, low-caste Indians, Mexican wetbacks, women with suffrage, paraplegics, teenagers—one group after another has been dubbed with that condescending tag. But, maybe, from this point of view the ordeal of the Jew is almost over, for he no longer occupies the number-one slot among the insulted and injured. Even the *New Yorker* has recognized that the Negro is, at the moment, *up;* and it is the Baldwins rather than the Bellows who have to wrestle now with the mystery of the failure of success in America. The general *détente* in the cold war between Gentile and Jew in the United States persists, and though other sentimental fashions challenge it, it remains chic in certain middlebrow, middle-class, middle-liberal quarters to be pro-Jewish. Philo-Semitism is required—or perhaps, by now, only assumed—in the reigning literary and intellectual circles of America, just as Anti-Semitism used to be required—and after a while only assumed—in the Twenties.

But the Judaization of American culture goes on at levels far beneath the literary and the intellectual. The favorite wine in Missoula, Montana, which does not have a dozen Jewish families, is Mogen David; and for years now, "Nebbishes" have stared out of the windows of the local gift shop from greeting cards, ash trays, beer mugs, and pen stands. And why not? Everyone digs Jules Feiffer and Mort Sahl, just as everyone tells "sick" jokes and sends "hate" cards to celebrate birthdays and weddings and national holidays. The "sick" joke and the "hate" card, however, represent the entry into our popular culture not only of certain formerly exclusive properties of the avant-garde (the mockery of bourgeois pieties, a touch of psychoanalysis) but also of Jewish humor at its most desperate. There is nothing entirely unprecedented here, of course; Potash and Perlmutter were best-sellers in the opening years of this century, and Charlie Chaplin's debut was almost contemporaneous with theirs. As a matter of fact, the Jew enters American culture "on the stage, laughing."

It might be possible, indeed, to make a graph showing, decade by decade, the point at which it became possible for Jews:

1) to act out travesties of themselves on the stage;

2) to act out travesties of other "comical" ethnic groups (Chico Marx as an Italian, Al Jolson in blackface);

3) to write popular songs and patriotic sub-poetry and begin the wholesale entry into universities as students;

4) to produce comic strips and popular novels;

5) to argue cases in court and judge them from the bench, to prescribe for the common cold and analyze the neurotic;

6) to write prose fiction and anti-academic criticism;

7) to teach in the universities and help determine official taste in the arts;

8) to write serious poetry, refuse to go to college, and write on the walls, "Down with the Jews!"

Presently all of these things are possible at once, for no new gain has canceled out another, our successes expand at dazzling speed. Huckleberry Finn becomes Augie March; Daisy Miller turns, via Natalie Wood, into Marjorie Morningstar; Eddie Fisher is drafted as the symbol of clean young American love, while Danny Kaye continues to play the blue-eyed jester; and finally we enter an age of strange conversions to Judaism (Marilyn Monroe, Elizabeth Taylor, Sammy Davis, Jr.), and symbolic marriages. Eros himself turns, or seems to for a little while, Jewish, as the mythical erotic dream-girls of us all yearn for Jewish intellectuals and learn to make matzo-balls.

Even more startlingly, the literature of busy males, of politicians and executives seeking at once relaxation and the reinforcement of their fantasies, is Judaized, too. The long dominance of the Western and the detective story is challenged by that largely Jewish product, science fiction. There are a score of Jewish authors among the most widely read writers in that popular genre as compared with practically none in the two older types of institutionalized fantasy. The basic myths of science fiction reflect the urban outlook, the social consciousness, the utopian concern of the modern, secularized Jew. The traditional Jewish waiting-for-the-Messiah becomes, in lay terms, the commitment-to-the-future, which is the motive force of current science fiction. The notion of a Jewish cowboy is utterly ridiculous, of a Jewish detective, Scotland-Yard variety or tough private eye, nearly as anomalous—but to think of the scientist as a Jew is almost tautological.

Much science fiction, set just before or after the Great Atomic War, embodies the kind of guilty conscience peculiar to such scientist-intellectuals (typically Jewish) as Robert Oppenheimer, while the figure of Einstein presides over the New Heaven and New Earth which such literature postulates, replacing an earlier Hebrew god who is dead. Even in its particulars, the universe of science fiction is Jewish; the wise old tailor, the absurd but sympathetic *yiddishe momme*, plus a dozen other Jewish stereotypes, whiz unchanged across its space and time. Even secret Jewish jokes are made for the cognoscenti: the police on a corrupt, trans-galactic planet are called, in the exotic tongue of that only half-imaginary world, *Ganavim* (thieves). And in the Superman comic books (the lowbrow equivalent of science fiction), the same aspirations and anxieties are projected in the improbable disguise of the Secret Savior, who may look like a *goy*, but who is invented by Jews. The biceps are the biceps of Esau, but the dialogue is the dialogue of Jacob.

Even for those who read neither books nor comics, Jewish culture lies in wait—not only in the gift shop and the saloon, but in what is our only truly living museum, the real cultural storehouse of the average man: the supermarket. There—even in the remotest hamlets—beside the headcheese, the sliced ham, the pseudo-hot-dogs composed of flour and sawdust, one finds kosher salami; beside the hardtack, Rye Krisp, and löfsa—matzos; beside the chocolate-covered ants, fried grasshoppers, anchovy hearts—Mother's Gefilte Fish. But whatever is in the supermarket, like whatever is in *Life* (both organized on the same pseudo-catholic principle: everything glossily packaged and presented without emphasis and distinction) is in the great democratic heart of America. In that heart, at least, Jewish culture, as defined by gefilte fish and Natalie Wood, the Jewish scientist and the Nebbish, has established itself as if it meant to stay. And it is in the light of this cultural fact that Jewish-American writers must assess the mounting sales of their books and the warm reviews which greet them; but the confrontation leaves the best of them amused, the second best embarrassed, and the worst atrociously pleased.

Yet this kind of success is, in a way, what the Jewish-American writer has all along desired—though for a long time he was able to depend on the realities of his situation, the exclusion from which he began, to protect him against his own lust for belonging. From the start, the Jewish-American writer has desired not only to create living images of his people in the imagination of all Americans, and to redeem them from psychic exploitation at the hands of anti-Semitic Gentile authors; but also, by creating such images and achieving such a redemption, to become himself part of the American scene, a citizen among citizens, one more author on a list which begins with Benjamin Franklin and Washington Irving. The very notion of a Jewish-American literature represents a dream of assimilation, and the process it envisages is bound to move toward a triumph (in terms of personal success) which is also a defeat (in terms of meaningful Jewish survival). If today Jewish-American writers seem engaged in writing not the high tragedy of Jewish persistence in the midst of persecution, but the comedy of Jewish dissolution in the midst of prosperity, this is because they tell the truth about a world which neither they nor their forerunners can consider themselves guiltless of desiring.

Yet at first the striving of the American-Jewish community, through its artists, to become a fact of the imagination as well as of the census seemed merely gallant and happily foredoomed. In the beginning, the Jewish author and the Jewish character, whether invented by Gentile or Jew, played only a slight and peripheral role in the literature of the United States and in the deep mind of the American people which that literature at once reflects and makes. This is in part the result of the simple sociological fact that Jews were, in the earliest years of our nation, few and insignificant and that, therefore, the mythology of the Jew, which we inherited along with the English language and the corpus of English literature, moved the popular American mind scarcely at all. What could the figures of the Wandering Jew, of Shylock and Jessica, Isaac of York and Rebecca, Riah and Fagin mean to a people whose own guilts and fears and baffled aspirations were projected onto quite different ethnic groups? Associated with the names of Shakespeare, Sir Walter Scott and Dickens, authors sometimes revered, even loved, but chiefly, alas, resented as required reading in the classroom, such figures assume the vicarious reality of classroom facts, of something learned for the first time out of books, rather than *recognized* in books as the truths of nightmare and dream.

It is those whom the white Anglo-Saxon Americans persecuted in the act of becoming Americans, even as the Europeans persecuted the Jews in the act of becoming Christians, who live in the American psyche as Shylock and the Wandering Jew live in the European one: the Indian and the Negro, who are facts of the American imagination from the moment that imagination is formed. The Anglo-Saxon immigrant could maintain only a theoretical anti-Semitism in the New World, just as he could maintain only a theoretical opposition to the aristocracy; his real struggles were elsewhere, and his attempts to project his own psychological difficulties onto the enemies of his ancestors never took root in literature. So, also, with later generations of immigrants, from other parts of Europe. The Germans, the Poles, the Czechs may have brought with them certain traditional anti-Semitic fantasies of their native lands; but at the moment that their assimilation to America moved from the social to the psychic level (and in the country of the melting pot this moment comes quite soon), they began to find their old nightmares driven out by new.

James Fenimore Cooper, greatest of American mythogaphers, tried to identify the evil Indian of the *Last of the Mohicans* with Shylock, and, in one of the last of his novels, portrayed the Indians as New World Jews re-enacting the crucifixion in the midst of the wilderness; but this major attempt to make transatlantic and cisatlantic attitudes of hatred and guilt reinforce each other failed. The Jew could not figure as the archetypal Other, the psychic whipping boy, in a society which was not bound to him by ancient and terrible guilts: guilts lived, as well as read about in schoolrooms or even sacred books. Exclusions from jobs and country clubs is no substitute for pogroms and massacres, and even the anti-Semitism implicit in Christianity has remained, in America, largely theoretical; an occasional schoolchild has been sent running home in tears with the cry of his classmates, "You killed our Christ!" ringing in his bewildered head; but practically nobody in the United States *has ever died from it!* And this is perhaps why in our classic literature, much concerned with precisely those conflicts from which men had indeed died, Jewish characters play such unimportant roles.

It is worth remembering that the poet who wrote and rewrote, from just past the middle of the last century to almost the beginning of ours, the four-hundred-page poem which declares itself the most broadly inclusive of all all-American poems, included no Jewish character or scene in his mythic world. There are no Jews in *Leaves of Grass;* and the single appearance of the adjective "semitic" recorded in the concordances to that work turns out to be an error. Whitman, meaning to describe the ideal American poet as "plunging his seminal muscle" into the "merits and demerits" of his country, miswrote "semitic muscle" the first time around, but changed it when some amused reader called it to his attention. White, red, and black make up his America, and even the yellow oriental makes an occasional appearance; but the Jew was represented by no color on his palette and constitutes no part of the myth he has left us. No more are there Jews included in that otherwise universally representative crew: the Manx, African, Irish, Spanish, Italian, Polynesian, and Middle-Eastern human flotsam of the world who, under a mad Yankee skipper, sail a ship called after a defunct Indian tribe in the pages of Melville's *Moby Dick.* Nor does Huck Finn meet a single Jew, either ashore or afloat on the great river whose course he follows down the center of civilized America.

There are, to be sure, occasional Jewish characters elsewhere in Melville, and in Hawthorne, Henry James, even Longfellow; but, by and large, these are either borrowed bugaboos, male and female, or inventions of a sentimentality which kept itself pure by keeping its Jews imaginary. In Melville's long narrative poem *Clarel,* for instance, one finds the major attempt to adapt for American uses the archetypal pattern story which has most appealed to the American imagination when it has sought at all to deal with things Jewish: the myth of Shylock and Jessica, the sinister Jew deprived of his lovely daughter. But the American imagination does not permit the Gentile hero to get the Jewish girl in a blithe Shakespearean ending; on this side of the ocean, a tragic blight falls over the European myth of assimilation: the dream of rescuing the desirable elements in the Judaic tradition (maternal tenderness and exotic charm: the figure of Mary) from the unsympathetic elements (patriarchal rigor and harsh legalism: the figure of the High Priest and Father Abraham with a knife).

The trouble is that the Jewish girl is thought of not in terms of Mary, but of Lilith, and becomes one with all those dark ladies (otherwise Latin) who are paired off against the fair, Anglo-Saxon girl: the former representing all the Puritan mind most longs for, and fears, in passion; the latter standing for a passionless, sexless love. At the very beginnings of our literature, Charles Brockden Brown could permit his hero to marry a Jewish woman, but neither Melville nor Hawthorne could forget his own pale, Anglo-Saxon bride long enough to follow Brown's example. Even in our presumably post-Puritan times, the protagonist of

Two for the Seesaw finally abandons his Gittel Mosca, Jewish embodiment of impulse and sexual generosity, to return like a good American to the Gentile wife he left behind.

But beside the nightmare of the Jew's alluring daughter flanked by the castrating father, there exists for the American imagination a dream of the "little Jew," too, enduring and forgiving under abuse—a kind of Semitic version of "Uncle Tom." Unfortunately, this is to be found nowhere in our serious writers and is, I suspect, an English importation where found, a spreading out and down of George Eliot's hortatory philo-Semitism. There appeared, at any rate, in the 1868 volume of the children's magazine called *Our Young Folks,* a poem which begins:

> We were at school together,
> The little Jew and I.
> He had black eyes, the biggest nose,
> The very smallest fist for blows,
> Yet nothing made him cry.

and which ends, after the speaker has thrust an apple under that "biggest nose" on Yom Kippur, mocking the child for his fast, and has then repented:

> Next day when school was over,
> I put my nonsense by;
> Begged the lad's pardon, stopped all strife.
> And—well, we have been friends for life,
> The little Jew and I.

A second-hand nightmare is answered by a borrowed dream.

The Jewish writer himself was engaged with these half-felt stereotypes in the latter half of the nineteenth century, and his responses seem as unreal, as far from the center of American psychic life, as those stereotypes themselves. Up to the end of the last century (and in a certain sense that century did not end for us until the conclusion of World War I), Jewish-American literature, the stories and poems written out of their own experience by those willing to call themselves Jews, or descended immediately from those so willing, remains not only theoretical but parochial. In this regard, it is like all the sub-literature which we customarily call "regional"—writing intended to represent the values and interests of a group which feels itself penalized, even threatened, by the disregard of the larger community. From one side, such writing constitutes a literature of self-congratulation and reassurance, intended to be consumed by an in-group which knows it is abused and suspect that it is hardly noticed by those who abuse it; and from another, it aims at becoming a literature of public relations, intended to "sell" that in-group to certain outsiders, who, it is assumed, will respond favorably only to "positive," i.e., innocuous or untrue, images of the excluded group.

Regional writing ceases to be sub-literary, however, not when those it portrays are made to seem respectable, but when they are presented as representative (in all their particularity) of the larger community: the nation, an alliance of nations, all of mankind. But this only begins to happen when regional writers stop being apologists and become critics, abandon falsification and sentimentality in favor of treating not the special virtues of the group from which they come, whether those virtues be real or fancied, but the weaknesses it shares with all men. Such writers seem often to their fellows, their very friends and parents, traitors —not only for the harsh things which they are led to say about those fellows, friends and parents in the pursuit of truth, but also because their desire for universality of theme and appeal leads them to begin tearing down from within the walls of a cultural ghetto, which, it turns out, he has meant security as well as exclusion to the community that nurtured them.

The plight is particularly difficult for those who are not even psychically exploited, not even used to represent certain deep uncertainties and guilts in the undermind of the larger community, but only psychically ignored, which is to say, blanked out of the range of vision of that larger community. They may, indeed, congratulate themselves on their social invisibility, taking it for a result of their own firm resolve not to be assimilated to the ways of strangers. Mythically invisible men, that is, tend to confuse their essential peculiarity, to which they are resolved to cling, with the psychic walls that make them invisible and which they know they must someday breach. They are, therefore, likely to think of those who first begin to breach these walls, in quest of the freedom to become the selves of their own imagining, as apostates from their ancestral identity and the values which sustain it.

The breakthrough to such psychic freedom and to the cultural assimilation which is its concomitant requires, then, a series of revolutionary acts as a critical point in the history of a minority group; but that critical point is determined not by the revolutionary writers alone. It is no more a mere matter of a certain number of heroic individual decisions than it is of the simple growth in size and prestige and power of the mythically non-existent community. The mass immigrations of Eastern European

Jews to the United States was over by 1910, and, some decades before that, a novelist who called himself Sidney Luska had attempted single-handed to transform various aspects of Jewish immigrant life in New York, which he had observed at first hand, into fictions capable of moving all Americans. Even the names of his novels, however (*As It Was Written, The Yoke of the Thorah,* etc.), are by now forgotten; for he had begun by imposing on the facts, as he knew them, a vision of the Jew as the infinitely sensitive artist and the herald of the future, compounded out of George Eliot's portrait of herself as a young Jew in *Daniel Deronda,* and the dreams of the Ethical Culturists of his time. And "Sidney Luska" was not really a Jew, only a disaffected white Anglo-Saxon Protestant who had affected what he took to be a "Jewish" beard as well as a "Jewish" name; and who, when confronted by the pettiness and weakness of actual Jews, returned to his own name, Henry Harland, and ended as an expatriate and editor of the *Yellow Book* and the author of a fashionably Catholic, anti-Semitic best-seller called *The Cardinal's Snuffbox.* It is the comic-pathetic catastrophe fitting to one hubristic enough to have attempted single-handed to give to Jews the status that only time and history could bestow.

The creation of Jewish characters able to live in the American imagination cannot be the work of Jewish writers, real or imagined, alone. As the Jewish writer goes out in search of his mythical self, he is bound to encounter the Gentile writer on a complementary quest to come to terms with him, the stranger in the Gentile's land. As collaborators or rivals, wittingly or not, Jewish author and Gentile must engage in a common enterprise if either is to succeed. The presence of talented Jewish writers concerned with Jewish life, and of a rich and complex Jewish life itself, are essential preconditions of the Jewish breakthrough into the deep psyche of Gentile America; but there is a necessary third precondition, too. At the moment of such a breakthrough, the Jew must *already* have become capable of projecting psychological meanings with which the non-Jewish community is vitally concerned, must already have come to represent in his mode of existence, symbolically at least, either a life lived and aspired to by those others— or at least (and more probably) one passionately rejected and secretly regretted by those others. But this is the job of non-Jewish writers, and for this reason we must look to such writers, rather than to the Jewish writers of the period, to understand just how the Jewish character became mythically viable during and just after World War I.

There were, to be sure, Jewish writers of varying degrees of talent who not only published during this period but were, in certain cases, widely read. In fiction, for instance, there were the mass entertainers: Fannie Hurst and Edna Ferber; middlebrow wits like Dorothy Parker; and even quite serious novelists like Ben Hecht (before his removal to Hollywood) and Ludwig Lewisohn (before his surrender to Zionist apologetics). The nineteenth-century "poetesses" from good Sephardic families, chief of whom was Emma Lazarus, were giving way to high school teachers with social consciences: Louis Ginsberg, James Oppenheim, Alfred Kreymborg. The minor achievements of such poets were preserved, along with the brittle verse of F.P.A. and Arthur Guiterman, the efforts of certain Village Bohemians of the Twenties (e.g., Maxwell Bodenheim), and the verses of Jewish prodigies like Nathalia Crane in the pages of Louis Untermeyer's earlier anthologies. In a time when poetry was in the process of becoming what was read in classrooms, certain Jewish journalists and educators compiled the standard classroom anthologies. Though these Jewish-American writers thus controlled American taste to some extent, they did not—in verse any more than in prose—succeed in making images of even their own lives that were capable of possessing the American mind. In any case, the writers anthologized by Untermeyer and others had little consciousness of themselves as Jews, were engaged, in fact, in assimilating themselves to general American culture by pledging allegiance to social or cultural ideals larger than their Jewishness, whether Bohemianism or socialism or humanism in its broadest sense.

No, the compelling images of Jews were made by writers who were not merely Gentiles but anti-Semites, interested in resisting this assimilationist impulse and keeping the Jews Jews. It is important to understand, however, the precise nature of their anti-Semitism. Quite different from working-class or populist, economic anti-Semitism, that "Black Socialism" of the American factory hand or poor farmer which identifies the Jews with Wall Street and international bankers, theirs was the cultural anti-Semitism of the educated bourgeois seeking status through a career in the arts; and it was, therefore, aimed not at expelling the money-changers from the Temple, but at distinguishing the Jewish exploiters of culture from its genuine Gentile makers, at separating the pseudo-artists (naturally, Jews) from the true ones (of course, Gentiles). This cultural anti-Semitism was the inevitable result of certain provincial Gentile Americans' moving toward the big city (Theodore Dreiser, for instance, and Sherwood Anderson) and discovering that the Jews had beat them to the artists' quarters of Chicago and New Orleans and New York; and it was exacerbated when still other provincial Gentile Americans, attempting expatriation (Pound and Eliot, Hemingway and Fitzgerald, and E. E. Cummings), found Jews even on the Left Bank, in the heart of what they had always dreamed of as Heaven. What the expatriates discovered in fact when they arrived at the Paris of their dreams was most vividly sketched not in a book by any one of them, but rather in one about all of them, Wyndham Lewis's *Paleface:* "Glance into the Dôme, anyone . . . who happens to be in Paris. You would think you were in a League of Nations beset by a zionist delegation, in a movie studio, in Moscow, Broadway or even Zion itself, anywhere but in the mythical watertight America . . ."

And when, in the Thirties, Henry Miller belatedly arrived in the same city, abandoned now, as far as Americans went, to the second-rate and the shoddy, he found the same overwhelming proportion of Jews in the expatriate community and exploded with baffled rage:

He is a Jew, Borowski, and his father was a philatelist. In fact, almost all Montparnasse is Jewish, or half-Jewish, which is worse. There's Carl and Paula, and Cronstadt and Boris, and Tania and Sylvester, and Moldorf and Lucille. All except Fillmore. Henry Jordan Oswald turned out to be a Jew also. Louis Nichols is a Jew. Even Van Norden and Chérie are Jewish. Frances Blake is a Jew, or a Jewess. Titus is a Jew. The Jews then are snowing me under. I am writing this for my friend Carl whose father is a Jew. All this is important to understand.

Of them all the loveliest Jew is Tania, and for her sake I too would become a Jew. Why not? I already speak like a Jew. And I am ugly as a Jew. Besides, who hates the Jews more than the Jew?

No wonder the German occupation forces in Paris made Miller a favorite author, finding in him not only sex but their favorite obsession with the Jew as the absolute Other. And, meanwhile, Miller's fellow German-American writer of the Thirties (one is almost tempted to say Nazi-American), Thomas Wolfe, was finding in New York City similar occasions for anti-Semitic outbursts, reacting with hatred and fear, and a lust of which he was ashamed, to the young Jewesses at New York University, forerunners of later Jewish coeds, who, a short generation later would be writing (under Jewish advisors) theses about the very anti-Semites of the decades before.

Even Jewish writers of the Thirties were more likely than not to produce hostile travesties of their own people, especially if—like Michael Gold, for instance, whose *Jews Without Money* was the first "proletarian novel" of the period—their Messiah was a Marxian rather than a Jewish one. The anti-Semitism so deeply implanted in Russian Communism during the Stalin regime was reflected in the American Communist Party, largely Jewish though it was, and in the literature which followed its line. Indeed, the presence of such anti-Semitism was taken as evidence that American Jewish Communists were emancipated from parochialism and chauvinism. In Michael Gold, at any rate, only the *yiddishe mamme,* the long-suffering maternal figure, comes off well; the Rabbi, the landlord, the pawnbroker are treated as egregious villains, and Gold's portraits of them disconcertingly resemble both those of European Jew-baiters like Julius Streicher, and native American provincials like Thomas Wolfe.

There are ironies involved here disturbing to both sides; for the anti-Semite, intending merely to excoriate the Jew, learns eventually that he has mythicized him. And the offended Jew realizes, after a while, that before the Jewish character could seem to author and reader in the United States an image of the essential American self, he had first to seem the essential American enemy. Nevertheless, it is depressing for the Jewish American to think how many of our most eminent and central writers in the decades during which we entered fully into world literature produced anti-Semitic caricatures, not from mere habit or tradition, but from conviction and passion. What a black anthology lives in his head: out of Cummings ("and pity the fool who cright/ god help me it aint no ews/ eye like the steak all ried/ but eye certainly hate the juse."); and Eliot ("And the jew squats on the window sill, the owner,/ Spawned in some estaminet of Antwerp,/ Blistered in Brussels, patched and peeled in London."), and Pound ("the yidd is a stimulant, and the goyim are cattle/ in gt/ proportion and go to saleable slaughter/ with the maximum of docility . . ."), and Hemingway ("No, listen, Jake. Brett's gone off with men. But they weren't Jews, and they didn't come and hang about afterward."), and Fitzgerald ("A small, flatnosed Jew raised his large head and regarded me with two fine growths of hair which luxuriated in either nostril. After a moment I discovered his tiny eyes in the half-darkness. . . . 'I see you're looking at my cuff buttons.' I hadn't been looking at them, but I did now. . . . 'Finest specimens of human molars,' he informed me."), and Michael Gold ("The landlord wore a black alpaca coat in the pawnshop, and a skull cap. He crouched on a stool behind the counter. One saw only his scaly yellow face and bulging eyes; he was like an anxious spider."), and Thomas Wolfe (". . . Jews and Jewesses, all laughing, shouting, screaming, thick with their hot and sweaty body-smells, their strong female odors of rut and crotch and armpit and cheap perfume . . .").

How hard it is, after Hitler, for any man of good will, Gentile or Jew, to confess that the most vivid and enduring portraits of Jews created in the period are not works of love and comprehension, but the products of malice and paranoia: Robert Cohen of Hemingway's *The Sun Also*

Rises and the multiformed Jewish usurer of Ezra Pound's *Cantos,* Boris of Miller's *Tropic of Cancer* and Abe Jones of Wolfe's *Of Time and the River*—anti-*goyim* and anti-artists one and all. And yet they are not all quite the same; though Hemingway and Pound, for instance, were motivated by a similar malice, and though both moved through the salons of Paris just after World War I, learning, as it were, their anti-Semitism in the same school, their ideologies must be sharply distinguished.

For writers like Pound and Eliot, on the one hand, it is European culture, particularly of the Middle Ages and the Renaissance, which represents the essential meaning of life when it is more than just "birth, copulation and death." And to them the Jew, excluded from the culture in the days of its making, is the supreme enemy; for as merchant-tourist and usurious millionaire, he desires now to appropriate what he never made, to buy and squat in the monuments of high Christian culture, fouling them by his mere presence. He is, therefore, felt and portrayed not only as the opposite to the artist but also to the aristocrat, who, traditionally, sustained the artist in his days of greatest glory.

To writers like Hemingway, on the other hand, to the devotees of raw experience who went to Europe to fish rather than to pray (though also, of course, to make books), the Jew stands for the pseudo-artist. Along with the homosexual, he seems to them to travesty and falsify their own real role; to help create in the public eye an image, from which they find it hard to dissociate themselves, of the effete intellectual, the over-articulate, pseudo-civilized fake. For them, too, the Jew represents the opposite of the Negro, Indian, peasant, bullfighter, or any of the other versions of the noble savage with whom such writers, whether at home or abroad, sought to identify themselves. When either the cult of the primitive or a genteel tradition is in the ascendancy, the Jew is likely to be regarded as the Adversary; for he is the anti-type of Negro and Indian, a projection of the feared intelligence rather than the distrusted impulse, and "genteel" equals Gentile in the language of the psyche. Neither paleface nor redskin, neither gentleman nor genital man, to what can the Jew appeal in the American imagination, which seems to oscillate helplessly between these two poles? Is he doomed to remain merely the absolute un-American, everybody's outsider?

This seems an unanswerable question at first; but it answers itself with the passage of time, and in the very terms in which it is posed. When Americans have grown tired of the neo-gentility, the selective ancestor worship and high-churchly piety of Eliot, and when they are equally sick of the white self-hatred and the adulation of blood sports and ignorance, but especially when they are sick and tired of the oscillation between the two, they can find in the Jewish writer and the world he imagines a way out. Through their Jewish writers, Americans, after the Second World War, were able to establish a new kind of link with Europe in place of the old paleface connection—a link not with the Europe of decaying castles and the Archbishop of Canterbury, nor with that of the Provençal poets and Dante and John Donne, nor with that of the French *symbolistes* and the deadly polite *Action Française*—for these are all Christian Europes; but with the post-Christian Europe of Marx and Freud, which is to say, of secularized Judaism, as well as the Europe of surrealism and existentialism, Kafka, neo-Chasidism—a Europe which at once abhors and yearns for the vacuum left by the death of its Christian god.

And through the same intermediaries, Gentile Americans discovered the possibility of a new kind of vulgarity unlike the old redskin variety, the when-the-ladies-are-out-of-the-room grossness of works like Mark Twain's *1601*, which depended upon naïveté and simplicity in writer and audience alike. The special Jewish vulgarity exemplified with greater or lesser skill from Ben Hecht through Michael Gold and Nathanael West to Norman Mailer and Philip Roth, is not merely sophisticated, but compatible with high complexity and even metaphysical transcendence. The Semite, someone once said (thinking primarily of the Arabs, but it will do for the Jews, too), stands in dung up to his eyes, but his brow touches the heavens. And where else is there to stand but on dung in a world buried beneath the privileged excretions of the mass media; and where else to aspire but the heavens, in a world whose dreams of earthly paradises have all come to nothing?

Moreover, the Jewish-American mind, conditioned by two thousand years of history, provides other Americans with ways of escaping the trap of vacillation between isolationism and expatriation, chauvinism and national self-hatred. Jewish-American writers are, by and large, neither expatriates nor "boosters"; and they do not create in their protagonists images of the expatriate or the "booster." More typically, they have begun to produce moderately cynical accounts of impatriation, the flight from the quasi-European metropolis to the provincial small town. This flight they have, indeed, lived, moving in quest of more ultimate exile not out of but *into* America, moving from New York or Chicago, Boston or Baltimore, to small towns in New Mexico, Oregon, Nebraska, and Montana.

After all, if it is a *difference* from what one is born to that is desirable, there is a greater difference between New York and Athens, Georgia, then between New York and Athens, Greece, or between Chicago and

Moscow, Idaho, than between Chicago and Moscow, Russia. Within the past couple of years the first fictional treatment of this new migration, a comedy involving an urban Jew in a small university community in the West, has appeared in the form of *A New Life,* the novel by Bernard Malamud which we have already noticed. But though Malamud's book begins with exile, it ends with return; for, like the expatriates of the past, the in-patriate of the present also ends by going home, returning East as inevitably as his forebears returned West.

All flights, the Jewish experience teaches, are from one exile to another; and this Americans have always known, though they have sometimes attempted to deny it. Fleeing exclusion in the Old World, the immigrant discovers loneliness in the New World; fleeing the communal loneliness of seaboard settlements, he discovers the ultimate isolation of the frontier. It is the dream of exile as freedom which has made America; but it is the experience of exile as terror that has forged the self-conscious-ness of Americans.

Yet it is the Jew who has best been able to recast this old American wisdom (that home itself is exile, that it is the nature of man to feel him-self everywhere alienated) in terms valid for twentieth-century Ameri-cans, which is to say, for dwellers in cities. The urban American, looking about him at the anonymous agglomeration of comfort-producing ma-chines that constitutes his home, knows that exile is what one endures, not seeks, and he is willing to believe the Jewish writer who tells him this. That the Jewish writer be his spokesman in this regard is natural enough, for he descends from those whose consciousness had already been radically altered by centuries of living in cities; and he stands at ease, therefore, in the midst of the first generation of really urban writers in the American twentieth century. Unlike those who made up the first waves of the movement in the United States, replacing the represen-tatives of proper old Boston and old New York, he is no provincial, no small-town Lewis or Anderson or Pound come to the big city to gawk; he is the metropolitan at home, though expert in the indignities, rather than the amenities, of urban life.

Therefore the American-Jewish writer chooses, characteristically, to work in neither the traditional tragic nor the traditional comic mode; for he feels both modes to be aristocratic, that is, pre-industrial, pre-mass-culture genres, reflecting the impulse of a reigning class to glorify its own suffering and to laugh at the suffering of others postulated as inferior to them, to treat only its own suffering as really real. The Jew, however, functions in his deepest imagination (influenced, of course, by the Gentile culture to which he aspires) as his own other, his own inferior;

and he must consequently laugh at himself—glorify himself, if at all, *by* laughing at himself. This is the famous Jewish humor, rooted in a humility too humble to think of its self-abasement as religious, and a modesty too modest to think of its encounter with pain as really real. But this is also the source of a third literary genre, neither tragedy nor comedy, though, like both, based on the perception of human absurdity—a genre for whose flourishing in recent American literature certain Jewish-American writers are largely responsible, though with thanks to Mark Twain as well as Sholom Aleichem.

We have similarly witnessed, over the last thirty years or so, the recasting in terms of second-generation American urban life certain American archetypal heroes and the rerendering of their adventures in an American English affected by the rhythms of Yiddish and shot through with a brand of wit conditioned by the Jewish joke. These great figures out of our deepest imagination, whom we had thought essentially American, we now learn are—or at least can be made to seem—characteristically Jewish as well. It is not a matter of cultural kidnaping, but of the discovery of cultural resemblances. What, for instance, has happened in the middle of the twentieth century to Huckleberry Finn: loneliest of Americans; eternally and by definition uncommitted; too marginal in his existence to afford either conventional virtue or ordinary villainy; excluded, by the conditions which shape him, from marriage and the family; his ending ambiguously suspended between joy and misery; condemned to the loneliness which he desperately desires? Reimagined by Saul Bellow for the survivors of the thirties, he comes now from northwest Chicago, works for petty Jewish gangsters, reads Kafka and Marx, goes to live with Leon Trotsky, and is called Augie March. Or reinvented yet again by J. D. Salinger for a younger and more ignorant audience, he comes from the west side of New York, a world of comfortably assimilated and well-heeled Jews (though his name cagily conceals his ethnic origin), plays hooky from an expensive prep school, slips unscathed through a big-city world of phonies and crooks, and is called Holden Caulfield.

Meanwhile what has happened to the most typical of all the heroes of American poetry? Conceived so deeply and specifically, expressed so passionately and intensely out of the self of the poet who first invented him, this mock-epic hero, crying the most pathetic and lovely of American boasts, "I was the man, I suffered, I was there," once seemed doomed to remain forever what he was to begin with—Walt Whitman, who was born of Quaker parents and moved through a world without Jews. But now, improbably reborn, he remembers listening beside his mother to Israel Amter, idol of the Jewish-American Communists of the Thirties, scolds America for what it has done to his Uncle Max, howls his rage at his father's world (the world of Jewish high-school-teacher-poets memorialized by Louis Untermeyer), and when he has symbolically killed it, writes a volume called *Kaddish,* title of the Hebrew prayer for the dead and tenderest of pet names by which a Jew calls his son. Walt Whitman, that is to say, becomes Allen Ginsberg.

Not only on the highbrow level of Bellow and Ginsberg, however, but on all levels of our literature, archetype and stereotype alike are captured by the Jewish imagination and refurbished for Gentile consumption. Norman Mailer and Irwin Shaw, for instance, have conspired to teach us that no platoon in the United States Army is complete without its sensitive Jew to suffer the jibes of his fellows and record their exploits, while Herman Wouk has made it clear that the valiant virgin beset by seducers, whom female Anglo-Saxondom once thought of as the pale projection of its own highest aspirations, is really a nice Jewish girl who has misguidedly changed her name. What Shaw and Wouk teach, the movies and *Time* magazine transmit to the largest audience; and who is to say them nay in a day when all rightminded men approve the fact of Israel and detest the memory of Hitler, a world in which Anne Frank, our latest secular saint, looks down from the hoardings on us all. Even the crassest segregationists sometimes combine their abuse of Negroes with praise for the Jews. "From the days of Abraham . . ." writes a certain Reverend G. T. Gillespie of Mississippi, "the Hebrews . . . became a respected people . . . and they . . . have made an invaluable contribution to the moral and spiritual progress of mankind." So the occasional anti-Semitic crank who still sends through the mail a cry of protest ("Every book that goes into print . . . is either written by, edited by, advertised by, published by—or what is common, all four—Jewish people . . . these publishers are at war with the American intelligence, as well as its Christian morality.") seems scarcely worth our contemptuous notice.

And there is no end. Very recently, for example, there has been an attempt, in the screenplay for *The Misfits* written by Arthur Miller, to adapt the classical American Western to new times and new uses. It is not merely a matter of making the Western "adult," as certain middle-brow manipulators of the form like to boast of their efforts on television, but of turning upside down the myth embodied in such standard versions of our archetypal plot as *The Virginian* and *High Noon.* In both of these, a conflict between a man and a woman, representing, respectively, the chivalric code of the West and the pacifism of Christianity, ends with the capitulation of the woman, and the abandonment of forgiveness in favor of force. In *The Misfits,* however, the woman is no longer the pious and pretty but flat-chested schoolmarm that Gentile Americans know their actual grandmothers to have been, but the big-busted, dyed blonde, life-giving and bursting with animal vitality; she is all that the Jew dreams the *shiksa,* whom his grandmothers forbade him as a mate. In Miller's film, that archetypal blonde was played by Marilyn Monroe (at that point Miller's wife and converted to Judaism), who, under the circumstances, was bound to triumph over the male Old West: the Gentiles' Saturday-matinee dream of violence and death, personified by Clark Gable, tamer of horses and females. What remained for Gable, after so ignominious a defeat, except, aptly, to die? Only the author lived on, though his marriage, too, was doomed by the very dream out of which he made a movie in its honor.

Generation after overlapping generation, American-Jewish writers continue to appear: Bellow and Malamud, Irwin Shaw and Arthur Miller and Karl Shapiro, followed by J. D. Salinger and Norman Mailer and Grace Paley, after whom come Philip Roth and Bruce Jay Friedman and Norman Fruchter, on and on, until at last Gore Vidal, himself a white Anglo-Saxon Protestant, writes in mock horror (but with an undertone of real bitterness, too) in the pages of the *Partisan Review,* where, indeed, many of these authors first appeared: "Every year there is a short list of the O.K. writers. Today's list consists of two Jews, two Negroes and a safe floating *goy* of the old American Establishment (often Mr. Wright Morris) . . ."

But it is the whole world, not merely *our* critics, who list, year after year, the two new Jews, plus the two Negroes and the one eternally rediscovered *goy.* The English boy in the sixth form of the Manchester Grammar School digs Norman Mailer; and his opposite number in the classical *liceo* in Milan sees himself as Salinger's *giovane Holden.* At the moment that young Europeans everywhere (even, at last, in England) are becoming imaginary Americans, the American is becoming an imaginary Jew. But this is only one half of the total irony we confront; for, at the same moment, the Jew whom his Gentile fellow-citizen emulates may himself be in the process of becoming an imaginary Negro. "Do we have to become Gentile Jews before we can become White Negroes?" an impatient and reasonably hip youngster from a college audience I addressed recently asked me; and he was only half joking.

DANIEL BELL (1919–   )

Daniel Bell has been an important social critic since his early experience as Managing Editor of The New Leader from 1941 to 1944. Born on May 20, 1919, Bell received his B.S.S. from the City College of New York in 1939 and his Ph.D. from Columbia in 1960. He has taught at the University of Chicago from 1945 to 1949, Columbia University from 1952 to 1958, and Harvard University since 1969.

Bell's work with magazines has been extensive. In addition to being the Editor of The New Leader, he has served as Labor Editor of Fortune Magazine from 1948 to 1958 and as a member of the editorial board of Daedalus and The American Scholar. His books include Marxian Socialism in America (1952), The New American Right (1957), The End of Ideology (1960), The Radical Right (1963), and The Reforming of General Education (1966).

Reflections on Jewish Identity

A PERSISTENT FEAR worried Jews of the early Diasporas and of Hellenistic times: the fear that a child of theirs might grow up to be an *am-haaretz*—a peasant, ignorant of Torah; or, even worse, an *apikoros*— a sophisticated unbeliever who abandons Jewish faith to indulge in rationalistic speculation about the meaning of existence. In either case, the danger felt was that such an individual would not only ignore the commandments and rituals, but that he would, in effect, have lost the sense of his past. Asked, in the classic question of identity, "Who are you?" the *am-haaretz* does not understand; and the *apikoros*, instead of giving the traditional response: "I am the son of my father" (Isaac *ben* Abraham), says: "I am I"—meaning, of course, I stand alone, I come out of myself, and, in choice and action, make myself.

A similar crisis of identity is a hallmark of our own modernity— except that not rationalism, but experience, has replaced faith. For us, sensibility and experience, rather than revealed utterances, tradition, authority, or even reason, have become the sources of understanding and of identity. One stakes out one's position and it is confirmed by others who accept the sign; it is no longer the hand of the father placed upon us—the covenant—that gives confirmation.

Not only the Jew, but all moderns, and particularly the intelligentsia, have made this decision to break with the past. Affecting first revealed religion, and later extended to all tradition and authority, the break has meant that the individual himself becomes the source of all moral judgment. But once experience is the touchstone of truth, then a "built-in" situation develops where alienation from society—which necessarily upholds the established, traditional values—is inescapable. This has meant, in the further fragmentation of society, that individuals have sought kinship with those who share both their sensibility and their experience—that is, with their own generation. The others have had a necessarily different experience. (Here we may see one reason why youth movements, a phenomenon unknown in previous times, are so characteristic a fact of modern life.)

Few of us can escape this mark. This is the way we have been bred. In us, especially the Jews, there has been a hunger for experience. The first generation fled the ghetto or the Pale—the second fled the past itself. For those of us whose parents were immigrants, there was the double barrier of language and culture to confront; and the double urgency of being not only thrust out on one's own, but having to make one's self in the course of discovering the world as home.

Yet no one wholly makes himself; nor is there such a thing as a completely cosmopolitan culture. The need to find parochial ties, to share experiences with those who are like ourselves, is part of the search for identity. There is an old truism that in some ways (biologically) we are like everyone else; in some ways (the idiosyncrasies of personality) like nobody else; and in some other ways still, like somebody else. In the parochial search for those like ourselves, the generation, the common age group, is only one tie. Neighborhood, city, country, vocation, political belief, family—these hold other ties. But prior to all—to begin with—one must come to terms with the past. One cannot wholly escape it. One may reject it, but the very mode of rejection is often conditioned by the past itself. A man is, first, the son of his father. In almost all tribal societies, the patronymic is part of one's name. And the sins of the fathers —in the psychological, if not the legal sense—are apt to be the burdens of the sons as well.

For the Jew, his relation to the past is complicated by the fact that he must come to terms not only with culture and history but with religion as well. For the religious tradition has shaped the others, providing both conscience and the continuity of fate. As an agnostic, one can, in rejecting religion, reject God; one may reject a supernatural or even a transcendental God. But as a Jew, how can one reject the God of Abraham, Isaac, and Jacob—without rejecting oneself? How, then, does a modern Jew continue to identify with the Jewish fate? And if such an identification is made and conditioned largely by experience, by a generational experience at that, what must be the consequences? The initial problem remains the religious one.

The simplest way of being a Jew is to be Orthodox—at least in ritual, if not always in faith. An esoteric legend ascribes to Maimonides the affirmation that one does not have to believe in God to be a good Jew, one merely has to follow halakhah—obey the law. This is in keeping, in traditional Judaism, with the derogation of the single individual. As the rabbi might say, "Who are *you* to say that you do or do not believe? Does the world exist for *you?*"

But it is in the confrontation with evil that the judging of God arises. In the *kaddish* of Reb Levi Yitzhak of Berditchev, the 18th-century Tsaddik refuses to speak the Sanctification of the Name until he first arraigns God for the suffering of His innocent Jews. And we know the accusation, two centuries later, of the fifteen-year-old boy who, in Auschwitz on Rosh Hashanah, cries, "Why should I bless Him? Because He kept six crematories working night and day, on the Sabbath and holy days?"*

Maimonides, in the *Guide to the Perplexed,* gave the classic answer to this recurrent cry:

Very often the throngs of the unreasonable will, in their hearts, put forth the claim that there is more evil than good in this world. . . . The cause of this error is that this foolish man and his unreasonable companions in the throng regard the whole universe only from the angle of individual existence. Thus every fool thinks that life is there for his sake alone, and as though nothing existed but him. And so, when anything happens that opposes his wishes, he concludes that the whole universe is evil. But if man would regard the whole universe, and realize what an infinitesimal part he plays in it, the truth would be clear and apparent to him. . . . It is of great advantage that man should recognize the measure of his worth, so that he may not fall into the error of believing that the universe exists only because of him. It is our opinion that the universe exists for the sake of the Creator. . . .

But if life is not present for *me,* if in the design of the universe "Man is like unto a breath," as the Bible puts it, then why fight at all against any injustice or evil? Orthodoxy leads to quietism; suffering is the badge, one accepts it as the mark of fate. One of the more disquieting facts about Jewish behavior in the death camps, as a number of writers have remarked, was the extreme passivity of the people. We know about the ways in which hunger, fright, privation, can depersonalize an individual. But the fatalism that comes out of the religious tradition violates one's conception of a personal autonomy. A modern man wants to believe that

* From *Night,* a memoir of Auschwitz, by Elie Wiesel.

some portion of the universe does exist for him, in the here and now. The Orthodox view of Judaism is too constricted for such a man to feel at home in.

The same pride of self leads to skepticism or rationalism as concerns a supernatural view of the world. To the extent that he must reject religion as superstition, myth, or "absurdity,"* to that extent is the modern Jew's loss of Orthodoxy the victory of philosophy over theology, of reason over faith.

A different mode of Jewish identification lies in accepting the ethical content of Judaism while rejecting the ritual. This has been the path of those who have sought to join the "human" side of faith with the potentialities of science—the path of reform. But if one is too much of a rationalist to accept Orthodoxy, one is too much of an irrationalist to accept the "merely" ethical side of religion. Orthodoxy's view of life may be too fatalistic, but that of ethical Judaism appears to some of us too shallow.

The ethical view is fundamentally syncretistic, drawing on all faiths, for to be valid, an ethical precept must be binding on every man and applicable to all men. Theologically, there is no more justification for a special Jewish ethic than for a Unitarian one, or for Ethical Culture, or for any non-ritualistic creed. The ethical dissolves the parochial, and takes away from individuals that need for the particular identification which singles them out and shapes their community in distinctive terms: terms which make possible a special sense of belonging shared by a group.

Ethical Judaism, in its often superficial rationalism, has taken some disturbing profundities of the Old Testament and transformed them into glossy moral platitudes. In ethical Judaism, a simplistic idea of human nature has led to the belief that there are few human ills which reason cannot remedy. But beyond that, the view of life represented by ethical Judaism is one of simple good and evil, unaware that a tragic component of choice is the fact that it must always involve some evil—a lesson

---

* There is, in the esoteric view, the interpretation that Maimonides views God as a necessary "myth" to hold the masses in check. Man, unrestrained, is a *b'hemah*, or animal, who gives way to his instincts and worships cruel gods. Where man regards himself as the measure, then all means, including murder, may be justified to achieve his unrestrained ends. Individual men could live without myth—the premise of stoicism —but the masses could not. Hence the need for the idea of God for the masses. But then is there not equally the question whether Maimonides, in the cunning of reason, may not have fashioned this rationale for private disbelief actually in order to seduce the *apikorsim*—the unbelievers—to public faith?

which has been taught us by recent 20th-century history. As Emil Fackenheim once put in these pages: "In the 20th century, men—all of us —find themselves compelled to commit or condone evil for the sake of preventing an evil believed to be greater. And the tragedy is that we do not know whether the evil we condone will not in the end be greater than the evil we seek to avert—or be identified with it."*

What is left, then, for one who feels himself to be a Jew, emotionally rather than rationally—who has not lost his sense of identification with the Jewish past and wants to understand the nature of that tie? A Jew, we are told by one existentialist thinker (Emil Fackenheim), is "anyone who by his descent is subject to Jewish fate"—the covenant; one who by *fate* is urged to *faith*. The ground here is still faith, though the ground is "absurd," in that the compulsions to belief are beyond one's control, shaped by descent and, therefore, by history. But this is an attempt to defend faith, not fate. Lacking faith, I myself can only "choose" fate. For me, therefore, to be a Jew is to be part of a community woven by memory—the memory whose knots are tied by the *yizkor,* by the continuity that is summed up in the holy words: *Yizkor Elohim nishmas oboh mori:*—"May God remember the name of. . . ."

The *yizkor* is the tie to the dead, the link to the past, the continuity with those who have suffered and, through suffering, have made us witnesses to cruelty and given us the strength of courage over pride. However much, as moderns, we reject the utterances of authority and the injunctions of ritual, the religious link with our fellows is not the search for immortality or other consolatory formulas against the fear of extinction—but is the link of memory and its articulation.

All societies have memorial occasions, a day that commemorates an event of the past, a day of mourning for the dead. A memorial day, a holy day, often becomes, in secular terms, a holiday and an escape from the past. The *yizkor* is different. It is recited not just on one day, but on a set of days whose occasions form the wheel of life. For the *yizkor* is said on four days: Passover, Shevuoth, Succoth, and Yom Kippur—the escape from bondage, the giving of the Law, the ingathering of the harvest, and the day of atonement, which is also the day of "at-one-ment."

One lives, therefore, as a Jew, through the meaning of the *yizkor,* through the act of commemoration, through the saying of a common prayer—but singling out in that prayer a specific name of one's own dead. In the *minyan* of my fellows, I am linked to my own parent. In the *yizkor,* through memory, I am identified as a Jew.

* "Can We Believe in Judaism Religiously?" December 1948.

If one is a Jew through filio-piety, is such a bond strong enough? Memory has its risks. The sense of the past is often merely the present read into the past. Memory is selective, it screens out the hurts, it throws roseate hues. Remembering what happened in one's lifetime is difficult enough; uncovering the past of history is even more so.

The greatest risk of memory is sentimentality, and Jewish life has paid dearly for its sentimentality. The lachrymose recollections of the *shtetl* (which are still with us) fail to recall its narrowness of mind, its cruelty, especially to school children (to which a whole series of memoirs, such as Solomon Ben Maimon's, testify), and its invidious stratification. In the same vein of nostalgia, there are the glowing reminiscences of the Lower East Side of Williamsburg, or Chicago's Maxwell Street—but they omit the frequent coarseness, the pushing, the many other gross features of that life. At its best, this parochial identification exists as a tie of memory through pity; at its worst, it may be the continuity of appetite—the lox, cream cheese, and bagel combinations; or through comedians' jokes.

A different form of filio-piety is in the satisfying of memory, when there is no faith, by "good works." One is a Jew, discharging one's obligations as a Jew, through membership in Jewish organizations. Here lies the second risk, of accommodation. In the *embourgeoisement* of Jewish life in America, the community has become institutionalized around fund raising, and the index of an individual's importance too often is the amount of money he donates to hospitals, defense agencies, philanthropic groups, and the like. The manifest ends are the community functions being served, but frequently the latent end is the personal prestige—*yichus*. This kind of institutional life may even lend itself to historic forms of corruption: of simony, when those who have risen high in Jewish organizations receive their rewards in appointive office in Jewish life; and of indulgences, when leadership is the simple reward of wealth. And in performance of charity as a way of Jewish life, self-satisfaction may take on the face of righteousness. The most sensitive of the Jewish agency professionals, lawyers, and businessmen have often deplored this situation, yet are trapped by the system.

But for the intellectual, the greatest risk of memory is its repression —the past is only allowed to come back in the form of self-hate, shame of one's parents, the caricaturing of Jewish traits (most notably verbal agility), the exaggerated thrust of ambition, the claims to superiority by the mere fact of being a Jew, and all the other modes of aggression that arise from the refusal to accept the tension of being in a minority, and the need to balance the insistent demands of the past with the needs of the present.

Coming to terms with this kind of repression often leads to alienation from Judaism, to the feeling of its insufficiency, even when one has some knowledge of its traditions. The alienated Jew is the Jewish orphan. He comes "out of himself," rather than out of a past. He is homeless. The present is his only reality. Lacking a past, he can have no notion of continuity, or any image of the future. For him there can be no *parousia*, no fulfillment. This has been the signet of Jewish fate, particularly in Central Europe, over the last forty years, and it foreshadowed the fate of a whole generation of intellectuals. As W. H. Auden once said of Kafka, "It was fit and proper that [he] should have been a Jew, for the Jews have for a long time been placed in the position in which we are all now to be, of having no home." The problem is spiritual, not territorial. Israel is no answer. The alienated Jew grew up in *galut,* and the world has been his home. Is it his fault that the world has been inhospitable —rejecting those who refuse to assert a distinctive parochial tie? Yet, in the awareness of his rejection, his life is Jewish, too: he is one of a community of exiles whose common experiences are molded by the common fate—and this becomes his parochial tie.

Finally, in this catalogue of risks, there is the risk of attrition. If, in order to give it meaning, Jewish involvement requires some encounter with tradition, so that one may be able to make choices, then succeeding generations, whose encounters are few and whose memories are hazy, must find themselves with fewer and fewer ties. They are in the most difficult position of all. It is not a question of assimilation, for that is a matter of choice, the choice of severing all ties, and one which is made consciously. Attrition is not chosen—it is a wasting away. There is a word, Jew, but no feeling. And this becomes the most tragic consequence of identification solely through memory.

If identification is an interplay of experience and memory, its shaping elements are in the successive generations themselves. Each generation has its own "entelechy"—its own inherent design, which gives the identification its distinct quality. In these days, generations succeed each other rapidly, and each succeeding one is also longer-lived. The characteristic fact about Jewish life today is the extraordinary palimpset which the different overlaying generational experiences have become. The different generations can be identified with one or the other of the different forms of response I have described (the five risks of memory) as a rationalization of their own experiences.

The basic shaping element of Jewish life in America has been the immigrant experience—an experience with an inner tension of anxiety and hope. The anxiety was an inevitable consequence of being uprooted and living in a strange land. At times it led, particularly for those who lived away from the large urban centers, to a sense of being "a guest in the house"—which in turn led to a minimizing of Jewish life, subduing an inherent drive and ebullience, temporizing with the neighbors—attitudes that have persisted in smaller Jewish communities in America and that have been repeated for a new mobile class in the suburbs.

For the bulk of Jewish immigrants, particularly those from Eastern Europe, the anxiety was translated into the struggle between fathers and sons. Few generational conflicts have had such an exposed nakedness, such depths of strain as this. The metaphor of Fathers and Sons that one finds in the Russian literature of the 1860's applied to political generations—there the "fathers" left home to go abroad, while the "sons," when they came of age, initiated the radical activity on the land; but both generations were within the boundaries of a common culture. In the American Jewish immigrant experience, it was the sons who left home, and the very boundaries of the culture came into question—the repudiation of the synagogue, the flight from the parents' language, the rejection of their authority, all of it intensified by the fact that both fathers and sons were living in a strange land.

If the immigrant generation was characterized by anxiety, the one after it was shaped by shame and guilt. However, the generational changes cannot be marked into exact historical periods, for generational time is interlinear. Thus the conflict of immigrant fathers and sons that took place before the First World War repeated itself during the depression of the 30's, when the children of those who came at the tail end of the immigrant wave grew up. And these parallels are refracted in the literature. The first immigrant generation found its literary spokesmen in the emotional outpourings of such writers as Sholem Asch and David Pinski, and the response in a Mike Gold or an Isidor Schneider; while the second wave—more wry, disenchanted, the twice-born—found meaning in Isaac Bashevis Singer, in his gothic, bittersweet, explorations of Jewish *shtetl* life, counterpointed to such revelations as Isaac Rosenfeld and Saul Bellow made in their unsentimental, even sardonic narratives of Chicago Jewish life.

Despite overlaying, three major time spans may be demarked. One may say that the first shaping element of the American Jewish experience came to maturity in the years from 1910 to 1930, the second achieved its awareness with the depression and the war, and the third, now coming into its own, emerged in the last decade and this one.

It was in the second of these generations that the rupture with the past was sharpest, the hunger for experience keenest. In its encounter with American life, the generation broke in two: some ran hard (the Sammy Glicks and the Harry Bogens); others, more openly alienated, became radicals. Ironically, both experiences proved to be a mirage. For those who felt that they had caught the world by the tail, using money as salt, the reality proved empty enough: all that was felt, finally, was the appearance of achievement. Those who left home to seek a new community in Marxism, in the expectation that revolutionary activity could be a vehicle for experience, found themselves caught in a net of abstraction and slogans. They had won their intellectual spurs, found places in the academies or in the world of publishing, but they were politically betrayed.

The failure of radicalism together with the death of six million Jews in the Nazi gas chambers brought the generation back. Still, coming to terms with the past proved difficult. For the middle class there was Jewish organizational life; for the intellectuals, theology. But the attractions of both have tended to wither. Those whose status has become tied to Jewish life have remained in the organizational milieux. For the intellectuals who once found meaning in theology (one remembers the intense debates about Simone Weil, Martin Buber, and neo-Orthodoxy in the pages of COMMENTARY ten years ago), such problems have worn thin; the discussion has turned to more modish topics as Zen or hipsterism, or it has lapsed, more privately, into political philosophy, art, or humanistic studies.

For many of this generation, the burden of shame and guilt has tended to become less heavy through the catharsis of psychoanalysis and self-awareness, and by the attenuating passage of time. What has remained is a stoic mood, perhaps the only possible response of whoever seeks to resist the innocence of naive hope and the harshness of disillusion. Whether the generation still has a further statement to make remains to be seen.

And for the third generation? If literature is still a mirror of life, one of the most striking things about recent decades has been the disappearance, as a genre, of the *roman fleuve*—the family chronicle. Who today undertakes to write a Forsyte saga or a Pasquier chronicle? The thread of family continuity has indeed been broken. In a recent attempt, André Schwarz-Bart's *The Last of the Just*, the family chronicle (about the ancestors of Ernie Levy) seems contrived and stilted; it is no longer within the range of actual experience; the memory is more literary than real.

This seems to be the fate of the third generation: either memory is fabricated, or there is none at all. In suburbia, one sees the signs of the false parochialism, the thin veneer of identity, which rubs off at the first contact with the world. Many new temples are built, and the children go to Sunday school—because "it is good for them." The fathers have made their accommodation—through their children. Yet it cannot last, for what is unreal to the fathers is doubly so, and hypocritical, to the child; the reckoning is yet to come.

There are no parochial ties and no memories for the children of the intelligentsia. They are driven to be educated (with the British tradition as the exemplar) and to be alienated, but without the moorings of the past that their fathers sailed away from. Just as there is something sorry about individuals who become "counter-revolutionaries" without having been "revolutionaries"—accepting someone else's rancor as one's own— so there is something pathetic about proclaiming one's alienation without having known the world one is rejecting. There is, one is told, a new radicalism among the young; but without a central vision of its own, such radicalism can only be a caricature of the past. The warning from Marx is that the repetition of history is farce.

I write as one of the middle generation, one who has not faith but memory, and who has run some of its risks. I have found no "final" place, for I have no final answers. I was born in *galut* and I accept—now gladly, though once in pain—the double burden and the double pleasure of my self-consciousness, the outward life of an American and the inward secret of the Jew. I walk with this sign as a frontlet between my eyes, and it is as visible to some secret others as their sign is to me.

And yet a disquieting fact remains. If this is an identity shaped by experience, what are the "limits" of my responsibility? The philosopher F. H. Bradley (according to G. R. G. Mure's memoir of him) once remarked late in life that, being so old, he no longer had much recollection of his undergraduate days, and if someone produced evidence of a sin he had committed at that time, he would refuse to accept responsibility for it—a reflection of his doctrine that responsibility rests on the sufficient continuance of personal identity.

How responsible am I for the Jewish past, and therefore for its future? My God—even the one of memory and not of faith—is a jealous God. Do I have to accept the sins of my fathers, and my children those of mine? This is not an academic question, for it confronts us everywhere, and most particularly in "our"—the American's, the Western's, the white man's—relations with peoples who now come forth to assert their own identity. About five years ago, a group of African Negro intellectuals met in Paris, under the sponsorship of the magazine *Présence Africaine,* to debate this very question. How far, some of them asked, can the sins of the fathers be visited upon the children? What these men were saying was that one could *feel* free only after becoming free, only by some overt act of revenge, symbolic or otherwise, against those who had, by deliberately imposing an inferiority complex upon the Negro, robbed him of his identity. And yet the white men alive now were not those who had committed the original sin—though they continued to benefit from it. Should they be responsible for those who did? And, in the accents of the older tribal morality, these Negro intellectuals asserted that responsibility held unto the third and fourth generations—that the act of revenge was not immoral.

All this has been played out before. Orestes, guiltless but guilty, is driven on to carry out the blood revenge by the primitive law of retaliation. And although at the end of the Oresteia a new order of disinterested justice prevails, it is never wholly satisfying, for one feels that though the Furies have been tamed, the personal act, the act created by one's obligation to the past, has now been dissolved as well. In the *Pirke Avot* is the famous saying of Rabbi Tarfon: "It is not thy duty to complete the work, but neither art thou free to desist from it. . . ." Is this the claim which the acceptance of any parochial tie imposes upon us? This is the question raised when one realizes that one does not stand alone, that the past is still present, and that there are responsibilities of participation even when the community of which one is a part is a community woven by the thinning strands of memory.

IRVING HOWE (1920–   )

Irving Howe is one of the important literary and cultural critics of the past thirty years. An eclectic scholar, Howe has written studies of Sherwood Anderson and William Faulkner as well as books concerned with politics and the novel, the American Communist Party, and Yiddish literature. As an editor of Dissent and a contributing editor of Partisan Review, New York Times Book Review and Harper's, he has been sensitive and responsive to contemporary social and literary movements, engaging at one time in a controversial exchange with Ralph Ellison or unleashing a vitriolic attack on Kate Millett's feminist study of modern literature. Howe is an embattled critic, and one of his most admirable traits has been the fearless honesty with which he has written of complex social problems.

"I was born in New York City in 1920," he has written of himself. "My parents were Jewish immigrants and now, in retrospect, I can see how important this was to my life. It meant, on the one hand, a home atmosphere of warm and binding love, and it meant, on the other hand, an atmosphere of striving, of struggle to appropriate those goods of American life which to others come almost automatically. On the whole, I suppose, the advantage was mine, since it was more important to inherit a valuable tradition and style of life, no matter how much I was later to deviate from it, than to receive a well-stocked but unread library.

"The great event of my childhood came when, during the depression years, my father lost his little grocery business and we were plunged into severe poverty. It was this which turned me to the world of books and ideas, which pulled me out of the unreflective routine of ordinary childhood. From the cast of seriousness that was thrown over me I have been unable to escape, nor do I wish to. During the years of my early adolescence, I read an immense amount of poetry, certainly more than I ever have since; and at the same time, like so many other youngsters of my generation I became interested in politics, developing a sympathy for socialism. Since then I have become a socialist, though in the course of years my conception of socialism has gradually been modulated and complicated. For a good part of my teens I was active in the various socialist youth groups, and unlike a good many of my contemporaries I feel no regret; never having succumbed to the falsities of Stalinism I have not had to fall into another extreme as a gesture of extenuation."

Howe attended the City College of New York from 1936–1940 and went on to take graduate courses at Brooklyn College; but, as he writes, he found "the routine of graduate study appalling and quit." After serving in the Army during World War II, he began to publish in Partisan

Review *and* Commentary. *His first full-length critical studies were* Sherwood Anderson, A Critical Biography *and* William Faulkner: A Critical Study; *both of these works were seminal, early accounts of the authors' fiction, and they are marked by an intellectual clarity that makes them still valuable. Howe's other work includes* Politics and the Novel (*1962*); The American Communist Party: A Critical History (*1957*), *with Lewis Coser;* A World More Attractive (*1963*); Thomas Hardy: A Critical Study (*1970*); Steady Work (*1966*); *and* Decline of the New (*1970*). *He is also the co-editor of* A Treasury of Yiddish Poetry (*1969*) *and* A Treasury of Yiddish Stories (*1954*). *Presently, Howe has a Guggenheim fellowship to complete a study of the Jewish immigrant experience in America. Throughout his career as an author, Howe has also been an active teacher, serving on the faculties of Brandeis (1953–1961), Stanford (1961–1963), and the City University of New York at Hunter College (1963–   ).*

Sholem Aleichem: Voice of Our Past

FIFTY OR SIXTY YEARS AGO the Jewish intelligentsia, its head buzzing with Zionist, Socialist and Yiddishist ideas, tended to look down upon Sholom Aleichem. His genius was acknowledged, but his importance skimped. To the intellectual Jewish youth in both Warsaw and New York he seemed old-fashioned, lacking in complexity and rebelliousness— it is even said that he showed no appreciation of existentialism. Sh. Niger, the distinguished Yiddish critic, tried to explain this condescension by saying that laughter, the characterisic effect of Sholom Aleichem's stories, is for children and old people, not the young. Perhaps so; the young are notoriously solemn. But my own explanation would be that the Jewish intellectuals simply did not know what to make of Sholom Aleichem: they did not know how to respond to his moral poise and his invulnerability to ideological fashions.

With the passage of the years embarrassment has been replaced by indifference. Soon we shall be needing an historical expedition, armed with footnotes, to salvage his work. Even today we cannot be quite certain that our affection for him rests upon a strict regard for the words he put on the page, rather than a parochial nostalgia.

It has been customary to say that Sholom Aleichem speaks for a whole people, but saying this we might remember that his people have not spoken very well for him. The conventional estimate—that Sholom Aleichem was a folksy humorist, a sort of jolly gleeman of the *shtetl*—is radically false. He needs to be rescued from his reputation, from the quavering sentimentality which keeps him at a safe distance.

When we say that Sholom Aleichem speaks for a whole culture, we can mean that in his work he represents all the significant levels of behavior and class in the *shtetl* world, thereby encompassing the style of life of the east European Jews in the nineteenth century. In that sense, however, it may be doubted that he does speak for the whole *shtetl* culture. For he does not command the range of a Balzac or even a Faulkner, and he does not present himself as the kind of writer who is primarily concerned with social representation. The ambition, or disease, of literary "scope" leaves him untouched.

Nor can we mean, in saying that Sholom Aleichem speaks for a whole culture, that he advances the conscious program of that culture. Toward the dominant Jewish ideologies of his time Sholom Aleichem showed a characteristic mixture of sympathy and skepticism, and precisely this modesty enabled him to achieve a deeper relation to the *folksmassen* than any Jewish political leader. He never set himself up as cultural spokesman or institution, in the style of Thomas Mann at his worst; he had no interest in boring people.

Sholom Aleichem speaks for the culture of the east European Jews because he embodies—not represents—its essential values in the very accents and rhythm of his speech, in the inflections of his voice and the gestures of his hands, in the pauses and suggestions between the words even more than the words themselves. To say that a writer represents a culture is to imply that a certain distance exists between the two. But that is not at all the relationship between Sholom Aleichem and the culture of the east European Jews: it is something much more intimate and elusive, something for which, having so little experience of it, we can barely find a name. In Sholom Aleichem everything that is deepest in the ethos of the east European Jews is brought to fulfillment and climax. He is, I think, the only modern writer who may truly be said to be a culture-hero, a writer whose work releases those assumptions of his people, those tacit gestures of bias, which undercut opinion and go deeper into communal life than values.

In his humorous yet often profoundly sad stories, Sholom Aleichem gave to the Jews what they instinctively felt was the right and true judgment of their experience: a judgment of love through the medium of irony. Sholom Aleichem is the great poet of Jewish humanism and Jewish transcendence over the pomp of the world. For the Jews of Eastern Europe he was protector and advocate; he celebrated their communal tradition; he defended their style of life and constantly underlined their passionate urge to dignity. But he was their judge as well: he ridiculed their pretensions, he mocked their vanity, and he constantly reiterated the central dilemma, that simultaneous tragedy and joke, of their exist- ence—the irony of their claim to being a Chosen People, indeed, the irony of their existence at all.

Sholom Aleichem's Yiddish is one of the most extraordinary verbal achievements of modern literature, as important in its way as T. S. Eliot's revolution in the language of English verse or Berthold Brecht's infusion of street language into the German lyric. Sholom Aleichem uses a sparse and highly controlled vocabulary; his medium is so drenched with irony that the material which comes through it is often twisted and elevated into direct tragic statement—irony multiples upon itself to become a deep winding sadness. Many of his stories are monologues, still close to the oral folk tradition, full of verbal by-play, slow in pace, winding in direc- tion, but always immediate and warm in tone. His imagery is based on an absolute mastery of the emotional rhythm of Jewish life; describing the sadness of a wheezing old clock, he writes that it was "a sadness like that in the song of an old, worn-out cantor toward the end of Yom Kippur"— and how sad that is only someone who has heard such a cantor and therefore knows the exquisite rightness of the image can really say.

The world of Sholom Aleichem is bounded by three major characters, each of whom has risen to the level of Jewish archetype: Tevye the Dairyman; Menachem Mendel the *luftmensch;* and Mottel the cantor's son, who represents the loving, spontaneous possibilities of Jewish child- hood. Tevye remains rooted in his little town, delights in displaying his uncertain Biblical learning, and stays close to the sources of Jewish sur- vival. Solid, slightly sardonic, fundamentally innocent, Tevye is the folk voice quarreling with itself, criticizing God from an abundance of love, and realizing in its own low-keyed way all that we mean, or should mean, by humaneness.

Tevye represents the generation of Jews that could no longer find complete deliverance in the traditional God yet could not conceive of abandoning Him. No choice remained, therefore, but to celebrate the earthly condition; poverty and hope. For if you had become skeptical of deliverance from above and had never accepted the heresy of deliverance from below, what could you do with poverty but celebrate it? "In Kasrilevke," says Tevye, "there are experienced authorities on the subject of hunger, one might say specialists. On the darkest night, simply by hearing your voice, they can tell if you are hungry and would like a bite to eat, or if you are really starving." Tevye, like the people for whom he speaks, is constantly assaulted by outer forces. The world comes to him, most insidiously, in the form of undesired sons-in-law: one who is poverty-stricken but romantic; another who is a revolutionist and ends in Siberia; a third—could anything be worse?—who is a gentile; and a fourth—this *is* worse—who is a Jew but rich, coarse, and unlearned.

Menachem Mendel, Tevye's opposite, personifies the element of restlessness and soaring, of speculation and fancy-free idealization, in Jewish character. He has a great many occupations: broker, insurance agent, matchmaker, coal dealer, and finally—it is inevitable—writer; but his fundamental principle in life is to keep moving. The love and longing he directs toward his unfound millions are the love and longing that later Jews direct toward programs and ideologies. He is the utopian principle of Jewish life; he is driven by the modern demon. Through Tevye and Menachem Mendel, flanked by little Mottel, Sholom Aleichem creates his vision of the Yiddish world.

There is a strong element of fantasy, even surrealism, in Sholom Aleichem. Strange things happen: a tailor becomes enchanted, a clock strikes thirteen, money disappears in the synagogue during Yom Kippur, a woman's corpse is dragged across the snow, a timid little Jew looks at himself in the mirror and sees the face of a Czarist officer. Life is precarious, uncertain, fearful, yet always bound by a sense of community and affection.

Sholom Aleichem came at a major turning point in the history of the east European Jews: between the unquestioned dominance of religious belief and the appearance of modern ideologies, between the past of traditional Judaism and the future of Jewish politics, between a totally integrated culture and a culture that by a leap of history would soon plunge into the midst of modern division and chaos. Yet it was the mark of Sholom Aleichem's greatness that, coming as he did at this point of transition, he betrayed no moral imbalance or uncertainty of tone. He remained unmoved by the fanaticisms of his time, those that were Jewish and those that were not; he lost himself neither to the delusions of the past nor the delusions of the future. His work is the fulfillment—pure, relaxed, humane—of that moment in the history of the Jews in which a people lives securely with itself, untroubled by any dualism, hardly aware of a distinction, between the sacred and secular.

The world he presented was constantly precarious and fearful, yet the vision from which it was seen remained a vision of absolute assurance. It was a vision controlled by that sense of Jewish humaneness which held the best of—even as it transcended—both the concern with the other world that had marked the past and the eagerness to transform this world that would mark the future. His work abounds in troubles, but only rarely does it betray anxiety.

In reading Sholom Aleichem one seldom thinks to wonder about his opinions. He stands between the age of faith and the age of ideology, but I doubt that there has ever been a reader naive enough to ask whether Sholom Aleichem *really* believed in God. For him it was not a living question, no more than it was for the people who read him. To say that he believed in God may be true, but it is also irrelevant. To say that he did not believe in God is probably false, but equally irrelevant.

What Sholom Aleichem believed in was the Jews who lived with him and about him, most of them Jews still believing in God. Or perhaps he believed in those Jews who lived so completely in the orbit of their fathers—fathers who had surely believed in God—that there was no need for them to ask such questions.

In Sholom Aleichem's stories God is there, not because He is God, not because there is any recognition or denial of His heavenly status, but simply because He figures as an actor in the life of the Jews. God becomes absorbed into the vital existence of the people, or to put it more drastically: God is there because Tevye is there.

But Tevye, does *he* believe in God? Another hopeless question. Tevye believes in something more important than believing in God; he believes in talking to God. And Tevye talks to God as to an old friend whom one need not flatter or assuage: Tevye, as we say in American slang, gives Him an earful.

Tevye, we may assume, makes God extremely uncomfortable—though also a little proud at the thought that, amid the countless failures of His world, He should at least have created a Tevye who can make him so sublimely uncomfortable. And how does Tevye do this? By telling God the complete truth. It is not a pretty truth, and if God would care to dispute anything Tevye has told him, Tevye is entirely prepared to discuss it with Him further. But whatever other mistakes He may have made, God is too clever to get into an argument with Tevye. God knows that Tevye does not fear Him: a Jew is afraid of people, not of God. So perhaps you can see how absurd it is to ask whether Sholom Aleichem *really* believed in God: —Sholom Aleichem who created a character to serve as the conscience of God.

All this comes through in Sholom Aleichem's stories as a blend of rapture and the absurd, sublimity and household ordinariness. Nor is it confined to Sholom Aleichem alone. In the poems of Jacob Glatstein, one of the great living Yiddish writers, there is a whole series of loving and estranged monologues to God. Glatstein writes: "I love my sorrowful

God/ My companion . . . I love to sit with Him upon a stone/ And to pour out all my words . . . And there He sits with me, my friend, my companion, clasping me/ And shares His last bite of food with me." Later, in the same poem, Glatstein adds: "The God of my unbelief is magnificent . . . My God sleeps and I watch over him/ My weary brother dreams the dream of my people."

Had Tevye lived through the events of the past thirty years, that is how he would have felt.

Sholom Aleichem believed in Jews as they embodied the virtues of powerlessness and the healing resources of poverty, as they stood firm against the outrage of history, indeed, against the very idea of history itself. Whoever is unable to conceive of such an outlook as at least an extreme possibility, whoever cannot imagine the power of a messianism turned away from the apocalyptic future and inward toward a living people, cannot understand Sholom Aleichem or the moment in Jewish experience from which he stems.

It is here that the alien reader may go astray. He may fail to see that for someone like Tevye everything pertaining to Jewishness can be a curse and an affliction, a wretched joke, a source of mockery and despair, but that being a Jew is nevertheless something to be treasured. Treasured, because in the world of Tevye there was a true matrix of human sociability.

The stories Sholom Aleichem told his readers were often stories they already knew, but then, as the Hasidic saying goes, they cared not for the words but the melody. What Sholom Aleichem did was to give back to them the very essence of their life and hope, in a language of exaltation: the exaltation of the ordinary.

When Tevye talked to his horse, it was the same as if he were talking to his wife. When he talked to his wife, it was the same is if he were talking to God. And when he talked to God, it was the same as if he were talking to his horse. That, for Tevye, was what it meant to be a Jew.

Between Sholom Aleichem and his readers there formed a community of outcasts: *edele kaptzunim*. Millions of words flowed back and forth, from writer to reader and reader to writer, for no people has ever talked so much in all recorded history; yet their companionship did not rest upon or even require words.

The last thing I wish to suggest here is an image of the sweetly pious or sentimental. Sholom Aleichem did not hesitate to thrust his barbs at his readers, and they were generous at reciprocating. Having love, they had no need for politeness. But the love of which I speak here is sharply different from that mindless ooze, that collapse of will, which the word suggests to Americans. It could be argumentative, fierce, bitter, violent; it could be ill-tempered and even vulgar; only one thing it could not be: lukewarm.

The Jews never fooled Sholom Aleichem. Peretz, I think, was sometimes deceived by the culture of the east European Jews, and Sholom Asch tried to deceive it at the end of his career. But with Sholom Aleichem, even as he was the defender of the Jews and their culture, there was always a sly wrinkle near his eyes which as soon as Jews saw it, they said to themselves: *Im ken men nisht upnaren,* him you cannot deceive. That is why, when you go through his stories, you find so little idealization, so little of that cozy self-indulgence and special pleading which is the curse of Jewish life. Between Sholom Aleichem and his readers there is a bond of that wary respect which grows up among clever men who recognize each other's cleverness, enjoy it and are content.

Middleton Murry once said of Thomas Hardy that "the contagion of the world's slow stain has not touched him." This magnificent remark must have referred to something far more complex and valuable than innocence, for no one could take Hardy to be merely innocent; it must have referred to the artist's final power, the power to see the world as it is, to love it and yet not succumb to it; and that is the power one finds in Sholom Aleichem.

NATHAN GLAZER (1923–   )

Nathan Glazer was born in New York on February 25, 1923. After graduating from the City College in 1944, he studied at the University of Pennsylvania (M.A., 1945) and at Columbia University (Ph.D., 1962).

During the 1940's and '50's, Glazer served on the editorial staff of Commentary *and published widely in the field of sociology. In 1948 he took a leave of absence from* Commentary *and collaborated with David Riesman and Reuel Denney on a study of mass communications which resulted, in 1950, in* The Lonely Crowd: A Study of the Changing American Character. *This study of "tradition-directed," "inner-directed," and "outer-directed" people was followed by interviews which were collected in* Faces in the Crowd. *Glazer's other books include* American Judaism *(1957),* Studies in Housing and Minority Groups *(1960),* The Social Basis of American Communism *(1961), and* Beyond the Melting Pot *(1963), with Daniel Moynihan. He has taught at many universities: the University of California at Berkeley, Bennington and Smith Colleges, Harvard, and Stanford.*

The Religion of American Jews

WHAT ELSE is there? What in the feelings and sentiments of Jews can we see as reflecting their ancestral religion?

We must begin with something that has not happened; this negative something is the strongest and, potentially, most significant religious reality among American Jews: it is that the Jews have not stopped being Jews. I do not now speak of the fact that they are sociologically defined as Jews; this is of small significance from the point of view of Jewish religion. I speak rather of the fact that they still *choose* to be Jews, that they do not cast off the yoke or burden of the Jewish heritage. Despite the concreteness of the words "yoke" and "burden," what I have in mind is something very abstract. It is not that most Jews in this country submit themselves to the Jewish law; they do not. Nor can they tell you what the Jewish heritage is. But they do not know it may demand something of them, and to that demand, insofar as it is brought to them and has any meaning for them, they will not answer. No. The significance of the fact that they have not cast off the yoke is that they are prepared to be Jews, though not to be the Jews their grandfathers were. The medieval world is gone and Orthodox Judaism is only a survival (as the anthropologists use the word) so far as the majority of American Jews is concerned. But they are prepared to be some kind of Jews; they are capable of being moved and reached and of transcending the pedestrian life that so many of them live in company with other Americans.

In my view, it is because of this negative characteristic, this refusal to become non-Jews, that we see today a flourishing of Jewish religious institutions. It is true that these institutions do not evoke or engage any deep religious impulses and find their greatest strength in a weak acceptance of the mores of middle-class life. Yet they are successful only because American Jews are ready to be Jews, because they are willing to be inducted into Jewish life.

We see the reality of this readiness in the fact that to every generation of recent times a different part of the Jewish past has become meaningful. At the same time, to be sure, other parts of that tradition, great chunks without which it seemed it must die, were rejected. And yet at no point has everything been rejected at once; a kind of shifting balance has been maintained whereby each generation could relate itself meaningfully to some part of the Jewish past. It has been the course of events that has dictated which part of the Jewish past should become more prominent at any given moment—at one time, and for some Jews, it was philanthropy; at another time, and for other Jews, Zionism or Yiddish-speaking socialism; or, as today, institutional religion. The son of the Reform Jewish philanthropist who gives up the last Jewish connections his father maintained may surprise us by becoming what his father never was, a Zionist. The son of the Yiddish-speaking socialist who abandons his father's movement may join the Reform temple. In this way, each generation shoulders a minimal part of the yoke.

There are even more complex patterns than this in the maintenance of a minimal relation to Judaism. There are American Jews who have been given a good traditional education and who, following the pattern of the twenties or thirties, have broken with all religious observance. They do not attend the synagogue, they do not observe the dietary laws, they do not mark the Jewish holidays, and they do not believe in the existence of God. When this kind of Jew has children, however, he will decide that they should have some sort of Jewish education.

Such a man is not succumbing to suburban middle-class pressures; he can resist them as easily as can the classic village atheist. He may tell himself—and believe—that the children should know what it means to be a Jew, for willy-nilly they will be considered Jews and they must know how to cope with anti-Semitism. But one sees at work here that obscure process whereby a minimal relation to Judaism is established. The mental calculus seems to be as follows: Since I myself have had a good traditional education, I can afford to be an agnostic or an atheist. My child won't get such an education, but he should at least get a taste of the Jewish religion.

Philanthropy, Zionism, Jewish organizational life, attachment to Yiddish, an interest in Hasidism, a love of Hebrew, formal religious affiliation, a liking for Jewish jokes and Jewish food—none of these has, on the surface, any particularly religious meaning. Each of them reflects the concerns of the moment. The Protestant social gospel, the needs of Jews in other parts of the world, varied philosophical movements, a tendency to take pride in one's origins—each finds an echo in American Judaism. It is easy to overlook any common element in the different forms of Judaism of the different generations and see only the reflection of movements in society and thought at large. Yet what binds all these shifting manifestations of Judaism and Jewishness together is the common refusal to throw off the yoke. The refusal to become non-Jews stems from an attitude of mind that seems to be—and indeed in large measure is—a stubborn insistence on remaining a Jew, enhanced by no particularly ennobling idea of what that means. And yet it has the effect of relating American Jews, let them be as ignorant of Judaism as a Hottentot, to a great religious tradition. Thus, the insistence of the Jews on remaining Jews, which may take the religiously indifferent forms of liking Yiddish jokes, supporting Israel, raising money for North African Jews, and preferring certain kinds of food, has a potentially religious meaning. It means that the Jewish religious tradition is not just a subject for scholars but is capable now and then of finding expression in life. And even if it finds no expression in one generation or another, the commitment to remain related to it still exists. Dead in one, two, or three generations, it may come to life in the fourth.

Or, indeed, it may not. Perhaps it is only an act of piety to preserve the relatedness to tradition. Perhaps nothing can come out of it any more, and all that remains for Jews is to act as the custodians of a museum. This is possible, too.

Yet if something were to happen, what would it be like? If the bland religious life of middle-class American Jews were to become, even to some small part of the Jewish population (we could not expect more), more alive and meaningful, what form would the change take? In the most tentative way, I would like to suggest what this form might be, by way of a description of one of the most exotic, and on the surface least significant, manifestations of Jewish religious life.

Up to now I have spoken almost entirely of what is, historically speaking, new in American Jewish life—the Reform movement, the Conservative movement, the suburban developments. I have said little of what is old—the Orthodox life of the ghettos of the big cities—because, indeed, there is little to say. It has survived—barely; and that we have said.

Today the areas of first settlement are, in all but the largest cities, deserted. The synagogues that were once churches are now churches again, or are boarded up. Negroes and Puerto Ricans now run through the corridors of settlement houses and schools in which a whole generation of Jewish business and professional men were educated. In the largest city, New York, perhaps two or three hundred thousand Jews still live in such "first settlement" neighborhoods.

The Orthodoxy of the areas of first settlement, as I have said, had almost no lasting hold on the children. As they grew up and married, they moved away—if their parents had not already moved away. If, thirty years ago, an authority had been asked to predict the future of the Lower East Side in New York and of Williamsburg in Brooklyn, he would have indicated the further decline of the Jewish population and its eventual replacement by Negroes or some new immigrant group. This is what had already happened to the neighborhoods of first Jewish settlement in smaller Jewish communities like that in Cincinnati.

In one of these areas of first settlement, however, there was a revival of an Orthodoxy of the most extreme sort that won over many of the children of the less extreme Orthodox—and even went beyond them. In Williamsburg, in Brooklyn, in a small area containing about twenty thousand people, three-quarters of them Jews, an Orthodox revival took place which, while it will never affect any but the most Orthodox fringes of American Jewry, still has something to tell us about the other variants of Jewish religious life in America.

In the middle and late thirties, the well-to-do of Williamsburg were moving out, and the half-dozen large synagogues, along with many small ones, were steadily losing members and support. A well-known and extremely Orthodox yeshiva, an all-day Jewish school for boys, and various other institutions of Orthodoxy remained. George Kranzler, writing about what happened in Williamsburg, points out that this neighborhood, undesirable to live in from almost every point of view, was attractive to Orthodox Jews because it permitted them to live a fully Jewish life as no other area did. They were willing to put up with decrepit and verminous tenement apartments, even though many could afford better elsewhere. The less Orthodox who improved their condition moved out; the more Othodox moved in. From the late thirties on, the latter included a larger and larger proportion of refugees from Germany, Austria, Czechoslovakia, and other countries overrun by Hitler. Soon the "natives" of Williamsburg, who had prided themselves on their Orthodoxy and considered themselves the most Orthodox element in American life, found themselves outflanked by even more Orthodox elements from Europe.

But this was only the beginning. As Hitler moved into eastern Europe, he reached the area around the Carpathian Moutains where

those European Jews least touched by Westernization and Western influences lived. Here Hasidism, the enthusiastic and mystical sect founded
in eastern Europe in the eighteenth century, was still strong. Many of
these Jews were dragged off to extermination camps. After the war, the
survivors gathered in the DP camps to study the Talmud again and re-
establish their communities around their surviving *rebbes*—as the leaders
of the Hasidic groups are called. In the late forties, a few Hasidic *rebbes*
who had settled with some followers in Williamsburg were joined by
rebbes of much greater fame and with many more supporters. The
Williamsburg norm of Orthodoxy was confirmed and heightened by this
influx. The Hasidic groups established kindergartens and all-day schools
for boys and girls and acquired large buildings to use as residences for
their *rebbes* and as synagogues.

Up to this point, we have been describing a situation in which a particularly backward and archaic group of Jews, uprooted by war, had
successfully re-established their old life in a small area. We know what
(generally) happens to such ethnic enclaves: the children go to public
school and no one generation or at most two is enough to make ordinary
Americans of them, except for those really exceptional groups like the
Mennonites who are capable of resisting the larger environment.

But there is more to this particular story, and it is its most interesting
part. First, Dr. Kranzler asserts, the children of this extremely Orthodox
element in Williamsburg remain loyal to Orthodoxy in proportions far
greater than ever before. One can partially understand this when one
realizes that almost none of them goes to public school. We have here,
for the first time, something that might become a Jewish equivalent of
the Mennonites but with a stronger potential appeal to other Jews than
the Mennonites have for other Protestants.

And, second, and this is quite unique in American Jewish religious
life, the Williamsburg Hasidim have made "converts." It is true the
Hasidim did not settle among Conservative or Reform or indifferent Jews;
we are not dealing with a modern religious miracle. As I have said, the
Jews of Williamsburg were already Orthodox before the Hasidic influx.
Young, somewhat pious Williamsburg Jews would attend the services of
a Hasidic *rebbe*, drawn by curiosity, and be swept up by the singing and
dancing, moved by the personality of the *rebbe*, and impressed by the
devotion of his followers; many would become followers themselves.

Jews from other districts would also come to see the Hasidim; on
occasion—very rare occasions—a young Jew not of Orthodox background,
seeking religious expression, who might in earlier years have been converted to Christianity, would visit the Hasidim and find some personal

fulfilment in following their way of life. We speak of Williamsburg, because we are guided there by Dr. Kranzler's excellent study; but actually the most important of the Hasidic *rebbes* to come to America, the Lubavitcher *rebbe* who leads the Habad Hasidim, did not settle in Williamsburg. This group has had remarkable success in establishing Jewish parochial schools, not only in New York City, but in communities throughout the country, and has been most successful in attracting the interest and even allegiance of young, American-born Jews.

The reason I have described this development is not that it strikes me as a stirring in distant parts that may some day influence the whole but that it illustrates a central pattern of Jewish religious life, a pattern which I believe is somewhat distinctive, particularly as compared with what we normally expect in Christianity. The role that in Christianity is played by God's grace—operating either directly or through inspired intermediates—is taken in Judaism by the holy community. It is that which touches and moves people, and brings them back to the faith. And the return to the faith, which in Christianity means the acceptance of beliefs—a creed, a dogma, or simply that Jesus saves—in Judaism means the return to the community, which is made holy because it lives under God's law.

The return to religion of the formerly secular-minded Yiddish writers that I spoke of in chapter vii also means the return to a community— not in this case to an actual Jewish community of today but to the community they recall from their childhood, somewhat idealized.

In Judaism, it is not God directly, found after an inner search, that changes man, but the example of the good and holy life, presented by the community of Jews, whether in actuality or as a historical myth or as an ideal. The disciples of the Hasidim in Williamsburg see this community before their eyes; the returning Yiddish writers recall it from the past.

But what of all the rest of American Jews, who find hardly anything attractive in either Hasidism or the Judaism of past ages, as defined by its 613 commandments? For them, the matter is far more difficult. Neither the living examples of today nor the examples of the past, of "normative" Judaism, seem viable in a modern society.

Nevertheless, the creation of examples proceeds, pragmatically and clumsily, within both the Conservative and the Reform groups. The Conservative movement struggles with the necessity of maintaining some of the practices of Orthodox Judaism, urges the use of Hebrew, speaks of the fellowship that should bind together the world-wide community of Jews. It has no desire to create a creed. Instead of depending on the attraction of a philosophy, which may convince people by reason or by giving them answers, it depends on the example of a Jewish life, which it is trying to create directly.

This is why Hebrew is so important to Conservative Judaism. What is the good, it has been asked, of taking children away for a summer to a Hebrew-speaking camp (as is done more and more frequently in the Conservative group) so that they may learn to say "Please pass the butter" in Hebrew? It makes one no more of a believer to know how to speak in Hebrew than in English. What is happening, however, is that the Conservative Jewish leaders, like the Hasidic *rebbes*, are trying to provide an example of a Jewish life so that it will not be necessary to argue and put out apologetic literature—it will only be necessary to point to a community that exists and that gives an example of what it is to be a good Jew.

In the same way, the Reform movement, once so concerned with formulating a creed, is now indifferent to that problem, but rather asks itself: What example of a Jewish life should we present, what rituals should we urge for the home, how much Hebrew should we require a Jew to know, what kind of ethical behavior should being a Jew impose on one?

Here we are, of course, very far from the Hasidim of Williamsburg, who need not ponder about what kind of Jewish life to live, though even they have certain problems in this respect. They are guided by tradition, and by leaders whose word is law. Among other Jews—and this includes Orthodox as well as Conservative and Reform Jews—the problem is the creation of a meaningful Jewish life whose power can make itself felt over those many Jews who remain, and wish to remain, open to the influence of an example. If Judaism is to become in America more than a set of religious institutions supported by a variety of social pressures, it will be by virtue of examples of Jewish lives that in some way are meaningful, that in some way permit one to be a Jew. It would be ridiculous to set up qualifications for these examples, to say that they may spring up in this or that grouping in American Jewish religious life and not in the other. What can fulfil a human life cannot be known in advance. All we can know, from the history of Judaism, is that the abstract demand to seek faith, to find God, tends to find little answer among Jews and that concrete examples of Jewish living must be given before religion has an impact on their lives. Once again, honesty requires one to say it is possible that no satisfactory example can be given in the modern world.

THEODORE SOLOTAROFF (1928–)

Of the literary critics who have addressed themselves almost exclusively to contemporary writers, Theodore Solotaroff has been among the most perceptive. Born in 1928 in Elizabeth, New Jersey, he was educated at the University of Michigan and the University of Chicago. He has taught at Indiana University and the University of Chicago, and he has served as an associate editor of Commentary, Book Week, *and the literary supplement of the* New York Herald Tribune.

Solotaroff is best known for his work as editor of New American Review, *which first printed large portions of* Portnoy's Complaint *and the work of other contemporary writers. He has edited* The Age of Enormity, Essays by Isaac Rosenfeld *and* Writers and Issues, Essays on the Sixties. *His own collection of essays and reviews is entitled* The Red Hot Vacuum.

Harry Golden and the American Audience

In October 1958 the Delphian Club of Forrest City, Arkansas, met for one of its literary teas. The "theme" of the program was "Americanism," which was illustrated by the floral arrangements and refreshments, and by the book that had been chosen for discussion—Harry Golden's *Only in America*. Since a considerable portion of Golden's book was occupied by his stand in favor of integration, it might seem curious that it should have been so honored by the ladies of a state which only a year before, at Little Rock, had threatened to oppose the desegregation of its schools by force of arms. No less curious, perhaps, was the fact that the recollections, attitudes, and tone of an unregenerate Lower-East-Side Jew should have been taken by these small-town Southern Protestant women as an exemplary expression of Americanism.

But the enthusiasm in the Delphian Club for Golden's liberal wit and Jewish wisdom was hardly exceptional and, by this time, hardly surprising. Published three months before, *Only in America*—a risky publishing venture at the start—had been the spectacular hit of the summer season. And the rush to the bookstores for this collection of snippets from the *Carolina Israelite*, Golden's one-man newspaper, seems to have been matched by the rush of the reviewers into print to praise it. Stamped across the cover of the 1,750,000 copies of the paperback edition sold in the first year (the sales of the trade edition ran to 250,000) was the legend: the "best seller which has taken all America by storm and which all America has taken to its heart"—and for once these time-worn claims appear to have been perfectly true.

Out of some several hundred reviews this writer has examined of

Only in America, exactly two declined to participate in the love feast between Golden and his audience. This "miracle . . . of receptivity"—as Nathan Ziprin, a syndicated Jewish columnist, called it—transcended not only regional prejudices but political, social, and intellectual ones as well. On the far left, the Communist *Worker* rejoiced in Golden's "lusty" way of "ridiculing Jim Crow hypocrisy and know-nothingism," while on the far right, the Chicago *Tribune* was delighted by the "sympathy and humor" with which Golden handled minority-group problems as well as the "approval," "tolerance," and "tart wisdom" with which he surveyed the American scene generally. He was praised as fulsomely by the *Nation* as by Hearst's Chicago *American,* just as he later charmed the skeptics both of *Time* and of the *New Yorker.* In the middle of a food column in the New York *Town and Village* (a solid, middle-class paper from Stuyvesant Town), the writer interrupted describing an experience with Italian sausages at the home of a friend to marvel at Golden's "warm and loving and thought-provoking philosophy"; meanwhile, across town in Greenwich Village's off-beat *Voice,* a writer applauded the acid satire with which Golden put down the hypocrisy of Brotherhood Week in the South. The Springfield (Massachusetts) *Republican* observed, that "there's still a lot of us who are neither eggheads nor beatniks, and Harry Golden says right out in print what we've been thinking." At the same time, intellectuals elsewhere were claiming this "urbane," "erudite" journalist as their own, in their own terms. Writing in the *Saturday Review,* Joseph Wood Krutch spoke of Golden's "amiable Rabelaisian streak," and wound up saying that "as a debunker . . . Mr. Golden is closer to Montaigne than to Mencken." Gerald Johnson found Golden to be less sentimental than Dickens, before running him through a battery of flattering comparisons with Socrates, Montaigne, and Anatole France.

And so it has gone with *For 2¢ Plain and Enjoy, Enjoy!,* Golden's next two collections of miscellaneous pieces from the *Carolina Israelite* and from the widely syndicated newspaper columns he began to write following the success of *Only in America.* Today, some two years after his rise to national fame, the tide of affection and approval may be falling slightly, but Golden's prestige is still such that *Life* selected him from among all the Jewish intellectuals and leaders in the country to stamp its publication of the Eichmann confession as kosher. It is still worth asking, then, why Golden looms as the most widely attractive writer to emerge in recent years.

Before looking into the more immediate sources of Golden's success, one ought to note that it probably owes something to the traditions of native American humor. From the *Farmer's Almanac* to Will Rogers, from Finley Peter Dunne to Sam Levenson, there has been a stream of humorists who, both in their kinds of wit and popularity, anticipate this "Yenkee Tarheel." American humor has, until fairly recently, been largely a marginal-group humor. During the nineteenth century such humorists mainly exploited the idiom and folkways of the Yankee farmer, the Southwest hunter or adventurer, the Far West prospector and gambler. The practice of out-group humor was so strongly entrenched that highly literate New Englanders like James Russell Lowell and Harriet Beecher Stowe and a host of bookish Southern lawyers like Augustus Longstreet, Joseph Baldwin, and Johnson J. Hooper usually turned to it when they were trying to be satirical or just funny.

Toward the end of the nineteenth century, a parallel tradition developed as the European immigrants settled in and began to produce their own comic spokesmen, who cast upon the American mind the exotic, incongruous images of the new form of marginal life. Relying upon ethnic rather than regional coloring, and creating a city rather than a rural humor, the Irish and Jewish comedians followed their native American prototypes in bringing their Gallaghers and Sheans, Potashes and Perlmutters into some sort of problematic relation with American society, and using the immunity of the clown to make some telling hits on its political, social, or moral follies. Also, they continued the traditional role of native humorists in keeping alive the sense of individuality and diversity, of a common touch and an uncorrupted shrewdness, all regarded as particularly American. Thus the redneck and the greenhorn provided America not only with most of its laughs but also with a considerable amount of self-criticism and even of self-definition.

These two parallel traditions of humorists have remained alive through the past five decades, becoming modified, to be sure, as regional and ethnic differences weaken and blur through their rapid assimilation by the cultural blender of the middle class. However, many of the major characteristics have continued to be fairly distinct and to maintain their appeal. For example, in the 1920's a champion long-run hit, *Abie's Irish Rose,* was manufactured by bringing together the two leading strains of immigrant life; and Milt Gross, Arthur Kober, Leo Rosten, Sam Levenson, among others, have gone on amusing a large audience by their comic presentations of the Jewish corner of the American scene. And now there has emerged the humorist who—if one is to accept the common description of Harry Golden as "the Jewish Will Rogers"—seems to have combined the native and immigrant traditions.

Anyone who is at all familiar with the history of American humor will not be surprised at the delight Golden calls forth by his demotic readings of history and literature (Cleopatra was the greatest call-girl in history, the Roman Empire fell because the women were left home with the "Senators and the 4-F's"); or by his whimsical nostrums for social ills (ending school segregation by removing the chairs from Southern class-rooms or destroying anti-Semitism by having the Jews threaten to convert); or by his good-natured inventory of the oddities and odd-balls of the ghetto and of the quirks and foibles of American society generally; or by the relish he takes in pointing out the chicaneries of politicians and in deflating a stuffed shirt; or, finally, by a homey touch which manages to merge Jewish "understanding" and American horse sense.

But to say there is a historical background for Golden's role hardly explains the magnitude of this popularity or covers its significance. Clearly, he speaks to and reflects a present-day state of mind. Since the reviewers of his three books have been largely preoccupied with the question of why they and their constituencies find him so pleasing and useful, a number of clues can readily be picked up from them.

Of the several areas of consensus, the leading one, perhaps, has to do with the reviewers' interest in and respect for Golden as an American Jew and as a raconteur of the delightful, instructive world of the erst-while Lower-East-Side ghetto. In his introduction to *Only in America,* Carl Sandburg remarks that it is an outstandingly "pro-Semitic book," a point that was echoed repeatedly in the newspaper reviews. The Chicago *Tribune* suggested that Golden's "tart wisdom" is "rooted in the mores of an Old Testament society." A writer for a Baptist Sunday-school book service in the South attributed not only Golden's delicious nostalgia but also his wisdom and penetration to his "Yiddish heart." And his "lovely Jewish slant on the world" was related by a host of reviewers to his grasp of history, to his compassionate understanding of the modern problem of Negroes and other minority groups, as well as of "the proud, embattled, defensive Presbyterians of Charlotte" because (according to Harry Ashmore) Golden himself is "the unapologetic product of a close-knit embattled defensive community." Other connections were made between his Jewishness and his reverence for family relations, his faith in the brotherhood of man, his optimism, his whimsical humor, his sense of paradox, his humility, his individuality, his perseverance, his erudition, his righteousness, his politics, and his appreciation of good food.

Telling its Jewish readers that *Only in America* "will make you proud to be a Jew," the Worcester (Mass.) *Sunday Telegram* left its other readers with the thought that Golden's pieces "increase your respect for the folk who have been with us since approximately the landing of the *Mayflower*." Here, as elsewhere, Golden's unabashed Jewishness was taken as the leading sign of his most widely celebrated quality—his "sincerity." A writer in the *Village Voice* summed up the over-all reaction, saying that "Golden's most important asset is that he presents his Jewish heritage in a manner that arouses admiration, amusement, and even envy."

Even envy? Well, the attitude reflected by Golden's reviewers is further evidence, perhaps the strongest yet, that for a writer to be recognizably Jewish in American today is an asset, that "the Jewish slant" is decidedly in vogue—whether the bourgeois pieties warmed over by Herman Wouk, or the tough, brooding moral imagination of Bernard Malamud, or the inspirational theology of Buber, or the folksy simplicity of Leo Rosten and Sam Levenson, or the sophisticated wit and candor of Saul Bellow and Philip Roth. It is significant that the attraction Golden exerts even touches, here and there, the prose of his reviewers: the Baptist woman in the South who uses the phrase "yiddishe heart" is not just characterizing Golden; in a small and subtle way, she is reaching out toward what she believes he possesses. To be sure, there is a hint here and there of the old condescension, as in *Time's* faintly patronizing puns about Golden as a "leprecohen" who is waging a "blintzkrieg." But the "Yiddishe heart" phrase is far more typical. One finds a four-square critic like Leslie Hanscom of the New York *World-Telegram,* among many others, straining after expressions that not only emulate Golden's prose but suggest the same kind of quasi-identification with the Jewish mentality.

None of this seems to have come as a surprise to Golden. In one of his more expansive interviews, for the *Jewish Post,* he remarks: "I knew the Jews would be lukewarm but that the goyim of America would go nuts over it." And he continues: "The names of the Americans who are pleading with me to accept them as Jews would amaze you." In the same interview he attributed the fascination of his Gentile readers as being partly

due to the fact that I have eliminated the "Jewish joke" of Sam Levenson and the dialect of Mr. Kober. These fellows are anachronisms. They will thrive for a little longer but basically they are on the way out. . . . The "Jewish" humor on the American scene is part of the humor involved in the entire American middle-class. I have eliminated the ghetto for good, I hope.

Golden's view of his work is quite accurate. His prose has only a flavoring touch left of the pungent Yiddish influence and is pretty much the English spoken by the second-generation businessman. Similarly,

Golden's humor tends to be a middle-class type that strains for effects and softens the edge, in contrast to the older Jewish humor with its abundant supply of natural, resonant incongruities. Golden will describe in detail the long, involved process by which a family finally bought a suit for their son, but it isn't really very funny because he is much more interested in explaining the Jews to the Gentiles than he is in portraying the special comedy and pathos of the ghetto for their own sake.

As for the ghetto itself, whether or not he has managed to "eliminate" it, he certainly has bent the shape and feeling of its life to his special uses. If his treatment of the Lower-East-Side has been one of the great selling points of his books, one reason seems to be that he has taken care to make the ghetto easily comprehensible to his Gentile readers—less ghetto, in fact, than a kind of incipient suburb where a steady stream of immigrants settled down to live family-centered, healthy, and responsible lives for the sake of their children. A review in the Columbus (Ohio) *Dispatch* offers a representative reaction:

> Most of his subjects make delicate but jolly humor of the heavy duty to Jewish family life that has been the subject of tragedy by so many other writers. And best of all, most of them carry a wonderfully gay and well-remembered picture of the immigrant Jewish family life in lower East Side New York.

There are, to be sure, occasional references in Golden to the overcrowding and the poverty, the sweatshops and the tuberculosis, but in his benign and invigorating Rivington Street, Golden portrays a satisfying way of life that both Gentiles and Jews today find to be instructive and— again judging by the reviews—inspiring.

The *New Yorker* reviewer was stretching it a bit when he said that Golden "recalls a romantic, vanished world full of drama and gallantry, something like the mythical Dixie. . . ." But what distinguishes Golden's Rivington Street from the so-called suburban "picture-window ghettoes" of today is not so much the noise, the grinding penury, the wear and tear on the nerves, but rather the vividness, energy, aspiration, discipline, and finally the warmth of its life—that is, precisely those qualities which are said to be declining in the modern middle-class family and suburb. The most frequently noted passage from *For 2¢ Plain* was the one in which Golden describes how as a boy he came home after staying away all day because he had lost five dollars on an errand; instead of punishing him, his mother kissed him and said, "It's better than giving it to a doctor." The fact that in Golden's childhood the title phrase *Enjoy, Enjoy!* meant "tomorrow" has also had a highly appreciative press. A writer for the

Chicago *Tribune,* for example, commented that such sentiments and ideas illustrate "a character pattern prevalent in the 1900's that gave these groups [of Jews] the stamina to rise above poverty and discrimination." And, as Golden frequently reminds us, that kind of "character pattern" is seriously wanting today.

Other reviewers have found that the value of Golden's recollections is simply that they let us look briefly at "a world we might not otherwise know." As a writer for the ILGWU *Justice* puts it: "No place else but in Harry Golden's wonderful book can the reader find essays on boiled-beef flanken . . . two cents plain and secondhand pants." Golden's anecdotes are crammed with the little details of what the Lower-East-Side Jews ate and slept on and took for medicine, of how they courted, voted, and shopped. His strong sense of detail, in fact, is one of the best things about him, and with its help he has been able to satisfy both Jewish nostalgia and Gentile curiosity. But what also sells his product, it is clear, is the packaging—the inspiriting morals drawn from Jewish experience in which he manages to wrap even such sordid happenings as the famous Triangle Shirtwaist fire. After describing how 146 girls perished and how the owners were then exonerated, Golden ends in a typical surge of upbeat moralizing by claiming that the disaster produced "fire-prevention legislation, factory-building inspection, workmen's compensation, liability insurance, and the International Ladies Garment Workers' Union."

Another leading motif that runs through the reception of Golden is the lament for the decline of ethnic variety, and the related loss of individualism, in America. A good many writers quoted Golden's statement that "we are heading for a ghastly sameness in our country, in which the magnificent Latins from the Mediterranean, the wonderful Swedes from Scandinavia, the brilliant Jews from Eastern Europe, and the effervescent Irish from the Auld Sod, will soon be indistinguishable from the Cape Cod Yankees. This is good?"

The reviewers didn't think it was and they jumped at the chance to corroborate this and other of Golden's criticisms of American sameness and conformity and to celebrate him as a notable exception. Martin Levin, writing in the *Saturday Review,* explained the appeal of *Only in America* as "offering an individual point of view . . . a refreshing phenomenon in a decade that has been thirsting for the humor of ideas and finds instead squibs on such yeasty themes as the rigors of commuting." In papers across the country, from the New York *Times* to the Detroit *News* to the Sacramento *Bee,* Golden's reviewers hailed him (in the words of William Du Bois) as a striking asset "in an era when the urge to conform is taking on the aspects of an epidemic." Taking their cue from Carl Sandburg's introduction to the book, in which he quotes Emerson's remark that "Whoso would be a man must first be a nonconformist" in order to praise Golden for being both, the reviewers made Golden's non-conformity their prevailing reason for touting *Only in America*.

It goes without saying that Golden's popularity was at the same time held to be an encouraging sign of life. William Hogan of the San Francisco *Chronicle* summed up this side of the reaction by suggesting that

the most interesting point about the popularity . . . is that in the ambitious, selfish, increasingly, uninteresting middle-class society we inhabit today so many people should turn to Harry Golden's simple honesty and warmth for some relief. Not since Will Rogers has there been such a people's philosopher.

In other words, Golden's "unorthodox" opinions—as several reviewers characterized them—such as his attacks upon the "platitudes and shibboleths" of American conformity have not apparently deprived him of being "the voice of unassuming millions." As the Springfield (Mass.) *Republican* went on to say, Golden's great following had been drawn by his "reassurances that there still were plain, sensible, kindly citizens . . . [who] wanted to be told that quiet, loving, family life wasn't out of style, but actually was rather well thought of in some circles." Heavily mixed in with the clippings that applauded Golden for the originality and independence of his thinking were those which, like one from the Evansville (Indiana) *Press*, asserted that "what Harry Golden thinks usually you think too, only you've been a bit shy about coming right out and saying it."

But how, then, does an outspoken non-conformist in a highly conforming society become the voice of its "unassuming millions"? Part of the answer lies in the ambivalences of the American audience that so many reviewers reflect: the desire to live freshly in the strangeness of the present but with the assurance of the past, and with this the development of a state of mind that seeks both criticism and approval. Just recently we saw how the psychic appeal of Kennedy's campaign was directed to one side of this ambivalence, that of Nixon to the other; the relatively small distance between the actual politics of the candidates themselves, and the virtual fifty-fifty split in the vote bear out the drift of the American psyche toward a misty equivocal blend of self-images and needs.

Harry Golden's success derives quite clearly from the successful way he confronts and bridges the two images. Just as his version of the Jewish

East Side both stimulates and soothes his middle-class audience, so does he soothe and stimulate by his musings upon the state of America. Here he tells us that our society is in trouble—it is bored, materialistic, frivolous, apathetic; there he tells us that this or that sturdy accomplishment of democracy or social progress could happen only in America. His collections are a handbook of contemporary bourgeois confusions; except for an occasional piece of direct and *meant* protest, his unorthodoxy, on examination, is seen to reside largely in the Jewish and the plain-truth-from-honest-James colorations of his tone. He speaks of America as being on "a huge breast binge," and says the "whole thing is psycho"—"the instinct to seek the safety and comfort of a 'mother.'" This, of course, is nothing new—even to readers of *Coronet* now. But a few pages later Golden imperturbably defends Mother and America against the denigrations and warnings of Phillip Wylie: "As long as the American boy continues to be dreamy-eyed every time he thinks of mother, just so long will our American freedom be safe." Here he talks about the sexual *angst* that gnaws away at the bourgeoisie; there he tells us that "if it were strictly a matter of virile, normal sex, all the pin-ups combined are not equal to one spinster school teacher with eyeglasses." If he is not forthrightly damning Governor Faubus and Senator Eastland, he is likely to be praising the "warm-hearted people of the South" who vote for them; if he is not telling us that popular culture today is corny and commercial, he is likely to be recording his "deep admiration and respect" for the "wonderful" way Robert Montgomery and Batten, Barton, Durstine and Osborne televised President Eisenhower's birthday party: the family sitting around the President while from off-stage came his favorite song, "Down Among the Sheltering Palms."

And so it goes. The American public, he says, is forever trying to escape from the realities that impinge upon it, but it is right and proper that the most important event of the next decade for most families will be getting the kids off to school. For the human story, as he tells us, is "a man and a woman and the love of a home." The 'Big Story' is about people who struggle to pay the rent and get up the tuition for a girl in college . . . about people who lose jobs and find better ones." Also it is about the home town, and Golden draws a bead on the *New Yorker* for failing to realize that home means "father, mother, sweetheart, past, present, future, and PARNOSSEH." The use of the Yiddish term for livelihood is fairly typical of Golden's approach and appeal: garnished with a little Manischewitz horseradish, the perplexed banalities of the middle class come back to them as the wisdom of the ages.

That Golden's own "platitudes and shibboleths" should be as immensely popular as they are is not too startling, then, for they occur on both sides of practically every issue that worries Americans today, without ever disturbing the desperately held notions that our society is fundamentally fine and the future, in any case, will somehow deliver us from our dilemmas. Yet Golden and his reviewers cannot help but reveal, all the same, anxieties endemic in our culture today—the loss of national energy and imagination, the conformity, soft-headedness, and even the joylessness of the people—before managing to gloss them over. The reviewers' glossing over is in their pointing to how many people read and swear by Golden; his is in applying the varnish of his much-admired "optimism."

It is perhaps to be expected that so many members of the American middle class—feeling that they have somehow lost the way despite what they tell themselves—should turn for pointers to the minority groups who they believe still possess some special vitality and individuality, some esoteric wisdom about how to live. For one group—the restless young— the supposedly "cool" self-contained style and highly instinctual behavior of the Negro have become the objects of envy and emulation, just as the Jews—to judge by the success of Wouk's *Marjorie Morningstar* and of Golden's essays—are currently thought to have the secret of why and how to lead the good, American family life, whether on Rivington Street or in Mamaroneck. So Golden says himself in the introduction to his latest book. Pointing to the thousand letters a week he receives these days, he tells us of the loneliness they testify to, the "unhappiness in a rootless society"; the most important meaning they disclose, he says, is that "the strongest memory of life is the *family*" (his italics). Thus his anecdotes of a family-centered childhood are a sedative, and offer hope as well, for, as he put it in a previous introduction, "I know with all my heart that whether you look down a path leading from a farmhouse near Fountain Run, Kentucky, or out of one of the magnificent residences in the Myers Park section of Charlotte . . . these pleasures and joys await you, too—'for 2¢ plain.'"

Yet another source of Golden's appeal as a commentator on American manners is his emphasis on success as natural, healthy, and self-justifying. For Golden's Jewish immigrant story is also the American Dream writ small and concrete. As the prose-poet of upward mobility, Golden once again translates the values of the older, parochial Jewish culture into terms that his affluent audience can find satisfying. Though he speaks now and then of the penalties of success, he nonetheless worships it about as uncritically as the first Jewish immigrants did. His essays are studded with accounts of how this lawyer and that doctor, this comedian and that song writer climbed to fame and fortune from the ghetto—accounts which are redolent of his persistent confusing of celebrity with merit. Within this compulsion for touting winners, virtually all distinctions collapse: "The New York *Times* . . . is one of the finest American institutions, along with Harvard, the New York Yankees, and the Supreme Court." When Golden tells us about an East Side boy who is now a lawyer whom "the oldest families in his city make . . . the administrator of their estates," there is nothing further to add. To be on top is to be on top, which is a wonderful place to be.

This is a dose of the good old soothing syrup in the America of today, where the problem of getting ahead has begun to make everyone nervous. Whether or not one wishes to relate this to some final assertion of American Puritanism, to the frequency with which success in America is revealed to have begun or ended in some form of fraud, or to the mass frustration of a people who at a vast cost to their pockets and their souls are constantly buying the symbols of success but never achieve its substance—the fact remains, as Leslie Fiedler has been telling us, that nothing fails in America like success. But by his examples and by his tone, Golden reaffirms the unsophisticated, guiltless ideal of success which has been characteristic of immigrant groups; and he does so most effectively, perhaps, when he prefaces his point that we were happier when we had iceboxes instead of status symbols in the kitchen, by saying that he learned this from all "the people who wrote me after they saw me on Ed Murrow's *Person to Person,* and on the programs of Dave Garroway, Jack Parr, and Arthur Godfrey."

What also makes Golden's presentation of success attractive, of course, is that—true to form—he occasionally debunks its more outrageous manifestations, poking fun, for example, at Elvis Presley; once he even downgrades Albert Schweitzer for not having been "on the firing line during the past two or there decades." But what he generally concentrates on is the more superficial problem of status, which, in most cases, can be handled as a humorous consequence of the magic American carpet of upward mobility, or as a less noxious and alarming by-product of the frustration, tension, and apathy that result when the possibilities for meaningful achievement are reduced or compromised.

In his critique of status-seeking, Golden depends as much on present-day Jewish life to make his points as he does upon the vanished ghetto to provide him with his morality and sample of success. "I use Jews as examples and rely upon Gentiles to get the point," he told one interviewer. Thus every ten pages or so there is some mention of bobbed noses or Ivy League *yarmulkes* or the quest for a blond rabbi. This is all very amusing to Golden: "They're worrying about a country club when Abe Ribicoff has gotten to be Governor of Connecticut." In general, the eager-beaver foibles and pretensions of the Jewish middle class provided him with another safe way of giving himself a critical voice. Golden's reviewers in the Jewish press do not appear to take offense over his gibes, and the Gentiles can examine their own silly search for status through an innocuous analogy. Also in this way, Golden emerges as a Jew who is not above criticizing his own people—another reason for the reviewers to praise him for his "fearless honesty."

But what is, finally, most interesting about all this is the success with which Golden has made the Jew seem entirely representative of the middle-class American—representative of a pattern that holds for the multitudes of Americans who in the course of their life have traveled from the lower to the middle class, from the closely knit enclave of the slum or the farm or the small town to the thinner, more mannered life of the suburb.

Here, as elsewhere, Golden reinforces the cultural situation he describes by the example of his own personality and career: the big-city boy who has settled in the provinces, the Jew who has had to make his way in the Protestant culture of the South, the son of the slums confronted by a highly organized pattern of middle-class life. Now, while he points to the Jews of today to evoke everybody's anxieties, he uses his frequently conveyed relish for the disparities and incongruities of his own position to allay the same anxieties. What makes the rest of the Jews nervous about their marginal status merely makes him rock with laughter; they wrestle foolishly and gloomily with the problem of identity, he stands fast in his happy acceptance of what he was and is; they trade their "marvelous" heritage for the dubious consolations of pseudo-Gentile attitudes and interests, he uses his heritage to make himself a respected, if off-beat, member of the community.

Moreover, in his "ease and naturalness in accepting joyously the fact that he is a Jew," Golden is able to exploit the traditional opportunities and immunities of the American humorist as the wise "original" whose very marginality arms him with the sensible, unvarnished truth. At the same time, as the "Yenkee Tarheel," Golden revives and flatters the declining notion of American variety and of a free society that is invigorated and kept on the beam by its robust minorities. (When Golden asked in his North Carolina newspaper whether he was a "Tarheel," he was answered by editorials all over the state which hastened to assure him that he most certainly was. And when Golden asked Governor Luther Hodges at a press conference how it "felt to be governor of a state where one-third of the population is embittered," Hodges turned to the other reporters and said, "Gentlemen, I think Harry Golden is one of the most valuable citizens of this state.")

As the freedom-loving Yankee in rigidly hierarchial Dixie, Golden is, in fact, as useful and appealing in his way as Mark Twain's energetic, ingenious, progress-minded émigré was to the tradition-ridden court of King Arthur. Unlike the hero of Twain's satire, Golden does not bring to his new home the industrial know-how and its social benefits that came to Camelot, but he does his part by celebrating the South's "day-to-day industrialization without parallel in the history of our country." In his role as a kind of one-man Chamber of Commerce reporting on Dixie's progress, Golden is also reminiscent of Twain's Connecticut Yankee in having to rely on some "stretchers" here and there. While one is willing to concede that "Tobacco Road today is full of TV antennas, with electric washing machines on every back porch," he may have trouble swallowing Golden's further claim that "Mrs. Jeeter Lester is getting dressed up for the Tuesday afternoon Garden Club or the League of Women Voters." This happy ambience of an up-and-coming South arises repeatedly from Golden's portraits of enterprising Southern manufacturers who are doing "more to end segregation than the NAACP" and of the states which are "spending fortunes to bring in new industry." Meanwhile the Southern Negro, according to Golden, no longer tips his hat as he walks "briskly along the street on his way to pick up his little girl at the dancing school, that is, if he's not arguing a new writ before a Federal judge."

It is within the context of a healthy, liberalizing society that Golden places the Negro question, a context that flatters the South while criticizing or lightly lampooning its intransigence on the matter of integration. There is also the good-natured blandness that operates along with the widely praised trenchancy of his satire. If Golden's famous plan for "vertical integration" was reprinted, as John Barkham claims, "in virtually every paper and magazine south of the Mason-Dixon line," it was surely not because the proposal to take the chairs out of Southern classrooms was—in the words of a Southern reviewer—"as mordant as, if slightly less savage than, Dean Swift's modest proposal for a solution to the Irish problem." Swift proposed that the Irish kill their starving children and sell them as delicacies to the English who kept the land in poverty; Golden's satire is a fairy tale by comparison. When the Greenville (North Carolina) *Daily Reflector* reflects a dozen Southern newspapers by speaking of this plan as "one of the best solutions to the segregation problem we have heard yet," it seems clear that Golden's value to the South lies largely in permitting a tolerance for the integrationists that comes easily because it costs nothing and endangers nothing. "If we were as impossible as we are often told we are," writes the Asheville (North Carolina) *Citizen Times,* "we wouldn't put up with this outsider coming here and poking fun at us."

Of course, Golden repays tolerance with more tolerance, constantly assuring the Southerners that he "understands" and respects their viewpoint. He understands, for example, how a young Southern engineer cannot reconcile himself to his children's attending an integrated school, though once he had driven a school bus and had had " 'a very bad time of it' " whenever a Negro mother had to train her child to sit in the back: " 'She would mount the bus again and again and lead it to the back again and again, until it understood.' " "Somehow I felt very close to that man," Golden concludes, "but I was anxious to see him go before we both started to bawl." His schmaltz along with his humorous ribbing of the incongruities of the segregationist position both end by leaving the nastier roots of Southern attitudes undisturbed (such as the one implied by the engineer's use of the neuter pronoun in speaking of a Negro child). "His barbed pen," according to the New York *World-Telegram,* always has "a soothing ointment as well"; the total effect is that of satire with the stinger removed—somewhere between a bite and a kiss.

Then there is the unction of his famous Jewish "understanding." "The segregationist needs your respect more, perhaps, because what he believes is less deserving," wrote Golden in *Pageant.* This trait is seen by Northern liberals and reactionaries and Southern traditionalists alike as a great virtue—the virtue of tolerance, concern, and "open-mindedness." "Golden has an open mind about practically everything except treason and dishonesty. He doesn't wait for the egghead butcher paper weeklies to make it up for him," writes the Chicago *American.* "Golden keeps his opposition off-balance by practicing the respect for others' racial, religious, and national heritage that he preaches," writes the New York *Post.* "You know he is concerned. Never does he stand outside and accuse," states the Greensboro (North Carolina) *Record.* But what this comes to in the pages of Golden's books is a tolerance that is so soft that any strong conviction is unable to stand upon it for more than a paragraph, and a mind that is usually so far open that it is unable to close decisively on the realities of racism. As one of Golden's rare critics put it, "with equal equanimity, he singes Klansmen's sheets and sings the praises of Southern White Protestants, liberals and otherwise." He is at his best in making a clear, convincing case of what segregation costs the South economically and morally; but otherwise one tends to find him explaining the South just as he explained the Jews.

All of which is not to say that Golden's approach is craven or that his opposition to segregation is ineffective. Because he lives in the South he has to measure the tone of his criticism carefully. And I am told by Southern friends that liberals such as Edward P. Morgan are right in saying that Golden's genial satire helps "to loosen the preposterous rigidity of the segregationists' stand." But it is hard to see that the "truth" he speaks, as the Kalamazoo *Gazette* puts it, is "the hurting, troubling kind." On the contrary: the truths he speaks about segregation, like those he speaks about America today, neither hurt nor disturb. Instead they flatter and tranquilize by making the reader think that he has come to grips with social problems when all he has done is to watch the issue of segregation or conformity or apathy being nudged lightly before he is hurried on to a joke about chocolate-covered matzos or to a plug for Shakespeare or for the Jewish authors of songs about Dixie, or to another rousing affirmation that Nixon's adoption of proposals which once landed their Socialist backers in jail is something that "could happen only in America."

Going through the bundles of enthusiastic reviews of Golden's books, one comes upon an occasional lonely voice, usually in an obscure newspaper, raised in dissent. Aaron Epstein, writing in the Santa Rosa (California) *Press Democrat,* points to the "specious wrestling match between the author and his subject" in which Golden relaxes his grip whenever there is any chance of a fall. Meier Ronnen, a visiting Israelis journalist, turns up in a Louisville newspaper to smile at Golden's knack for presenting "the obvious as philosophy," and adds that "as a philosopher, his sharp stylus does little more than scratch the surface of his schmaltz-covered tablet." Mortimer J. Cohen in the *Jewish Exponent* notes the "sameness" of Golden's three collections which he convincingly argues comes from "the relatively narrow range of his emotions." Cohen also finds that Golden is a little "too full of love for people," that, for all his highly touted "sweetness and light," there is "an obsequiousness in his voice." And a young man in Park Forest, Illinois, begins a review: "This is tantamount to being un-American or something" and goes on to say that Golden "is to prose all that Edgar Guest is to poetry."

Much else might be added. There are the glib or sometimes idiotic discussions of history and literature: Brutus was "a neurotic who spent his entire life worrying about whether Caesar was his father"; *The Merchant of Venice* is, in reality, a philo-Semitic play; modern poetry is so untopical that only Benét and Sandburg have given us "a sense of time and place" to match Longfellow's "Listen my children and you shall hear,/ Of the midnight ride of Paul Revere." There is also the forcing of relationships that allows Golden to relate Jewish history or "ideas" to almost anything under the sun. Jews and Gentiles alike have hailed the goodwill toward the Jews that Golden has elicited, but a more extended treatment would want to show how he has accomplished this by presenting the Jewish mind in an advanced stage of vulgarization, which probably explains why his stiffest critics have been Jews.

But what is most disheartening about the Golden case is not the books themselves nor the mindless praise of them but rather the malaise of American consciousness which these books and their success reflect. "The wonderful progress of science has brought no improvements in the hearts of men," says Golden. Where do we seem to have heard that platitude before, that special quality of affable flatulence? Golden has been described by several reviewers as "the court jester of American democracy," but I would be more specific and call him the court jester of the Eisenhower Age. He is very much a phenomenon of a period in which great national success came to bland, homey Americans who could best soothe anxieties, provide a confident if vague sense of direction, and preside over the evasion of issues. For all the supposed vitality and alertness in Golden's writing, there is a softness in his prose and in his thought, a steady veering away from complexity and controversy to the safe banality or the nice sentiment, and a power of accommodation that eventually occupies both sides of the question, which give his books much of the eerie feeling of an Eisenhower press conference or a Nixon speech. But perhaps the narrow election of Kennedy and the fact that some of Golden's reviewers are becoming mildly irritated both point to the same surfeit of tranquilizers. As two of his readers have suggested, he should call his next book "Enough Already."

NORMAN PODHORETZ (1930–   )

Although Norman Podhoretz has written interesting criticism, collected in Doings and Undoings (1964), and an autobiographical account of his rise in the New York literary world, entitled Making It (1968), his primary role as cultural critic has been established as the Editor of Commentary from 1960 until today. He shifted Commentary's anti-Communist posture of the 1950's toward a strongly liberal direction reminiscent of social criticism in the thirties. "I determined to take Commentary out of the hands of the largely academic types on whom it had come to rely so heavily and to bring it back into the family." The "family" included most of the writers represented in this volume: Paul Goodman, Lionel Trilling, Alfred Kazin, Irving Howe, and Hannah Arendt. Just as Edgar Allan Poe, William Dean Howells, H. L. Mencken, Philip Rahv and William Phillips represented editorial positions that were particularly sympathetic to the great writers of their time, Podhoretz caught the pulse beat of intellectual life in the sixties. Although the writers of the Jewish-American renaissance published in all the well-known journals, they did appear frequently in Commentary, and the editorial policy of the magazine, more than that of any other, mirrored their thought.

Norman Podhoretz was born in the Brownzeville section of Brooklyn, New York, on January 16, 1930, of parents who were East European immigrants. He graduated from Columbia University and the Jewish Theological Seminary in 1950 and went to Cambridge University in England, where he studied under F. R. Leavis. On returning to the United States in 1953, he began his career as a literary critic by publishing in Commentary and other well-known journals; his reputation grew quickly because of iconoclastic, controversial reviews of novels like Saul Bellows's The Adventures of Augie March and Nelson Algren's A Walk on the Wild Side. In 1955, he was made an assistant editor of Commentary; he left the magazine in 1958 but returned in 1960 to assume the editorship made vacant by Eliot Cohen's suicide.

Jewishness and the Younger Intellectuals

INTRODUCTION: In February 1944—some two years after America's entry into World War II and less than two years before the end of the war—COMMENTARY's forerunner, the *Contemporary Jewish Record*, published a symposium entitled "Under Forty: American Literature and the Younger Generation of American Jews." The theme of the symposium was apparently a literary one, for the editors in their introductory statement announced that their intention was to cast light on the question of whether there was any important difference between the work produced by American writers of Jewish descent (who had only recently become "full participants in the cultural life of the country") and that of their "Christian colleagues." It seems clear, however, that this approach was something of a stratagem employed by the editors to get at another and more elusive question—a question at which they merely hinted in asking "to what extent, and in what manner, has [the Jewish writer's] awareness of his position as artist and citizen been modified or changed by the revival of anti-Semitism as a powerful force in the political history of our time?" What lay behind this question, I feel sure, was the editors' awareness that most of the writers they had invited to contribute were assimilationists and that their assimilationism was grounded in the belief that the "Jewish problem"—as it used to be called—was on its way to being solved in the modern world. The Dreyfus Case had persuaded Theodor Herzl that assimilationism would never work; surely the Nazis ought to have taught American Jews the same lesson. And if a Jew becomes convinced that there is no escaping the disabilities of Jewish birth, isn't he then required to abandon assimilationism as a program, even for himself, and search for some other solution?

The eleven contributors to the symposium included some of the most gifted and brilliant members of the younger generation of writers and critics in America—Lionel Trilling, Alfred Kazin, Delmore Schwartz, Isaac Rosenfeld, Louis Kronenberger, Clement Greenberg—and it is therefore no surprise that they should have understood the true nature of the apparently academic questions they were being asked to consider. Yes, they all said—and here I am going beyond the explicit comments some of them made and into the implications of their remarks—we now know that integration into the surrounding culture is not the answer to anti-Semitism. But where the good 19th-century emancipated Jew could find an alternative answer in the principle of national sovereignty—not only because he thought it would work but also because he *believed,* along with so many of his contemporaries, in nationalism as a creative and benevolent force—we have learned (thanks partly to the Nazis) to be repelled by nationalism in any form whatever. The Zionists we have met are generally "dreary middle-class chauvinists"—the phrase is Alfred Kazin's—and we have no wish to associate ourselves with them or what they stand for. What, then, is left? You speak of the "Jewish heritage" and ask whether we have been shaped by it. Certainly we have been shaped by the fact of our Jewish birth, but we are by no means sure that you are not confusing the experience of being the child of immigrants with the experience of being a Jew. And what is this Jewish heritage? Whatever it may have been in the past, today in America it has deteriorated into nothingness, or worse than nothingness. It has been integrated into a culture which is itself inferior and vicious, and it has taken on all the worst qualities of that culture while retaining nothing valuable of its own.

Out of modern Jewish religion, said Lionel Trilling, "there has not come a single voice with the note of authority—of philosophical, or poetic, or even of rhetorical, let alone of religious, authority," and "as the Jewish community now exists, it can give no sustenance to the American artist or intellectual who is born a Jew." Said Clement Greenberg: "Jewish life in America has become, *for reasons of security,* so solidly, so rigidly, restrictedly, and suffocatingly middle-class that behavior within it is a pattern from which personality can deviate in only a mechanical and hardly ever in a temperamental sense. No people on earth are more correct, more staid, more provincial, more commonplace, more inexperienced; none observe more strictly the letter of every code that is respectable; no people do so completely and habitually what is expected of them. . . ." Who is the American Jew? asked Alfred Kazin. "What is Jewish in him? What does he believe, especially in these terrible years, that separates him at all from our national habits of acquisitiveness, showiness, and ignorant brag? . . . What a pity that he should feel 'different,' when he believes so little; what a stupendous moral pity, historically, that the Fascist cutthroats should have their eyes on him, too, when he asks for so little—only to be safe, in all the Babbitt warrens."

These were severe and merciless indictments (though one could find their equal in Zionist literature and worse in the Hebrew prophets), and certainly they were motivated in part by the bitterness these young American Jews felt over the fact that the Jewish community should have been no better than the middle-class America from which so huge a proportion of its most gifted artists and intellectuals had always felt estranged.

Indeed, the few positive statements made by the contributors—for example Delmore Schwartz's: "And thus I have to say (with gratitude and yet difference because it has been so different for other Jews, different to the point of death) that the fact of Jewishness has been nothing but an evergrowing good to me, and it seems clear to me now that it can be, at least for me, nothing but a fruitful and inexhaustible inheritance" —had less to do with Judaism or the Jewish community than with the advantages to a modern writer of having been born into a marginal culture. The Jewish writer in America was doubly schooled in the experience of alienation and so, paradoxically, could speak as the quintessential modern man.

The word alienation supplies the real key to understanding the 1944 symposium. Not all the contributors were socialists—of the ones I have selected for analysis, only Clement Greenberg actually said that the Jewish problem was a version of "the alienation of man under capitalism" and could only be solved in a socialist society—but it has not in our time been necessary to embrace socialism in order to repudiate the life and culture of the middle class throughout the Western world. Thus it was the middle-classness of the Jewish community which more than anything else accounted for the harsh words the young writers of 1944 had for their fellow Jews in America. Below the harsh words, however, lay an assumption obviously shared by most of the contributors—that, by committing themselves to the Ideal in culture and politics, they were being more truly Jewish than the community which called itself Jewish.

That they were unfair and one-sided in their judgments a large number of these writers themselves later came to acknowledge. One has only to skim through the back files of COMMENTARY to see how far many of the contributors to the 1944 symposium (and others like them) went in revising their estimate of the "Jewish heritage." Though in 1944 they would probably have all agreed with Trilling's flat assertion that modern Jewish religion had produced nothing of value, ten years later at least half of them had become enthusiasts of Martin Buber, while the whole of the New York literary world was ringing with praise of the Yiddish storytellers, the Hasidim, Maimonides, medieval Hebrew poetry, and even the Rabbis of the Talmud. (Trilling himself wrote an essay called "Wordsworth and the Rabbis.") The relation of the Jewish writer to his Jewishness had shifted dramatically, and by 1955, after the work of Saul Bellow and Bernard Malamud—to mention only two names—had begun to appear, Kazin could not have said, as he did in 1944, that "When I read a novel by an American Jew that is at least as grounded in the life it rejects as Farrell's *Studs Lonigan* or Dreiser's *Sister Carrie,* I shall believe in the empirical fact of our participation." The work of these writers was not only grounded in American Jewish life, but in many instances it even struck an affirmative stance, celebrating—as did Kazin's own autobiographical book about Brownsville, *A Walker in the City*—the richness and color of the immigrant urban experience.

What had happened? To some extent, no doubt, the new relation to Jewishness and Judaism that was expressed by the literary intelligentsia of the 50's developed merely as a consequence of the passage of years: what a man flees in youth he often learns to love in middle age. But the main factor operating here, I believe, was the widespread retreat among intellectuals from the whole complex of attitudes symbolized by the term alienation. The new relation to Jewishness, in other words, was an aspect of the new and more positive relation to America which was bred in large part by the menace of Soviet totalitarianism on the one side and the change (or apparent change) that had taken place in the character of the American middle class.* A symposium published in 1952 in *Partisan Review,* "America and the Intellectuals," provides extensive evidence of this new relation, which might be described psychologically as a great willingness by the intellectuals to acknowledge and *value* the American in themselves—a willingness that extended quite naturally, in the case of those who were also Jews, to the Jew in them. It ought to be said, however, that the new attitude toward the American middle class in general —which was seen as having overcome its Babbittry and which was now

* I have discussed these developments at greater length in several articles: "Jewish Culture and the Intellectuals," COMMENTARY MAY 1955; "The Young Generation," the *New Leader,* March 11, 1957; and "The Intellectuals and Jewish Fate," *Midstream,* Winter 1957.

thought of as the great bulwark against totalitarianism—was never quite extended to the American Jewish community. If most of the contributors to the 1944 symposium later came to discover great fascination and virtue in traditional Jewish culture, very few of them ever acknowledged the unfairness of the charge that Jewish life in America bore no trace of the admirable characteristics of the Jewish past. For whatever else may be said of the American Jewish community, it does—in the fantastically elaborate network of social, welfare, and educational institutions it supports (a network that no other group even begins to parallel), in the rescue work it has done, and in the generosity it has consistently shown toward the oppressed and the homeless whenever called upon to do so— maintain in a very active and vivid way the traditions of communal responsibility and social service which in past contexts have been singled out as among the most attractive qualities of "the Jewish heritage." And one could easily expand the list of traditional Jewish qualities that persist in one form or another among the Jews of America.

While all this was taking place in the generation that is now between forty-five and fifty-five years old, a new generation of American Jews was beginning to make its appearance on the scene—a generation which on the whole was at least one remove from the immigrant experience and which emerged into consciousness in an atmosphere that contrasted very sharply with that of the 30's. Radicalism and rebellion were probably less fashionable among the young than ever before in modern history; a much publicized religious revival was in process; the State of Israel was in existence and fighting for its life; and the Jews in America had arrived. Discrimination had declined sharply; anti-Semitism was in great disrepute (after having been fashionable for so long even among the educated); and the somewhat premature claim made in 1944 by the editors of the *Contemporary Jewish Record,* that Jews had become "full participants in the cultural life of the country," was now finally and wholly true. Jews were active and prominent in every sphere of activity in America, including the arts; what Benjamin DeMott recently observed in these pages concerning Jewish writers—that they now have a "place in the establishment"—could be said with equal justice of Jewish musicians, painters, doctors, lawyers, politicians.

The editors of COMMENTARY were curious to know how the generation of Jewish intellectuals who came to maturity in such an atmosphere and under such conditions felt about its relation to the Jewish heritage and to the community which is committed to preserving and extending that heritage. Since Jewish intellectuals are now prominent in all fields, we did not limit our inquiries to literary people, but rather tried to extend the occupational range of our sample as far as possible—with the intention, however, of finding young men and women who, in some sense which is rather difficult to define with precision, correspond in type and distinction (or promise of future distinction) with the 1944 group. Assuming—perhaps foolishly—that a Jew with a definite religious commitment of any kind would regard the sort of questions we wished to ask either as irrelevant to him or as self-evidently answerable, we did not invite any representatives of the younger religious intelligentsia (though when one of the people we did invite turned out to our surprise to be a member of that group, we decided to publish his reply anyway). We also decided to invite only native-born Americans, but here again one respondent (and possibly more) turned out not to fit the specifications; his contribution nevertheless appears below. The age limit we set was forty, though I believe that most of the contributors are much younger than that and only three or four are over thirty-five. In any case, the intention was to question young people who seemed to us—from what we knew of their work—to have been formed or shaped by the characteristic conditions of the postwar period rather than by some earlier ethos. We sent out about fifty questionnaires, expecting ten or fifteen replies; instead we received a total of thirty-one, and they are all printed below, in alphabetical order.

This is, of course, by no means a "scientific" sampling; perhaps it is not even representative. The symposium does, however, bring together a random group of the most talented and most articulate younger intellectuals of Jewish birth in America today. Their backgrounds—geographical, social, and religious—are remarkably diverse; they come from all classes, and their parents range from rabbis to militant atheists. Their occupations, too, are highly varied. Almost all the academic disciplines are represented (including science); there are novelists, poets, critics, publishers, and editors; there is a film producer, a newspaperman, a Congressional assistant, a psychiatrist. Many of the contributors are married (in some cases to non-Jews) and have children, which means that they have been forced to confront such problems as whether they wish to give their children a Jewish education: the problem of Jewishness for them has therefore become "existential" and urgent where it once may have been theoretical.

How, then, do these third- and fourth-generation American Jewish intellectuals—these children of the "neo-conservative" age, the age of the religious revival and the rediscovery of America—differ in their relation to Jewishness from their elders, the children of the immigrants and the depression and the militantly anti-religious atmosphere of the various radical movements of the 30's? The answer is—hardly at all. To be sure, there is far less bitterness in the pieces below than one might find in the 1944 symposium; on the whole, the contributors to the present symposium are neither vigorously rejecting Jewishness nor enthusiastically rushing toward it. Most of them have something good to say for the Jewish heritage, though very few express any sense of living commitment to it—and like their forebears of 1944, they assume easily, and incorrectly I think, that the American Jewish community is indistinguishable from the middle-class American community in general and bears no sign of the former attributes of the Jewish people. Again, like the 1944 group, they are against "chauvinism" (though the overwhelming majority express a great sympathy for Israel) and "parochialism," feeling that they properly belong to a much wider world than is encompassed by the Jewish community—or, indeed, by America itself. Except in some of the older contributors (who in this respect are closer in tone to the preceding generation), there is scarcely a trace of the idea that a man must have strong local or "parochial" attachments before he can achieve a true universalism of spirit.

But what is most surprising and, to my mind at least, most reassuring is the atmosphere of idealism that permeates this symposium, an idealism that many of the contributors themselves associate with the fact of their Jewishness. Believing (on the basis, it should be emphasized, of an obviously scant acquaintance with the literature and history of Judaism) that the essence of Judaism is the struggle for universal justice and human brotherhood, these young intellectuals assert over and over again that anyone who fights for the Ideal is to that degree more Jewish than a man who merely observes the rituals or merely identifies himself with the Jewish community. This, really, is what the 1944 group was also saying, that the essential tradition of Judaism came to be embodied in modern times not in the committed Jewish community but in the great post-Emancipation figures who rushed out of the ghetto to devour and then recreate the culture of the West: Marx, Freud, Einstein.

How do they feel about the future? By and large, they are perfectly well aware that their kind of Jewishness provides little hope for the survival of even those Jewish traditions which they admire; as some of them actually point out, they are living off the religious and cultural capital of the past. They seem to think, however, that the best Jewish traditions are no longer the unique possession of the Jewish people—obviously one can be an idealist without being a Jew. And many of them would agree with Jason Epstein, who says that *all* "the conventional groupings," national, religious, and ethnic, "are on the way out," that the world is in a state of revolutionary change, and that its contours are bound to re-form themselves during the next fifty or a hundred years. To paraphrase Elihu Katz's striking remark about Israel: the trouble with the Jews is that they are such a big idea in the perspective of world history and such a little idea in the perspective of modern history.

But are the Jews such a "little idea" in the perspective of modern history? In some sense, of course, they are; so, for that matter, are Protestants and Frenchmen. Yet the demise of the Jewish people has been predicted with equal confidence so many times in the past two thousand years that one simply hesitates to be persuaded by still another plausible case for its inevitable disappearance. I do not believe—if I may conclude by joining the symposium myself—that the Jews are destined to disappear, though I would be extremely hard put to argue the matter convincingly. Nor do I believe that a Jew does himself, or the world, any great service by an indifference to the future of the Jewish people. Let me make it as clear as I possibly can that in my view any man has an absolute moral right to choose his loyalties, even if this means violating the law of the land and incurring the disfavor of his fellows. At the same time it would be disingenuous to ignore the fact that certain choices bring with them unpleasant human consequences, and especially those choices which involve the willful tampering with things that are somehow too big and too mysterious to be controlled by individual reason. I know of course that this argument has been used by kings to justify divine right, by the rich to justify the existence of the poor, and in general by those who have tried to stem the tide of social change. Nevertheless, there *are*—there must be—in the life of every individual areas that are sacred, and demands before which the only proper attitude is piety or reverence. After four thousand years of existence, the Jews are indeed a very big idea in the history of the world, and no person born into this idea can dismiss it or refuse to acknowledge the loyalties and responsibilities it imposes on him, without doing himself some violence. I will not pretend that anything very concrete in the way of program or philosophy follows from such piety. But I will register my conviction that one ought to feel a sense of "historic reverence" to Jewish tradition even, or perhaps especially, if one is convinced that the curtain is about to drop on the last act of a very long play.

Jewishness and the Younger Intellectuals

Herbert Gold

(1) FIFTEEN YEARS AGO anti-Semitism was still a semi-acceptable social attitude. Now the pressure from outside on individual Jews to remain separate from other Americans has been much diminished. If they still remain partly separate, it is less likely to be because of ghetto habits or fears; but it may also arise from the positive belief that, within the Jewish tradition of finding virtue here and soon, on earth, rather than in heaven, there is an important guide to all the perplexed.

Jewish pleasure in the senses, Jewish risk-taking and daring, Jewish generosity and originality all provide sources of my own non-religious pride in a family tradition. The State of Israel gives special support to a history of holding fast. Today the Jew has an exhilarating choice among several alternatives: to accept Judaism as a religion and/or a national identification, to accept assimilation, or to draw a complex strength from solidarity with Jewish history while remaining nonetheless unambiguously committed to the fate of America. (These complicated choices overlap, of course. No important choice is pure.)

Platonic idealism in various corrupt forms has led the world to the edge of suicide. I hope that something like Jewish practicality—present also in non-Jews!—can build both personal and social means toward the preservation of humankind on earth.

(2) Jewish intellectual socialism was often a curious outcropping of abstraction against a mountain of practical injustices and horrors. The intensity of the Jewish radical's rebellion against a day-to-day confrontation

---

For a biographical note on Herbert Gold see p. 292.

of reality ran an exact parallel to the intense day-to-day struggle of the majority of American Jews in the commercial community. An element of reaction against the Jewish community will probably diminish as the intellectual's bond with that community is weakened. Middle-class, time-serving, togethered Jews are too much like all other time-serving, to-gethered Americans to be singled out for despair. There is a danger here: much of the originality of Jews seemed to come from this tension between their aspirations in the middle—Jewish and non-Jewish hostility at either end. What a waste if psychological homogenizing reduces passion and discipline!

(3) My experience as a Jew partly locates me as an American—especially with the practical, meliorative, answer-seeking side of Americans. It has protected me from the passivity of much of American life: I *know* that there is no heaven, that like a peddler I can carry only what is on my back and in my head, that what I do is what I am, that I am responsible for my fate. This Jewish acceptance of what the world offers, an energetic rather than a passive acceptance—a continual redefinition of the terms of life—contributes an important element in the American style. As a writer, I find Mark Twain and Thoreau "Jewish" in this way. The Jewish contribution reinforces a general pattern in American life, with individual men of genius sounding their individual notes.

(4)–(5) The implications of Jewish religious doctrine and ritual are important to me. For example, the weakness of the rabbi in the synagogue I find very appealing; the fact that every man follows his own lead in prayer is a significant difference between Judaism and most forms of Christianity. But this pride in Jewish individualism is very far from faith in doctrine. My identification with Jewish aspiration, suffering, and dignity is far from providing a total identification for myself as a Jew. Because of my own history, I choose to describe myself as a Jew—it is a part of my fiber—but I see no way of turning history back for my children. They will know other pains and joys of growth in a different period of history. Vividness cannot be willed outside of the given possibilities of a life. I believe it unlikely that my children will convert to any religion. I would be puzzled if they became religious Jews, also. I suspect that the Temple branch of the Girl Scouts does not provide much stimulus for religious crisis.

The special values which the Jewish people have created and transmitted will survive, if at all, through other institutions than the religious ones. The problems of our lives are political, social, economic, and also moral. I see no chance of solving the ethical problems through a Jewish community life in which the normally religious element has inevitably been "adjusted" to the fact that it is no longer a serious matter except for isolated individuals. Chicken soup and Yiddish jokes will tarry awhile. But the history of the Jews from now on will be one with the history of everybody else.

(6) I feel both a sentimental and social connection with the State of Israel: sentimental because of my history as a Jew, social because of a hope for Israel's growth as an exemplary force. To some extent this personal interest in Israel is contradictory. But family feeling is strong and can perhaps be justified simply as a fact of human nature (the alternative is the perversity—"Do I contradict myself? Very well, then I contradict myself"—explored in the Platonic dialogue, "The Euthyphro").

The freshness of danger, the vigor and intelligence disposed for public purposes, the sense of public hope which permeates life in Israel—these elements bring me closer to Israel than to the American Jewish community. Though for it too I suffer complex family attitudes, as I do for all of American life, which I despise, hate, fear, admire, relish, love. The American Jewish community is most important to me as a writer because it is a mirror in which the rest of America can be seen. Like all mirrors, it invites distortion.

WALLACE MARKFIELD (1926–)

Wallace Markfield was born on August 12, 1926. He studied at Brooklyn College (B.A., 1947) and New York University (1948–1950). He was a film critic for The New Leader *from 1954–1955. His one novel is* To An Early Grave *(1964). He has also written short fiction and criticism.*

Jewishness and the Younger Intellectuals

On Fridays, an hour or so before sundown, The Collector would limp into my mother's kitchen and take what there was to take from the *pushkeh*. Wasted, gloomy-eyed, wearing the thinnest of coats and unlaced sneakers in all weathers, he might have been lifted, kicking and nagging from the pages of a Malamud story. He would stack the coins—pennies, nickels, once in a while a dime, quarters never—sweep them into a shopping bag, and, with the remnant of a pencil scratch out his meager receipt: *From Markfield, a Contribution.* Thereupon he would sway and sigh and drop a few heavy hints about hard times. How the boys in the yeshiva lived on day-old bread and the cheapest of meats, how egg crates served them as study tables, how they could not afford, *nebach,* to replace a light bulb. Before he was gone my mother would promise to do better, far better in the weeks to come, while, I deft pilferer of the *pushkeh* pennies, would swallow down a bitter lump of guilt.

Though he is dead probably these twenty years, I nevertheless expect The Collector, like Bardamu's Robinson, to pop up in my life again. I see, with appalling clarity, a fund-raising affair, the kick-off dinner, say, of the National Council for the Comfort of Jewish Lonely (NCCJL). The waiters have cleared the tables, the pledge cards are in place, and all eyes turn upon the dais. Nervously rasping, the chairman fiddles with his notes, gives a few healthy bangs with the gavel. "Order, please, ladies and gentlemen, a little bit of order!" He is met by the scrape of chairs, the chime of glassware. But soon the hullabaloo dwindles into a reverent hush. "Distinguished guests," says the chairman, as the photographer hoists his strobe unit, "distinguished guests and fellow officers—" When all of a sudden The Collector, his hour come round at last, shlumps on floppy sneakers across the vast expanse of ballroom, drawing slowly near the dais, his pencil poised, his shopping bag open . . .

Admittedly, I am a special case. From my cubicle in the publicity mill of one of the medium-sized Jewish philanthropic agencies I see the American Jew and the American Jewish community as a fish might see the world from his tank—clouded, freakish, sometimes smaller, sometimes larger than life. In my time I have catered to and cajoled a thousand big givers, filled them with compassion and passion, brought to their eyes tears enough to irrigate the Negev. I have raised up images of Auschwitz and Buchenwald, of sun-bronzed sabras gallantly picking oranges under sniper fire, of forlorn Jewish aged wasting their golden years on park benches, of scapegoats and pariahs, of the broken families and chronically ill seeking help in time of need. Who can say, at this point, if I have chronicled these agonies or created them? And that golden-ager on that park bench—where have I seen him before? No matter; as one publicity director pointed out in a masterful memo on the use of stock photos:

"Many illustrations may be used for more than one field of service. For example, a change of words in the caption and heading can transform a community center illustration into a child care photo: a care of the aged picture may be used equally well to depict vocational rehabilitation, etc., etc."

Once each week I scan scores of Anglo-Jewish newspapers. From year to year and community to community the lead stories seem to issue from one mind and one mimeograph machine. There is the crisis ("Morocco Revokes Exist Visas; No Aid to Emigration of Jews"); the remembrance of things past ("Twenty Years Ago: Maimonides Hospital Opens Out-Patient Wing"); the celebration of the present ("Combined Jewish Appeal Pledges Top $750,000 Mark"); the anxious peek toward the future ("Jewish Culture Taking Back Seat, Study Group Charges"); the invocation of the name ("Feldman Takes PPJS Helm for Second Term"). A blurred four-column cut dominates the bottom of the page; President Kennedy is receiving a laminated, illuminated scroll from the Daughters of Israel.

The inside pages are made of warmer, more intimate and *heimishe* stuff: S. Lawrence Layman's trip to Israel, the Temple Sisterhood bazaar, the Junior Hadassah production of *The Wall*, the recent Center lecture by Maurice Samuel on "Jewish Types and Stereotypes in the American Novel." Next I cast a coll eye upon the editorials, passing, without a tremor in transition, from the solemn, Max Lerner-type moralizing (". . . somehow we are *all* responsible"), to the orotund optimism of Benet-*cum-*

Macleish-*cum*-Corwin ("out of the ashes of the crematoria there rises a phoenix in Israel"), to the catchy parallelism-into-half-truth style of the Luceman ("In an age of anxiety, a time for greatness") and thence to the somber sociological speculation ("Is not our status-seeking and object-hunger drawing us farther and farther from the faith of our forebears?").

It is the social news that holds me longest, the chit-chat about births and brides and Bar Mitzvahs. How I envy Andrew William, Edwin Bruce, Don Craig, and Michael Adams as they pose in *talleisim* and bow ties! No *rebbe* cracked their knuckles or meted out arid stretches of *chumash* to memorize, no bearded, brooding, vindictive Jehovah fevered their dreams. Percival Goodman designed their Sunday schools, John Dewey laid out the rules for their instructors, and that Old Testament God has long since grown affable and even-minded; his beard is gone and now resembles Norman Vincent Peale. And soon, all too soon, Andrew William will be paired off with Linda Jane, Edwin Bruce with Susan Lynn, Don Craig with Sandra Lee, and Michael Adam—somehow I wouldn't be surprised if Michael Adam marries a *shikse*.

The mothers and fathers bother me, though. I linger and linger over the smooth, bland, untroubled faces that preside over installations and elections, Sisterhoods and Brotherhoods, fashion shows and theater parties. Something, something is amiss in these faces, but what and why? For in six thousand years has there ever been so large, so powerful and prosperous a Jewish community? What needs are there yet to meet, what agencies remain to be created? What tension, what anxiety lies beyond the surveys and statistics of the social worker and human relations expert . . . ?

Meanwhile, my old Collector has reached the dais. He is lifting a hand and pointing a prophetic finger at those who sit on boards and those who sit on committees, at those who give and those who get others to give. He has come to tell them all one thing, and one thing only: *Es vell dir gornisht helfen.*

Jewishness and the Younger Intellectuals

Philip Roth

SMALL MATTERS ASIDE—food preferences, a certain syntax, certain jokes—it is difficult for me to distinguish a Jewish style of life in our country that is significantly separate and distinct from the American style of life. (I am thinking of the urban and suburban middle classes.) What a Jew wants and how he goes after it, does not on the whole appear to differ radically from what his Gentile neighbor wants and how he goes after it. There does not seem to me a complex of values or aspirations or beliefs that continue to connect one Jew to another in our country, but rather an ancient and powerful disbelief, which, if it is not fashionable or wise to assert in public, is no less powerful for being underground: that is, the rejection of the myth of Jesus as Christ. Not only does this serve to separate the Jew from his Christian neighbor on the one side who accepts Jesus, but also from the man on his other side who is indifferent, and even from the fellow across the street, the downright atheist, whose tradition, whose social history and bias, do not lead him to reject the Christian savior with quite the same quality of willfulness, zeal, and blood certainty.

And wherein my fellow Jews reject Jesus as the supernatural envoy of God, I feel a kinship with them. It is not the sort of kinship, however, that produces solidarity and trust between us—for the strength with which Jesus continues to be rejected is not equalled by the passion with which the God who gave the Law to Moses is embraced, or approached. What passion remains is neither for the Law nor the God, as for a few

---

For a biographical note on Philip Roth see p. 302.

festive holidays and nostalgic ceremonies, and here, too, there is not so much evidence of passion, as of duty and guilt, a kind of religious tolerance toward one's own religion; surely this is no more true of Jews in our country than of Christians; however, it is not less true. How can it be otherwise? If indeed there were a *religious* connection between us as Jews there would be a cultural one as well: for a moral and political and social character of one's own springs not from disbelief, but faith and conviction. The result is that we are bound together, I to my fellow Jews, my fellow Jews to me, in a relationship that is peculiarly enervating and unviable. Our rejection, our abhorrence finally, of the Christian fantasy leads us to proclaim to the world that we are Jews still—alone, however, what have we to proclaim to one another?

Piety about "the tradition" does not satisfy. The values of the tradition—the laws of human conduct, the light of human intelligence— have not for a very long time now been the special property of any one people, if they ever were. I cannot but value and respect my forebears where they have struggled tenaciously against chaos and ignorance and cruelty, and value their tenacity as well; but this has not been *all* of the Jewish tradition that has been passed down to me. Nor has it been the only tradition: where the Jewish past has informed my spirit and imagination, so too has the political and cultural past of America, and the literary past of England. Neither reverence toward the tradition, nor reverent feelings about the Jewish past seem to me sufficient to bind American Jews together today.

Whatever awe and grief we feel in contemplating the arc of Jewish experience, the cycle of expulsion, wandering, and suffering, the history of a people is finally its history, and its purpose is to give us some measure of our place in the world, how it has happened that we are here, acting as we do. One cannot *will* oneself into a community today on the strength of the miseries and triumphs of a community that existed in Babylonia in the 7th century B.C.E. or in Madrid in 1492, or even in Warsaw in the spring of 1943; and the dying away of anti-Semitism in our own country, its gradual ineffectiveness as a threat to our economic and political rights, further disobliges us from identifying ourselves as Jews so as to help present a proud and united front to the enemy. And that is a good thing, for it enables a man to *choose* to be a Jew, and not to be turned into one, without his free accession, by a hostile society.

Since one need not commit oneself to this religion so as to help protect its rights; since one cannot commit oneself to it simply because one's ancestors did—what then? For myself, I cannot find a true and honest place in the history of believers that begins with Abraham, Isaac, and Jacob on the basis of the heroism of these believers, or of their humiliations and anguish. I can only connect with them, and with their descendants, as I apprehend their God. And until such time as I do apprehend him, there will continue to exist between myself and those others who seek his presence, a question, sometimes spoken, sometimes not, which for all the pain and longing it may engender, for all the disappointment and bewilderment it may produce, cannot be swept away by nostalgia or sentimentality or even by a blind and valiant effort of the will: how are you connected to me as another man is not?

General Studies

Alter, Robert. *After the Tradition: Essays on Modern Jewish Writing.* New York: E. P. Dutton, 1969.

Fiedler, Leslie A. *The Jew in the American Novel.* New York: Herzl Press, 1959.

Guttmann, Allen. *The Jewish Writer in America—Assimilation and the Crisis of Identity.* New York: Oxford University Press, 1971.

Liptzin, Solomon. *The Jew in American Literature.* New York: Bloch, 1966.

Malin, Irving. Editor (with Irwin Stark). *Breakthrough—A Treasury of Contemporary American-Jewish Literature.* New York: McGraw-Hill, 1964.

———. Editor. *Contemporary American-Jewish Literature*—Critical Essays. Bloomington: Indiana University Press, 1973.

———. *Jews and Americans.* Carbondale: Southern Illinois University Press, 1965.

Mersand, Joseph. *Traditions in American Literature—A Study of Jewish Characters and Authors.* Port Washington, N.Y.: Kennikat Press, 1968.

Pinsker, Sanford. *The Schlemiel as Metaphor—Studies in the Yiddish and American Jewish Novel.* Carbondale: Southern Illinois University Press, 1971.

Schulz, Max F. *Radical Sophistication: Studies in Contemporary Jewish-American Novelists.* Athens: Ohio University Press, 1969.

Sherman, Bernard. *The Invention of the Jew—Jewish-American Education Novels* (1916–1964). New York: Thomas Yoseloff, 1969.

Author Bibliography

The following is a selective list of works by the authors represented in this volume.

ISAAC MAYER WISE

The Cosmic God. Cincinnati: Office of *The American Israelite and Deborah,* 1876.

The Essence of Judaism. Cincinnati: Bloch & Co., 1861.

History of the Hebrews' Second Commonwealth with Special Reference to Its Literature, Culture, and the Origin of Rabbinism and Christianity. Cincinnati: Bloch & Co., 1880.

History of the Israelitish Nation, from Abraham to the Present Time. Albany: J. Munsell, 1854.

Hymns, Psalms and Prayers in English and German. Cincinnati: Bloch & Co., 1868.

Judaism: Its Doctrines and Duties. Cincinnati: Office of *The American Israelite and Deborah,* 1872.

Liturgy and Ritual. Editor. The divine service of American Israelites for the Day of Atonement. Cincinnati: Bloch and Co., 1866.

The Martyrdom of Jesus of Nazareth: A Historic-Critical Treatise on the Last Chapters of the Gospel. Cincinnati: Office of *The American Israelite and Deborah,* 1874.

Reminiscences. Ed. and translated by D. Philipson. Cincinnati: L. Wise & Co., 1901. Rev. ed., 1945, 1969.

Selected Writings. Ed. D. Philipson and L. Grossmann. Published under the auspices of the Alumnal Association of the Hebrew Union College. Cincinnati: The R. Clarke Co., 1900.

Selected Writings of I. M. Wise. New York: Arno Press, 1969.

The World of My Books. Cincinnati: American Jewish Archives, 1954.

PENINA MOISE

Fancy's Sketch Book. Charleston: J. S. Burges, 1833.

Secular and Religious Works of Penina Moise, with brief sketch of her life. Compiled and published by Charleston Section, Council of Jewish Women. Charleston: N. G. Duffy, 1911.

ADAH ISAACS MENKEN

Infelicia. New York: J. L. Williams, 1868.

EMMA LAZARUS

Admetus, and other poems. New York: Hurd & Houghton, 1871.

Alide: an Episode of Goethe's life. Philadelphia: J. B. Lippincott Company, 1874.

Emma Lazarus: Selections from Her Poetry and Prose. Ed. Morris U. Schappes. New York: Cooperative Book League, 1944.

Letters to E. Lazarus in the Columbia University Library. Ed. Ralph L. Rusk. New York: Columbia University Press, 1939.

The Poems of Emma Lazarus. Boston: Houghton Mifflin Company, 1889.

Songs of a Semite, The Dance to Death, and Other Poems. New York: Office of The American Hebrew, 1882.

ABRAHAM CAHAN

Hear the other side: a Symposium of Democrtaic Socialist Opinion. Editor. New York: 1934.

The Imported Bridegroom, and Other Stories of the New York Ghetto. Boston: Houghton Mifflin Company, 1898.

Palestine. New York: Forward Press, 1934.

Raphael Naarizoch. New York: Forward Press, 1907.

Rashel. New York: Forward Press, 1938.

The Rise of David Levinsky. New York: Harper & Brothers, 1917.

A Tale of the New York Ghetto. New York: 1896.

The White Terror and the Red; a Novel of Revolutionary Russia. New York: A. S. Barnes & Co., 1905.

Yekl: a Tale of the New York Ghetto. New York: D. Appleton & Company Inc., 1896.

MARY ANTIN

From Plotzk to Boston. Boston: W. B. Clarke & Co., 1899.

The Promised Land. Boston: Houghton Mifflin Company, 1912.

They Who Knock at Our Gates: a Complete Gospel of Immigration. Boston: Houghton Mifflin Company, 1914.

LUDWIG LEWISOHN

Adam. New York: Harper & Brothers, 1929.

An Altar in the Fields. New York: Harper & Brothers, 1934.

The American Jew. New York: Farrar, Straus & Co., 1950.

Among the Nations. Editor. New York: Farrar, Straus & Co., 1948.

Anniversary. New York: Farrar, Straus & Co., 1946.

The Answer: the Jew and the World. New York: Liveright Publishing Corporation, 1939.

Breathe Upon These. Indianapolis: The Bobbs-Merrill Company, Inc., 1944.

The Broken Snare. New York: B. W. Dodge & Co., 1908.

The Case of Mr. Crump. Paris: E. W. Titus, 1931.

Cities and Men. New York: Harper & Brothers, 1927.

Creative America. Editor. New York: Harper & Brothers, 1933.

The Creative Life. New York: Boni & Liveright, 1924.

The Defeated. London: T. Thornton Butterworth, Limited, 1927.

Don Juan. New York: Boni & Liveright, 1923.

The Drama and the Stage. New York: Harcourt, Brace and Company, Inc., 1922.

For Ever Wilt Thou Love. New York: The Dial Press, Inc., 1939.

German Style, An Introduction to the Study of German Prose. Editor. New York: Henry Holt and Company, Inc., 1910.

The Golden Vase. New York: Harper & Brothers, 1931.

Haven. New York: The Dial Press, Inc., 1940.

In a Summer Season. New York: Farrar, Straus & Co., 1955.

The Island Within. New York: Harper & Brothers, 1928.

Israel. New York: Boni & Liveright, 1925.

A Jew Speaks: An Anthology from L. Lewisohn. Editor. J. W. Wise.

Jewish Short Stories. Editor. New York: Behrman House, 1945.

The Last Days of Shylock. New York: Harper & Brothers, 1931.

The Magic Word. New York: Farrar, Straus & Co., 1950.

Mid-Channel: an American Chronicle. New York and London: Harper & Brothers, 1929.

A Modern Book of Criticism. Editor. New York: Boni & Liveright, 1919.

The Modern Drama. New York: B. W. Huebsch, 1915.

The People. New York: Harper & Brothers, 1933.

The Permanent Horizon. New York: Harper & Brothers, 1934.

The Poets of Modern France. New York: B. W. Huebsch, 1918.

Rebirth: a Book of Modern Jewish Thought. Editor. New York: Harper & Brothers, 1935.

Renegade. New York: The Dial Press, Inc., 1942.

Roman Summer. New York: Harper & Brothers, 1927.

The Spirit of Modern German Literature. New York: B. W. Huebsch, 1916.

Stephen Escott. New York: Harper & Brothers, 1930.

The Story of American Literature. New York: Harper & Brothers, 1937.

Theodor Herzl: a Portrait for This Age. Cleveland: The World Publishing Company, 1955.

Trumpet of Jubilee. New York: Harper & Brothers, 1937.

Upstream: an American Chronicle. New York: Boni & Liveright, 1922.

What Is This Jewish Heritage? New York: B'nai B'rith Hillell Foundation.

WALDO FRANK

America Hispana. New York: Charles Scribner's Sons, 1931.

The Art of the Vieux Colombier. Paris: Nouvelle Revue Française, 1918.

Birth of a World: Bolivar in Terms of His People. Boston: Houghton Mifflin Company, 1951.

The Bridegroom Cometh. New York: Doubleday, Doran & Company, Inc., 1939.

Bridgehead: the Drama of Israel. New York: George Braziller, Inc., 1957.

Chalk Face. New York: Boni & Liveright, 1924.

Chart for Rough Water. New York: Doubleday, Doran & Company, Inc., 1940.

City Block. New York: Charles Scribner's Sons, 1932.

Cuba: Prophetic Island. New York: Marzani & Munsell, 1961.

The Dark Mother. New York: Boni & Liveright, 1920.

Dawn in Russia. New York: Charles Scribner's Sons, 1932.

The Death and Birth of David Markand. New York: Charles Scribner's Sons, 1934.

Dot: a Comedy in Four Acts. New York: Z. & L. Rosenfield, 1913.

Holiday. New York: Boni & Liveright, 1923.

In the American Jungle (1925–1936). New York: Farrar & Rinehart, Inc., 1937.

The Invaders. New York: Duell, Sloan & Pearce, Inc., 1946.

Island in the Atlantic. New York: Duell, Sloan & Pearce, Inc., 1946.

The Jew in Our Day. New York: Duell, Sloan & Pearce, Inc., 1944.

New Year's Eve. New York: Charles Scribner's Sons, 1929.

Not Heaven. New York: Hermitage House, 1953.

Our America. New York: Boni Liveright, 1919.

Rahab. New York: Boni & Liveright, 1922.

The Re-discovery of America. New York: Charles Scribner's Sons, 1929.

The Re-discovery of Man. New York: George Braziller, Inc., 1958.

Salvos. New York: Boni and Liveright, 1924.

South American Journey. New York: Duell, Sloan & Pearce, Inc., 1943.

Time Exposures. New York: Boni & Liveright, 1926.

The Unwelcome Man. Boston: Little Brown, and Company, 1917.

Virgin Spain. New York: Boni & Liveright, 1926.

MICHAEL GOLD

Battle Hymn: a Play (with Michael Blankfort). New York: Samuel French, Inc., 1936.

Change the World! New York: International Publishers Company, Inc., 1937.

Charlie Chaplin's Parade. New York: Harcourt, Brace & Company, Inc., 1930.

The Damned Agitator. Chicago: Daily Worker Publishing Co., 1926.

The Hollow Men. New York: International Publishers Company, Inc., 1941.

Jews Without Money. New York: Horace Liveright, 1930.

Life of John Brown. Girard, Kan.: Haldeman-Julius Co., 1924.

Mike Gold: a Literary Anthology. Ed. Michael Folsom. New York: International Publishers Company, Inc., 1972.

The Mike Gold Reader. New York: International Publishers Company, Inc., 1954.

Money. New York: Samuel French Inc., 1929.

120 Million. New York: International Publishers Company, Inc., 1929.

BEN HECHT

Actor's Blood. New York: Covici, Friede, Inc., 1936.

A Book of Miracles. New York: The Viking Press, Inc.

Broken Necks: Containing More "1001 afternoons." Chicago: P. Covici, 1926.

The Cat That Jumped Out of the Story. Philadelphia: John C. Winston Company, 1947.

The Champion from Far Away. New York: Covici, Friede, Inc., 1931.

Charlie: the Improbable Life and Times of Charles MacArthur. New York: Harper & Brothers, 1957.

Christmas Eve. New York: Covici, Friede, Inc., 1928.

The Collected Stories of Ben Hecht. New York: Crown Publishers, Inc., 1945.

Concerning a Woman of Sin, and Other Stories. New York: Avon Book Division, The Hearst Corporation, 1947.

A Child of the Century. New York: Simon & Schuster, Inc., 1954.

Count Bruga. New York: Boni & Liveright, 1926.

Erik Dorn. New York: G. P. Putnam's Sons, 1921.

Fantazius Mallare. Chicago: Covici, McGee, 1922.

The Florentine Dagger. New York: Boni & Liveright, 1923.

The Front Page (with Charles MacArthur). New York: Covici, Friede, Inc., 1928.

Fun to be Free (with Charles MacArthur). New York: Dramatists Play Service, Inc., 1941.

Gaily, Gaily. Garden City, N.Y.: Doubleday & Co., Inc., 1963.

Gargoyles. New York: Boni & Liveright, 1922.

The Great Magoo. New York: Covici, Friede, Inc., 1933.

A Guide for the Bedevilled. New York: Charles Scribner's Sons, 1944.

Hollywood Mystery! New York: Bartholomew House, 1946.

Humpty Dumpty. New York: Boni & Liveright, 1924.

I Hate Actors! New York: Crown Publishers, Inc., 1944.

In the Midst of Death. London: Mayflower Books, 1964.

A Jew in Love. New York: Covici, Friede, Inc., 1931.

Letters from Bohemia. Garden City, N.Y.: Doubleday & Co., Inc., 1964.

Miracle in the Rain. New York: Alfred A. Knopf, Inc., 1943.

Perfidy. New York: Julian Messner, a division of Simon & Schuster, Inc., 1961.

The Sensualists. New York: Julian Messner, a division of Simon & Schuster, Inc., 1959.

Tales of Chicago Streets. Girard, Kan.: Haldeman-Julius Co., 1924.

A Thousand and One Afternoons in Chicago. Chicago: Covici, McGee, 1922.

To Quito and Back. New York: Covici, Friede, Inc., 1937.

A Treasury of Ben Hecht. New York: Crown Publishers, Inc., 1959.

HENRY ROTH
Call It Sleep. New York: R. O. Ballou, 1934.

DANIEL FUCHS

Homage to Blenholt. New York: Vanguard Press, Inc., 1936.

Low Company. New York: Vanguard Press, Inc., 1937.

Summer in Williamsburg. New York: Vanguard Press, Inc., 1934.

Three Novels. New York: Basic Books, Inc., Publishers, 1964.

West of the Rockies. New York: Alfred A. Knopf, Inc., 1971.

CLIFFORD ODETS

The Big Knife. New York: Random House, Inc., 1949.

Clash By Night. New York: Random House, Inc., 1942.

Country Girl. New York: The Viking Press, Inc., 1951.

Golden Boy. New York: Random House, Inc., 1937.

Night Music. New York: Random House, Inc., 1940.

Paradise Lost. New York: Random House, Inc., 1936.

Rocket to the Moon. New York: Random House, Inc., 1939.

Six Plays. New York: Random House, Inc., 1939.

PAUL GOODMAN

Adam and his Works. New York: Vintage Books, Random House, Inc., 1968.

The Break-up of Our Camp. New York: New Directions, 1949.

Communitas: Means of Livelihood and Ways of Life. Chicago: The University of Chicago Press, 1947.

Days, and Other Poems. New York: Paul Goodman, 1955.

The Facts of Life. New York: Vanguard Press, Inc., 1945.

Five Years. New York: Brussel & Brussel, 1966.

The Grand Piano. San Francisco: The Colt Press, 1942.

Growing Up Absurd. New York: Random House, Inc., 1960.

Hawkweek: Poems. New York: Random House, Inc., 1967.

Kafka's Prayer. New York: Vanguard Press, Inc., 1947.

Like a Conquered Province. New York: Random House, Inc., 1967.

The Lordly Hudson: Collected Poems. New York: The Macmillan Company, 1962.

Making Do. New York: The Macmillan Company, 1963.

Mass Education in Science. Los Angeles: University of California Press, 1966.

Our Visit to Niagara. New York: Horizon Press, 1960.

People or Personnel. New York: Random House, Inc., 1945.

Seeds of Liberation. New York: George Braziller, Inc., 1965.

The Society I Live in Is Mine. New York: Horizon Press, 1962.

Speaking and Language: Defence of Poetry. New York: Random House, Inc., 1971.

The State of Nature. New York: Vanguard Press, Inc., 1946.

The Structure of Literature. Chicago: The University of Chicago Press, 1954.

BERNARD MALAMUD

The Assistant. New York: Farrar, Straus & Cudahy, Inc., 1957.

The Fixer. New York: Farrar, Straus & Giroux, Inc., 1966.

Idiots First. New York: Farrar, Straus & Co., 1963.

The Magic Barrel. New York: Farrar, Straus & Cudahy, Inc., 1958.

A Malamud Reader. New York: Farrar, Straus & Giroux, Inc., 1967.

The Natural. New York: Harcourt, Brace and Company, Inc., 1952.

A New Life. New York: Farrar, Straus & Cudahy, Inc., 1961.

Pictures of Fidelman. New York: Farrar, Straus & Giroux, Inc., 1969.

The Tenants. New York: Farrar, Straus & Giroux, Inc., 1971.

SAUL BELLOW

The Adventures of Augie March. New York: The Viking Press, Inc., 1953.

The Dangling Man. New York: Vanguard Press, Inc., 1944.

Great Jewish Short Stories. Editor. New York: Dell Publishing Co., Inc., 1963.

Henderson, the Rain King. New York: The Viking Press, Inc., 1959.

Herzog. New York: The Viking Press, Inc., 1964.

The Last Analysis: a Play. New York: The Viking Press, Inc., 1965.

Mosby's Memoirs and Other Stories. New York: The Viking Press, Inc., 1968.

Mr. Sammler's Planet. New York: The Viking Press, Inc., 1970.

Seize the Day. New York: The Viking Press, Inc., 1956.

The Victim. New York: Vanguard Press, Inc., 1947.

ARTHUR MILLER

After the Fall. New York: The Viking Press, Inc., 1964.

All My Sons. New York: Reynal & Hitchcock, Inc., 1947.

Collected Plays. New York: The Viking Press, Inc., 1957.

The Creation of the World and Other Business (Broadway, 1972 season).

The Crucible. New York: The Viking Press, Inc., 1953.

Death of a Salesman. New York: The Viking Press, Inc., 1949.

Focus. New York: Reynal & Hitchcock, Inc., 1945.

I Don't Need You Any More. New York: The Viking Press, Inc., 1967.

Incident at Vichy. New York: The Viking Press, Inc., 1965.

A Memory of Two Mondays. New York: Dramatists Play Service, Inc., 1956.

The Misfits. New York: The Viking Press, Inc., 1961.

The Price. New York: The Viking Press, Inc., 1968.

Situation Normal. New York: Reynal & Hitchcock, Inc., 1944.

A View from the Bridge. New York: The Viking Press, Inc., 1955.

In Russia (with Inge Morath). New York: The Viking Press, Inc., 1969.

GRACE PALEY

The Little Disturbances of Man. Garden City, N.Y.: Doubleday & Company, Inc., 1959.

NORMAN MAILER

Advertisements for Myself. New York: New American Library, Inc., 1959.

An American Dream. New York: The Dial Press, Inc., 1965.

The Armies of the Night. New York: New American Library, Inc., 1968.

Barbary Shore. New York: Rinehart & Company, Inc., 1951.

Cannibals and Christians. New York: The Dial Press, Inc., 1966.

Deaths for the Ladies and Other Disasters. New York: G. P. Putnam's Sons, 1962.

The Deer Park. New York: G. P. Putnam's Sons, 1955.

Maidstone: a Mystery. New York: New American Library, Inc., 1971.

Miami and the Siege of Chicago. New York: World Publishing Company, 1968.

The Naked and the Dead. New York: Rinehart & Company, Inc., 1948.

Of a Fire on the Moon. Boston: Little, Brown and Company, 1970.

The Presidential Papers. New York: G. P. Putnam's Sons, 1963.

The Prisoner of Sex. Boston: Little, Brown and Company, 1971.

Why Are We in Vietnam? New York: Putnam's Sons, 1967.

HERBERT GOLD

The Age of Happy Problems. New York: The Dial Press, Inc., 1962.

Birth of a Hero. New York: The Viking Press, Inc., 1951.

Fathers. New York: Random House, Inc., 1966.

Fiction of the Fifties: a Decade of American Writing. Editor. Garden City, N.Y.: Doubleday & Company, Inc., 1959.

First Person Singular: Essays for the Sixties. Editor. New York: The Dial Press, Inc., 1963.

The Great American Jackpot. New York: Random House, Inc., 1969.

Love and Like. New York: The Dial Press, Inc., 1960.

The Magic Will. New York: Random House, Inc., 1971.

The Man Who Was Not With It. Boston: Little, Brown and Company, 1956.

The Optimist. Boston: Little, Brown and Company, 1959.

Salt. New York: The Dial Press, Inc., 1963.

Stories of Modern America. Editor (with David L. Stevenson). New York: St. Martin's Press, Inc., 1961.

Therefore Be Bold. New York: The Dial Press, Inc., 1960.

WALLACE MARKFIELD

To an Early Grave. New York: Simon and Schuster, 1964.

Teitlebaum's Window. New York: Alfred A. Knopf, Inc., 1970.

PHILIP ROTH

The Breast. New York: Random House, Inc., 1972.

Goodbye, Columbus, and Five Short Stories. Boston: Houghton Mifflin Company, 1959.

The Great American Novel. New York: Holt, Rhinehart and Winston, 1973.

Letting Go. New York: Random House, Inc., 1962.

Our Gang. New York: Random House, Inc., 1971.

Portnoy's Complaint. New York: Random House, Inc., 1969.

When She Was Good. New York: Random House, Inc., 1967.

IRVIN FAUST

The Steagle. New York: Random House, Inc., 1966.

Roar Lion Roar, and Other Stories. New York: Random House, Inc., 1965.

The File on Stanley Patton Buchta. New York: Random House, Inc., 1970.

Willy Remembers. New York: Arbor House, 1971.

DELMORE SCHWARTZ

Selected Essays. Ed. Donald A. Dike and David H. Zucker. Chicago: The University of Chicago Press, 1970.

Summer Knowledge: New and Selected Poems, 1938–1958. Garden City, N.Y.: Doubleday & Company, Inc., 1959.

MURIEL RUKEYSER

Beast in View. Garden City, N.Y.: Doubleday, Doran & Company, Inc., 1944.

Body of Waking. New York: Harper & Brothers, 1958.

Come Back, Paul. New York: Harper & Brothers, 1955.

Elegies. Norfolk, Conn.: New Directions, 1949.

The Green Wave. Garden City, N.Y.: Doubleday & Company, Inc., 1948.

I Go Out. New York: Harper & Brothers, 1961.

The Life of Poetry. New York: Current Books, 1949.

One Life. New York: Simon & Schuster, Inc., 1957.

The Orgy. New York: Coward-McCann, Inc., 1965.

Orpheus. San Francisco: Centaur Press, 1949.

The Outer Banks. Santa Barbara: Unicorn Press, 1967.

Selected Poems. New York: New Directions, 1951.

The Speed of Darkness. New York: Random House, Inc., 1968.

Theory of Flight. New Haven, Conn.: Yale University Press, 1935.

The Traces of Thomas Hariot. New York: Random House, Inc., 1971.

A Turning Wind. New York: The Viking Press, Inc., 1939.

Waterlily Fire: Poems, 1935–1962. New York: Macmillan Company, 1962.

Willard Gibbs. Garden City, N.Y.: Doubleday, Doran & Company, Inc., 1942.

KARL SHAPIRO

American Poetry. Editor. New York: Thomas Y. Crowell Company, 1960.

A Bibliography of Modern Prosody. Baltimore: The John Hopkins Press, 1948.

Beyond Criticism. Lincoln: University of Nebraska Press, 1953.

The Bourgeois Poet. New York: Random House, Inc., 1964.

English Prosody and Modern Poetry. Baltimore: The Johns Hopkins Press, 1947.

Essay on Rime. New York: Reynal & Hitchcock, Inc., 1945.

In Defense of Ignorance. New York: Random House, Inc., 1960.

Person, Place and Thing. New York: Reynal & Hitchcock, Inc., 1942.

The Place of Love. Malvern, Australia: The Bradley Printers, 1942.

Poems. Baltimore: Waverly Press, 1935.

Poems: 1940–1953. New York: Random House, Inc., 1953.

Poems of a Jew. New York: Random House, Inc., 1958.

Trial of a Poet, and Other Poems. New York: Reynal & Hitchcock, Inc., 1947.

V-letter, and Other Poems. New York: Reynal & Hitchcock, Inc., 1944.

HOWARD NEMEROV

The Blue Swallows. Chicago: The University of Chicago Press, 1967.

A Commodity of Dreams. New York: Simon & Schuster, Inc., 1959.

Endor. New York: Abingdon Press, 1961.

Federigo: or, The Power of Love. Boston: Little, Brown and Company, 1954.

Guide to the Ruins. New York: Random House, Inc., 1950.

The Homecoming Game. New York: Simon & Schuster, 1957.

The Image and the Law. New York: Henry Holt and Company, Inc., 1947.

Journal of the Fictive Life. New Brunswick, N.J.: Rutgers University Press, 1965.

The Melodramatists. New York: Random House, Inc., 1949.

Mirrors and Windows. Chicago: The University of Chicago Press, 1958.

New and Selected Poems. Chicago: The University of Chicago Press, 1960.

The Next Room of the Dream. Chicago: The University of Chicago Press, 1962.

Poetry and Fiction. New Brunswick, N.J.: Rutgers University Press, 1963.

Poets on Poetry. New York: Basic Books, Inc., Publishers, 1966.

The Salt Garden. Boston: Little, Brown and Company, 1955.

A Sequence of Seven with a Drawing by Ron Slaughter. Roanoke: Tinker Press, 1967.

The Winter Lightning. London: Rapp & Whiting, 1968.

ALLEN GINSBERG
Ankor Wat. London: Fulcrum Press, 1968.

Empty Mirror. New York: Totem Press, 1961.

Howl, and Other Poems. San Francisco: City Lights Pocket Bookshop, 1956.

Kaddish, and Other Poems: 1958–1960. San Francisco: City Lights Books, 1961.

Reality Sandwiches, 1953–1960. San Francisco: City Lights Books, 1963.

T.V. Baby Poems. New York: Grossman, 1968.

LIONEL TRILLING
Authenticity and Sincerity. Cambridge, Mass.: Harvard University Press, 1972.

Beyond Culture. New York: The Viking Press, Inc., 1965.

E. M. Forster. Norfolk, Conn.: New Directions, 1943.

The Experience of Literature. Editor. Garden City, N.Y.: Doubleday & Company, Inc., 1967.

Freud and the Crisis of Our Culture. Boston: Beacon Press, 1955.

A Gathering of Fugitives. Boston: Beacon Press, 1956.

The Liberal Imagination. New York: The Viking Press, Inc., 1950.

Matthew Arnold. New York: W. W. Norton & Company, Inc., 1939.

The Middle of the Journey. New York: The Viking Press, Inc., 1947.

The Opposing Self. New York: The Viking Press, Inc., 1955.

PHILIP RAHV

Discovery of Europe. Editor. Boston: Houghton Mifflin Company, 1947. Rev. ed., 1960.

Image and Idea. New York: New Directions, 1949. Rev. ed., 1957.

Literature and the Sixth Sense. Boston: Houghton Mifflin Company, 1969.

Modern Occasions. Editor. New York: Farrar, Straus & Giroux, Inc., 1966.

The Myth and the Powerhouse. New York: Farrar, Straus & Giroux, Inc., 1965.

The Partisan Review Anthology. Editor (with William Phillips) New York: Holt, Rinehart and Winston, Inc., 1962.

Russian Short Novels. Editor. New York: The Dial Press, Inc., 1951.

ISAAC ROSENFELD

An Age of Enormity: Life and Writings in the Thirties and Forties. Ed. Theodore Solotaroff. Cleveland: The World Publishing Company, 1962.

Alpha and Omega. New York: The Viking Press, Inc., 1966.

Passage from Home. Cleveland: The World Publishing Company, 1961.

ALFRED KAZIN

Bright Book of Life. Boston: Little, Brown and Company, 1973.

Contemporaries. Boston: Little, Brown and Company, 1962.

F. Scott Fitzgerald: the Man and His Work. Editor. Cleveland: The World Publishing Company, 1951.

The Inmost Leaf. New York: Harcourt, Brace and Company, Inc., 1955.

Nathaniel Hawthorne: Selected Short Stories. Editor. Greenwich, Conn.: Fawcett Publications, Inc., 1966.

On Native Grounds. New York: Reynal & Hitchcock, Inc., 1942.

The Open Form. Editor. New York: Harcourt, Brace & World, Inc., 1961.

The Portable Blake. Editor. New York: The Viking Press, Inc., 1946.

Starting Out in the Thirties. Boston: Little, Brown and Company, 1965.

The Stature of Theodore Dreiser. Editor (with Charles Shapiro). Bloomington: Indiana University Press, 1955.

A Walker in the City. New York: Harcourt, Brace and Company, Inc., 1951.

LESLIE FIEDLER

The Art of the Essay. Editor. New York: Thomas Y. Crowell Company, 1953.

Back to China. New York: Stein and Day Incorporated, 1965.

Being Busted. New York: Stein and Day Incorporated, 1969.

The Collected Essays of Leslie Fiedler. New York: Stein and Day Incorporated, 1971.

The Continuing Debate. Editor (with Jacob Vinocur). New York: St. Martin's Press, Inc., 1964.

An End to Innocence. Boston: Beacon Press, 1955.

The Jew in the American Novel. New York: Herzl Press, 1959.

The Last Jew in America. New York: Stein and Day Incorporated, 1965.

Love and Death in the American Novel. New York: Criterion Books, Inc., 1960.

No! in Thunder. Boston: Beacon Press, 1960.

Pull Down Vanity, and Other Stories. Philadelphia: J. B. Lippincott Company, 1962.

The Return of the Vanishing American. New York: Stein and Day Incorporated, 1968.

The Second Stone. New York: Stein and Day Incorporated, 1963.

The Stranger in Shakespeare. New York: Stein and Day Incorporated, 1972.

DANIEL BELL

The End of Ideology: on the Exhaustion of Political Ideas in the Fifties. New York: The Free Press, 1960.

The New American Right. Editor. New York: Criterion Books, Inc., 1955.

The Reforming of General Education: the Columbia College Experience in its National Setting. New York: Columbia University Press, 1966.

Work and Its Discontents. Boston: Beacon Press, 1956.

IRVING HOWE

The American Communist Party: a Critical History, 1919–1957. Boston: Beacon Press, 1957.

Edith Wharton: a Collection of Critical Essays. Editor. Englewood Cliffs, N.J.: Prentice-Hall, Inc., 1962.

The Idea of the Modern in Literature and the Arts. Editor. New York: Horizon Press, 1967.

Modern Literary Criticism. Boston: Beacon Press, 1958.

Politics and the Novel. New York: Horizon Press, 1957.

The Radical Imagination. Editor. New York: New American Library, Inc., 1967.

Sherwood Anderson. New York: William Sloane Associates, 1951.

Steady Work. New York: Harcourt, Brace & World, Inc., 1966.

Thomas Hardy. New York: The Macmillan Company, 1967.

A Treasury of Yiddish Stories. Editor (with Eliezer Greenberg. New York: The Viking Press, Inc., 1954.

The U.A.W. and Walter Reuther. New York: Random House, Inc., 1949.

William Faulkner: a Critical Study. New York: Random House, Inc., 1952.

A World More Attractive. New York: Horizon Press, 1963.

NATHAN GLAZER

American Judaism. Chicago: The University of Chicago Press, 1957. Rev. ed., 1972.

Beyond the Melting Pot. Cambridge, Mass.: The M.I.T. Press, 1963.

Cities in Trouble. Editor. Chicago: Quadrangle Books, Inc., 1970.

Faces in the Crowd (with David Reisman). New Haven, Conn.: Yale University Press, 1965.

Remembering the Answers: Essays on the American Student Revolt. New York: Basic Books, Inc., Publishing, 1970.

The Social Basis of American Communism. New York: Harcourt, Brace and Company, Inc., 1961.

THEODORE SOLOTAROFF

The Red Hot Vacuum. New York: Atheneum Publishers, 1970.

Writers and Issues. Editor. New York: New American Library, Inc., 1969.

NORMAN PODHORETZ

Doings and Undoings. New York: Farrar, Straus & Co., 1964.

The Commentary Reader. Editor. New York: Atheneum Publishers, 1966.

Making It. New York: Random House, Inc., 1967.

Index

INDEX